"UNthkg respect for AUTHORITY is the greatest ENEMY of truth." —ALBERT EINSTEIN—

Self-Determination

"Tst Everybody, but cut the cards." — Finley Peter Dunne —

"UNTIL YOU undstd A writer's ignce presume yourself ignt / his undstdg." —Samuel Taylor Coleridge—

Thomas Pink offers a new approach to the problem of free will. Do we have control of how we act, so that we are free to act in more than one way, and does it matter to morality whether we do? Pink argues that what matters to morality is not in fact the freedom to do otherwise, but something more primitive—a basic capacity or power to determine for ourselves what we do. This capacity might or might not take the form of a freedom to act in more than one way, and it might or might not be compatible with causal determinism. What really matters to morality is that it is we who determine what we do. What we do must not simply be a function of powers or capacities for which we are not responsible, or a matter of mere chance. At the heart of moral responsibility is a distinctive form of power that is quite unlike ordinary causation—a power by which we determine outcomes in a way quite different from the way ordinary causes determine outcomes. Pink examines how this power is involved in action, and how the nature of action permits the operation of such a power to determine it.

Thomas Pink studied history and philosophy at the University of Cambridge. After a short career in banking he became a research fellow of Churchill College, Cambridge, and has since taught at the University of Sheffield and at King's College London. He has published on the philosophy of action and free will, on ethics and political philosophy and on the history of philosophy. He has recently published an edition of Francisco Suarez's moral and political works, and is editing *The Questions Concerning Liberty, Necessity and Chance* for the Clarendon Edition of the works of Thomas Hobbes.

Self-Determination

The Ethics of Action, Volume 1

Thomas Pink

OXFORD
UNIVERSITY PRESS

OXFORD
UNIVERSITY PRESS

Great Clarendon Street, Oxford, OX2 6DP,
United Kingdom

Oxford University Press is a department of the University of Oxford.
It furthers the University's objective of excellence in research, scholarship,
and education by publishing worldwide. Oxford is a registered trade mark of
Oxford University Press in the UK and in certain other countries

First Edition published in 2016
First published in paperback 2019

Published in the United States of America by Oxford University Press
198 Madison Avenue, New York, NY 10016, United States of America

British Library Cataloguing in Publication Data
Data available

Library of Congress Cataloging in Publication Data
Data available

ISBN 978-0-19-927275-4 (Hbk.)
ISBN 978-0-19-884307-8 (Pbk.)

Contents

Acknowledgements

This book owes much to criticism and discussion at a number of academic institutions including the Collège de France, Institut Jean Nicod Paris, and the Universities of Amsterdam, California at Riverside and at Santa Barbara, Chicago, Fribourg, Glasgow, Heidelberg, Helsinki, Leuven, London, Ludwig Maximilian Munich, Keio, Oxford, Queen's Belfast, Princeton, Reading, St Andrews, Sheffield, Southampton, Stirling, Sussex, Trinity College Dublin, Uppsala, Valencia.

I have learnt from discussion with too many philosophers for a comprehensive list to be possible. Some individuals are acknowledged by name in the text and footnotes. But I must mention, in particular, my colleagues in the Philosophy Department of King's College London who, in our weekly seminars and in private conversations, have done much to inform this work. I am also very grateful to many colleagues in the other colleges within London University. I benefited especially from discussion with those, from London and elsewhere, who attended a seminar on an earlier version of the book.

There is also my debt to friends and colleagues within the historical community. The study of history is crucial to philosophical understanding, especially in the fields of ethics and moral psychology. Both as philosopher and as historian I have learnt from many fellow students of the late medieval and early modern scholastic tradition and of Thomas Hobbes.

Among those who have read various versions of the book I am very grateful for their comments to Peter Adamson, Randolph Clarke, Erasmus Mayr, Timothy O'Connor, Constantine Sandis, and Martin Stone, as well as to anonymous readers from Oxford University Press.

My especial thanks go to Peter Momtchiloff of Oxford University Press for his invaluable editorial counsel and support and for his great patience.

Most of all, the advice and support of my wife Judy has been essential. The research for this book on self-determination and its companion on normativity would never have been embarked on, still less this book completed, without her.

List of Figures

List of Tables

Introduction and Summary

This book, *Self-Determination*, and a forthcoming companion volume, *Normativity*, will together form two volumes on *The Ethics of Action*, and will examine the significance of action within ethics. Does action matter ethically in a way that is distinctive, and if so, how?

This general question has to do both with the nature of action and with the nature of ethical standards. How might what we do or refrain from doing differ from other aspects of the self, and in ways that are of moral significance? And how might morality or the ethical be concerned with such differences?

One issue is central. Is action the locus of some power of self-determination—some power to determine for ourselves what we do? The existence and nature of such a power is, of course, the heart of the free will problem. And there is obviously one way such a power might be of ethical significance. The power might be the basis of a special, moral responsibility for what we do or omit—a responsibility that could in turn be for meeting some correspondingly distinctive kind of ethical standard that is specifically on how we act, such as moral obligation.

So we have, on the one hand, a problem about the self and its psychology and the place of action within that psychology; and then a problem about the nature of ethical standards and the way these standards engage with various aspects of the self. These two problems, about action and about ethical standards, though related, are nevertheless different, and have built up substantially distinct philosophical literatures. Many philosophers address the nature of action as a question within the metaphysics of the mind and of free will, but without giving much detailed attention to ethical theory. Equally, many other philosophers address the nature of ethical standards without much critical examination of action theory. If the nature of action is discussed at all, action is taken, without much argument, to be equivalent to something called 'the voluntary' and to be something that occurs as an expression and effect of prior motivating 'attitudes'—and there the issue is left.

The mutual separation of much contemporary work in ethics and in the theory of action and free will poses dangers. On the side of philosophy of action and free will, there is the serious temptation to assimilate ethical standards to a single kind. For example, it is tempting to suppose that if free will matters to ethics at all, there is a general dependence of ethical standing on its reality. But there are, as I shall argue, many different forms of ethical standard, involving various kinds of direction and criticism, and not all of them seem to presuppose any metaphysically distinctive capacity for self-determination. And there are dangers in the separation for moral philosophers too. We should not take it for granted that action is, by its very nature, the voluntary expression of prior motivations. Such a theory of action is highly debatable, both as an account of the true metaphysics of action and as an account of our ordinary psychological belief. The theory is a comparatively recent development, and is peculiarly a product of the English-language philosophical tradition. This book will be subjecting this theory of action to detailed criticism. It is a theory that is in deep tension with our ordinary thinking, not least about ethics.

Contemporary ethical theory has become notably detached from inquiry into the metaphysics of free will. This detachment is an important development, reflected in the changing history of the university curriculum. Any student attending a European university in the early modern period, whether Catholic or Protestant, there to be instructed in natural law as the dominant form of ethical theory, would have come across an account of human action and free will as the basis of the entire ethics course, and fundamental to its moral psychology. Take Pufendorf's *On the Law of Nature and of Nations*.[1] Pufendorf's work was as important to the ethical and political curriculum of seventeenth- and early eighteenth-century Protestant Germany and Scandinavia as Rawls is to that of contemporary America. Pufendorf's treatise begins in its first book with a thorough and foundational discussion of human action and the will, and of the will's freedom. Things are quite different in the British and American universities of the present. Now the free will problem is often treated just as an introductory part of metaphysics—with even many aspirant metaphysicians paying it little attention thereafter. In ethics, there will be a general treatment of responsibility, but often in a form that leaves the possible relevance of freedom as a metaphysical power deeply unobvious.

Modern ethics has been detached from a concern for free will for the same reason as it has adopted a conception of action as the voluntary expression of prior motivation. Fundamental is Thomas Hobbes' brilliant and highly innovative attack both on the very possibility of free will, as also on its ethical significance. It is largely thanks to the long-term influence of this attack, especially within English-language philosophy, that so much modern moral, political, and legal theory altogether sidelines the problem of free will, and indeed any real debate about the nature of action itself.

But Hobbes' metaphysics and psychology are highly problematic, not least because he aggressively confuses two projects that are, in fact, importantly distinct. The first is to provide a metaphysical account of the way the world really is. For Hobbes this account includes the central claim, with radical implications for ethics and psychology, that ordinary efficient causation is the only power to be found in nature,

---

[1] Samuel Pufendorf, *De iure naturae et gentium* (Amsterdam, 1688).

human nature included. The second project is conceptual, to recover the content of our ordinary psychological and ethical conceptions or ideas. Hobbes merges the two projects by assuming that properly understood this content must be metaphysically unobjectionable, by Hobbes' lights. Any claims that appear to differ from his metaphysics are dismissed by Hobbes as really contentless verbiage, and as having nothing to do with anything we might intelligibly think. But of course these two projects, to determine the true metaphysics and to recover content, are not the same. It could be that the true metaphysics and what we ordinarily think are very different: that our thought contains elements that have a clear content that is ethically important but that is, nevertheless, false and that fails to apply. It could be that it really does matter to our ethics that we possess some power of self-determination, despite the fact that such a power does not, and perhaps, never could, actually exist.

This volume, *Self-Determination*, will principally address psychological issues. The emphasis is on recovering the content of our ordinary belief about human action. What kind of phenomenon do we ordinarily take intentional human action to be? As for the possible existence of some ethically significant power of self-determination, we need to determine what forms such a power might take. It is often thought, even by many sceptics about the reality of human freedom, that if moral responsibility depends on some metaphysically distinctive power of self-determination at all, it must depend on our possessing full-blown libertarian free will—a power that is over alternatives, and that causal determinism would remove. But it could be that moral responsibility, though it does depend on a power of self-determination, need not specifically depend on this power taking the form of libertarian free will. If many people do nevertheless naturally believe in libertarian freedom, this may not have very much to do with ethics. Important elements of our beliefs about our actual capacity to determine action for ourselves may have a non-ethical origin.

Indeed, regarding the classic issue of freedom's compatibility with causal determinism, this book does not in the end side either with incompatibilism or compatibilism. Rather it suggests a new way of looking at this debate that explains its peculiar intractability, especially as the debate is currently conducted by philosophers.

At the heart of the free will problem is an unresolved debate within the English-language philosophical tradition about the nature of power. Is all power like that of ordinary causation—the power of stones to break windows or of fire to melt ice? Or are we committed to the existence of forms of power in non-causal form, including possibly the power of freedom? How might we learn about the existence and nature of various kinds of power, and are certain forms of power, such as, for example, freedom and causation, experientially or phenomenologically presented to us? Thanks to the immense influence of the work on power and action of Hobbes and Hume, these questions have been neglected by many modern theories of freedom. But these questions are fundamental to resolving the free will problem.

The second volume, *Normativity*, will then address in more detail the question of ethics and the nature of ethical standards. That further volume will look at various different kinds of ethical standard, including obligation, and at how these standards might be normative, making some sort of call on us to meet them. To understand ethical standards and their normativity, we shall need an account both of the standards themselves and of the various kinds of human capacity they might govern and direct. One modern approach to normativity is that of ethical rationalism—the project, suggested by the work of philosophers such as Scanlon and Raz as well as by the work of many consequentialists, of understanding ethical normativity simply in terms of some model of reason, and so too of understanding ethical standards as addressing just various forms of a capacity on our part to respond to reason. But there is another, very different approach—that of David Hume, who sought to understand ethical normativity as something quite different from a normativity of reason, and who accordingly located the ethical life in quite other aspects of psychology than our capacity to respond to reason.

The two approaches to normativity, ethical rationalism and Humean reason-scepticism, are obviously opposed. But we shall see that they share a common concern: to distance ethics from any commitment to self-determination—to our possession of a power to determine for ourselves how we act. Because of this, volume two will argue, the distinctive ethical significance of action poses difficulties for both approaches to normativity. Neither ethical rationalism nor Hume's reason-scepticism can explain the special significance for morality of what we actually do or omit doing. Nevertheless both approaches to normativity are important, for each highlights vital aspects of normativity neglected by the other. Hume's theory of normativity is of especial importance, for there really is much of ethical and moral significance in human life that has nothing directly to do with reason or our capacity to respond to reason. Hume's reflections on the relation between virtue and talent exhibit, in particular, a profound grasp of the significance within ethics of the non-rational—or so I shall argue.

The contrasting inadequacies of ethical rationalism and reason-scepticism will lead us back to the very much more complex accounts of normativity of the pre-Enlightenment—especially those involved in the natural law theory of medieval and early modern scholasticism, which combined appeals to reason with appeals to other, importantly different kinds of capacity. These further capacities include self-determination, but other capacities too, none of which is a function of our reason.[2]

The chapters of *Self-Determination* are in outline as follows:

1. Action and Its Place in Ethics

This chapter explores why action might be the proper object of moral blame, and raises the issue of self-determination as a power presupposed by blame. Two

---

[2] For a preliminary discussion, see Thomas Pink, 'Law and the normativity of obligation', *The Jurisprudence Annual Lecture 2014, Jurisprudence* 5, no. 1 (2014): pp. 1–28.

conceptions of action are introduced. The *voluntariness-based* conception goes back to Thomas Hobbes, and dominates contemporary philosophy. This takes action to be an expression and effect of prior motivation—action is conceived as an effect of the passive. The opposing *practical reason-based* conception takes intentional action to be a distinctive and action-constitutive mode of exercising reason.

2. Freedom and Purposiveness

We should distinguish two very different phenomena associated with action. The first is self-determination, or the power or capacity of an agent to determine for herself what she does, which is a relation of agent to action. The second is purposiveness or goal-direction, which is a relation of action to object—of an action to its goal—where the goal is an object of thought. What is the relationship within the theory of action between a theory of self-determination and a theory of purposiveness? And how might this relation matter to the nature of self-determination? The chapter examines the possibility that self-determination might take the form of freedom, a power to determine alternatives, and introduces the problems raised by such a conception of self-determination.

3. Motivation and Voluntariness

Two elements to action as goal-directed or purposive doing are distinguished: motivation, involving psychological attitudes and the agent's orientation towards goals; and voluntariness, the production of outcomes on the basis of a motivation or will so to act, and so in a way explained by that motivating orientation towards goals.

What is the relation between motivation and voluntariness, and how might motivation explain what we do voluntarily? It seems that motivation is itself non-voluntary—not itself subject to the will as is the voluntary action it explains. Is action to be found exclusively in what we do voluntarily; or can action occur as non-voluntary motivation too?

4. The Non-Voluntariness of the Will

The possible distinctiveness of one particular kind of motivation is discussed—motivations of the will understood as our capacity for decision and intention. If motivation is non-voluntary, does that include decisions and intentions? The chapter argues that decisions and intentions, as Hobbes rightly supposed, are not voluntary themselves. Discussion centres on Kavka's toxin puzzle and its implications for the theory of action.

5. The Voluntariness-Based Model of Action

The chapter centres on Hobbes' radical project in action theory, which has dominated English-language action theory since—of identifying action and its purposiveness with voluntariness. To do something as a means to an end is to do it on the basis of a will to do it, and so as an effect of passive pro attitudes towards doing it. The chapter discusses the implications of this model, and the peculiar difficulties it poses, very much pressed by Hobbes himself, for the intuition that, though non-voluntary, decisions to act are themselves goal-directed actions—deliberately taken for the purpose of ensuring performance of the action decided upon.

6. Freedom and Scepticism: Incompatibilism

The chapter addresses freedom as a form of self-determination that involves power to determine alternatives. One form of modern scepticism about the existence of such a power assumes incompatibilism about freedom—our very concept of freedom is taken to be an incompatibilist one—and then infers freedom's unreality from this incompatibilism. The chapter discusses this scepticism in Galen Strawson, and also a further sceptical error theory of how, if entirely without application, an incompatibilist or libertarian concept of freedom could ever have arisen—an error theory that appeals to an intrusion of misguided ethics into psychology. Doubts are raised about the viability of such an error theory. It looks as though our conception of self-determination may be ethically underdetermined. Important elements of our conception of self-determination may come instead from outside ethics. These elements feed into ethics and they may shape ethical theory; but they are not ethical in origin.

7. Freedom and Scepticism: Alternatives

This chapter discusses a different form of scepticism about freedom—a scepticism directed not at freedom conceived in specifically incompatibilist terms, but at the very idea of a power to determine alternatives. Is such a power over alternatives possible?

Modern philosophy often assumes that all power, any capacity to produce or determine outcomes, is by its very nature a causal phenomenon; and that this is both a conceptual truth, about our very concept of power, and a metaphysical truth, about what kinds of power the world can contain.

It is suggested that whatever may be the truth regarding metaphysics, our concept of power clearly allows for power to take non-causal form, and such non-causal forms of power are still central to common-sense psychology and ethics, as they were once central to scholastic ethical and psychological theory. Self-determination, as ordinarily conceived, is a central case of non-causal power—non-causal because conceived by us as operating to determine outcomes in a way radically unlike ordinary causation.

Much scepticism about freedom that is ostensibly concerned with incompatibilism turns out, on examination, really to be targeted at freedom understood in just this way—as a power over alternatives operating differently from ordinary causation.

The chapter examines various projects to distance self-determination from freedom's supposedly problematic involvement of alternatives. One such is the rationalist project of identifying self-determination with our capacity for reason. Against this rationalist project, the capacity for reason is shown to be quite different from any capacity for self-determination. Self-determination involves our exercising power; whereas our capacity for reason subjects us to power, rather than constitutes our possession of it.

8. Moral Responsibility and Reduction

This chapter examines the attempt to replace freedom or power over alternatives as a basis of moral responsibility with other, supposedly less problematic, forms of ordinary causal power—such as voluntariness as a causal power of our will or motivation to determine us to act as willed.

A distinction is drawn between an old project, associated with Calvin, of proposing voluntariness as a substitute basis of moral responsibility when freedom is lost or absent; and a modern and highly counter-intuitive project, associated with Frankfurt, of showing freedom to be irrelevant to moral responsibility even when freedom is present.

The second and modern project is shown to have its roots in a reductive approach to freedom characteristic of English-language compatibilism. Freedom as a power over alternatives is reduced to a complex form of voluntariness. This reduction guarantees the irrelevance to moral responsibility of the freedom to do otherwise. But the reduction is questionable, for that very reason, as an account of our ordinary conception of freedom, which takes the freedom to do otherwise to be, when present, very relevant to moral responsibility.

It is conceptually possible, however, that there could be a power of self-determination distinct from ordinary causation and clearly sufficient to base moral responsibility, but without involving, by its very nature, the freedom to act or determine otherwise. If we nevertheless believe that in our case self-determination does so involve a freedom to do otherwise, this belief seems not to be required by ethics, nor by the very concept of self-determination. The source of this belief lies outside ethics.

9. The Practical Reason-Based Model and Its Past

Though decisions are non-voluntary, we still think of decisions to act as themselves actions that we can determine for ourselves—unlike other equally non-voluntary motivations, such as desire, that are passive.

Scholastic action theory identified decisions, or actions of the will, as action in its primary or true form, and the point at which we directly exercised our freedom or control; our control over the voluntary actions decided upon was seen as indirect, being exercised wholly through our control of the decisions that gave rise to those voluntary actions. This *volitionist* theory of action is a mirror image of Hobbes' theory of action as nothing more than voluntariness, and seems at least as objectionable. The Hobbesian theory privileges voluntary action, while the volitionist theory privileges non-voluntary actions of the will. But common sense seems to view both non-voluntary decisions to act and the voluntary actions decided upon as equally cases of action.

The chapter argues that the volitionism of scholastic action theory was a merely surface feature of it. In fact, scholastic action theory deployed an underlying theory of intentional action that was not volitionist at all, and that, properly understood, applies equally to decisions to act and to voluntary actions, privileging neither over the other. This is a practical reason-based model of intentional action as involving a distinctively action-constitutive mode of exercising reason. Hobbes' assault on scholastic action theory was very perceptively directed, not at its surface volitionism, but at the underlying and much more plausible theory of action's relation to practical reason.

10. Intention and Practical Reason

This chapter argues that intention is a reason-applying attitude, and that because of its reason-applying role intention is essential to the occurrence of genuinely intentional action. The chapter builds on, but goes beyond, Michael Bratman's planning theory of intention. The peculiarly reason-applying role of intention is identified through a contrast with what Brian O'Shaughnessy has characterized as subintentional action—action that is purposive but in no way intentional, and which bypasses our capacity for reason. Intention plays a very distinctive role in the motivation of voluntary action; and it is that distinctive role, and its importance to action rationality, which explains why motivation by intention is essential to voluntary action being properly intentional.

11. The Action-Constitutive Exercise of Reason

The distinctive role played by intention in the motivation of voluntary action has implications for the rationality of intention and intention-formation itself. Intention involves a special form of rationality—a form which incorporates purposiveness. We arrive at a new account of the purposiveness involved in intentional agency—an account that explains purposiveness not as voluntariness and not as an effect or expression of passive motivation, but as a special mode of exercising reason.

This model of purposiveness allows for purposive action to occur in non-voluntary form, as decision-making or intention-formation, and independently of passive causes.

12. Action and Its Motivation

This chapter examines the implications of the practical reason-based model of action for the modern debate about action motivation.

Much contemporary discussion assumes a model of motivation as something provided for action by prior attitudes—by content-bearing occurrences that are distinct from the action that they motivate. The debate then centres on what might connect action to the distinct attitudes that provide it with its motivation. Are the motivating attitudes causes of the action that they motivate? Or is there some non-causal link between attitudes and action?

This chapter argues for a more complex picture. Motivation may involve attitudes as occurrences distinct from the action motivated. But motivation may be internal to action itself. And in either case motivation may also involve the operation of motivating power: the goals at which action is directed may *move*—determine or influence us—to perform that action. Motivating power may be causal, being exercised through prior attitudes; but, at least as conceived in common-sense psychology, motivating power can take non-causal form as well, arising just from the action's object.

13. Voluntariness and Freedom of the Will

Freedom and voluntariness are quite distinct forms of power. Voluntariness is a power of the will or of motivation to get us to act as willed. Freedom is a power exercised by us to determine not only voluntary actions, but non-voluntary motivations of the will itself—our decisions and intentions.

That freedom extends to non-voluntary motivation is an essential feature of freedom, as ordinarily understood. It is up to us how we act only because we have a capacity to decide how we shall act, and it is up to us how we decide to act. Freedom of action depends on a freedom specifically of the will. But why?

And if freedom really is understood by us as something exercised over non-voluntary motivations, why have so many philosophers still tried to tie freedom and self-determination to voluntariness? Why have these philosophers supposed that if X is up to us or within our control, X must be subject to our will?

The inclination to tie freedom to voluntariness is shown to arise from the profound salience to us as rational agents of action in its voluntary form. Our idea of freedom is not, as Bernard Williams and others have suggested, a development out of some more primitive conception of self-determination as voluntariness. Rather our primitive conception of self-determination is of freedom as a power that can be exercised non-voluntarily; and the philosophical inclination to tie self-determination to voluntariness is the subsequent development.

14. Freedom and Causation

This chapter addresses the randomness problem—the worry, which goes back at least to Hume, that if we remove causal determination from human action, we are left not with freedom but with randomness or mere chance. This problem is shown to be spurious and the product of the assumption that all power is causal—that to determine an outcome is to determine it causally. The non-causal nature of self-determination is further argued for in this chapter, and parallels are developed between freedom and other forms of non-causal power.

15. Freedom as a Power

We conceive of self-determination as taking the form of a power of freedom—a power to determine alternative outcomes; and many of us also tend to an incompatibilist conception of the power. Why? The book argues that our ethics, and in particular our conception of moral responsibility, does not require self-determination to involve either alternatives or incompatibilism. So why are we so inclined to conceive of self-determination as involving both?

In this chapter our conception of self-determination as involving both alternatives and incompatibilism is traced to experience and the imagination—and in particular to the way these represent to us the operation on us of causal forces from outside the will. The modern free will debate has been shaped by the assumption, going back at least to Hume, that power, and the relations between one power and another, are never directly represented to us in experience. This 'aphenomenalism' about power is crucial to modern attempts to resolve the free will problem—a problem centrally about the relation of one power, freedom, to another, causation—entirely conceptually, rather than by reference to experience. The attempt to bypass experience has been especially distorting for incompatibilism which, through reliance on dubious conceptual argument, such as the consequence argument, has come to be understood by philosophers in ways that sharply conflict with experience, and in particular with the way we experience the operation of our will. Future progress on free will requires a better epistemology and phenomenology of power.

1

Action and Its Place in Ethics

1.1 Action and Reason

Action is not something arbitrary or groundless. There are justifications or reasons why we should do some things and avoid doing others, or so we ordinarily suppose. In which case there is such a thing as a practical or action-directive reason. As adult humans we have the capacity both to recognize this directive reason in the specific justifications that constitute it, and to be guided into performing those actions which are sensible and supported by reasons, and refraining from those actions that the available justifications oppose.

So our capacity for action, it is natural to think, is one part of our general rationality. To act is one way in which we can exercise our capacity to respond to reasons. This is something that we can do competently, when we act sensibly and in ways that are justified; or incompetently when, despite our sensitivity to reason and our general capacity to do what is sensible, we ignore reason and do what is foolish instead.

But action is only one mode by which, competently or incompetently, sensibly or foolishly, we exercise our rationality. For we can also arrive at beliefs, experience desires, and come to feel emotions. And all these psychological states or attitudes are similarly governed by reason, and can also be formed by us in response to reasons for and against. The evidence drives me to arrive at a particular conclusion about what happened, the tempting attractions of an offer bring on a desire to accept it, which for a while almost grips me, the obvious danger of my situation overwhelms me with fear. These situations involve perfectly good justifications for belief, for desire, for fear. And in forming the belief, the desire, the fear, I am again exercising a capacity to respond to these justifications—to exercise rationality. But I am not performing any action.

When, for example, on being made a tempting offer I immediately feel a strong desire to accept it, my reason certainly is involved. I can be responding as a rational animal to a perfectly good rational justification—to features of the offer which do make accepting it, in some respects at least, very desirable. But feeling this strong desire to accept the offer is hardly going, just on that basis, to count as my own deliberate doing. The desire to accept is surely something which just comes over me—which my receptivity to these justifications just lands me with. Simply learning of the tempting details of the offer is enough to leave a desire to accept it arising irresistibly within me. That such a desire arises within me constitutes no intentional or deliberate doing on my part; nor would the failure of such a desire to arise constitute an omission of action.

Desire is a mode of exercising rationality. Desires can be sensible or foolish, and there can perfectly well be reasons for and against wanting things. But desire is nevertheless a mode of exercising rationality that is *passive*. By *passive* I mean here merely that the event of coming to have a desire is not an action, and correspondingly that the persisting state of desire that results is not a state whose beginning constitutes action. As passive, desires are things which happen to us without being directly our doing.

Action and desire formation are both modes of exercising reason. Yet they are otherwise as different as what we ourselves do is from what happens to us. What then explains the distinctive nature of action; and how among other ways of exercising reason might action stand out?

1.2 Moral Responsibility and Blame

There is one field in which this question obviously matters—and that is in ethics. For morality seems centrally concerned with how we act. Moral standards seem to involve reasons for acting this way rather than that. If we were not capable of performing actions at all, but were merely passive observers of the passing scene, it is hard to imagine us being answerable to moral standards, or subject to moral appraisal and criticism.

Our moral responsibility, in particular, is for action—or so it is common to think. It is for how we act that we are morally responsible—not for what happens to us independently of our own doing. This has been a widespread intuition. But nowadays the intuition is often challenged. One contemporary challenge is based on a philosophical doctrine about action and, especially, its ethical significance—a doctrine that appeals to action's role as one mode of exercising reason among many. The doctrine is that as far as our moral accountability for what we do is concerned, there is nothing to privilege action (and our responsibility for it) over any other mode of exercising rationality. If moral responsibility is understood properly, we are responsible, not just for what we deliberately do or refrain from doing, but for any rationally appraisable attitude. And so T.M. Scanlon argues with especial clarity, in his *What We Owe to Each Other*. Responsibility, he thinks, is not for actions and omissions alone, but for something more general. Responsibility is for how we exercise our capacity for rationality—something we do, not just in our actions, but more generally in forming psychological attitudes of belief, desire, emotion, and the like. What we are responsible for is how we exercise our reason: '"being responsible" is mainly a matter of the appropriateness of demanding reasons…'.[1] So moral responsibility is something that we possess not just for our actions but also for our prior passive attitudes:

---

[1] T.M. Scanlon, *What We Owe to Each Other* (Cambridge MA: Harvard University Press, 1998), p. 22.

For this reason, one can be responsible not only for one's actions but also for intentions, beliefs and other attitudes. That is, one can properly be asked to defend these attitudes according to the canons relevant to them, and one can be appraised in the light of these canons for the attitudes one holds. The 'sting' of finding oneself responsible for an attitude that shows one's thinking to be defective by certain standards will be different in each case, depending on our reasons for caring about the standards in question. But the basic idea of responsibility is the same.[2]

In fact, on Scanlon's view, it is primarily attitudes that are rationally appraisable, and it is primarily in attitude formation that we exercise our reason: 'Judgment-sensitive attitudes constitute the class of things for which reasons in the standard normative sense can sensibly be asked for or offered.'[3] Whereas actions occur only as expressions of prior attitudes, and it is only as such expressions that they count as rationally appraisable at all:

Actions are the kind of things for which normative reasons can be given only insofar as they are intentional, that is, are the expression of judgment-sensitive attitudes . . . it is the connection with judgment-sensitive attitudes that makes events actions, and hence the kind of things for which reasons can sensibly be asked for and offered at all.[4]

The implication for moral responsibility is clear. According to Scanlon, what we are responsible for is not agency as such, but the rationally appraisable. Since our actions are rationally appraisable only as expressions of priorly rationally appraisable attitudes, Scanlon's view implies that we are responsible first of all for attitudes as things which occur within us prior to and independently of how we act; and we are responsible for our actions only as expressions of these prior and passive attitudes. Responsibility for non-actions comes first. And then responsibility for actions follows.

But I suspect that this is really the reverse of our ordinary view. For surely we ordinarily think that our moral responsibility is primarily for how we act—for what we ourselves do or fail to. It is what we ourselves do or refrain from doing and the consequences of this that is our responsibility—not what happens independently of our own doing. In which case any responsibility we might have for our passive attitudes is derivative, and based on the extent to which we have been in a position to use prior actions to influence some of those attitudes. To make our moral responsibility for what we ourselves do a secondary and derivative case of responsibility—this is to turn our ordinary view of moral responsibility upside down.

Ethical rationalism is the view that the ethics of action are entirely to be explained in terms of general reason. Moral standards are just one kind of rational standard among others, and they govern action as one mode among others of exercising reason. To meet and conform to moral standards is no more than to exercise a general capacity for rationality—our capacity to respond to any standard of reasonableness. And to criticize someone morally is just to criticize them for some form of irrationality or

[2] *What We Owe to Each Other*, p. 22. [3] *What We Owe to Each Other*, p. 21.
[4] *What We Owe to Each Other*, p. 21.

unreasonableness—some failure in the exercise of reason. In so far as he equates moral responsibility with rational appraisability—'"being responsible" is mainly a matter of the appropriateness of demanding reasons...'—Scanlon is a clear ethical rationalist.

But this equation of moral responsibility with rational appraisability must be a mistake, at least as an interpretation of our ordinary ethical thinking. What shows this is the nature of blame—the criticism we make of people when we hold them responsible for having done wrong.

When we blame people for wrongdoing, we are not merely alleging some fault or deficiency in their response to reasons. And this is because of something that is quite central to the content of blame. Blame does not just report a deficiency in the person blamed. It further states that this deficiency was the person's fault—that they were 'to blame' for it. Blame, which asserts one's moral responsibility for what one is being blamed for, not only detects a fault. It also condemns the fault in one as one's own fault. The attribution of a fault as not only a fault in the person, but their fault, is essential to anything recognizable as genuine blame.

This fact about blame is key to what distinguishes moral responsibility from any mere rational appraisability. For Suppose someone is subject to ordinary rational criticism. Suppose, for example, that they have committed some error of reasoning. It is always a *further* question whether that they made this error was their fault. Are they responsible and to blame for the fact that they made it?—or did they make the mistake through no fault of their own? They were certainly being foolish or less than sensible; it is, after all, their reasoning which was bad. But we can still ask whether it was through their own fault that they reasoned incorrectly. The question of one's moral responsibility for one's attitudes remains open, even when one's rational appraisability for those attitudes is admitted. In which case Scanlon must be wrong. The kind of responsibility assumed in blame does not reduce to the appropriateness of rational appraisal.

Robert Merrihew Adams makes the same mistake as Scanlon—that of confusing blame with more general rational or ethical criticism. In his 'Involuntary sins' Adams has suggested that people can be blamed for attitudes, such as selfish motivations, that are not of their own doing.[5] Now certainly people can be criticized simply for being selfish, and that criticism of them is clearly moral. Selfishness is, after all, a deficiency in one's response to the interests of others. But Adams supposes that such criticism is not only moral, but always amounts to blame:

Perhaps for some people the word 'blame' has connotations that it does not have for me. To me, it seems strange to say that I do not blame someone though I think poorly of him, believing that his motives are thoroughly selfish. Intuitively speaking, I should have said that thinking poorly of a person in this way is a form of unspoken blame.[6]

---

[5] Robert Merrihew Adams, 'Involuntary sins', *Philosophical Review* 94, (1985): p. 21.
[6] 'Involuntary sins', p. 21.

But contrary to what Adams claims, to be criticized as selfish does not itself amount to being blamed. For again the selfishness of someone's motivation does not of itself settle the question which is raised in blame—namely their responsibility for the motivation they possess. Their selfishness, certainly a moral failing, is one thing. It is still a further question whether their possession of such a character is their fault. For there is no inconsistency at all in criticizing someone as having a selfish character, while wondering or doubting whether their possession of this character really is their fault. Just as someone can be criticized as poor at reasoning without this being supposed to be their fault, so they can be criticized as selfish without this being supposed to be their fault.

1.3 Self-Determination

When we ask whether a fault in someone, such as selfishness or reasoning error, is that person's fault, what does this question involve? What distinguishes general ethical criticism that detects a fault in someone—criticism of someone as unreasonable or selfish—from blame, where the fault is put down to them as their fault?

General ethical criticism of someone as unreasonable or selfish operates at just one level. It criticizes the person just by reference to some normative or ethical deficiency in a state or occurrence in their life. We criticize someone as unreasonable because they hold or are disposed to hold attitudes that are unreasonable. Similarly we criticize someone as selfish just because their motivations are selfish: their motivations disregard the interests of others. The criticism is of defective states and of the person just as possessing those defective states.

Blame, on the other hand, puts a person's possession of such states down to them as their fault. This supposes something more—a problem not fundamentally with events and states in the agent's life, but beyond these specifically with the agent. This problem with the agent cannot amount simply to normative or ethical deficiency at the level of their attitudes. For as we have seen, that sort of failure is already tracked by the ordinary ethical criticism that criticizes the agent as unreasonable or selfish just by reference to such deficiency. When we go on to ask whether unreasonableness or selfishness is the agent's fault, we are no longer appraising that agent just by reference to the nature of their attitudes. We are asking about the agent's further responsibility for those attitudes. We are examining the agent's role, not as a simple attitude-holder, but as a determiner of what attitudes they hold.

What the person is blamed for is put down to them as their fault—and their fault as mere unreasonableness or selfishness need not be. But if they are to blame this means that they must have been in a position in some way to determine or prevent the unreasonableness or selfishness for themselves—and determine in a way that goes beyond any mere exercise of their capacity for reason. Why else would the thing be their fault as an ordinary exercise of reason need not be? So at issue then is some power that they possessed over what they are being blamed for—a power distinctively to determine its occurrence or prevent it.

And this power, it seems, is exercised through agency. The special responsibility asserted in blame involves action or omission of action. Failing to respond in one's beliefs or motivations to reasons is one thing. Being responsible for that failure as occurring through one's fault, is another. What settles whether someone is so responsible? How, for example, to establish that it was through the bad reasoner's own fault that their reasoning was faulty? It seems clear enough how. We would raise questions about their action and omission and about how this might have affected their responsiveness to reason in this case—questions such as the following: what if they had taken greater pains at the time, such as by attending more carefully or taking longer to reflect; or had prepared themselves better beforehand, such as by working harder at practising this form of reasoning? Did the error arise from their failure to do any of these things? If on the other hand they would make the error whatever care they took, if they are simply not good enough at this kind of reasoning, then their making the error, though it certainly lays them open to rational criticism, is clearly not their fault. And so generally: we are responsible for a faulty response to reason only if this faulty response is brought about as or through some action or omission of our own. We are responsible for it only if it arises as our doing.

Responsibility of the sort invoked in blame, the idea of something's being one's fault, does seem to be tied to agency. We can always sensibly ask whether something already admitted as mistaken or bad, such as a reasoning error, or a selfish disposition, really has arisen through the person's own fault. And the answer to the question then depends, at least in part, on doing. We are responsible for the bad occurrence only if it arises as or out of our own action or omission.

Blame asserts a responsibility that is based on power—a power to determine outcomes for ourselves. If blame is for how we act, then that will be because this power to determine things for ourselves applies specifically to how we act, but not to the exercise of our rationality in general. If we are directly morally responsible for our actions and our failures to act, but not for non-actions such as mere desires, that is because the power of self-determination which moral responsibility presupposes is exercised in and through how we act, but is not exercised simply in coming to have a desire. It is this power and its link with action which explains our special and moral responsibility for how we act. If we exercise this power, or if, despite possessing it, we fail to exercise it, then we ourselves can be responsible and can be truly to blame. What happened as a result can truly have been our fault.

At the heart of our ethical thinking there lies an idea of power. Our moral responsibility for how we act presupposes a kind of power to determine for ourselves how we act. The bearer of the power is a person; and action is both the thing over which this power is immediately exercised and, in so far as we determine other things through how we act, a medium for the exercise of this power over those other things. It is the existence of this power which explains, if anything does, why it should in particular be for our actions and omissions of action that we are responsible.

The ethical rationalist characteristically denies that this supposed self-determination has any real moral significance. There is no kind of ethical criticism, such as blame, nor any kind of ethical standard, such as moral obligation, that might presuppose some special power to determine things for oneself. Such rationalist suspicion of self-determination is immediately based on that power's distinction from our basic capacity for reason. In the rationalist's view we can understand our capacity to respond to ethical standards entirely in terms of a capacity to respond to reasons or justifications. And just responding to reasons, the ethical rationalist plausibly maintains, seems not to involve any distinctive power to determine for ourselves what we do. For, as we have seen, we can respond to reasons or justifications through our general attitudes—attitudes that need not be determined by us. We do not determine for ourselves what desires we feel. Yet those desires can be responses to justifications nevertheless.

But the attempt to ring-fence ethics from self-determination is not peculiar to modern ethical rationalism. It has deep roots within the English-language ethical tradition. The ring-fencing of ethics from what are taken to be metaphysically extravagant powers and capacities goes back to Hobbes and Hume—and to views of the self that threaten to undermine not only belief in self-determination, but even the rationalist's own belief in the capacity for reason.

1.4 Scepticism about Self-Determination

We find suspicion of self-determination in philosophers who are equivocal about or even hostile to appeals to reason in ethical theory. Hume also thought that ethical appraisal is primarily of attitudes and mental character, not actions:

> If any *action* be either virtuous or vicious, 'tis only as a sign of some quality or character ... Actions themselves, not proceeding from any constant principle, have no influence on love or hatred, pride or humility; and consequently are never consider'd in morality.[8]

And Hume too viewed blame as involving no appeal to self-determination. Blame, for Hume, involved nothing more than negative evaluation. Just as much as Scanlon, then, Hume also refused to recognize the distinguishing feature of blame—that not only is the agent criticized or negatively evaluated for a fault, but the fault is put down to them as their fault, because they had the capacity to determine the fault's

---

[7] Not all rationalists take this view. There is a rationalism, not about ethical standards, but about self-determination, that sees our very capacity for rationality as constituting a power on our part to determine for ourselves what actions we perform and what attitudes we form. I discuss this particular form of rationalism in chapter 7.

[8] David Hume, *A Treatise of Human Nature*, ed. P.H. Nidditch (Oxford: Clarendon Press, 1978), p. 575.

occurrence or non-occurrence for themselves: 'A blemish, a fault, a vice, a crime; these expressions seem to denote different degrees of censure and disapprobation; which are, however, all of them, at the bottom, pretty nearly of the same kind or species.'[9]

But unlike Scanlon, Hume denied that moral standards were standards of reason, or that in governing motivation and action they in any way addressed a capacity on our part to respond to reason. In Hume's view, motivations and actions involved no such capacity for rationality.

Suspicion of appeals to self-determination in ethical theory need not then be based on a view of ethical standards as just standards of reason. The suspicion can have quite another source instead. The suspicion can come not from rationalism, but from some form of metaphysical naturalism. By metaphysical naturalism I mean the view that there is nothing metaphysically distinctive about deliberate human agency, or indeed about human psychological processes generally. The powers and capacities involved in human nature and action are no more than special cases of powers and capacities found in wider nature. Naturalism places self-determination under suspicion, not because self-determination—'determining things for oneself'—is surplus to what is involved in simply being reasonable, but because self-determination is too radically unlike capacities and powers found elsewhere.

Ethical rationalism and metaphysical naturalism are importantly different theories. Ethical rationalism is, at least immediately, a theory of the content of our ethical thought—of what we really mean when we propose moral standards and convey moral criticism. And rationalism sees this content as concerned simply with reason and rationality. Whereas metaphysical naturalism is a theory of what powers and capacities are actually to be found in the world, and in human beings in particular. But ethical rationalists may well be encouraged by metaphysical naturalism and its contemporary appeal. For in so far as metaphysical naturalism tends to discredit belief in the very possibility of self-determination, the ethical rationalist can claim to be presenting an account of morality that detaches the content of our ethics from commitment to a metaphysically dubious form of power—a form of power that appears completely absent from the rest of nature.

But the alliance between naturalism and rationalism is an uneasy one, and not nearly so convenient as it might immediately appear. For of course the same worries that the naturalist has about self-determination might be had about the capacity for reason itself. Just like the capacity to determine for oneself what one does, the capacity to respond to justifications seems peculiar to humans, or at best to humans and the higher animals. And though the capacity for reason may not require self-determination on our part, it may still involve other modes of power and determination radically unlike ordinary causation.

---

[9]   David Hume, *An Enquiry Concerning the Principles of Morals*, ed. P.H. Nidditch (Oxford: Clarendon Press 1975), p. 322.

There is anyway a second question mark over the alliance. If self-determination—a power on our part to determine for ourselves what we do—really is a fiction, it would be pleasant if our ethical thought were not committed to its reality. But in fact there is nothing to rule out the possibility that our ethics presupposes much that is false, including our possession of a capacity for self-determination. The truth of metaphysical naturalism would not suffice to prove ethical rationalism true too. Naturalism may deny our possession of a power to determine actions and outcomes for ourselves; and it may even be right in this denial. But that does not establish the ethical rationalist's claim that no such power is presupposed by moral blame. It may yet be that the content of moral blame presupposes powers and capacities that do not actually exist. These powers and capacities may turn out to be fictions, and so to be denied by the best metaphysics; but they may still be central features of our ethics, and essential to moral responsibility nonetheless. We must beware of assuming that the best metaphysics is any very reliable guide to the content of our ethics.

Indeed the possibility that our ethical thought involves metaphysical fictions is central to a modern project of explaining where, if it is so erroneous, the belief in our possession of a capacity for self-determination comes from. The more it is felt that self-determination, as we ordinarily understand it, is too radically unlike anything else in nature to be real, the greater the temptation to develop an error theory of our belief in it—a theory that traces our conception of this power of self-determination, not to the way the world reveals itself to us, but to our ethical thinking instead. According to this error theory, we believe in self-determination only because of an ethical commitment—to a theory of a distinctively moral responsibility for what we do. We believe in self-determination as a condition of blaming people, and putting faults down to them as their fault.

So there is no necessary association between ethical rationalism and metaphysical naturalism. Far from it: to the extent that individual ethical rationalists might want not only to understand the content of our ethical thought, but to vindicate it too, metaphysical naturalism may be a threat to those rationalists' own belief in rationality; and in any case, even if naturalism is true, that may establish nothing in the rationalist's favour about the actual content of our ethics.

Nevertheless, within the English-language philosophical tradition, ethical rationalism and metaphysical naturalism have long been linked historically. And the figure most responsible for this linking was Thomas Hobbes. Hobbes opposed the very existence of self-determination as a power because, in his view, human nature is continuous with the rest of nature, and no such power exists in wider nature. In particular, any attempt to understand self-determination in terms of ordinary causal power would, Hobbes argued, end in absurdity. But, exactly as Hume and Scanlon were also later to suppose, blame in any case involves no presupposition of any such power:

[Why do we blame people?] I answer because they please us not. I might ask him, whether blaming be any thing else but saying the thing blamed is ill or imperfect . . . I answer, they are to be blamed though their wills be not in their power. Is not good good and evill evill though they be not in our power? And shall I not call them so? And is that not praise and blame? But it seems that the Bishop takes blame not for the dispraise of a thing, but for a praetext and colour of malice and revenge against him that he blameth.[10]

Our everyday ethical conceptions involved, in Hobbes' view, no thought of any power or capacity that the true metaphysics would not also countenance. For powers or capacities, such as self-determination, that were, in Hobbes' view, fictional or absurd, were simply not represented to us in our experience, and so nor were they represented in the imagination that depends on experience, and that, in his view, alone provides our capacity for thought. Reference to powers of self-determination was literally empty talk—philosophical jargon. Whatever words we might utter, we really did not think actual thoughts about determining our actions for ourselves. For Hobbes, metaphysics and the retrieval and interpretation of the content of our ethical conceptions were one and the same enterprise.

But more than that, Hobbes saw no tension between either enterprise and a fundamentally rationalist account of the content of ethical thought. He was extremely hostile, as we shall see, to powers apparently associated with the capacity for reason as we ordinarily understand it—just because these powers were in such tension with his naturalism. But he continued to view ethical standards as standards of reason nonetheless, and to attribute to us a capacity to respond to ethical standards so conceived.

Hobbes did not deny our capacity for reason. He simply avoided serious examination of the metaphysical demands made by such a capacity as ordinarily conceived. He never subjected the very idea of such a capacity to the same hostile examination as he gave to self-determination. But he did nonetheless seek to shrink the scope of our capacity for reason, and to avoid appeals to ideas of reason and rationality in his characterization of human psychology and action. Hobbes may not have done what Hume did later—which was to exclude reason entirely from motivation and action. Hobbes certainly did not deny the capacity for practical reason altogether. But he did restrict and relocate that capacity—to the passive. And in this he was a decisive influence on subsequent philosophy, and on action theory in particular.

1.5 Rationalism, Naturalism, and the Theory of Action

One of the central historical links between metaphysical naturalism and ethical rationalism lies in a shared theory of action. This is the action theory bequeathed to both traditions by Hobbes. The Hobbesian theory of action is not something that ethical rationalism is committed to just by its central doctrine—that ethical standards

---

[10] Thomas Hobbes in Thomas Hobbes and John Bramhall, *The Questions Concerning Liberty, Necessity and Chance, clearly stated between Dr Bramhall Bishop of Derry, and Thomas Hobbes of Malmesbury*, (London 1656), p. 40.

are responded to by us simply through the exercise of reason. Yet ethical rationalists such as Scanlon tend to accept the theory nonetheless. And this Hobbesian theory of action, once accepted, makes a coherent account of self-determination far more difficult. It is this theory of action which, in particular, lies behind Scanlon's highly counter-intuitive reversal of ordinary intuition about moral responsibility—his strange doctrine that moral responsibility for action is secondary to and derivative from a prior moral responsibility for attitudes.

This theory of action was openly appealed to by Scanlon in the passage quoted above:

Actions are the kind of things for which normative reasons can be given only insofar as they are intentional, that is, are the expression of judgment-sensitive attitudes . . . it is the connection with judgment-sensitive attitudes that makes events actions, and hence the kind of things for which reasons can sensibly be asked for and offered at all.[11]

According to Hobbes' and Scanlon's shared theory of human agency, action occurs only as an expression and effect of prior motivation—of psychological attitudes which as precedent to action are passive, not themselves our doing, but which are what move us to act in the way that we do. To act is to be moved to do something by prior beliefs and desires or other pro attitudes. It is these prior attitudes that make what we do count as a genuine action and, indeed, as any kind of exercise of reason. It is only through these prior beliefs and desires—attitudes that are passive antecedents of action and not actions themselves—that we count as exercising rationality in what we do.

This model makes it problematic how self-determination as ordinarily understood can occur at the point of action or be of ethical significance. It is clear from the outset where the threat might lie, at least in general terms. For according to the theory, it is only through prior motivations, through passive attitudes that move us to act, that action ever occurs. By its very nature, then, action occurs as the expression and output of a lot of events and states not of the agent's own doing. It is these events and states that produce the action and explain why the agent does what he does. In which case it looks as though it might really be these events and states, and not so much the agent, that determine action. The action-determining agent threatens to be pushed aside by the passive attitudes that define the very nature of action—and define it precisely as those factors that explain why the agent performs the actions that he does.

Not only is very little room left for self-determination. Responsibility for action is clearly left derivative from responsibility for the passive. On this theory, all that happens when we act is that a passive exercise of our rationality which occurs in and through our prior motivations is given outer expression—in the action that those motivations determine and produce. As Scanlon acknowledges, action is no more than the final expression of an exercise of our reason which was already made before, in and through the formation of attitudes within us that were not themselves our

---

[11] *What We Owe to Each Other*, p. 21.

doing. It was at that point, prior to action, that we responded or failed to respond to any reasons for action that moral standards might provide. As a response to moral standards, what we ourselves do is entirely parasitic on the passive—on attitudes within us which precede any action of our own. So why should action be any more our responsibility than are those attitudes? And surely it will then be true that any responsibility we might have for our actions is indeed derived from a prior responsibility for attitudes.

It was a form of naturalism that attracted Hobbes to this view of action. He could characterize human action, without appeal to any normative notions, and especially without appeal to any theory of practical reason, simply as an effect and expression of prior motivations—and so as an expression of the passive. But the consequences of the view were profound—for theories of rationality as well as for views of self-determination. Not only was self-determination made to appear a highly problematic phenomenon, but human reason was importantly detached from action. Practical reason was not yet denied altogether, as it was to be by Hume. But reason directed action only by virtue of directing and being responded to through motivations that were passive. This theory of action as an expression of the passive is not compulsory for ethical rationalists. As I shall show, they could have retained their view that we respond to ethical standards simply through the exercise of reason, but resisted Hobbes' theory of action and its consequence—the further, strange Scanlonian doctrine that our responsibility for action is actually secondary to and derivative from our responsibility for the passive. But history did not work in this direction. Borrowing Hobbes' action theory, ethical rationalism came to take a distinctively Hobbesian form.

1.6 Power and Reason

Our practice of blaming and holding morally responsible presupposes quite a different theory of action. For, as our consideration of blame has shown, at the heart of our ordinary thinking about action and its morality is an opposing intuition. Action really is ethically distinctive. To perform an action, actually to do something, is morally speaking quite different from simply being passively motivated so to act. And what makes action morally so very different is, indeed, its link to self-determination. When we act we may not only be doing something, as opposed to having something happen to or within us. We may also be exercising a power—to determine outcomes for ourselves. We can determine for ourselves what happens in our lives; and we do this not through the beliefs, desires, and feelings that come over us independently of our own doing, but in and through our very intentional agency itself—in and through what we deliberately and intentionally do or refrain from doing. It is this power of self-determination, exercisable in and through our action, that makes us so peculiarly responsible for what we do.

Action as we ordinarily understand it is ethically distinctive, then. Its ethical significance lies not just in its being a mode of exercising rationality—though it is indeed that—but in its being a mode of exercising self-determination. In action it is we who are in charge. But how might action as we ordinarily conceive it leave space for self-determination? How can action have an independence from prior happenings not of our own doing—enough independence to be something genuinely determined by us, as opposed to being a mere expression of those prior happenings?

This book will argue that our ordinary conception of action leaves clear room for self-determination—and it does so by identifying action not as a kind of effect or expression of motivations, but through according it a special and distinctive place within the human capacity for reason. Crucial is the distinctive way that reason is involved in the performance of human action. Of course the self-determination which we exercise in action must, on our ordinary understanding, involve more than just the exercise of reason. This has to be true, since otherwise self-determination and the moral responsibility which it bases would not be specific to how we act, but apply to any mode of exercising reason. Nevertheless, it is still the theory of rationality which is key to uncovering the nature of the action through which our power of self-determination is exercised. What makes self-determination possible, on our ordinary conception, is that as a mode of exercising rationality action is quite distinctive. Intentional action, as we ordinarily understand it, is not any expression of prior motivation, but a special mode of exercising rationality in its own right—one which is distinct from and importantly independent of any other.

Scanlon would certainly admit that action is a mode of exercising rationality—that in acting intentionally we are exercising a capacity for responding to justifications. But as we have seen he is committed to denying that what distinguishes action and separates it from the passive is the way that reason is involved in how we act. To perform an action is certainly not to exercise reason in any very special way, since, on his view, the rationality with which we act is no more than an expression of the rationality with which we are first passively motivated to act. The rationality of action is entirely parasitic on and derivative from the rationality of prior motivation. So in fact our capacity for rationality is exercised in the same way in our motivating attitudes and in our actions. Action stands out only in its relation to these passive motivations—as being their expression, as being what they have motivated us to do.

But on the theory of action that forms part of psychological common sense, there is a clear distinction between action and any merely passive exercise of rationality. What makes action genuine action is not its being an expression of some prior exercise of rationality in passive motivation, but its being a distinctively practical, action-constitutive exercise of reason in its own right. Action can then occur in a way that is significantly independent of prior attitudes, determined to occur not by them but by ourselves (Figures 1.1 and 1.2).

Figure 1.1. Ethical rationalism.

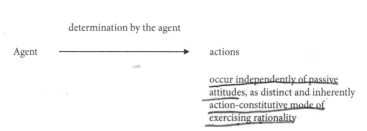

Figure 1.2. Action as ethically distinctive.

We can be responsible and accountable for how we act and for the consequences of how we act as we are responsible and accountable for nothing else—and this is so only because action occurs as a distinctive mode of exercising reason in its own right, a mode that is peculiarly practice- or action-constitutive. And this has profound implications both for the nature of action itself, and for the nature of normativity. Hobbes helped to remove self-determination from ethical theory by removing action from its place at the heart of our capacity for rationality. To recapture the true ethical significance of action as a locus of self-determination, we need to undo Hobbes' legacy, and restore action to a central and distinctive place in the theory of our reason.

Beyond that, we need to understand better the phenomenon of self-determination itself. For self-determination can be exercised by us through action only as a very special kind of power—one of a range of very distinctive powers entertained in common-sense psychology. Our ordinary ethical and psychological thought involves a complex theory of powers involved not just in self-determination, but in ethical life more widely—including our very capacity for rationality. These powers, as ordinarily understood by us, are conceived in ways that distinguish them sharply from ordinary causation. These powers may or may not actually exist, and since they seem absent from wider nature outside specifically human life, it is the programme of metaphysical naturalism to demonstrate their unreality. But even if such a demonstration can be given, these powers deserve the attention of the moralist nonetheless. For whether they are real or not, power in non-causal form is a central feature of our ethical self-conception, and is as fundamental to the rationality that ethical rationalism endorses as it is to the self-determination that ethical rationalism rejects.

2

Freedom and Purposiveness

2.1 Action and Self-Determination

It is sometimes supposed that action is by its very nature something self-deter-mined—that for a human, or even for an animal, deliberately and intentionally to do something is *ipso facto* for them to determine some outcome for themselves.[1] But that is not obviously true. I intentionally retreat from coming danger. Yet what moves me to retreat may be overpowering fear. And a fear can so naturally be described as overpowering because especially intense cases of it are felt not only as motivating action, but as overwhelming our capacity to determine for ourselves what we do. We may do something deliberately and intentionally, but feel driven to do it by an emotion, and not by ourselves.

There are two aspects to human agency that are importantly distinct—and which were once carefully distinguished by many past action theorists, but which, since Hobbes, modern English language action theory has tended to assimilate. These two aspects are purposiveness and self-determination. The intuitiveness of the possibility of performing actions, but without determining those actions for ourselves—instead being driven or compelled to act by something else—is very much bound up with the difference between purposiveness and self-determination.

An action is a change—change that an omission of the action would avoid. But change can be passive. It can happen to someone, as opposed to being done by them. What makes a change count as one's own doing? The answer seems to lie in purposiveness. To be employing some change as a means, in order to attain some goal, is to be involved in action. It is to be doing something as a means to an end. Not only is change made as a means to an end always action; but action itself is always goal-directed or done as a means to some end—even if the goal just is the perform-ance of the action itself, as when an action is performed for its own sake.[2] Likewise, omission, when not a mere absence of action but a genuinely negative exercise of the

---

[1] Thus Helen Steward proposes a view of action as by its very nature up to the agent:

'An action is to be thought of as an input into the course of events such that it is essentially up to its agent whether or not it occurs...' *A Metaphysics for Freedom*, (Oxford: Oxford University Press, 2012), 'Overview', p. xi.

[2] The goal-direction of action is the doctrine with which Aristotle begins the *Nicomachean Ethics* at 1094a, in *The Complete Works of Aristotle*, ed. Jonathan Barnes, (Princeton: Princeton University Press, 1984) vol. 2, p. 1729.

capacity for agency, the deliberate avoidance of change, will take a similarly purposive form. Omission occurs as agency when, for example, I remain very still not because I am asleep or out cold, but for a purpose—in order to evade detection. It is this employment of means to ends that distinguishes action and agency generally from non-agency. In particular it distinguishes genuine agency from mere inclinations to act or to refrain. I may be attracted towards doing or omitting doing something—I have some desire to do or omit—without yet having been involved in actual agency. And that is because a desire is not something I form as a means to any end—which is why simply in coming to want something I am not yet properly 'doing'. What I want is merely an object of attraction. It is not a goal that my desire is being used to attain.

A theory of action is going, then, to be a theory of purposiveness—of what it is for an event or change to constitute the employment of some means towards an end. It will characterize action in terms of its distinctive relation to a goal. A theory of self-determination, by contrast, is very different. True, a theory of self-determination also relates action or omission to something else. But the entity to which it relates action is very different from any goal, as is the manner of relation. A theory of self-determination is a theory of an action or omission's relation, not to a goal, but to its agent as someone who determines its occurrence.

purposiveness/goal-direction:

> action—goal

freedom/self-determination:

> agent—action

The relation of an action or omission to its goal is not at all the same as that of an agent to the action or omission that he determines. Besides the action or omission itself, involved as a *relatum* in both cases, the other *relata* are quite different. In the one case we have an actual substance, a determining agent; but in the other case, we have something that need not be actual in the same way. The goal of an action is something that may or may not ever occur, for the action, though aimed at the goal's attainment, may prove unsuccessful. The goal of an action seems then to be, in itself, just an object of the agent's thought.

Considered as a relation between an occurrence and an object of thought—what is being aimed at—purposiveness seems to have important parallels. We seem in the goal-directedness of action to have a particular case of a wider phenomenon—what philosophers refer to as intentionality at the level of the mental, or mental direction at an object of thought. Actions are directed at objects of thought as are beliefs and desires and other attitudes. What might distinguish action, if we apply this parallel to provide a theory of agency, is the way that action is directed at its object. A belief is directed at its object as true, a desire is directed at its object as something good or desirable; and an action is directed at its object as a goal. The task for a theory of action is then to characterize these various modes of intentionality or mental direction, and the action-constitutive one in particular. What is it for a psychological attitude, or the event of its formation, to be directed at an object as its goal—to be employed, in other words, as a means to an end?

In all these cases of intentionality or mental directedness—action, belief, desire—we have some mode of direction at an object that need not be actual. By contrast, where the exercise of self-determination is concerned, the relation of an agent to the action he determines is a relation where both entities are actual. Here what is required is not a theory of intentionality or mental directedness, but of power, and of the relation between someone exercising a power and an entity—an action—that they are using that power to make actual—to produce. And it is far from obvious that each of these two very different relations, between action and object and between agent and action, involving, besides the action, two such very different *relata*, should be constituted in the same way or explained by one and the same theory.

If this is the right way to understand action, then there seems no reason why an action need be determined by its agent. If the right way to understand action is indeed via a theory of mental intentionality—of various modes of psychological direction towards mental objects—it is not obvious that an account of purposiveness need involve appeal to any kind of power on the agent's part to determine the action's occurrence. What is immediately crucial is the particular way in which an action or attitude is related to its non-actual object. Whether the agent is exercising some sort of power to determine the occurrence of an event with that particular mode of direction is another and further question. The action's relation to an object of thought seems one thing; the agent's relation to the action as determinant of it seems quite another.

And indeed historically, as we shall see, much action theory outside the English-language tradition respected this intuitive difference in subject matter. This is especially true of pre-Hobbesian action theory—the action theory of scholastic Aristotelianism that Hobbes set out to oppose. Scholastic action theory carefully allowed for actions or purposive doings that were not determined by their agents; and avoided making the theory of action and its purposiveness do duty for a further theory of self-determination. Purposiveness was understood, in just the way I have proposed, to involve a distinctive mode of intentionality—a distinctive mode of psychological direction at an object of thought—and one that need not be determined by the agent. Self-determination itself was then clearly identified as involving something importantly different—a distinctive power to determine the very occurrence of that form of intentionality. And since the theory of action was importantly distinct from the theory of self-determination, there could easily be a general consensus about the nature of action itself, but widespread and quite radical disagreement about the nature of self-determination. And that, in the scholastic tradition, is what we find. Scholasticism maintained a consensus about the nature of action and its purposiveness, as involving a distinctively goal-directed mode of exercising reason. But there was then considerable disagreement about the nature of self-determination, a disagreement that centred largely on the relation between the power of agents to determine outcomes and their capacity for rationality.

Modern English-language action theory has taken an importantly different direction. It tends to take as basic either a theory of purposiveness or a theory of self-determination, and then seeks to make this one theory do all the work. One modern strategy, though very much a minority option, has been to attempt to sideline the project of giving an account of action in terms of purposiveness, and characterize action simply as a mode of self-determination. Action is often seen to involve a distinctive power to determine more than one outcome, perhaps under conditions where that outcome was previously undetermined.[3] But most modern English-language action theory has taken the opposite course. The dominant approach has been to start with an account of action that appeals to a theory of purposiveness, and then employ that theory of purposiveness to provide an account of self-determination too: self-determination is, in effect, purposiveness in some suitably souped-up form.

This second approach, of using purposiveness to explain self-determination, is the result of a radical change, which we owe to Hobbes, in the theory of purposiveness. Thanks to Hobbes, action and its purposiveness was no longer seen as involving a distinctive mode of intentionality. For action was no longer taken to be object-directed in the same way that beliefs or desires are object-directed. As Scanlon's casual drawing of the distinction suggested, it came to be thought that actions are one thing, and attitudes are quite another.

Taken in themselves, on much modern post-Hobbesian English-language action theory, actions have no object-direction of their own at all. Actions are not attitudes themselves. Actions come to be directed at goals only through being suitably related to prior occurrences distinct from them that are attitudes and that do possess object-direction in their own right. These attitudes are passive motivations that determine or influence causally how the agent acts. Causation links the object-directed motivations to the (inherently objectless) actions, so that the objects of the motivating attitudes can count as the 'objects' too—the goals—of the actions that those motivations cause.

We have here a quite different theory of purposiveness. Instead of goal-direction being understood as a distinctive form of intentionality at the point of action, it is now understood as something produced by causal power, with the action gaining its purpose or goal-direction from mental causes—causes that are prior and passive motivating psychological attitudes within the agent's mind, and whose contents provide the action with its goal. But since purposiveness, on this model, now involves the exercise of a causal power to determine action, and this power is possessed by the

---

[3] For this programme in action theory see Helen Steward, *A Metaphysics for Freedom* and Maria Alvarez, 'Actions, thought experiments and the "Principle of Alternate Possibilities"', *Australasian Journal of Philosophy* 87, (2009): pp. 61–82.

agent, or at least by attitudes within the agent, the theory of purposiveness promises to deliver a theory of self-determination as well—of how actions are determined by the agent. The agent's power to determine his action is supposed 'really' to be just the power of his motivating attitudes to cause action. It remains to be seen whether such a model is viable, whether as a theory of self-determination or even as a theory of purposiveness.

MULTI-WAYNESS

2.2 Self-Determination as Freedom

Any discussion of self-determination has to discuss the nature of power. And that is because to determine for ourselves how we act is surely to possess and exercise some kind of power over what we do. What, then, is the nature of the power? I have just mentioned a theory of it as a causal power of our motivations. But such a theory is a philosopher's construction. Our everyday idea of the power is very different. As we ordinarily understand the power, its bearer is not a motivation but the agent himself. And our immediate conception of the power is not as causal but as a power that involves alternatives. *IN WIll cntrl or up to us

In everyday life we talk of our action as being within our control or as being up to us. The phrase *up to us* is naturally followed by *whether…or…* introducing a range of alternatives or contrary options, each of which we could use our power to perform. It is up to me whether I raise my hand or lower it, or perhaps do something else entirely. Indeed this involvement of alternatives seems central to our conception of the power. If asked to characterize what our power to determine our action consists in, our immediate conception of it will be as a control of which actions we perform—as that power that leaves it up to us what we do. In which case it seems that there is a single power, control, which could be used either to do one thing or else to refrain from it and even, perhaps, to do another. The very same power that I employ to raise my hand could also be employed to lower it, the power leaving it up to me which I do. We interpret freedom's involvement of alternatives in terms of *multi-wayness*—the existence of a single power that could under any given circumstances operate in more than one way, to produce more than one outcome.

Notice too that this power is ordinarily understood to include not just the actions we choose between and decide on, such as raising a hand or lowering it, but also the prior decisions so to act. It is up to me whether I raise my hand or lower it just because I can decide which I do, and it is up to me how I decide. Since control is exercised by us in relation to what we do, as opposed to what happens to us, that conception of control exercised at the point of decisions themselves involves an understanding of those decisions to act as intentional actions themselves—as things that we deliberately take, just as we deliberately or intentionally perform the actions decided upon.

Philosophers refer to this power of control or up-to-usness as *freedom* or *free will*. But this use of terms such as *freedom* is fairly removed from everyday expression, and raises questions of its own. *Freedom* and its equivalents were not always used to characterize our power of self-determination. The application of terms such as *up to us* to pick out the power is older and more general. In the *Nicomachean Ethics* Aristotle was already deploying the Greek equivalent of *up to us*, *eph hemin*, to convey our power over how we act. By contrast, the first use by the Greeks of an equivalent of *freedom* to pick out our power over our decisions and actions occurred only after Aristotle, in the Hellenistic period, when philosophers came to apply *eleutheria*, a Greek term that had previously been used to pick out political freedom, to convey this capacity to determine for ourselves what we decide and do.

This reminds us that not only is *freedom* a specifically philosophical term of art for the up-to-us-ness of our action, or our control over what we do, but that the term can also be used for other things that even if related to freedom as a power of control, are not obviously forms of power at all. Instead of being used to pick out a metaphysical power we possess over our own actions, *freedom* can be used for something as importantly different as political liberty—not a power to determine outcomes that comes with human nature, but instead a legally constituted political condition. Why there is this varied use of the term *freedom*, and what connections there are between these various uses is itself an important question which a complete account of human freedom must address.[4] But our present topic will remain simply freedom as a power or capacity to determine how we act.

Again the term *free will* involves a distinctive psychological vocabulary of motivation that while present in everyday English has come to take on a highly specialized significance within philosophy. The Germanic word *will* and the related Latin term *voluntas* have come to pick out a specific inner motivational faculty as the supposed immediate location of any exercise of our power of control—hence the identification of the power of freedom as freedom of the will. This faculty of will is proposed to provide an account of, *inter alia*, our capacity to take decisions to act. But the claim that we possess a faculty of will seems very much more controversial than the simple idea that we make decisions or make choices. The idea of such a faculty is not obviously found in Aristotle, and seems again to emerge within the Hellenistic period or later. We shall have to explore what precisely 'will theory' might add to our everyday conception of deciding and choosing, and how much of this addition we might wish to retain.

Freedom as a power then is, as control or up-to-usness, a capacity to determine more than one outcome at the point of action. And this feature of the power, its involvement of alternatives, highlights what, rightly or wrongly, is treated as the central issue in the modern debate about freedom's nature—the relation of freedom

---

[4] The question is addressed in *Normativity: The Ethics of Action, volume 2*. For a preliminary discussion see Thomas Pink, 'Thomas Hobbes and the ethics of freedom', *Inquiry* 54, (2011): pp. 541–63.

to causal determinism. Because freedom depends on a capacity to determine otherwise, causal determinism is widely, though controversially, viewed as a threat to it. If it is already causally determined that I will do A rather than B, then, in the view of many, I must altogether lack the power to do B—in which case it can no longer be up to me which I do. If how I act is already causally determined by prior occurrences not of my own doing, then I must lack the capacity to do otherwise, and so the capacity to determine for myself what I do. For many philosophers—incompatibilists about free will as they are called—the causal predetermination of human action by prior occurrences outside their control would remove human freedom.

not true

how does determinism eliminate freedom of choice?

This issue of the compatibility or incompatibility of free will with causal determinism is widely supposed to be a conceptual issue. Incompatibilists think that the incompatibility of free will with causal determinism is not at all a contingent matter, but a necessity to be recognized through one's grasp of the concept of an 'ability to do otherwise'. Whereas compatibilists, who claim the compatibility of freedom with causal determinism, correspondingly claim that it is this compatibility which is conceptually true. Indeed, modern compatibilism commonly comes with a proposed conceptual reduction of what it is to act freely—a reduction that characterizes freedom in terms of other concepts supposed to be entirely consistent with causal determinism.

Finally, whether philosophers are compatibilists or incompatibilists about freedom—whether they suppose free will to be consistent or inconsistent with causal determinism—there is a widespread assumption that freedom is itself a form of causal power:

The exercise of active control is essentially a causal phenomenon.[5]

In which case

The view that free actions have uncaused volitions at their core is prima facie puzzling. If it is uncaused, if it is no sense determined to occur by anything at all, then it is not determined to occur by me in particular. And if I don't determine it, then it's not under my control.[6]

And that is because it is very widely supposed that power by its very nature is a causal phenomenon, so that any form of power is a form of causation.

in the first place, the notions of power or disposition are already causally laden notions and it can thus reasonably be argued that unless one already has a grasp of causation, one cannot have a grasp of power. Powers, indeed, are often called causal powers.[7]

---

[5] Randolph Clarke, *Libertarian Accounts of Free Will* (Oxford: Oxford University Press, 2003), p. 151.

[6] Timothy O'Connor, *Persons and Causes: The Metaphysics of Free Will* (Oxford: Oxford University Press, 2000), p. 25.

[7] Rom Harre and E.H. Madden, *Causal Powers: A Theory of Natural Necessity* (Oxford: Blackwell, 1975)—as cited and endorsed in Stephen Mumford and Rani Lill Anjum, *Getting Causes from Powers* (Oxford: University Press, 2011), p. 7.

Now this position that power in general and freedom in particular are forms of causation would be trivial if 'causation' were being used to mean no more than power, so that a power to determine was trivially a power to determine causally. But then the claim that the notion of power is 'causally laden' would not be a substantial claim worth making; and that a conception of power presupposes a conception of causation would not have to be 'reasonably argued'. But by *causation* modern philosophers mean something rather more substantial than just power in general. They mean not simply power, but a power of the same kind as is involved in what Aristotelians called efficient causation—the power of fire to melt ice and burn wood, of stones to break windows, of objects before one to produce visual experiences of them. As we shall see, considerable efforts have been made by many philosophers to model freedom as a form of efficient causation.

Central to the modern debate about freedom then is a debate, widely taken to be conceptual, about the role of causation in human action, and, in particular, about how to understand freedom in terms of causation. How is freedom itself to be realized through causation, and is freedom so realized consistent with causal determinism in wider nature?

But concentration on causation and on the issue of causal determinism may miss what is more fundamental. Central to our ordinary understanding of the power that is freedom is not its relation to causation but just its involvement of alternatives and its apparently multi-way nature, as a single power of control that can be employed to produce more than one outcome and do more than one thing. The involvement of alternatives—its being up to us whether or not we do something—seems a genuinely universal feature of our understanding of self-determination, and something that even compatibilist theories of it have tried to accommodate.

It is arguable that freedom's involvement of alternatives—its identity as a power of control over which actions we perform—is more central to our conception of freedom than any allegiance to incompatibilism. For freedom's involvement of alternatives turns up immediately, as incompatibilism does not, in a central locution that we use to refer to our power to determine action—in our talk of its being 'up to us whether we do A or B'. This locution seems to identify the power as by its very nature a single power that is multi-way, that can under any given circumstances operate to produce more than one outcome. Incompatibilism, by contrast, has to do not so much with the nature of the power of freedom in itself, but its relation to other powers—the powers attaching to prior causes distinct from the agent. Now it is true that incompatibilist intuitions are certainly very common. But they are not shared by everyone. While the involvement of alternatives seems much more plausibly essential to the nature of freedom in itself, and is a far less contentious feature of our ordinary understanding of it.

It may even come to seem that power over alternatives is essential not only to freedom but to self-determination in any form. What else is it for us to be able to determine for ourselves what we do but to have the power to act or to refrain? But it is by no means clear, as we shall see, that self-determination and freedom are quite the same. Self-determination—the capacity, sufficient to base moral responsibility, to determine outcomes for oneself—may prove to take many possible forms, of which a power over alternatives is only one. The relation between what self-determination strictly requires, as a matter of conceptual necessity, and the particular form in which we possess that capacity is far from clear. Equally unclear, as I shall show, is the purely conceptual nature of the relation between self-determination and causal determinism, as well as the supposedly causal nature either of freedom or of self-determination in general.

But besides freedom or self-determination there are other kinds of power involved in action. These are forms of power involved in action's purposiveness or object-direction. And whatever recent English-language action theory may have supposed, these forms of power, far from explaining self-determination, appear, in some cases at least, even to threaten it. For these forms of power are not exercised by agents themselves. They belong instead to other entities—entities that motivate the agent, thereby determining how the agent will act. The purposiveness that seems so central to agency appears to involve the opposite of self-determination. Purposiveness seems to involve agents being subject to power rather than exercising it. So before we return to the nature of freedom and self-determination, we need to examine further the nature of purposiveness, and the role played in action by motivating power.

3

Motivation and Voluntariness

3.1 Actions and Attitudes

We have noted that the goal-direction or purposiveness of action could be understood in two quite different ways. Purposiveness could be understood as a special mode of direction at an object of thought, hence treating action as involving a distinctive kind of attitude. Or alternatively purposiveness could arise not as a distinctive kind of attitude, but as something that is merely expressive of attitudes—on the most common version of this view, occurring as an effect of the attitudes expressed.

It should be no surprise that these two ways of understanding purposiveness exist. They reflect two distinct elements involved in the performance of human action, and a fundamental debate about how these two elements are related. One element, motivation, involves psychological attitudes and content. The other, voluntariness, involves the production of outcomes—and can be specified without reference to any particular attitude. It is very natural, indeed, to suppose that whatever might be the case for action in general, voluntariness in particular occurs as something distinct from any attitudes, simply as their expression. Theories of action that sharply distinguish actions from attitudes are theories that identify action exclusively with voluntariness conceived in just this last way. This was Hobbes' conception of action—and it still remains the dominant conception of action today.

The debate about the nature of human action that Hobbes began involves two related issues. The first has to do with what occurrences in human life involve content and count as genuine attitudes in their own right. We find Hobbes excluding action itself from the field of the content-bearing, just as Hume was later to go even further and exclude from bearing content not only actions but even motivations. In each case their exclusion of aspects of the mind and action from counting as content-bearing had important implications for the theory of practical reason.

The second issue has to do with the location of action. Where does the division come between passive and active—between what happens to us and what we ourselves do? Does human action occur only as voluntary action—as voluntariness—as Hobbes and his many modern followers maintain? Or does action occur also at the point of motivation for the voluntary; or even, as Hobbes' scholastic opponents thought, at least in its primary or immediate form, exclusively as a form of inner motivation, distinct from, though generative and explanatory of, what we do voluntarily on the basis of that motivation?

Through all these disputes we shall find various differing accounts of what motivation and voluntariness each involve, and of how they are related. These involve disagreements about how human actions are explained, and about how the human capacity for reason is involved in their performance. We need therefore to begin by looking at motivation and voluntariness, and to uncover some fundamental common ground about these two elements to human agency. Then we can see how this common ground can be developed theoretically in directions that are radically different.

3.2 Motivation and Voluntariness

Consider what is involved in the successful performance of an action. Let us consider a very ordinary example. Coming to a road I have a choice between crossing it or not, and so I deliberate about which to do. Wanting to buy some food, perhaps having even already decided to do so, I spot a shop of the right kind on the opposite side. So I decide and form an intention to cross the road, and then cross it on the basis of that decision, in order to reach the shop on the other side.

My crossing of the road is an obvious case of action. But it is action in a very distinctive and important form that I shall term, following Hobbes, as voluntariness. *Voluntariness* as used by Hobbes refers to what is done on the basis of a will or desire to do it, the sphere of the voluntary being what is subject to will or desire. My crossing of the road counts as done voluntarily or is a case of voluntariness because it is something I do on the basis of having decided or desired to do it. To perform an action A *voluntarily*, I shall say, is to do A on the basis of an attitude by which I favour doing A, such as on the basis of a desire or decision on my part to do A. More generally, the category of the *voluntary* is the category of what is subject to our motivation or will—of what we can do voluntarily, on the basis of our having an attitude, such as a decision or intention or desire, that favours or is *pro* its doing.

The voluntary, I shall claim, is, in a sense, what action is all about. Not only is what we do voluntarily, such as crossing the road, a clear case of action, but it seems to be action in the form that immediately matters to us as practical reasoners—as people reasoning or deliberating about how to act. It is with the voluntary that we as practical reasoners, deliberating about how to act, are primarily concerned. And it is to the performance of the voluntary that all our action is directed, and in and through this performance that our action as a whole is successful. So the voluntary is fundamental to action. Performance of the voluntary provides the goal at which all our action is aimed, and constitutes the point at which all our action succeeds or fails.

But besides voluntariness, there is another essential element to action—motivation. Action, and rational action even more, would not be possible at all without motivation. It is only through motivation that actions possess purpose or goal-direction, and so count as genuine actions. Take the road crossing itself. If it is a genuine action the road crossing is going to be purposive and goal-directed. But just describing it as someone's crossing of the road does not specify what, if any, goal is involved. All that is reported is the production of an outcome, not the purpose for which it is produced. It might be that, as in this case, the agent is crossing the road in order to reach the shop on the other side and get food to eat; or alternatively he might be crossing the road in order to escape what he takes to be pursuers chasing him on this side. Or someone could be crossing the road without meaning to, quite absent-mindedly.

An action's motivation can be described just by giving the objects or goals at which the action's performance is directed. These supply the answer to the question why— that is for what purpose—the action is performed. Now we can specify these objects or goals simply by using the *in order to* construction followed by the objects: he was crossing in order to get to the chip shop, or in order to evade pursuers. But besides the object itself, we can also describe in psychological terms *how* the action is directed at that object—by referring to various kinds of psychological attitude that might be taken to the object. The agent might be crossing the road because he *wants* to obtain food, or because he *intends* to escape pursuers. Whenever a voluntary action is directed at an object as its goal, we can always report that goal-direction by referring to a particular kind of psychological attitude directed at that same object, and describe the voluntary action as motivated by that psychological attitude. So the action's performance counts as motivated both by its objects or goals and by the attitudes directed at those objects. My crossing the road is motivated both by its goal, getting to the chip shop, say, and the desirability of that; and also by some attitude of mine in favour of that goal, such as my intention to get to the chip shop.

So motivation involves attitudes. What all these attitudes have in common is something that seems essential to the goal-directedness of action. The attitudes all involve the agent in favouring their object, the goal of the action being motivated. All these motivating attitudes are *pro attitudes*, as Davidson and others have termed them. But though pro attitudes are all attitudes in favour of their objects, they may otherwise involve very important psychological differences. Some pro attitudes might be cognitive, a motivating belief that it would be desirable or good to do something. Other pro attitudes might be as different from beliefs as could be, being mere non-cognitive urges or passions—mere desires to act. One especially important kind of pro attitude is intentions to act, the action-determining motivations that we can form by taking decisions to do this rather than that. Notice that when philosophers talk of the will, particularly when they talk of the will as a locus of freedom and agency—as when they talk of the possible freedom of the will—they generally have in mind, not our pro attitudes in general, but decisions and intentions in particular. And this discrimination is in many ways fully justified. Intentions and the decisions which form them are very distinctive pro attitudes, and we shall be examining just how very distinctive they are. But I shall also be counselling against taking the genuine differences too far and imagining the will as a faculty within the mind wholly unlike other sources of motivation. For in a number of crucial respects decisions and intentions do resemble other action-motivating pro attitudes, and are usefully to be placed in the same class.

We have then the voluntary action—the production of an outcome, such as the crossing of the road, which can, however, be specified as just that, abstracting from any specific purpose or goal-direction. At the same time there is the motivation with which that voluntary action is performed—the action's goal-direction, the goal being an object of thought. And in relation to that object of thought there are the various motivating psychological attitudes directed at it and that, through motivating the voluntary action, leave that action directed at it too. Any theory of action must explain the relation between these elements—the action as involving the voluntary production of an outcome, the action as directed at some motivating object, and the particular psychological pro attitudes favouring that object that leave the action motivated directed at it too.

3.3 Motivation and Explanation

One thing seems clear. Motivation is understood by us as explanatory of voluntary action. An agent's mental direction at the production of certain outcomes in some way explains his actual production of them. Why was she crossing the road? She was doing it in order to reach the shop on the other side and get food. What immediately provides the explanation here is the action's object, which is the goal at which its performance is directed.

What form does this explanation take? The explanation seems immediately to do what any explanation must do, which is to render what it explains intelligible. And that is surely what lies at the heart of action explanation. When we supply the goal or goals at which an action's performance was directed, we render its performance intelligible, at least to a degree. But that raises two obvious, and related, questions. First, how does the action get to be directed at that object; in other words, how does an action come to be performed for that particular purpose? And secondly, in what way does the action's direction at that object explain it?

It is possible to take a theoretically minimalist view of these questions. One might take the goal-direction of actions as just a brute fact about them, of which no further account need be given. There is, on this view, nothing to be said about what an action's goal-direction involves beyond the fact of the goal-direction. As for the way in which an action's goal-direction explains its performance, that would similarly be treated simply as involving a primitive form of explanation. We would say no more about this form of explanation than that it involves the explanation of action in terms of its goal; we might simply label this as teleological explanation—and there things would be left. However, this is not, on the whole, what philosophers have done. They have striven to relate action explanation to other forms of explanation. And they have done this because common-sense psychology makes a number of parallels with other forms of explanation especially compelling.

One approach builds on a view that we have already mentioned—the view that action occurs as a distinctive kind of attitude, so that actions are related to their objects as are attitudes generally. On this model, the goal-direction of an action is given by a content that is internal to it, as the particular attitude that it is. To explain the action is to report that content. And that involves an obvious model of action explanation—as interpretation. The explanation of an action in terms of its goal involves, as with interpretation generally, uncovering content to be found in what is being explained or made intelligible. This view of action explanation and motivation has historically been of considerable importance. It lies at the heart of scholastic action theory's appeals to formal causation. In scholastic action theory, the goal or object of an action is seen as giving it content and psychological definition and thereby intelligibility. Put in Aristotelian terms, the object is understood as providing *form* for the action's *matter*.

But we can make something intelligible other than by interpreting it. We can also make the occurrence of something intelligible by showing it to be the outcome of the exercise of some power, possessed by something else, to determine that occurrence or at least to influence it. And such an idea of power certainly seems part of our ordinary understanding of motivation. Motivation is what *moves* me to do something—and that suggests an idea of something imparting a force or power to influence me to do that thing, a power or force applied and exercised by whatever it is that is moving one. We often talk of desires as inclinations, or as inclining one to act as desired. And this seems to involve the idea of, at the very least, a mild kind of push. Very strong desires or emotions are described as exercising even greater motivating force—power that is more than merely influencing or inclining, but outright action-determining. We talk of someone being *gripped* by an intense fear or desire to escape, and of being *impelled* by that desire into fleeing the danger.

This provides another way of relating the object to the action. The action as directed at that object comes to be performed only because something other than the action, either the object itself or some prior attitude directed at it, determines or influences the agent so to act. The action is performed because the agent is subjected to some form of motivating power.

The Hobbesian model of action that has dominated modern English-language philosophy has run with the intuition that motivation really does *move*—that it does indeed involve the agent being subject to a kind of power. Hobbesians then give this intuition a very specific reading. On the Hobbesian view motivation not only involves power, but specifically causal power—and the power belongs to the agent's own psychological attitudes as causes of the actions they explain. Motivating object-direction comes to actions from prior attitudes of the agent which exercise causal power or force to determine or influence which actions that agent then performs. The explanation of the action therefore does not strictly speaking involve interpretation of the action itself. The action lacks the content required for it to be a possible object of interpretation in its own right. Interpretation is of the action's causes. To explain action in terms of its goals is then to specify the attitudes, with their contents, that have caused the agent to act as he has.

To say someone did something intentionally is to describe the action in a way that bears a special relation to the beliefs and attitudes of the agent; and perhaps further to describe the action as having been caused by those beliefs and attitudes.[1]

There is one obvious support for the Hobbesian view. We do understand much motivation as indeed involving psychological events or states distinct from the voluntary actions they explain, both preceding those actions in time, and even persisting after the actions have been performed. These psychological occurrences interact in their own right with other psychological events and states, such as beliefs about means. The motivations thus exist and operate apart from and independently of the voluntary actions motivated. For example, I come to feel an increasing desire to go to Spain next year on holiday, a desire which constantly leads me to think and read about places in Spain. Eventually because of this persisting desire I finally decide to go to Spain next year, which decision leads to further planning and decision about where in particular to go and how to get there. And then, eventually, these motivating attitudes lead me to act as planned—and I finally go.

It is very natural to think of this process as involving a complex causal chain leading from the initial desire to a decision to attain some end; and then through my beliefs and other desires, to a further complex and action-coordinatory series of decisions about means. We shall return later to look at the causal nature of what is going on, and of the power involved. But it does seem that the desires and decisions are states or events doing what causes standardly do, which is to raise the chances of, or even outright determine in advance, the occurrence of specific later states or events, such as the performance of the action desired or decided upon. And again in relation to emotions such as fear or particularly strong desires, terms such as *grip* and *impel* are deeply associated with familiar kinds of causal process and power. Some cases of motivation do indeed seem to involve psychological events and states within the mind that are quite distinct from the voluntary actions they explain, and that possess causal powers in their own right—including motivating causal power over later action.

The conception of motivations as causes is, then, not obviously a gratuitous invention of philosophy. It seems deeply natural for us to think of motivation in terms of the operation of some motivating power or force, and to understand this force causally. Not only do we think of emotions and desires as driving or pushing us into action; in ways that we shall be examining further, we also understand our own

---

[1] Donald Davidson, 'The logical form of action sentences', in *Essays on Actions and Events* (Oxford Clarendon Press, 1980), p. 121.

decisions and intentions as bearers of causal power—and especially in relation to the actions intended. The Hobbesian model of motivation being provided by attitudes as causes of the actions motivated does seem to have a real basis in everyday psychological thought.

If motivation involves power, this means that action is associated with two importantly different forms of power. The first kind of power, already introduced, is self-determination—agents' power to determine action for themselves. The second is a power of whatever provides the agent's motivation—a power to move the agent to perform the action. This is not, or not obviously, a power of the agent, but a power of something else—whatever does the motivating—exercised over the agent. And it looks as though the two forms of power could be in some tension. The tension does not arise just because two powers are involved. After all, it could simply be that something—a motivation—moves or even determines the agent; and then the agent, thus moved, in turn determines the action. The tension arises from the particular way we conceive of self-determination—from the thought that agents determine actions *for themselves*. What does 'for themselves' suggest, but a form of independence on an agent's part in the way that they determine their action—an independence that might be threatened by their own subjection to the motivating power of something else? And here we come to a central question within the debate between compatibilists and incompatibilists—namely the relation of motivation to self-determination. Does the motivation essential to human action really involve a form of power exercised over the agent? If so, what kind of power is this? And does the agent's subjection to this power threaten his own power to determine for himself what he does?

So we have two models of motivation and of the action-explanation that it provides. There is the model of motivation as involving content internal to the action as an attitude in its own right, where the explanation involves the action's interpretation in terms of that content. The other model involves some motivating entity exercising a power over the agent, and the explanation is of the action as produced through the exercise of that motivating power. We shall need to examine these two models further. Notice that each model may sometimes apply. Sometimes motivation may be through content internal to the action. But sometimes it may also involve the exercise of some power by some other motivating entity to determine or produce the action's performance. There may even be cases where the two models apply together. In those cases motivation may involve both content internal to the action and some entity exercising power to produce the action. The possibility of such a combination of the two models was a central feature of scholastic action theory.

Partly because of the threat to self-determination, there have been many attempts in the recent theory of motivation to sever the link between motivation and the subjection of the agent to motivating power, especially causal power. But these attempts have characteristically retained the distinctively Hobbesian picture of action as a non-attitude that derives its object-direction from prior attitudes. So instead of appealing to a theory of goal-direction as internal to the action which it explains, motivation is still seen as exclusively provided for the action from without—from attitudes distinct from the action they explain. However, these attitudes are not seen as causes of the action they explain, or as exercising a power to produce it. The link between attitudes and the distinct actions they explain takes instead another form. We shall be returning in Chapter 12 to consider a number of such views.[2] Such theories view motivation as explaining action neither as internal to the action nor through the exercise of motivating power. It remains to be seen whether there really is some further way of understanding action explanation to be had.

3.4 Motivation and Rationality

Besides the role of power in human action, we need also to consider the role played by the human capacity for reason. And that again involves looking at the relation between motivation and voluntariness. For not only is the very occurrence of action dependent on motivation, but the rationality or reasonableness of an action's performance depends on the nature of that motivation too—on the specific purposes for which it is being performed.

Practical reason's primary concern is with the voluntary. We reason or deliberate, not about what desires or intentions or other motivations to hold, but about possible objects of such motivations—such as about whether to cross the road or about whether and where to go on holiday. So the justifications that we consider in reasoning about how to act are to do not with our motivations themselves, but with the goals or outcomes which will be attained by us on the basis of our motivations. Someone deliberating or reasoning about how to act will consider a range of options by way of voluntary action, and the various ends that might be furthered by those voluntary actions. Should I cross the road or remain on this side? Crossing the road might be risky, as staying on this side would not be. But crossing would get me to that chip shop, and allow me to buy food. And so forth.

When deliberating about the voluntary, we consider both what the voluntary actions are like in themselves, and what further ends or outcomes they might help us attain. We come to see certain voluntary actions rather than others as desirable or good actions to perform, either in themselves, or as means to further desirable ends. The source of practical reasons or justifications, then, is to be found in features of the voluntary—whether in the nature of the voluntary actions themselves, or in the fact that there are various further ends which those actions would or might attain. These are features of the voluntary which make its performance desirable in some way,

---

[2] See for example Scott Sehon, *Teleological Realism: Mind, Agency, and Explanation* (Cambridge, MA: MIT Press, 2005); Timothy O'Connor, *Persons and Causes: The Metaphysics of Free Will* (Oxford: Oxford University Press, 2000); Hugh McCann, *The Works of Agency: On Human Action, Will, and Freedom* (Ithaca: Cornell University Press, 1998).

either as an end in itself or as a means to further ends. Crossing the road might be fun in itself; or it might help to get us somewhere worth visiting on the other side.

Practical justifications come, then, from possible voluntary actions and from the features that make those actions desirable. However, these features must also justify, not merely the voluntary actions themselves, but motivations to perform them as well—the motivating pro attitudes that have those voluntary actions as their objects. For it is only in and through forming and holding those motivating attitudes that we ever perform the actions justified. A justification for crossing the road only gets me to act as justified by leading me to become motivated so to act—to aim at crossing the road, and so to hold attitudes directed at that object. So if they are to move us, practical justifications for the voluntary must equally be justifications for becoming motivated to perform the voluntary (Figure 3.1):

Motivation or will   *Voluntary action*

motivation to do A   doing A

justify   ◄──────   features F, G... of doing A

Figure 3.1. The structure of practical justification.

If practical justifications could not address our will or motivation with the same force that they address the voluntary—if they could not provide the same support for being motivated to do A which they provide for doing A—they would bypass the motivation which explains our doing of A and, by providing it with goal-direction, makes it count as genuine action. If justifications for crossing the road did not support becoming motivated to cross the road as well, then they would bypass one's very capacity to respond to such justifications as an agent. Reason could not take a genuinely practical form.

Motivation matters not just to the actual performance of action, but also to the rationality of that performance. Suppose that it is sensible for me to cross the road, but *only* because that way I shall reach a shop I need to get to on the other side of the road. If an argument citing this justification is to get me not only to perform the intentional action of crossing, but to perform it rationally, in response to that justification for crossing, then that argument will again need to persuade me into the specific motivation required. I need to become motivated to cross the road, and for the right reason—as a way to get to the shop. So, again, the argument must justify not just the voluntary action but also an intention or like pro attitude towards getting to the shop and to crossing the road as a means to that particular end. In this case, only if I cross the road in order to get to the shop will my road crossing not only be something which there is justification for doing, but also something done by me rationally or reasonably, for the only purpose that in this case would justify its doing.

The desirable features of a given voluntary action, then, only count as justifying its performance insofar as there is also the possibility of their providing the same justification for being motivated to perform it. Justifications for performing a voluntary action must be able to constitute equal justifications for the motivation so to act. Only so can reason ever direct and move us into performing, and performing reasonably or rationally, this voluntary action rather than that.

It should certainly not be supposed that practical justifications justify *only* motivations—that they do not justify voluntary actions as well. For voluntary action is very plainly something which people can be argued or reasoned into. We argue people into acting voluntarily by arguing or reasoning them into the motivation, such as an intention so to act, which will lead them into performing the voluntary action concerned. Consider, furthermore, how the intention is justified. The intention is justified by the fact that its object, the action intended, is desirable—a good action to perform. Since the basis on which practical reason argues us into forming intentions to act, then, is that it would be good for us to act as intended, in so directing us to form an intention to act, practical reason is clearly just as much directing us into acting as intended.

It follows that the justifications which practical reason supplies for deciding or intending to perform a voluntary action equally count as justifying the actual performance of that voluntary action thereafter. And, in fact, it must be practical reason's direction of us towards and justification of the voluntary which is fundamental—because the final goal which reason presents to us is not the possession of this or that motivation, but our successful performance of the right voluntary actions; and it is from the character of those voluntary actions which any justification for prior motivations derives.

So, in summary, what does the exercise and application of practical reason involve? Obviously, when done successfully it involves conforming to the relevant practical justifications. That is, it involves managing to do what practical reason justifies doing; and it involves doing it in response to practical reason, precisely because practical reason has justified doing it. Hence the successful application of practical reason takes place at two levels. One level is that of our motivational response to practical reason, in becoming motivated to perform those voluntary actions for which we have rational justification. The second level occurs in the voluntary production of outcomes—the final goal of the process, when, as motivated, we manage voluntarily to do what we have rational justification for doing. And the second level, the stage of successful voluntariness, is clearly necessary for the exercise of our practical rationality to be successful as a whole. All the deliberation and decision-making that motivates us to cross the road has that successful road crossing as its real point and goal. If we do not manage actually to cross the road, the exercise of our practical reason will have failed—and at the point which matters.

But remember—the goodness or desirability of performing a voluntary action still only counts as justificatory of that action insofar as it can also be justificatory of motivation for the action. For it is only in virtue of the justification which exists for the motivating attitude that voluntary action can ever be performed on the basis of reason or argument at all. The desirability of the voluntary action can only direct and lead rational agents into performing it as directing and leading them into becoming motivated to perform it.

Moreover, though to fail to perform those voluntary actions which are justified is to fail, and fail quite fundamentally, in the application of our practical reason, the cause of that failure need not lie in our rationality itself. It need not lie in any folly or lack of sense on our part. In failing to perform the voluntary actions justified, we may have failed fully to apply and execute reason—to do all that we had justification for doing. But we need not have done so through any irrationality.

Suppose, for example, that we are rationally justified in performing some voluntary action such as crossing the road, and in adopting various means, such as looking both ways before crossing, towards ensuring that we manage successfully so to act. If we are rational, we will respond to these justifications, and become motivated both to cross the road and to employ all the appropriate means. Now, once we have become fully motivated to do all this, our practical rationality is confirmed and established as far as performing this action is concerned. We have formed and retained all the relevant action-explanatory attitudes for which there is rational justification. Whether after all this we actually succeed in doing all that we have very sensibly become motivated to do—this then depends not on our practical rationality but on other factors. It depends on whether we avoid a sudden heart attack or stroke, on whether our nerves and muscles otherwise operate as they should, on whether the precautions which we have rationally taken do actually protect us against the risk of speeding cars and the like. If not because of any irrational motivation but because of sheer bad luck as regards these other factors we still fail to act as motivated—perhaps despite all our precautions some car running at an unusual speed unexpectedly hits us halfway across—we will have failed to apply practical reason successfully. We will have failed to do all that we had justification for doing. But we will still have been acting wholly rationally.

The rationality with which we act depends on the rationality of the motivations on the basis of which we act. We must be rational in holding these motivations and being moved into action by them. Provided that is the case, our rationality does not further depend on our actually managing to do all that practical reason justifies our doing. So the element in our action that fixes our basic rationality as agents is not what we manage voluntarily to achieve, dependent as that is on non-rational factors such as luck and our actual strength and resources. What fixes our rationality in practical terms—the rationality with which we act—is what we are motivated to do or to attempt. To be acting rationally we need simply to be motivated to attain the right ends through the right means.[3]

---

[3] In his 'Intention and permissibility: Scanlon's principles', *Aristotelian Society Supplementary Volume* 74, (2000), Jonathan Dancy denies that practical justifications must, by their very nature, be able equally to

3.5 The Non-Voluntariness of Motivation

Motivations are pro attitudes—attitudes directed at voluntary actions and outcomes, and which are responsive to and justified by the desirability of these voluntary actions and outcomes. Based as they are on pro attitudes towards performing them, voluntary actions are correspondingly performed in response to their own desirability, either in themselves or as means to further ends (Table 3.1).

Table 3.1. Motivation and voluntary action

Motivations to do A	explain	Voluntarily doing A
Pro attitudes to doing A—either in itself or as means to further ends.		Based on pro attitudes towards doing A.
Objects (derived from contents): doing A and ends to be attained by doing A.		Objects *qua goals*: objects of motivations for doing A.
Responsive to and justified by desirability of objects.		Responsive to and justified by its own desirability.
Rationality of motivation depends on desirability of its object.		Rationality with which A is done depends on rationality of motivation for doing it.

Since pro attitudes must, by their very nature, occur in a way which is responsive to whether or not their objects are desirable, it seems to follow that motivating pro attitudes towards the voluntary are not formed voluntarily themselves. We form pro attitudes non-voluntarily, in a way responsive to the desirability of their objects; not

serve as justifications for motivations too. He claims to find an instance 'of a (sort of) action ruled out by a reason, in a way that does not pass *via* the ruling out of a judgment-sensitive attitude' (p. 323). His supposed instance is that there are actions (like treading on the neighbour's baby) which we have reason not to do *even by accident*.

But there is no counterexample here. Granted, treading on the neighbour's baby is something which we have reason not to do, period, whether we do it deliberately or accidentally. But this practical justification can perfectly well exist and be responded to as a justification for motivations. We are justified in being motivated not to tread on the baby at all, not even accidentally; and so, in particular, we have reason to be motivated to take due care to exclude even an accident.

If we do tread on the neighbour's baby, even by accident, we have done what we had every justification not to do. But of course, as I explained in the main text, if our treading on the baby was wholly accidental, and occurred *despite* our being fully motivated not to do it even by accident and so despite our being motivated to perform all actions involved in taking due care to that end, we may have done what we had justification for not doing—but we will still not have acted irrationally. Our motivation, and so too our action, will have been rational. We will have been unlucky, not unreasonable, in doing what we did.

Dancy also supposes (p. 322) that the doctrine that practical justifications must be for attitudes implies the claim—which I agree is plainly false—that practical justifications cannot be for voluntary actions as well. But there is no warrant for supposing this, as I have also argued in the main text. Justifications for raising one's arm must be able to constitute, and be responded to as, justifications for being motivated to raise one's arm; but they are still, nonetheless, justifications for raising one's arm.

voluntarily, out of a desire or decision to do so, and just in response to the desirability of holding those attitudes themselves. We are moved to desire to do A by the desirability of doing A and the ends which we expect doing A to further—not by the desirability just of desiring to do A.

The claim that pro attitudes are non-voluntary themselves should not be too controversial for many pro attitudes. Few think of desires or emotions as voluntary. We cannot form desires and feel emotions at will, just on the basis of deciding to do so. But some seem to think that the case is different for intentions and the decisions that form them. For there certainly are philosophers who would place decisions and intentions within the voluntary. But they would be wrong to do so. There are very good reasons why decisions and intentions cannot be voluntary—why, in this respect, they are pro attitudes just like any other. So the next chapter will address the non-voluntariness of these decisions and intentions of the will.

4

The Non-Voluntariness of the Will

4.1 Is the Will Voluntary?

This chapter will argue that decisions and intentions are not voluntary and that in this they are no different from other pro attitudes. Now this may seem counter-intuitive to some philosophers. For some philosophers are inclined to describe decisions and intentions as voluntary attitudes—even as pre-eminently voluntary attitudes.[1] So I need to say something about their intuition.

Part of the problem may be purely terminological. These philosophers have a clear, and in my view, perfectly correct intuition that decisions and intention formations are intentional actions. But, like many others, they have also come to use the term 'acting voluntarily' as a synonym of 'acting intentionally'. So they will naturally express their intuition by talking of decisions and intentions as 'voluntary' attitudes. In so doing, they are proposing no particular doctrine about what intentions are like, or indeed about what actions are like. They are saying no more than that intention-formation counts as a form of action. And I have no disagreement with their view, though I differ with their choice of terminology.

For I mean by 'voluntariness' not simply 'agency', but something rather different—a property the identity between which and agency is very much a matter of dispute. By 'voluntariness' I specifically mean voluntariness as it has been understood so far in this book—the very important property of an action's occurring on the basis of a pro attitude to its performance. For A to be done voluntarily is for the doing of A to be motivated by some pro attitude to its doing, such as a desire or decision to do A. And I am interested in this kind of voluntariness because voluntariness understood in just this way has been employed by English-language philosophers from Hobbes to Davidson as the basis of a substantial model of what human agency in general involves. For Hobbes and his followers, then, whether the formation of an intention to do A can be an intentional action depends entirely on whether forming that intention can be something that we do voluntarily, on exactly my understanding of voluntariness.

---

[1] As for example, in a private communication, Robert Kane described them to me.

Now I shall be arguing that in my sense of 'voluntary', decisions and intention formations are not voluntary at all, at least directly—something Hobbes and David-son have openly argued as well. And this is for a very fundamental reason, namely the role played by decisions and intentions in responding to and applying practical reason. So I shall be in clear and substantial disagreement with any philosopher who is working with my understanding of what voluntariness is, but who neverthe-less still thinks that decisions and intentions fall directly within the voluntary so understood. To these philosophers—and there certainly are such philosophers—I shall have three arguments to make.

First, everyday common-sense psychology provides no support whatsoever for supposing that intentions and decisions fall within the voluntary as I understand it: there just are no clear cases of directly voluntary intention-formation. This is a point which Thomas Hobbes understood with particular clarity.

Secondly, there is an equally clear and convincing rationale for why this should be so—for why decisions are not taken and intentions are not formed voluntarily—a rationale based on a common-sense psychologically natural view of the role which decisions and intentions play in our mental life. This is the view that decisions and intentions of the will have a reason-applying function. Their central function is to apply practical reason as it governs the voluntary actions decided upon.

Thirdly, we may have an intuition that taking a specific decision to act is itself an intentional action—is something which we do deliberately or intentionally. And this intuition may initially suggest that therefore decisions and the intentions which they form must themselves be voluntary. But in fact, as later chapters will make clear, this intuition that decisions are actions really provides no support at all for thinking that the taking of such a decision is done voluntarily, as I understand voluntariness. For there is a way of understanding action that makes no appeal to voluntariness—which explains how actions can perfectly well occur in non-voluntary form.

Philosophers do have a marked tendency to link something's being an action to its being voluntary. This tendency was widespread long before Hobbes, and even among philosophers who would not have sought to explain the nature of action just in terms of voluntariness as Hobbes did. Though they in no way identified action with voluntariness, even many pre-Hobbesian philosophers were very liable to infer from something's being an action to at least the possibility of its being done voluntarily.[2] To counteract this tendency to link agency to voluntariness, we shall need to explain why the tendency has so often arisen and been so marked, and why, nevertheless, the tendency is mistaken. We shall explain the tendency as arising from a kind of perspectivally generated illusion—an illusion that is caused by the marked salience of voluntariness as a constituent of human action. And that will be a task for a later part of the book.[3]

---

[2] As I discuss further in Chapter 13.   [3] See, especially, Chapter 13.

4.2 The Will Is Not Voluntary

Let me develop the first point—that decisions and intentions simply do not occur on a directly voluntary basis. If decisions themselves were taken voluntarily—if they were voluntary actions exactly like the voluntary actions which they explain—then a decision could itself be taken just on the basis of a pro attitude towards taking it, such as a desire or a decision or intention to take that particular decision. If decisions were voluntary actions then they too would be subject to the will just as are the actions that they explain. Yet it is utterly and abundantly clear that our decisions to act this way rather than that are not so subject to the will. As Hobbes observed, decisions are not themselves things we take voluntarily. My decision to raise my hand, for example, is not something I take on the basis of a decision to decide to raise my hand. As Hobbes put it, using the seventeenth-century term *willing* for our modern *deciding*: 'I acknowledge this liberty, that I can do if I will, but to say, I can will if I will, I take to be an absurd speech.'[4]

And Hobbes was surely right on one point at least. Decisions to act are not voluntary. They are not directly subject to the will. They cannot be taken just on the basis of decisions or desires so to decide. For example, I cannot decide that in precisely five minutes' time I shall then take a decision to raise my hand—and sensibly expect that in five minutes, at the appointed time, I shall take the decision decided upon, and take it voluntarily, just on the basis of my earlier decision that I shall take it.

And this is connected with another feature of decisions which also distinguishes them from what we really can do voluntarily—from what we really can do on the basis of a prior decision or desire to do it. Just as decisions are not directly subject to the will, so they are not in general directly subject to command as uncontroversially voluntary actions are. I cannot sensibly command you to take a particular decision just like that, such as a decision to raise your hand, and then expect you to take the decision commanded exactly as commanded and simply in order to obey my command. Suppose, for example, I commanded you thus:

In five minutes' time take a decision to raise your hand tomorrow—and then, after a further minute, abandon that decision, and instead decide not to raise your hand tomorrow. Then, after yet a further minute, abandon that decision too.

You would surely react to my command with some bewilderment. You would be quite incapable of carrying it out. Decisions are not things that can be taken simply in order to obey commands that they be taken.

The fact that decisions cannot sensibly be commanded 'just like that' is obviously connected with the fact that decisions cannot be taken at will, just on the basis of a

---

[4] Thomas Hobbes in *The Questions Concerning Liberty, Necessity and Chance, clearly stated between Dr Bramhall Bishop of Derry, and Thomas Hobbes of Malmesbury,* (London 1656), p. 29.

desire or decision to take them. For if decisions could be taken voluntarily, then you could perfectly well take decisions simply in order to obey my decision commands. You need only decide to take whatever decisions I commanded you to take, and then obeying my decision commands would be easy. Once I commanded you to take a particular decision, such as a decision to raise your hand, you would simply take that decision voluntarily, on the basis of a decision to take it, just as a means to fulfilling my command.

It is very clear why decisions cannot be taken to order. To get you to take a particular decision, to decide on a particular action, I cannot just command you to take the decision in question. If I want to get you to decide to raise your hand, I cannot simply order you, 'Decide to raise your hand!' If I am to get you to decide to raise your hand, you have to be convinced that acting as decided, raising your hand, would be a sufficiently good idea. There must be something that could move you to raise your hand.

So one way for me to get you to decide to raise your hand is for me to show or make it clear to you that raising your hand would have benefits. And one way to do that, of course, is to *make* it true, and obviously true, that raising your hand would have benefits. For example, I could offer you a reward for raising your hand. That could get you to decide to raise your hand. Or if I have the necessary authority to do so, I could simply issue a command. Not a command to decide to raise your hand, but a command that would give you a reason to act as decided and actually raise your hand. I could simply command you to raise your hand. Given this command, there would be one possible benefit to your raising your hand, one reason why you should raise it—namely, that in doing so you will manage to obey my authority. And by giving you this reason to raise your hand, I could again get you to decide to raise it.

So Hobbes was quite right about the non-voluntariness of decisions. We cannot take a particular decision to act at will, just because we have decided to take it. We should not be distracted from appreciating this by the fact that there is something else connected with decision-making that we can do voluntarily. This is not taking a particular decision to act, but something which is very easily confused with it but which is, nevertheless, importantly different—namely making up our mind one way or the other what to do.

I can perfectly well decide today that in five minutes' time I will make up my mind one way or the other about whether to raise my hand—and then, in five minutes' time, make my mind up on the basis of that earlier decision. Making one's mind up one way or the other, then, is something that very clearly can be done voluntarily, on the basis of a prior decision to make one's mind up. But that does not show that the taking of a particular decision can be voluntary too. Making up my mind, after all, is a process. And it initially involves deliberating or at least seriously considering the options—something which is done preparatory to making any particular decision. It is this which can be done voluntarily. But which particular decision I then arrive at is not a voluntary matter. If when I make my mind up I decide to raise my hand rather than lower it, this is not something I can have done on the basis of some earlier decision to arrive at that particular decision rather than its opposite. I can decide in advance *that* I shall make my mind up; but I cannot effectively decide in advance *how* I will make my mind up. Deciding to do this rather than that is something entirely non-voluntary, just as Hobbes supposed. Deciding to do this rather than that is something I do in response to the options as I see them at the time—in response to their potential benefits, real or apparent—and not on the basis of some earlier decision to decide this particular way rather than the other.

4.3 Why the Will is Not Voluntary—The Will as a Reason-Applying Capacity

The clear non-voluntariness of decisions and intentions has a rationale—and it lies in the function of decision-making. After all, in ordinary life we do treat decision-making as something with one central clear purpose to it. There is an obvious point to bothering to take decisions about how we shall act. And that is to ensure that we end up performing the right voluntary actions—so that, as a result of our decision, we do the right thing and avoid doing the wrong one. Decisions have a *reason-applying* function in relation to voluntary action. One central point to taking decisions about which action to perform is to apply practical reason as it refers to the voluntary actions decided upon—to ensure that one performs voluntary actions which reason supports or at least does not oppose.

This reason-applying function is a fundamental feature of decision-making as we ordinarily understand it. It constrains the forms that decision-making can take. Whatever other roles decisions can fulfil in our lives, they must be consistent with this reason-applying function. And the reason-applying function shows up in one key way in particular. We naturally tie the justifiability of deciding to do A to the justifiability of remaining motivated to do A thereafter and of finally doing A. We never ordinarily agree with a decision to do A while leaving the question of whether to do A still open. To endorse someone's decision to do A as the right decision is always to endorse their doing A thereafter as the right action. To agree with how someone has decided to act is—by clear implication—to agree with their going on to perform the action which they have decided upon.[5] And that is not surprising if one essential function of decisions is to apply reason as it concerns the voluntary; for if that is always a decision's function, a decision to perform some voluntary action A can only be justified if doing A thereafter would be justified too.

---

[5] Assuming, of course, as I am throughout, that we are considering appraisals of the decision and of the act decided on made from the same information-base. Having endorsed someone's decision we can, *later on*, perfectly well come to advise them not to act as decided. But that is because new information has come in meantime—information which, if available earlier, would have prevented our original endorsement of the decision too.

Voluntary actions are justified, I have supposed, by features of them which make performing them good or desirable. To argue someone into, say, going to the bank, you need to make out that going to the bank would be desirable, either in itself, or as a means to further desirable ends. It follows that, in so far as decisions serve to apply reason as it concerns the voluntary, decisions have to be guided and justified by how desirable their objects are. Justification for deciding to do A must be tied to the desirability of subsequently doing A: for the decision to be justified, subsequently doing A must be on balance desirable.

That is why the considerations or reasons to which decisions are sensitive have to do with the desirability, not simply of the decision itself, but of its object. And so that in particular is why decisions to do A are not responsive to commands to take those decisions 'just like that', but are responsive to commands to do A. For it is these last commands that affect how desirable doing A might be. It is these commands that plainly can give us reason to do A.

The tie between the rationality of a decision and the desirability of its object rules out decisions being voluntary themselves. To see how, we need to consider Kavka's toxin puzzle, which nicely illustrates the tight link between the non-voluntariness of decisions and their reason-applying function.[6]

4.4 Kavka's Toxin Puzzle

Kavka's well-known toxin puzzle involves the offer of a $1mn prize for taking a particular decision to do A, a prize to be won just for taking that decision and irrespective of whether A is subsequently done. The action A decided upon is, considered overall, mildly undesirable: in Kavka's example, it involves taking a mild toxin one or two days later. On the other hand, winning the prize would be very desirable—desirable enough even to make up for the mild ill effects of the toxin. And that seems to leave the decision a very desirable one to take. It might still be very desirable to take it even were the decision sure to be carried out, so that the mild discomfort from taking the toxin would certainly follow.

The puzzle is about whether we could take the decision simply in order to win the prize: is a decision something we can take voluntarily, just because it would be very desirable to take it? And secondly and connectedly the puzzle is about whether the prize offer could ever justify so taking the decision. I shall argue that it is plain, from what we have already said, that the decision could not be taken voluntarily, simply in order to win a prize—that we can't take specific decisions just because taking those decisions would be very desirable; and that the decision could not be justified by its desirability as a means to winning the prize—and that the two facts are interdependent, and bound up with the reason-applying function which decisions have. A central

---

[6] Gregory Kavka, 'The toxin puzzle', *Analysis* 43, (1983).

function of decisions is to apply reason as it concerns the voluntary actions decided upon; and that means that decisions cannot be justified just by prizes for taking them. Whereas if *per impossibile* decisions were voluntary, they would be justified by decision prizes, and so would no longer serve this reason-applying function. The reason-applying function of decisions implies, therefore, that decisions cannot be taken voluntarily.

If the decision to do A were voluntary, then one could take that decision at will, in direct response to the desirability of taking it. One could take that decision simply because one wanted or had decided to, because taking it would win the prize. Now to exercise any such capacity for voluntariness, if one did possess it, in such a prize-winning way, would surely be perfectly rational. Even if the prize-winning decision did lead one to enact it—to take the mild toxin—the toxin's mildness would guarantee no lasting damage, and any temporary ill would be far outweighed by the huge sum won through the decision itself. The decision is clearly a desirable one; and so if decisions could be taken voluntarily, in response just to their desirability, taking this particular prize-winning decision would surely be fully justified. But, in such a case, once the prize was won there would be every justification not to retain the decision thereafter or enact it: in itself the toxin would be unpleasant, and nothing would be gained by taking it, the prize having already been secured. Taking the toxin would be wholly undesirable. In which case, a voluntary decision to take the toxin could be taken, and taken with full justification, in order to win the prize; but though the decision was justified, acting as decided, taking the toxin thereafter, would not be justified at all.

If decisions were voluntary, the justifiability of deciding to do A would no longer imply that subsequently doing A was justified too. To endorse someone's decision to do A would no longer be to endorse their doing A thereafter. Since the rightness of a decision clearly does imply the rightness of the act decided on—to endorse someone's decision is to endorse their doing what they have decided—decisions cannot be voluntary.

The non-voluntariness of decisions and intentions evidently has the same general basis as the non-voluntariness of other motivations, such as desires. Decisions are the formations of content-bearing attitudes—of intentions to act. And, as with desires to act, the object of a decision or intention to act is a voluntary action—some action which, when we decide to perform it, we are responding to in a way appropriate to, and to be justified in terms of the action's desirability. If decisions are non-voluntary, that must be because, as much as any desire-formation, they are content-bearing events which are responsive to the goodness or desirability of their objects, the voluntary actions decided upon.

Kavka's puzzle arises as such a puzzle because of an apparent clash of two intuitions. On the one hand we have the intuition that decisions are pro attitudes which have a reason-applying function—that decisions are centrally about applying reason as it governs the voluntary. And, for the reasons just given, this intuition means that decisions cannot be voluntary themselves. Without this intuition that decisions have to be responsive to the desirability of their objects, of course, the puzzle would not arise. There would be no obstacle to allowing that decisions could be taken voluntarily, simply in order to win prizes just for taking them. On the other hand, we have the intuition that decisions are themselves actions. And this intuition appears to clash with the first to the extent that we see the status of being an action as implying voluntariness. Hence the puzzle—how to resolve these conflicting intuitions?

The common conviction that a decision is an action is crucial to generating the puzzle. This kind of puzzle does not arise nearly as compellingly for other more intuitively passive pro attitudes such as desires—though justifications for those pro attitudes are similarly tied to the desirability of their objects. Fewer people, I suspect, are willing to toy with the idea that desires might be formed at will and voluntarily, simply in order to win prizes for forming them. The reason for the difference is clear enough. We see desire formation as something passive. Since coming to desire or want to do something does not itself appear to be a kind of action, we have less of an inclination to voluntarize it—to model its motivation and rationality on that of voluntary action.

The key to a final resolution of Kavka's puzzle lies, then, in how we interpret and make sense of the idea that a decision is indeed an action. For as long as we feel inclined to adhere to this idea, and then go on to infer from it to the voluntariness of decision-making, so our intuitions will remain in conflict and so the puzzle will remain. We will remain torn between the idea of decisions as voluntary, and the commitment to their non-voluntariness which comes from our belief in their reason-applying role.

One way to resolve the puzzle would of course be to show that decisions are not actions after all. But our belief in their nature as actions is not easy to get rid of. Another and, in the end, far more intuitive way to resolve the puzzle is to detach action from voluntariness. That way we can explain how decisions can be actions while remaining reason-applying motivations that are non-voluntary. And that means showing how the supposed tie of action to voluntariness really arises through some kind of illusion. Any resolution of the toxin puzzle depends, then, on the argument of the remainder of this book.

4.5 The Non-Voluntariness of Deciding and the Voluntariness of Trying

The question of the bounds of voluntariness is deeply connected with the problem of the extent of content within psychology, and of what in human action and its psychology counts as a genuine attitude and what does not. For motivations such as decisions are non-voluntary just because they are content-bearing pro attitudes;

they are directed at objects to the desirability of which they are responsive. There is a kind of occurrence that could easily be confused with decisions but which perfectly illustrates the contrast between genuine voluntariness and motivations that are non-voluntary because they are pro attitudes. Compare trying to do something and deciding to do it.

Hume denied that motivations are content-bearing states. On Hume's view, motivations or 'passions' are no more than contentless feelings, and to talk of their 'objects' is no more than to refer to their causes and effects. Talk of the 'object' had nothing to do with an object of thought to which the motivation was directed as a content-bearing and rationally appraisable attitude. 'When I am angry, I am actually possest with the passion, and in that emotion have no more a reference to any other object, than when I am thirsty, or sick, or more than five foot high.'[7] Now Hume may have been wrong to take this view of motivation. But he would have been right to take a correspondingly sceptical view of tryings as attitudes in their own right. We may reject the Humean theory of the contentlessness of passion. But we should endorse a Humean theory of the contentlessness of trying.

That there is a contrast between trying and deciding may not be obvious. For at first sight tryings look very like decisions. Tryings, after all, are reported exactly like decisions. Just as we talk of deciding *to raise one's arm*, so too we talk of trying *to raise one's arm*—both the decision and the trying being reported by reference to a voluntary action which they are apt to produce.

If trying were exactly like deciding, then just as a decision is a pro attitude towards acting as decided, so too an attempt would be a pro attitude towards acting as attempted. As with a decision, the attempt would have a content of its own—a content which specified the action attempted as the object of the attempt, and which left the rationality of the attempt dependent on that object's desirability. Just as decisions to do A have to be responsive to the desirability of doing A, so too would attempts at doing A. Trying to do A would never be done by us in a way responsive simply to the desirability of so trying. Trying to do A would never be done by us simply because we wanted or had decided so to try.

But tryings are not pro attitudes. And what shows this is that, unlike deciding, trying is something which can perfectly well be done voluntarily. We may not be able voluntarily to decide to do something, taking that particular decision on the basis of a decision or intention so to decide. But we certainly can voluntarily *try* to do something, making that particular attempt on the basis of an intention so to try. And then that particular trying counts as something we do voluntarily—as a voluntary action.

If trying to do A really were a pro attitude towards doing what was attempted, then, as with any genuine pro attitude, it would be by reference to desirability of what

---

[7] David Hume, *A Treatise of Human Nature*, ed. P.H. Nidditch (Oxford: Clarendon Press, 1978), p. 415.

was attempted that the rationality of the attempt was determined. But in reality the rationality of an attempt is determined in the same way as in any other case of voluntary action—by reference to the motivations on which the attempt is being based and to the rationality of those motivations, and so by reference to the desirability of the objects which those motivations have. And, as with any voluntary action, it is those same motivations and their objects that provide the attempt with its real object—with the goal at which the attempt is being directed. The goal of an attempt is determined, not by what it is an attempt to do, but by the pro attitudes on which the attempt is based.

To see this, consider the following conation experiment—an experiment to study unsuccessful tryings or conations. One's aim, in this experiment, is to determine what happens when one tries to raise one's arm and fails. One is therefore trying to raise one's arm—but only after first having had one's arm tied down. In this experiment one is in no way rationally committed to raising one's arm being desirable. For the aim of the experiment has nothing to do with actually raising one's arm. The whole experiment is predicated on one's arm's *not* rising. Raising one's arm would in fact, in the context of the experiment, be very undesirable; if one did manage to raise one's arm, the whole experiment would have failed. The goal of the trying is given, then, not by what it is an attempt to do, but by the content of the intention on which the trying is based—which in this case is an intention to try to raise one's arm without actually raising it. Making the attempt and failing—that is our goal in making the attempt and so that object at which our attempt is really being directed. And it is on the rationality of that intention that the rationality of the attempt depends—a rationality which depends in turn on the desirability of the intention's object. It is on the desirability of the intended outcome, an outcome in which the attempt is unsuccessful, that justification for the intention and so too for the intended trying depends. It is that goal, and that alone, to which one is rationally committed.

When we try to do A, we are not forming a further rationally appraisable pro attitude towards doing A, the action attempted. All that is happening is that on the basis of genuine pro attitudes, such as our intention to do A now, or perhaps our intention merely to try to do A now, our nerves, muscles, and limbs are engaged in ways that would standardly lead to A's being successfully done. The action or doing attempted is not the real object of the attempt, but simply its standard outcome or effect—an effect in terms of which the attempt is reported and identified, but not something at which the attempt need be directed or aimed. And this standard effect, taken in itself, is irrelevant to the trying's justification and rationality—as the content-provided object of a genuine pro attitude would not be to that pro attitude's rationality.

Of course, in most cases, when we try to do A, the rationality of our making the attempt really does depend on A being a sufficiently desirable thing for us to do. But that is only because an attempt normally is motivated by a pro attitude towards performing the action attempted. It is still the pro attitude motivating our attempt which is providing it with its true goal-direction; and it is on the rationality of that motivation and so on the desirability of that motivation's object, the real goal of the attempt, that the rationality of the attempt depends.

Table 4.1 sums up the differences between deciding and trying:

Table 4.1. Deciding and trying

Deciding to do A	Trying to do A
Cannot be done voluntarily	Can be done voluntarily, on the basis of pro attitudes towards trying to do A
Object (derived from content): doing A	Object *qua goal*: object of motivation for the trying—not necessarily doing A
Rationality depends on desirability of doing A	Rationality depends on the rationality of the motivation for the trying, and so on the desirability of that motivation's object

Trying shows very clearly what voluntary agency is like. As the case of trying has shown, voluntary actions take their goals from the contents and objects of the pro attitudes that motivate and explain them. Voluntary actions derive their goal-direction and their rationality as actions from the object-direction and rationality of the pro attitudes on which they are based.

Deciding is quite different. Decisions and the intentions which they form are content-bearing attitudes in their own right. So they are directed at objects provided by their own content. And their rationality depends on these same content-provided objects, and in a way which implies their non-voluntariness. Unlike tryings, the object-direction and rationality of our decisions is not simply inherited from further motivations on which those decisions are based—a point about decisions that is of fundamental importance and to which we shall return.

In fact this difference in their rationality and object-direction between decisions and tryings will be central to the argument of the remainder of this book. No plausible theory of decisions can plausibly treat them as just another case of voluntary action. Decisions are very plainly quite unlike voluntary actions. To voluntarize decisions and assimilate them to tryings would be a mistake, as would doing the reverse and devoluntarizing trying by assimilating it to deciding. The differences between decisions and attempts are fundamental. They typify and represent the differences between non-voluntary motivation and voluntary action.

4.6 Where Does Action Occur?

To sum up so far. Voluntary action is action performed on the basis of pro attitudes to its performance—pro attitudes by which we respond to the desirability of performing this voluntary action rather than that, and from which voluntary actions derive their goal-direction and their rationality. As responsive to the desirability of their objects these motivating desires and intentions are uniformly non-voluntary themselves. Deliberate or intentional action, then, involves voluntariness that arises out of and is explained by motivations that are inherently non-voluntary.

Where disagreement now begins, is about where in these two elements of motivation and voluntariness intentional action is to be found. Is our capacity for intentional agency first exercised—as the *voluntariness-based* model maintains—only in action which is performed voluntarily, on the basis of pro attitudes towards its performance, so that the categories of action and voluntariness are one and the same? Or is our capacity for intentional agency also exercised non-voluntarily, and independently of any motivating pro attitudes towards performing it?

The test case for this dispute is the will—our capacity for decision and intention-formation. The will seems to be exercised non-voluntarily. But it also seems to be regarded by us as a capacity for agency in its own right. If action can be detached from voluntariness, it must be at the point of the will.

5

The Voluntariness-Based Model of Action

5.1 The Voluntariness-Based Model

We have seen that fully executed intentional action involves both motivation and voluntariness. But where in these two elements do we find intentional action itself? So far I have been relying on this fundamental claim; that actions are distinguished from other events in one central way—by goal-directedness. Goal-directedness involves more than an event's serving a function. For example, the beating of a heart serves to circulate the blood and keep a body oxygenated. But the beating of a heart does not exemplify the goal-directedness we find in genuine agency. The goal-directedness that distinguishes agency involves, not simply an event's serving an end, but the event's being motivated by that end. An action is an event that has an object— an object at which the agent is directing the action's performance; and this object is what motivates the action's performance, being the goal at which the agent is aiming, and which he is using the action to attain.

So where do we find the deliberate and intentional employment of means to attain ends? One place where we may certainly find such goal-directed events is in voluntary action. Goal-directedness is undoubtedly to be found in what we do on the basis of a pro attitude towards doing it. And this voluntary goal-directedness comes from the pro attitude that is moving us to act. The objects qua goals of our voluntary actions are the content-determined objects of our motivating pro attitudes (Table 5.1):

Table 5.1. Motivation and voluntary action

Motivations to do A	Voluntarily doing A
	Goal-directed
Objects (derived from contents): doing A and ends to be attained by doing A.	Objects *qua* goals: objects of motivations for doing A.

But what of the motivating pro attitudes which give rise to our voluntary actions? Could forming a particular motivation to act ever be a goal-directed action—something which we do as a means to an end? In many cases at least, motivation-formation is not something goal-directed. That is very clearly so in those cases where we also suppose that the motivation's formation is passive, and not something that we intentionally do. Desires are passions. Coming to hold a specific desire, such as a desire to accept an offer, is something which happens to one, rather than something which one deliberately does. And the connection between goal-directedness and action gives part of the story why. Forming a desire to accept the offer is not an action because it does not constitute the adopting of means to pursue any end. In so far as I want to accept the offer I am of course attracted to accepting it. But that attraction is all that my attitude involves. The desire-formation is not an action because in forming the desire I am simply responding to its object, what I want, as something desirable or good. I am as yet merely attracted by it. In forming the desire I am not yet pursuing that object as my goal. The object of a desire is not a goal which the desire is being formed in order to attain.

But if desire formation is not goal-directed—is not something employed as a means—whereas the voluntary action of accepting the offer would be, what is the difference? What is it intentionally to do something as a means to an end?

Modern English-language philosophy has historically been dominated by a simple answer to that question—the answer given by the voluntariness-based model of intentional action. This model says that goal-directedness just is voluntariness. Goal-directedness always arises in voluntary action; and it always comes from the content of some motivating attitude—a pro attitude in which we respond to what we are doing as something desirable, either in itself, or as a means to further ends. Intentionally to do A for the sake of some end, whether for its own sake or as a means towards some further goal, is always to do A voluntarily, on the basis of a pro attitude towards doing A. In other words, our capacity for action is nothing more than a capacity to do things through wanting or deciding to do them.

The voluntariness-based model allows us, then, to see very clearly why simply in coming to want to accept the offer I am not pursuing any goal. And that is because the desire is not formed voluntarily and in a way responsive to its own desirability, on the basis of some pro attitude towards so desiring. The desire is instead formed non-voluntarily, as a response to its object, the action of accepting the offer. It is that object which is being responded to as something desirable.

As for desires, so, on the voluntariness-based model, for our non-voluntary motivating pro attitudes generally—whether cognitive or non-cognitive, whether mere desires or full-blown intentions. Classic supporters of the voluntariness-based model such as Hobbes and Davidson have been happy to assimilate all the pro attitudes, intentions and the events of their formation included, to the same general class of passive attitudes as desires. All are passive because all are non-voluntary. The forming of a specific motivation to do A rather than B is not something which ever directly counts as our own intentional doing—precisely because the motivation is formed non-voluntarily.

If the occurrence of a particular intention or desire is ever our deliberate or intentional doing, that can only be so indirectly—because the pro attitude is the effect of some prior voluntary action which can be deliberately used to cause that specific attitude. I can, for example, increase my desire for food by intentionally and voluntarily taking a run; or by concentrating my mind on inviting mental imagery of delicious tastes and smells. In these cases inherently non-voluntary feelings and motivations can, to a degree, be our own voluntary doing—though only indirectly, as intended effects of prior actions that were voluntary. But aside from the indirect manipulation of ourselves into holding them by prior voluntary action, these feelings and motivations can only be formed by us non-voluntarily. And so, on the voluntariness-based model, none of these feelings and motivations can count as actions on their own account.

Thomas Hobbes relied on his identification of action with voluntariness to argue against any form of freedom of or agency of the will. Hobbes claimed, rightly in my view, that we lack the liberty to decide as we will. We cannot decide to do A rather than B just on the basis of having decided or wanted so to decide. But then, relying on a voluntariness-based model of action, from the lack of a liberty to decide as we will he inferred that we lack a liberty of the will altogether. For Hobbes, to decide to do A rather than B is not something that we can do freely or intentionally, as a means to any end.

We find the same voluntariness-based model in modern English-language philosophy, in the work of Davidson. Consider what it is, in Davidson's view, for an agent to perform an action for a reason:

Whenever someone does something for a reason, therefore, he can be characterised as (a) having some sort of pro attitude towards actions of a certain kind, and (b) believing (or knowing, perceiving, noticing, remembering) that his action is of that kind.[1]

In Davidson's view, as things done for reasons, actions are performed voluntarily, on the basis of pro attitudes to their performance.

For Davidson, the forming of a particular intention is not a case of intentional action—any more than is coming to hold a particular desire. Why not? The same answer is given for intentions as applies to desires. In Davidson's view, forming an intention is no action because the formation of particular intentions, like desire-formation but unlike the performance of the actions intended, is non-voluntary: 'The coming to have an intention we might try connecting with desires and beliefs as we did other intentional actions ... But the story does not have the substantial quality of the account of intentional action ...'[2] And that is because the most plausible account of intention-motivation, in Davidson's view, is that particular intentions to act aren't formed voluntarily, in a way appropriate to the desirability of so intending—but

---

[1] Donald Davidson, 'Actions, reasons and causes', in *Essays on Actions and Events*, pp. 3–4.
[2] 'Intending' in *Essays on Actions and Events*, p. 90.

non-voluntarily, in a way appropriate to the desirability of the action intended and decided upon.[3]

In fact, in his 'Intending' Davidson wants to identify intentions with outright judgements that the voluntary action decided upon is good or desirable, desires being prima facie judgements to the same effect. And in his view the formation of none of these judgements is an intentional action, because all are formed non-voluntarily.

A number of lines of thought support identifying action with voluntariness. To begin with, what else is it to act towards a goal than to act on the basis of pro attitudes—pro attitudes in which what we do is favoured, either as an end in itself or as a means to further ends? The story about how goal-directedness arises in the voluntary case is obvious and intuitive. It is not immediately clear what other story there is to be told.

Moreover, and as we have already noted, it is with agency and goal-directedness in this familiar form that our practical deliberation—our deliberation about how to act—is primarily concerned. Deliberation about how to act, is, we have seen, centrally deliberation about the voluntary. We consider which voluntary actions to perform, and not which non-voluntary motivations to hold. We deliberate about whether to cross the road; not about whether to desire or intend to cross the road. But if deliberation about how to act is deliberation about the voluntary, does that not suggest that voluntariness is just what action is? To act intentionally, on this view, is always to act voluntarily, on the basis of some pro attitude towards doing what one is doing.

There are evident and systematic dissimilarities between our non-voluntary motivations, on the one hand, and the voluntary actions which they explain. Voluntariness and the pro attitudes which motivate it form naturally distinctive and distinct categories. On the one hand we have motivating psychological events and states, and on the other what we do through these motivating attitudes, as an object at which those attitudes are directed, and in a way responsive to the desirability of doing it. Could we do justice to what is special and distinctive about agency, and in particular to the intuition that cases of intentional agency form one single kind, if the category of agency straddled this evident divide between voluntariness and non-voluntariness? If someone did offer another story about what goal-directedness comes to—a story which applied to some non-voluntary motivations—it seems that it would have to be very different from the story which applies to the voluntary case. The story would certainly have nothing to do with voluntariness. Indeed, at least as applying to non-voluntary motivations, it might even have to appeal to features that actually exclude voluntariness. Once such a story was told, would goal-directed

---

[3] 'If someone intends to polish his right shoe, it must be because there is some value he wants to promote by polishing his right shoe...and he believes that by shining his right shoe he has a chance of promoting what he wants.' Davidson's replies in *Essays on Davidson*, eds B. Vermazen and M. Hintikka (Oxford: Oxford University Press, 1985), pp. 213–14.

agency in this non-voluntary form still count as, in any interesting sense, the same kind of phenomenon as agency in the voluntary case? How could agency consist, at one and the same time, both in voluntariness and in something else quite different, perhaps even voluntariness-excluding?

The voluntariness-based model has a number of consequences—consequences which will be important for the rest of the book and which supporters of the model have, on the whole, recognized and been willing enough to draw. That all these consequences really do follow is, however, controversial enough to require some discussion.

5.2 The Passivity of Decisions and Intentions

I have already mentioned one straight consequence of the model's identification of action with voluntariness. The motivations which explain our voluntary actions, being non-voluntary, are themselves passive. The non-voluntary event of forming a particular pro attitude is not itself an action.

As for pro attitudes in general, so for decisions and intentions in particular. Forming an intention to do A rather than B is not something that I do intentionally, as a means to attaining any goal. And it is clear enough why. Goal-directed action in general is being modelled on goal-directedness in its voluntary form. To do something intentionally, as a means to an end, is to do it voluntarily, on the basis of a pro attitude towards doing it. But we form intentions non-voluntarily, in a way responsive to the desirability of their objects, and not voluntarily, on the basis of a pro attitude towards forming them and in a way responsive just to the desirability of those intentions themselves.

Now, as we have seen, this straight consequence of the model—that to form a particular motivation is a passive occurrence, and does not constitute an intentional action—was openly drawn by Hobbes. It has also been explicitly taught by many other supporters of the model, down to the voluntariness-based model's most eminent and influential modern defender, Davidson. As a result there has been within English-language philosophy a powerful tradition of disbelief in the occurrence of actions of motivation or will. We find this scepticism in Gilbert Ryle, and more recently in Daniel Dennett, Galen Strawson, and Bernard Williams.[4] Belief in an agency or freedom of motivation or of will is viewed as a myth—and one generated by a dubious metaphysics of the mind or by dubious ethical theory. This myth is thought importantly connected with our common understanding of freedom as a freedom specifically of the will—a conception of self-determination which, again,

---

[4] See especially Gilbert Ryle, *The Concept of Mind* (London: Hutchinson, 1949); Daniel Dennett, *Elbow Room* (Oxford: Oxford University Press, 1984); Galen Strawson, *Freedom and Belief* (Oxford: Oxford University Press, 1986); and Bernard Williams, *Shame and Necessity* (Berkeley: University of California Press, 1993).

is regarded as mythical and erroneous. We shall be examining these sceptical claims in the chapters which follow. But such a tradition of scepticism is hardly surprising. The voluntariness-based model which dominates thinking about action makes such widespread scepticism inevitable, by leaving it very difficult to understand how motivation could be a locus of agency, let alone of self-determination.

However, there are other modern philosophers who share Hobbes' and Davidson's allegiance to the voluntariness-based model, but who nevertheless also want to hold onto the very natural idea that if some motivations, such as desires, are passive, others are active—that what we decide and intend, in particular, is or can be directly our deliberate doing.[5]

Of course it is not surprising that people should wish to hold onto the idea that decisions are actions. For surely our very own decisions about how we shall act are our own deliberate self-determined doing if anything in our lives is. When I decide to stay in, rather than go out, it is I myself who determine that I take that particular decision rather than the other. The occurrence of that particular decision to act is just as much determined by me, and so just as much my own deliberate doing, as is the further action which results.

If decisions are actions, then they must be directed at some goal. But what goal might that be? Whatever else decisions are used to do, any decision must have one end at least—to ensure that one acts as decided. That, after all, is the point of deciding to do A rather than B; to ensure that one does eventually do A, not B. A decision to act has an end, to which its taking is a means—the end of ensuring that one performs the particular action decided upon. And in this respect taking decisions contrasts markedly with forming desires. For as we have already observed, just as desires are intuitively passive, so they lack goal-direction. To form a desire is not to employ any means to an end. We are merely attracted to the objects of our desires. Simply in wanting something, we are not yet doing anything to attain it.

To make sense of a deliberate agency of decision-making or intention-formation, then, we need to explain how it is that, unlike the formation of a desire, a decision counts as a goal-directed event—an action performed in order to ensure the subsequent performance of the action decided upon. But however we explain it, one thing seems clear. Decisions are taken non-voluntarily. Unlike the actions which decisions explain, decisions are not themselves taken at will, motivated just by the agent's pro attitude to so deciding. So if decisions themselves are actions too, the voluntariness-based model must be false. Or must it?

In fact the voluntariness-based model is now far too well dug into the intellectual culture for it to be readily abandoned. So even those philosophers convinced that decisions are genuine actions generally try to stay with some version of the model.

---

[5] The view that decisions are or can be actions is defended within the framework of the voluntariness-based model by many philosophers, including David Lewis, Alfred Mele, David Velleman, Hugh McCann, and Randolph Clarke. The main text will discuss the various strategies adopted.

They try somehow to make sense of the agency and goal-directedness of decision-making in voluntariness-based or at least quasi-voluntariness-based terms. So let us now consider how this might be done, and the costs and benefits of the various available strategies. I shall suggest that while some of these strategies may not be straightforwardly incoherent, they are all profoundly unattractive. For they all involve assimilating decisions to the voluntary in ways that are, at best, ad hoc—that lack any very convincing rationale in what we independently know about the nature of decisions themselves.

5.2.1 Decisions as straightforwardly voluntary actions

One strategy just turns to the voluntariness-based model in its unqualified form—and claims that what makes decisions actions is simply that decisions are voluntary. That I decide to do A rather than B is my intentional doing, on this view, in that what motivates me to take the decision is nothing other than the fact that I want or intend so to decide.

For example, David Lewis takes this very position. In his view, we can take specific decisions at will, in response to the real or apparent desirability of taking them, simply on the basis of wanting or deciding so to decide.[6]

Now anyone who teaches the voluntariness of decisions and intention-formations must pay a price—a price that Lewis himself is perfectly willing to pay.[7] They must give up a fundamental intuition: that a central point of deciding what to do is not to take the decisions we want to take, but to ensure that we do the right thing—that the function of the will is to apply reason as it governs the voluntary, so that the rationality of deciding to do A guarantees the rationality of doing A thereafter.

We have seen why this price must be paid. If decisions are motivated and justified by reference to their own desirability, and not by reference to that of their objects, the rationality of deciding to do A and that of subsequently doing A must fall apart. For the fact that a particular decision would be a desirable one to take does nothing to guarantee the desirability of acting as decided thereafter.

My view is that the price is simply not worth paying. That decisions and intentions play an essentially reason-applying role in relation to the actions decided upon and intended is basic to the common-sense psychology of the will. It is at least as basic as the intuition that decisions are self-determined actions. And it implies that even if decisions are actions, they cannot be voluntary.

What of the claim, made by Hugh McCann, that decisions and intention-formations are inherently active—actions by their very nature—because *reflexively* or *internally* voluntary? Decisions count as actions not because they are effects of distinct and prior decisions or intentions to hold them—McCann sees such a view as

---

[6] See David Lewis, 'Devil's bargains and the real world', in *The Security Gamble: Deterrence in the Nuclear Age*, ed. Douglas MacLean (Ottowa: Rowman and Allenheld, 1984), pp. 141–54.

[7] See Lewis, 'Devil's bargains and the real world', p. 143.

threatening a vicious regress—but because any state of intending to do A is by its very nature also a state of intending to intend to do A: 'When I decide, I intend to decide, and I intend to decide exactly as I do.'[8]

The problem with this proposal is not just that it has no immediate support from common sense, though that is importantly true. We do not normally think of ourselves as intending to intend, let alone intending to intend to intend. The more fundamental problem is that the proposal is inconsistent with the nature and function of intention.

The function of an intention is give rise to the intention's object—what is intended—and to do so in a way responsive to that object's desirability. So the function of an intention to do A is to be responsive to the desirability of doing A. But an intention so to intend would not be responsive to the desirability of that object. Its function would be to be responsive not to the desirability of doing A, but to the desirability of intending to do A. And that indeed is precisely the way such intentions to intend are formed—on the relatively uncommon occasions when we do actually form them.

Offer me a prize for forming tomorrow an intention to take a toxin and, if I think there is some chance of somehow engineering the prize-winning intention within myself, perhaps through some drug or hypnosis, I may well form the intention to do just that—to manipulate myself into acquiring the prize-winning intention. In other words, I will form an intention to intend to take the toxin. Now the beliefs that move me to form this intention to intend have to do with the intended prize-winning intention. They are to do with intending to take the toxin, and the desirability of that. Whereas any beliefs that directly motivated the prize-winning intention itself—that directly motivated me to intend to take the toxin—would be have to be importantly different. They would have to include beliefs about taking the toxin and the desirability of that. Which is why forming the intention to intend won't of itself guarantee forming the further intention intended, and why some intervening manipulation may be required to induce that last intention.

Intending to do A and intending so to intend are very different cases of intention, and are motivated in very different ways. To form the one is not necessarily to form the other. That is because they have quite different objects, and so, since their objects are different, the considerations to which they are responsive are quite different too. Each intention is responsive to the desirability of its own object. But a single state cannot sensibly be responsive to both these objects at once since, as we have seen, the desirability of doing A and the desirability of intending to do A can fall apart. Hence

---

[8]   Hugh McCann, 'The formation of intention' in *The Works of Agency*, p. 163. This claim that intention-formation is inherently and reflexively intended has been made by earlier action theorists. The inherent and reflexive voluntariness of decisions was, for example, taught by Francisco Suarez—see Thomas Pink, 'Suarez, Hobbes and the scholastic tradition in action theory', in *The Will and Human Action: from Antiquity to the Present Day*, eds Thomas Pink and Martin Stone (London: Routledge, 2004).

it is not surprising that we do not normally regard intentions to do A as by their very nature intentions so to intend.[9]

McCann wants to explain how decisions are actions, but can think of no other way than to appeal to voluntariness. To get round the evident fact that decisions cannot be directly motivated by prior decisions to take them—they certainly cannot be voluntary in the ordinary way—he postulates instead a special and internal kind of reflexive voluntariness. But the proposal is ad hoc in that he has no independent grounds for this kind of internal voluntariness. Indeed the proposal is worse than ad hoc. For we have seen that there is argument against it. If the function of the will is to be responsive to the desirability of its objects, intentions cannot be reflexively voluntary. They cannot have their own occurrence as their intended object as well as the actions intended.

5.2.2 The appeal to the voluntariness of deciding one way or the other

There is one thing at least which, it seems, I can do voluntarily—namely to arrive at a decision one way or the other about whether to do A. The intention on which a decision to do A is based may not be an intention to take that particular decision. But it may perfectly well be an intention to make up one's mind—to decide, one way or the other, about whether to do A. So, as Robert Kane, Alfred Mele, and Randolph Clarke[10] have all suggested, cannot the status of deciding to do A as a goal-directed action be explained in terms of its being an effect of an intention or other pro attitude towards making up our minds—towards arriving at a decision one way or the other?

This proposal simply fails to address the problem. It does nothing to vindicate the voluntariness-based model, because it does nothing to establish the voluntariness of deciding specifically to do A. And it is the voluntariness of that which would need to be established if the voluntariness-based model is to accommodate our ordinary conception of how we ourselves can determine our own wills. For we naturally think that not only do we determine for ourselves whether we take a decision at all. We also determine for ourselves both what specifically we decide and, in so doing, too, how we shall act thereafter. Which means that our taking of these specific decisions must be something that we deliberately and intentionally do—and do as a means to ensuring that we perform the actions decided upon.

---

[9] I do not of course rule out the possibility that intentions have objects that are specified *by reference* to their being intended. Thus, as Gilbert Harman has argued in his 'Practical reasoning' (*Review of Metaphysics*, 29 (1976), pp. 431–63), it might be true that to intend to do A is *ipso facto* to intend to do A as a result of so intending. But here the object of the intention, to the desirability of which the intention is responsive, is still doing A—this time considered as based on a prior intention so to intend. It is to the desirability of so acting that the intention is responsive—not to the desirability of intending to do A in the first place. The object of the intention is that, given that the intention is held, the action intended be performed as an effect of that intention—not that the intention be held in the first place.

[10] See Randolph Clarke in *Libertarian Accounts of Free Will* (Oxford: Oxford University Press, 2003), p. 26; also Robert Kane, *The Significance of Free Will* (Oxford: Oxford University Press, 1998), pp. 138–9; and Alfred Mele, *Motivation and Agency* (Oxford: Oxford University Press, 2003), p. 205.

So it is not enough for it to have been our deliberate goal-directed doing that we took a decision at all. It must have been our deliberate goal-directed doing that we took *this* decision rather than *that*. And that means, on the voluntariness-based model, that what we specifically decide has to be voluntary too. The model, after all, is all about understanding intentional goal-directedness, doing things intentionally in order to attain ends, in terms of voluntariness. To do something as a means to ends is understood as doing it voluntarily, on the basis of a pro attitude towards doing it. So if the model works, it must apply to every case of goal-directed action. There cannot be goal-directed actions, things done as means to ends, which simply cannot be done voluntarily. But the taking of a specific decision, though a goal-directed action, though done as a means to an end, though done in order to ensure that we perform the action decided upon, is, it seems, no more subject to our prior will or decision than what we specifically want. We can no more take specific decisions at will than we can form specific desires. At the level of specific decisions, the voluntariness-based model, and its conception of what agency involves—acting as we decide or want—has not been shown to apply.

In any case, many of our intentions are not based on prior intentions to make our minds up. Indeed, on pain of a vicious regress, not all our intentions could be so motivated. Sometimes we simply take a decision without having had any prior intention of making up our minds. We just make up our minds on the spot, as soon as options occur to us, without having had first to form a prior intention to arrive at a decision. But are decisions so taken the less our own doing for that? In such cases are we the less able deliberately to determine for ourselves which decision we take?

5.2.3 Decisions as quasi-voluntary actions

Let us accept that we cannot take specific decisions just on the basis of deciding or wanting to take them, in a way responsive simply to the desirability of so deciding. As Hobbes put it so bluntly: the will is not voluntary.[11]

If then decisions are actions, as desire-formations are not, that cannot be because the voluntariness-based model of action in its classic form is true. If decisions are actions, that model must be false. There must be some things that we can do intentionally, as means to ends, without being able to do them voluntarily and just because we want to do them. But even if the voluntariness-based model in its unqualified form is false, perhaps something like it, a heavily qualified version of the model, might still be true.

Decisions may not be voluntary. We may not be able to decide just as we decide or want to. But that does not mean that some sort of pro attitude towards the taking of

---

[11] 'Can any man but a schoolman think that the will is voluntary?' Hobbes in *The Questions Concerning Liberty, Necessity and Chance, clearly stated between Dr Bramhall Bishop of Derry, and Thomas Hobbes of Malmesbury*, (London 1656), p. 256.

specific decisions cannot play a part in their motivation. And perhaps it is only because of the motivating role played by such pro attitudes towards them that decisions do count as intentional actions.

What kind of pro attitude might move us to take a decision? It cannot be any pro attitude whatsoever towards taking the decision—otherwise we would return to the voluntariness-based model in its unqualified form. If decisions are to be responsive to the desirability of their objects, decisions cannot be taken just on the basis of their own general desirability. But perhaps a decision is always taken on the basis of its desirability in one specific respect—as a means to attaining its object. The pro attitudes which motivate a decision to do A, then, must always include a particular kind of desire so to decide. They must always include a desire so to decide which is *pro tanto* in a particular way—which is directed at the decision insofar as it provides a means to attaining the further desired end that A be done. What makes decisions to do A actions, and gives them their goal-direction—towards the goal that A be done— is their being motivated by desires to do A, and to take the decision to do A as a means to this end.[12]

The voluntariness-based model says that actions are performed in response to the desirability of performing them, motivated just by our desiring or deciding so to act. Put so simply, this model is false of decisions. But a qualified version of it is true. Decisions are taken in response to their desirability in one particular respect—as means to the desirable end of acting as decided—and on the basis of desires to use them as means in just this way.

On this view, we have no unqualified capacity to decide as we desire or want. Deciding or desiring to take a specific decision will not necessarily motivate us to take it. But certain desires to decide do still play a role in motivating our decisions. We can and do take decisions on the basis of wanting to take them; provided that our desire to take those decisions is always for one reason in particular—to use them as means to ensuring that we later act as decided.

This theory of how decisions are actions is more faithful to common-sense psychology than Lewis's view—the view which treated decisions simply as voluntary actions. It respects decisions' character as events responsive to the desirability of the acts decided on—as events which therefore cannot be straightforwardly voluntary themselves. Moreover, unlike the view of Clarke, Kane, and Mele, it does something to address the point at issue—our capacity to determine how we decide by inten- tionally taking one specific decision rather than another. The status of specific decisions as goal-directed actions is made to rest not, irrelevantly, on the unqualified voluntariness of something else, but on a qualified or quasi-voluntariness of those decisions themselves. But the theory still faces serious criticisms.

---

[12] What such a theory of decision motivation needs, of course, is a story about why decisions should have to be motivated by these desires in particular—a story which is not ad hoc, but is based on a plausible account of what kind of event a decision is. It is not immediately obvious what this story would be.

There is one immediate problem with the theory. It too seems ad hoc, and it is obvious enough why. At least in the usual or everyday case, decisions do not seem to be taken on the basis of desires to decide at all, or on the basis of beliefs about what ends our decisions might help us attain. In general, decision makers consider simply the action to be decided upon, and what ends that action might attain. They don't think about the decision itself at all. Any desires that explain decisions to do A are normally desires to do A, and to attain various ends through doing A. Decisions to do A are not normally explained by desires so to decide and to attain various ends through so deciding.

What, after all, ordinarily moves decision makers? Surely, concerns to do with the subject matter of their deliberation—with what they are worrying and deliberating about whether to do. Yet ordinary practical deliberation is concerned not with decisions themselves, but with their objects. We worry and deliberate about whether to go for a walk, not about whether to decide or form an intention to go for a walk. Indeed in many cases not only are decision makers unmoved by desires to decide. There seems no clear evidence of such desires even having been formed or held.

Even if such desires did exist, our ordinary belief in the status of our decisions as actions seems not to appeal to them in any way. We think of our decisions as actions, but without postulating motivating desires to decide as we do so. Any desires we do postulate are to do with our decisions' objects, and not to do with the decisions themselves. Our belief in the status of our decisions as active motivations seems to have nothing to do even with this kind of quasi or qualified voluntariness.

It might be conceded that ordinary decisions seem not to be formed even quasi-voluntarily. If any prior desires motivate our decisions to do A, it is desires to do A and to attain ends through doing A, and not desires to decide to do A.[13] But some philosophers might still want to hold onto one element of the voluntariness-based theory, and claim that what makes decisions actions is the fact that they are explained and motivated by pro attitudes. No weight, though, is put on the claim that these pro attitudes are directed at the decision itself. The motivating desires that explain our decisions and constitute them as actions are allowed simply to be what they ordinarily appear to be—pro attitudes just to the decision's own object. Decisions to do A are actions simply as events explained and motivated by desires to do A and to attain various ends by doing A. In other words, the idea that decisions are actions because they are taken voluntarily is being given up entirely. All that is being relied on is the idea that decisions are motivated by further attitudes.

The problem with this compromise is obvious. A decision to do A is supposed to be motivated by a desire to do A. But why should this leave the decision a goal-directed action—something which is done as a means to ensuring the subsequent doing of A? The appeal to voluntariness explained this at least—by applying a thoroughly familiar

---

[13] For this view of how desires motivate decisions and intentions, see again Davidson in *Essays on Davidson*, pp. 213–14.

and, when it does apply, very intuitive model of goal-directedness to the case of decisions themselves. What we do voluntarily, on the basis of a pro attitude towards doing it, either for its own sake or as a means to further ends, is clearly being aimed at as a goal. But this vital element of voluntariness has now been abandoned. And what is left is certainly not enough to give us goal-direction and agency. After all, passive desires to do A can themselves be motivated—if not by desires to do A (such motivations would require that the desire already be held), then by desires for the ends that doing A might be thought to attain. But such desires do not seem to be goal-directed actions on that account.

The appeal to some kind of voluntariness was not, then, a dispensable luxury. If it is further motivating attitudes that make decisions actions, these motivations had better include desires specifically to decide. Yet appeal to such desires to decide is unattractive. It paints a rather complicated picture of how decisions are ordinarily motivated—a picture that looks rather implausible. And the theory faces other difficulties as well.

5.2.3.1 THE AGENCY OF DECISION-MAKING IS LEFT QUALIFIED

Those of us who do have an intuition that our decisions are actions—that what we decide is our own doing—do not normally see the agency of our decisions as a thinner or qualified version of the agency of the actions decided upon. That we take a decision to go for a walk, rather than deciding to stay at home—this is just as much something that we deliberately do, and just as much something which we determine for ourselves, as is our eventually going out rather than staying in. After all, normal, everyday decision-making seems to provide a locus of self-determination par excellence—a case of self-determination in its most vivid and immediately intuitive form. To decide what we shall do is, in general, precisely to determine for ourselves what we shall do. Now if our ordinary decisions provide particularly clear cases of self-determination, and self-determination presupposes action—something self-determined must be our very own doing, and not something which merely happens to us—then our decisions must be as clear and full-blooded cases of action as any. If the everyday taking of specific decisions to act offers a paradigm case of self-determination, how could the taking of those decisions exemplify the defining features of intentional agency, of what counts as our own deliberate doing, only marginally? How could decisions exemplify those action-constitutive characteristics less fully than do the actions which decisions explain?

Unfortunately, the agency of decision-making turns out, on the quasi-voluntary theory, to be just a heavily qualified analogue of agency in another more full-blooded form—the subsequent and fully voluntary actions which our decisions explain. And it is clear enough why. The quasi-voluntary theory still understands the capacity for agency exercised in decision-making as a capacity to do things on the basis of wanting to do them. It is only because decision-making involves such a capacity, in however qualified a form, that it counts as a case of genuine action at all. But, as the theory admits, the capacity for doing things on the basis of our wanting to do them which is exercised in our decision-making really is limited or qualified—and deeply so compared to the capacity exercised in our fully voluntary action. For it still remains very much the case that, as Hobbes made so brutally clear, the mere fact that we want to take a given decision does nothing of itself to motivate us to take it; and decisions are never taken simply on the basis of our holding pro attitudes to taking them. Which is why decisions behave so much like other non-voluntary attitude-formations such as desire-formations, and so little like the genuinely voluntary actions which they explain. In the case neither of intentions nor desires are we generally able to form these attitudes on the basis of wanting to form them.

Like the voluntariness-based model proper, the quasi-voluntary theory still understands action in the same highly debatable way—as the exercise of an ability to do things through wanting to do them. But at best and even on the quasi-voluntary theory's own terms, decision-making involves such an ability only very restrictedly. Such an ability is exercised in full-blooded form only in our performance of the voluntary actions decided upon. That leaves the agency of decision-making a thinner, qualified version of the agency of voluntary action. If we want it to be anything more, we need a different model of agency entirely—not a model of it as doing what we want, but something quite different.

5.2.3.2 THE GRATUITOUSNESS OF APPEAL TO DESIRES TO DECIDE

In the case of action that is obviously and uncontroversially voluntary, goal-direction clearly does come from pro attitudes motivating the action—such as from desires or intentions so to act—and from the contents of those attitudes. Appeal to such motivations, then, is central to understanding action in its genuinely voluntary form. For without goal-direction, there can be no action at all. If an event's goal-directedness wholly depends on such motivations then so too must its very status as action. But this condition on the goal-directedness of actions that are undoubtedly voluntary—that it be provided by pro attitudes towards so acting—is just not true of decisions. With decisions the postulation of desires to decide, or indeed of any such further motivations at all, does not seem to be necessary in the same way. It is not similarly needed to give decisions their goal-direction.

Take some voluntary bodily action, such as crossing the road. If we are to make sense of that action as something goal-directed—as intentionally done as a means to an end—we shall need to appeal to some pro attitude towards so acting. And it is clear enough why. Without such a pro attitude and its content, there would be no object at all at which the agent's movement was being aimed. For it seems that the voluntary action involves no content and object of its own beyond that provided by the pro attitudes which motivate it. Which is why in seeing such a voluntary action as goal-directed, we naturally relate it to pro attitudes on which its performance is based; we naturally convey that goal-direction by referring, for example, to 'the intention with which the action is being performed'.

Of course, not all that we do voluntarily lacks a content and object of its own. Suppose that I imagine or visualize a scene in my mind's eye, and do so voluntarily, on the basis of a decision to visualize it. There is here an object of the imagination—the scene which I imagine. But the object of an imagining is not by that fact a goal which the imagining of it is aimed at attaining. Taken in itself, an object of an imagining is simply that; a state of affairs which I merely imagine, and not necessarily—indeed, not usually—a state of affairs that the imagining is directed at bringing about. Indeed, an imagining need not be a goal-directed action at all. It may be an event without any purpose, an event which has simply intruded itself passively into my mind. To show that the imagining is a goal-directed action and to determine what its goals might be, we have to leave the imagining's own content, and find pro attitudes on the basis of which the visualization is occurring. It is these pro attitudes and their contents which give the imagining its goal-direction. These might be pro attitudes towards visualizing a scene of that kind, and perhaps towards attaining various ends thereby—such as remembering something experienced once before or even, in some cases, if the agent really thinks the visualizing can have this effect, making a scene of the kind to be imagined come true. It is the objects of these motivating pro attitudes which give my imagining its goal-direction—not the object which my imagining has in its own right.

As for imaginings, so for something else that we can do voluntarily—deliberating. When, for example, we deliberate practically, we entertain a sequence of thoughts—thoughts with objects of their own, namely the various options between which we are deliberating, conceived by us in the way that we believe them to be. Now if in entertaining these thoughts I really am acting intentionally—I am intentionally deliberating about what to do—this whole process will have a further object. It will have an object in the sense of a goal towards attaining which all my thinking is being intentionally directed by me—the goal of finding out how best to act. But this goal and the direction of the thoughts towards it is not constituted by the mere fact that I am entertaining these thoughts with the objects which they have in their own right—the relevant options as I believe them to be. For the having of thoughts with such objects need not be my deliberate doing at all. I need not be using these thoughts as a means to any goal. The thoughts could simply be passing undirectedly through my mind. The goal, if there is one, at which these thoughts are being intentionally directed must come from some pro attitude on the basis of which the thoughts are occurring—such as a desire or intention to find out which option is best. So, just as before, the goal-direction of what we do voluntarily comes from the pro attitudes which motivate it—and not from anywhere else.

As we saw in Chapter 4, trying provides another example of how the goal-direction of what we do voluntarily always depends on the content of a pro attitude on which the voluntary doing is based. Trying, again, is something that we can do voluntarily, on the basis of a decision or desire to try. And when we try there is always something that we are trying to do. But that action attempted does not, simply as what is attempted, provide the trying with its goal. We have again to turn to the pro attitudes on which the trying is based. And those may not include pro attitudes towards doing what is attempted at all. I might try to do something intending to fail. As in the conation experiment, my goal might be precisely not doing what I am attempting to do.

Where actions of road crossing, imagining, deliberating, trying, and the like are concerned, the intentional pursuit of goals does depend on pro attitudes motivating the action, and cannot be understood in other terms. But decisions are quite different. Intuitively, any decisions we take count as our very own doing—and as our own doing as much as anything is. Decisions, as we ordinarily understand them, are actions by their very nature. And as actions, these decisions must have goal-direction. Moreover there is a particular goal-direction that decisions also have by their very nature. For as we have already noted, as actions, there is one immediate goal at which decisions must always be directed—namely, performance of the action decided on and intended. The point of deciding to do A is always to ensure that one does subsequently do A. But this immediate goal is the very object which the decision has as a content-bearing event in its own right—the goal is simply what the decision is a decision to do, the object being provided not by the content of some further pro attitude motivating the decision, but by the decision's own content. Decisions are the formations or initiations of content-bearing states—of intentions—and share the contents of the states they form. So the immediate goal of a decision comes, not from the content of some pro attitude to the decision, but from a content that the decision has in its own right.

We can see why genuinely voluntary action is dependent on pro attitudes to its performance for its nature as action. Without those motivations and their contents, it would have no goal-direction at all. For its goal-direction is entirely derived from those contents. But the same seems not to be true of decisions. The immediate goal-direction of our decisions is determined by contents that they have in themselves. And this suggests that what makes decisions actions—events with some goal-direction—is not any further attitudes that might be motivating the decisions, but simply the kinds of content-bearing events which decisions themselves are.

We have been considering a watered down and qualified version of the voluntariness-based model. But the model in this qualified form is still objectionable. For it is tying the status of a decision or intention-formation as an action to something beyond the nature of the decision itself—to the decision's being motivated by further attitudes. But a step that makes sense for genuinely voluntary actions—which in their case is unavoidable, in fact—lacks the same rationale where decisions are concerned. Further motivations are just not needed to give decisions some basic or immediate goal-direction. Decisions have that goal-direction anyway—from their own contents, and not just from the contents of other attitudes.

By contrast to cases of genuine voluntariness, such as road-crossings, imaginings, and the like, it really is not clear that our belief that our decisions are goal-directed events rests on the existence of further motivations for taking them. It may be that decisions get their basic goal-direction, and so their status as actions, in a quite different way from any voluntary action. It may be that this basic goal-directedness comes from within, from the contents that they possess as psychological attitudes in their own right, and from the relation they bear to those contents as the particular kind of attitudes that they are.

5.2.4 Decisions as parts of voluntary actions

Suppose it is admitted that decisions are not voluntary themselves. It might still be claimed, nonetheless, that what makes them actions is their occurrence as components of or parts of more inclusive wholes that are actions; and that these more inclusive wholes are actions because they have other parts which are voluntary—namely, the actions decided upon. It is this status as parts of events which also contain voluntariness that makes decisions actions. So the status of decisions as actions is still being explained in terms of voluntariness.[14]

But this move is question-begging. Decisions themselves are supposed to count as genuine doings by us. And, according to the view proposed, what is supposed to make them doings is that they occur as parts of what we do. But why should we admit that they are parts of what we do unless it has already been shown that decisions are indeed things done by us? After all, if decisions were passive non-doings, far from being parts of what we do, they could only be non-active antecedents or accompaniments of what we do. In other words, we have here nothing to explain what makes decisions actions—but merely an ontological proposal which depends on the assumption that they are. And, far from showing that decisions are actions, any linkage between agency and voluntariness, a linkage which the theory is striving to retain, suggests the opposite. For, as has been admitted, decisions themselves are not voluntary.

Secondly decisions can occur well in advance of the occurrence of any voluntary action, and even without the agent managing to do anything voluntary. Through ill luck the agent may never manage to act on his decisions. So there can perfectly well be decisions unconnected to any voluntariness then or later. But, intuitively, such decisions count as actions nonetheless.

5.2.5 Summary

If we identify action with voluntariness, then the logic of our position is inescapable. Motivating pro attitudes are not formed voluntarily. So they must be formed passively. Where decisions are concerned, we might try to smuggle in a qualified or

---

[14] My thanks to an Oxford University Press reader for proposing this theory.

quasi-voluntariness. But that quasi-voluntariness has to be smuggled in. It is not clearly part of our ordinary conception of how we take decisions. And on a voluntariness-based model of action a qualified kind of voluntariness will at best get us no more than a qualified kind of agency.

We have also uncovered a vital feature of decisions—something that distinguishes them from all genuinely and unqualifiedly voluntary actions. This is that if they do have goal-direction at all, then some basic goal-direction seems internal to them, and part of their very nature as having the kind of content and mode of direction to that content that they do. Deciding to do A always has as its goal the object which its own content provides—that A be done. And this raises a serious and fundamental issue: whether a model of agency that derives an action's goal-direction from pro attitudes towards the action—a model that certainly does apply to agency in uncontroversially voluntary form—is at all appropriate for decisions.

5.3 Motivation, Action, and the Voluntary

What does the voluntariness-based model imply for the relation between action and its motivation? According to the model, the motivation for an action always comes from pro attitudes to the action and to ends furthered by the action. And these motivating pro attitudes must be distinct from the voluntary action they explain.

Notice that attitudes do not have to be distinct from the voluntary action they motivate just because the attitudes themselves are non-voluntary. As we shall see, once we abandon the voluntariness-based model and allow for action to take non-voluntary form, then what we ourselves do as a means to ends can include non-voluntary motivations as well as voluntary actions based on those motivations—and each, non-voluntary motivation and voluntary action, can be purposively done aspects of one and the same action. It is the voluntariness-based model and what it implies that forces us to treat non-voluntary motivations as occurrences that are distinct from the voluntary actions they explain. For on the non-voluntariness-based model, the non-voluntariness of motivation—the impossibility of forming a pro attitude just on the basis of a pro attitude to holding that pro attitude—straightforwardly implies passivity. It is not as if motivations could be aspects of what we do that just happen not to be done deliberately, or as a means to ends, but might have been our own purposive doing. Motivations are essentially non-voluntary, and so, indirect manipulation through prior action aside, could never be formed by us for a purpose, as means to any ends. That means that motivations must always be like desires that come over us. They must be passions—occurrences that happen to us rather than being directly our own doing; and so as passive and not our own doing motivations must be distinct from what is our own doing—the action that those motivations explain.

That rules out any view of action as a kind of purposive attitude, with its goal-direction coming from content internal to it. Action derives its object solely from the contents of motivations that are passive—and that as passive must be distinct from it. And if those motivations are distinct from the action they explain that then raises the issue of the action's connection to those motivations. How do the objects provided by contents that are internal to these motivations come to count as objects of the action? Those objects belong immediately to the motivations, after all, and not immediately to the action. So something else must connect the action to the motivations, to allow the objects of the motivations to become the action's objects too.

Davidson is well known for having argued that this connection must involve something more than the fact that the motivations constitute pro attitudes to the action's performance. As he puts it, something more is required than the fact that the motivations *rationalize* the action's performance. Such rationalizing attitudes can be present, he argues, without actually providing the goals or objects at which an action's performance is directed. As we shall be discussing further in Chapter 12, I can want to attain some end E, believe that doing A would attain E—attitudes that leave me favouring doing A and so rationalize doing A—but perform A for quite different ends and out of a quite different motivation. The additional element required for attitudes to count as the attitudes that actually motivate what I do and provide it with its goal-direction is, in Davidson's view, causation: the motivations that provide an action's goal-direction must do so as causes of its performance.

Davidson's argument is very important to the modern philosophical literature on motivation, and is central to current discussion of whether motivations must be causes. But remember that there is another much older line of thought that connects motivation to causation. For the Hobbesian voluntariness-based tradition was inclined to view motivations as causes of the actions they explain in any case, long before Davidson came forward with this particular argument. This is because, as we have already observed, there is strong association in common-sense psychology between motivation and power: we are *moved*—influenced or determined—into action. Now on the voluntariness-based model, motivations and the actions they explain are distinct occurrences. And the natural way of conceiving of the exercise of power by one occurrence to determine or influence another is to appeal to causation—to power in causal form. For how else does one occurrence influence or determine another distinct from it than by causing it?

We shall return to consider again the issue of how motivation relates to action and to voluntary action in particular, as well as the general problem of power and its relation to causation. But the dominant version of the voluntariness-based model has undoubtedly been one in which actions, as voluntary doings, derive their goals exclusively from without—from motivations that as passive are not only distinct from the actions they explain, but are also causes of the actions they explain, and whose contents provide those actions with their goals. So goal-direction occurs, by its very nature, as an effect of a power that is causal, and that attaches to passive motivations.

5.4 Practical Reason and the Passive

We saw in the last chapter what it is to apply practical reason. It is to exercise a capacity to respond and conform to practical or action-governing justifications. Now, as we have seen, such a capacity is exercised when we act voluntarily—but not only then. It is also exercised when we become motivated to act voluntarily. For, as we have seen, justifications for the voluntary can only move agents to act if they equally justify the motivation which that voluntary action presupposes and requires. We can only respond to justifications for doing voluntary A if we become motivated to do A—a motivation which those same justifications must also support.

On the voluntariness-based model, however, that motivation, as formed non-voluntarily, must count as something passive—as a motivation which happens to us, and the formation of which is not our direct and intentional doing. It follows, on the voluntariness-based model, that our motivational response to practical justifications is passive; and that our response, at the point of action, occurs as an expression and effect of that response at the point of passive motivation (Figure 5.1).

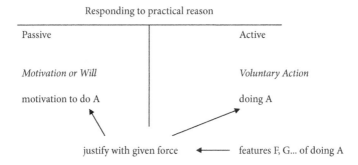

Figure 5.1. Responding to practical reason.

This point still holds even if, contrary to what Hobbes and many others and I myself have all argued, we class some motivating pro attitudes—decisions and intentions—among our voluntary actions. For as voluntary actions these attitudes too will presuppose prior pro attitudes towards forming them—motivating pro attitudes which must be formed if those decisions are to be taken, and which if the theory is not to be infinitely regressive must themselves be passive. And so, if it is to move us to decide, any practical justification for taking a decision must also justify the passive motivation which the decision requires, be it a desire to decide or whatever. And in responding to this justification the agent must first do so passively, by forming that required motivation.

If we take what I regard as the more principled voluntariness-based view, and classify all motivation as passive, a further consequence follows. We saw earlier that we can fail in our application of practical reason without the failure lying strictly in our reason itself. For the failure may occur outside our motivation. It may lie, not in any lack of practical rationality, but in some other factor—such as in our health or strength, or in the unexpected intervention of others. Provided our practical reason has left us motivated us to do all that we have justification for doing, then even if we do not succeed in doing what we had justification for doing, we can still count as acting rationally. Our rationality as agents, then, depends on and is fixed by the motivations with which we act. Which means that, on the voluntariness-based model, if those motivations are formed passively, and not through intentional action, so our rationality as agents is determined passively and not actively.

The voluntariness-based model of action certainly does allow that actions can be performed rationally or irrationally—but explains this rationality in action in terms of our rationality or irrationality at the level of the passive. We count as acting rationally only to the extent that the passive attitudes that motivate our action are rational. Rationality or irrationality in action is a function of a prior rationality or irrationality in passive motivation.

As Allan Gibbard has put it:

In short, then, we appraise as rational or irrational things that are clearly involuntary, like beliefs and attitudes—and there is no special reason to think we are mistaken. Even in the case of action, appraisals of rationality apply primarily to states of mind that are not straightforwardly voluntary.[15]

5.5 The Voluntariness-Based Model in Summary

On the voluntariness-based model, then, in its most principled and consistent form, the systematic differences between non-voluntary pro attitudes and voluntary actions are turned into differences between passions and actions as such (Table 5.2).

Table 5.2. Voluntariness-based model

Passive motivation	causes	Intentional action
Motivation to do A		doing A
(counts as passive because non-voluntary)		(counts as active only because done voluntarily, as effect of motivations)
object (derived from content)	*provides*	object *qua* goal
passive rationality	*determines*	rationality of action

The model divides active from passive in a way that leaves action entirely dependent on passive causes for its goal-direction and rationality—for its character as intelligible action. On the one hand we have the motivating psychological attitudes

---

[15] Allan Gibbard, *Wise Choices, Apt Feelings* (Oxford: Oxford University Press, 1990), p. 40.

whose rationality determines our rationality as agents and whose contents alone provide the goals towards which we act—all these, according to the model, are passive. And on the other hand we have actions, which as exclusively voluntary derive their goals from the contents of those passive attitudes.

Actions have objects—goals towards which they are directed. But actions are linked to those goals only through being motivated and explained by events and states distinct from them that are content-bearing—through being motivated by attitudes which are entirely passive. And it is the content of these passive attitudes, and not any distinct content which actions have in their own right, which gives actions their goal-direction. Talk of objects of action is not on a level with talk of objects of belief and desire. Objects of belief and desire are a function of the contents which beliefs and desires have in their own right as genuine attitudes. Whereas, on the voluntariness-based view, the object of an action, its goal, comes not from any content which the action might have in its own right, but rather from the contents of the pro attitudes which cause it.

As T.M. Scanlon observes—action-explanatory attitudes are one thing, and actions are another; and actions are rationally appraisable and rationally justifiable by reference to their objects, the goals at which they are directed, only insofar as they are events which are expressive of and motivated by prior attitudes:

I have said that judgment-sensitive attitudes constitute the class of things for which reasons in the standard normative sense can sensibly be asked for or offered. Actions might be cited as a class of glaring exceptions to this claim, on the ground that they are not themselves attitudes yet are clearly things for which standard normative reasons can be given. But they are only an apparent exception. Actions are the kind of things for which normative reasons can be given only insofar as they are intentional, that is, are the expression of judgment-sensitive attitudes . . . it is the connection with judgment-sensitive attitudes that makes events actions, and hence the kind of things for which reasons can sensibly be asked for and offered at all.[16]

It is very clear why supporters of the voluntariness-based model have historically taught the passivity of decision and intention. In its unqualified form, the model entails that intentions are indeed passive; and that is because intentions are certainly not voluntary. It is equally clear why able supporters of the model such as Hobbes were not interested in fudging or qualifying the model to let decisions or intentions slip in. What point is there to giving decisions or intention-formations the status of actions on second-rate terms?—and then do so through relying on claims about their motivation, supposedly through pro attitudes towards taking them, which as conditions on agency have a clear rationale only for the case of voluntary action proper? If we really are convinced that decisions are actions, and no less so than the voluntary actions which they explain, we need a quite different model of action.

---

[16] *What We Owe to Each Other*, p. 21.

We may need a quite different model of action for another reason, too. Just as the intuitive agency of our decisions is not naturally explained in voluntariness-based terms, neither is our freedom. As the next chapter will explain, a very natural understanding of our freedom seems deeply inconsistent with any conception of agency that is voluntariness-based—that views action as by its nature an effect and expression of the passive.

6

Freedom and Scepticism
Incompatibilism

6.1 Moral Responsibility and Freedom

Most people assume that within the limits of their knowledge and intelligence, physical capacities and resources, it is indeed up to them what they do. In our everyday lives we effectively assume the existence of freedom as a power over alternatives, and it is in terms of this power over alternatives that we naturally conceive self-determination. We can determine for ourselves how we can act because we have control over how we act. And our moral responsibility for action depends on our possession of this control. Or so we ordinarily suppose.

Freedom is understood by us to be a power that is agency-specific—exercised in and through deliberate agency. True, as we have already noted, not all action is within our control to perform or not. Causal determinism, compulsive desires, emotions in overpowering form, the manipulations of others, physical obstacles, and incapacities—though there will be disagreement about how far all these factors are threatening to freedom, some at least of these factors might remove or reduce our control over what we manage to do. But any exercise of freedom must certainly be through agency that is intentional—through some deliberate action or deliberate refraining from action. Not only to possess, but actually to be exercising control over whether the lights are on or off, for example, there must be something that I am deliberately doing, or deliberately refraining from doing, such as throwing a switch, that would determine or influence whether or not the lights are on. If there is nothing that I am deliberately doing or refraining from doing that could in any way influence whether the lights are on or off, that I cannot be exercising any control over whether they are on or off.

And so freedom can provide a ready explanation for why it is for our actions and omissions that we are directly morally responsible—but not, say, for desires or other non-actions. Suppose we can be morally responsible only for what we control, and for what arises through our exercising or failing to exercise this control. Then, since we possess control only over how we act and the possible consequences of how we act, our actions and omissions and their consequences are all we can be held morally responsible for.

Our distinctive moral responsibility for how we act depends on and is explained by our capacity to determine action for ourselves. And freedom—a power of control over alternatives—seems the immediately natural conception of what self-determination comes to. We naturally identify the agent with the exercise of his freedom. It is the agent, after all, who is in control. And it is action for which we are responsible because it is action which we control. Moral responsibility is explained by and depends on the freedom to do otherwise.

We might eventually conclude that, in the end, our moral responsibility for how we act is not after all really explained by nor dependent on any freedom to do otherwise. But whether or not this proves to be the case, one thing is nevertheless clearly true. In appealing to freedom to explain the scope of our moral responsibility, we are managing to make what is a perfectly meaningful and, for many people, immediately intuitive claim about why actions and omissions might be blameworthy, but not non-actions such as what we desire or how we feel or what objects we believe surround us: namely, that we can control our actions—but not, except in so far as they are indirect consequences of prior actions, ordinary beliefs, desires, or feelings. It is a very important fact that, be it true or be it false, the appeal to freedom to explain moral responsibility is so intuitive—a fact that will tell us much about the nature of freedom.

The idea that we are responsible for our actions because it is our actions that we control—that we can be held accountable for how we act because how we act is up to us, so that we are free to act otherwise than as we actually do—may seem utterly natural and appealing. But though the dependence of moral responsibility on freedom is highly intuitive, this supposed dependence is also widely doubted by philosophers. Even amongst those philosophers who still tie moral obligation and responsibility to action, there is no consensus that the tie has anything to do with freedom.

Philosophical doubt about the supposed dependence of moral responsibility on freedom is very general. And there is one obvious reason why. There is widespread scepticism about the very possibility of freedom. If, for whatever reason, suspicion grows that the freedom to act otherwise may not only not exist but be downright impossible—something just incoherent, and that we could never possess—then the idea of a dependence of moral responsibility on freedom can start to look especially bad news. We may be tying moral responsibility and blame—central features of our ethics and of our social organization—to something as absurd and impossible as a round square. So we must now turn to consider why so many people have come to disbelieve in the very possibility and coherence of freedom.

6.2 Incompatibilism and Scepticism

The main source of modern scepticism about freedom is undoubtedly the debate about whether freedom as a power to do otherwise is compatible with causal determinism—with our being causally determined to do what we actually do. And what drives the scepticism is the plausibility of incompatibilism—the view that freedom is not so compatible.

The truth of incompatibilism is often taken to be both obvious and obviously conceptual. Our very concept of freedom as involving a freedom to do otherwise is supposed to deliver an incompatibility between freedom and causal determinism. Nor is this view peculiar to libertarians—to those who believe that we actually possess freedom as incompatibilistically understood. Much modern scepticism about freedom also endorses incompatibilism as a supposedly conceptual truth, and works from it.

The difficulty with freedom, according to modern sceptics, is not simply the threat that causal determinism might actually be true. For the truth of causal determinism is unobvious, and would in any case seem to be contingent; and the modern sceptic is certainly not saying that freedom is something we merely happen contingently to lack. The real worry about freedom lies deeper. Modern scepticism about freedom is in fact a marriage of incompatibilism to elements associated with compatibilism—and especially to certain assumptions about the nature of power and of action that the English language compatibilist tradition, in particular, has tended to make. These assumptions lead the modern sceptic to claim that freedom conceptually requires determinism, just as many English-language compatibilists have long claimed that it does.[1] But the sceptic also accepts that we have a concept of freedom that excludes determinism, just as incompatibilism teaches. So freedom is conceptually impossible.

Why does freedom require determinism? Suppose, as incompatibilist freedom would require, that our actions are not causally determined in advance. Then that seems to mean that how we finally act is a matter of simple chance. For there are but these two alternatives. Either an action is causally determined. Or, to the extent that it is causally undetermined, its occurrence depends on nothing more than chance. As David Hume put it: '... liberty, by removing necessity, removes also causes, and is the very same thing with chance.'[2] But chance alone does not really constitute freedom. On its own chance comes to nothing more than randomness. And one thing does seem to be clear. Randomness, the operation of mere chance, clearly excludes control. For example, if we are to count as exercising control over a process, that process cannot simply be developing at random. If a process is just random, then it must be taking place outside our control. Randomness is at least as much a threat to freedom—to our exercising control over how we act—as determinism might be. If our actions are no more than chance occurrences, then how can our action involve an exercise of control on our part?

---

[1] See for example R. Hobart, 'Free will as involving determinism and inconceivable without it', *Mind* 43, (1934).

[2] David Hume, *A Treatise of Human Nature*, p. 407.

Indeed, the worry goes even deeper. It is not simply that undetermined actions look no better than random. It seems that if what we think of as our actions were undetermined, they could not really be *actions* at all—they could be no more than mere blind motions.

Suppose, for example, that my hand goes up. What has to be true if my hand going up is to be, not a mere happening, but a genuine *action*—something that I intentionally do, a deliberate raising of my hand by me? As we have seen, for me to count as raising my hand intentionally, there must be a purpose behind my hand going up. If I am intentionally raising my hand, I must be doing so for the sake of some goal or end. Perhaps I am raising my hand simply for its own sake—just for the sake of raising it. Or perhaps I have some further purpose in mind. Perhaps I am raising my hand in order to signal to you. But there had better be some purpose in what I am doing if it is to count as a genuine action—a deliberate and intentional doing of something by me.

What, then, makes it true that our action is aimed at a given goal? The voluntariness-based model provides an answer. Essential to purposiveness, on this model, is that I am performing the action because and as an effect of a particular desire or motivation—a desire for or motivation towards that very goal. If my raising my hand is to count as having signalling to you as its goal, it must be my desire to signal to you that is causing my hand to go up. Movements of our body that are not caused by our desires—that occur whether or not we want them to—are not goal-directed actions, but mere blind motions such as twitches or reflexes.

To the degree that our actions are causally undetermined, so they will fail to be influenced by our prior desires, and the less how we move about and do things will depend on what beforehand we desire or want. And that means, on this causal model of purposiveness, that these so-called actions will look less like genuine actions, and more like blind motions or reflexes. And how can blind motions or reflexes be free? How can blind motions or reflexes be genuine exercises of our control?

It seems then that if incompatibilism is true, we cannot be free. For either our actions are causally predetermined, in which case—incompatibilism says—they are imposed on us by past history, and we cannot be performing them freely. Or our actions are undetermined, in which case they are no more than blind, random happenings and only actions so-called. So, again, we cannot be performing actions freely.

Incompatibilism is a very natural theory of freedom. But incompatibilism seems to raise serious problems for the possibility of freedom. It is not just that for freedom to obtain, causal determinism must be false—that our actions are not causally determined in advance. There is another, even more serious problem. Suppose causal determinism is indeed false. We must be able to explain how the causally undetermined events which are supposed to be free actions really are that—genuine free actions. We must explain how, despite its being to some degree chancy whether they occur, these purported free actions differ from movements, such as reflexes and twitches, that are blindly random. But libertarianism, non-sceptical incompatibilism, has not yet provided this vital story—a story of how incompatibilist freedom can be embodied in action that, though causally undetermined just as is any mere chance motion, is nevertheless genuine free action. Libertarianism needs to explain how an action can be causally undetermined by past events without, however, being merely random or blind. And many philosophers have doubted that any such story can be given.

But there is a further element to our everyday conception of freedom that we must also explore—an element that is equally puzzling and equally in need of explanation. It involves the possibility of actions of the will. For it seems that as we ordinarily understand our freedom, there is a close link between freedom in general and a freedom specifically of the will.

Suppose, for example, that in the morning, just as you get up, you take a decision about what you will do in the afternoon—you decide to go the bank in the afternoon, as opposed to staying at home and reading. This decision taken in the morning then determines or leads you, in the afternoon, actually to go to the bank. What in this process do you control?

Plausibly you do not just control whether, in the afternoon, you actually go to the bank. Equally up to you is your decision, taken in the morning, to go to the bank. When you get up, it is within your control whether you decide to go to the bank or decide to stay at home. How you decide to act is as much up to you as are the subsequent actions that result from what you decide. And it is not surprising that we should think this. For, as the last chapter discussed, we think of our decisions as our own deliberate doing. And like any other deliberate action of ours, we suppose they fall typically within our control.

But there is more. This decision control is not a mere optional extra—an add-on to a control of other things that we would possess anyway. It is hard to see how you could have the action control at all without the decision control. Imagine that the decisions that guide and determine your actions were just passive occurrences that came over you, like feelings, entirely outside your control. Imagining this, it is hard to hold on to the thought that, nevertheless, the actions that result are still within your control. If your decision to go to the bank really were no more than a kind of feeling, something which just comes over you, so that you have no control over whether it occurs, and if it were this wholly uncontrolled feeling which determined whether you go to the bank, how could whether you go to the bank still be within your control?

In fact the following is just a natural thought to think, something that we ordinarily do believe. It is up to us how we act only because we can decide for ourselves how we shall act, and it is up to us what we decide.

It seems, then, that, as we ordinarily conceive things, our freedom of action depends on a freedom of decision-making in particular. Now our capacity for decision-making, our will, is a mental or psychological capacity. And that means that our ordinary conception of freedom of action is what I shall term a *psychologizing* conception: it makes the freedom even of a bodily action such as whether or not we walk to the bank, depend on a prior strictly *psychological* freedom—on a freedom of whether or not we *decide* to go to the bank. Freedom of action depends on a freedom specifically of the will.

It also follows that our everyday conception of our freedom is linked to an important complexity in our ordinary conception of action. And that is a commitment to the existence of actions specifically of the will—exactly the kinds of action with which, we saw, the voluntariness-based model of agency has the most difficulty. Freedom or control, we have seen, is exercised in and through action. But if, prior to performing any of the actions between which we are to decide, we have already to be exercising control over which decisions we take, then it must be true that decisions are themselves actions.

If this is indeed our ordinary understanding of our own freedom, it raises an obvious question. Why does the power of freedom, the power we have over our own actions, have to be exercised through action-determining actions of the will—actions of decision that we must in turn have the power to determine for ourselves? Such a dependence is very worrying. If freedom of action does depend on a freedom of a higher order, action-generating action, then why should this dependence stop? If freedom of action depends on freedom of will, then why would freedom of will not itself depend on the freedom of a higher order, will-generating will? In which case, free agents will need to be able to take not only decisions to act, but also decisions to decide. This psychologizing conception of our freedom looks worryingly and viciously regressive—besides committing us to a conception of our own agency that is hard to accommodate within the voluntariness-based model of action that most modern philosophers accept.

6.3 A Construction Out of Voluntariness?

Sceptics deny the very possibility of libertarian free will—a freedom of decision-making or will understood in incompatibilist terms, as ruling out the causal prede-termination of how we act by prior occurrences outside our control. But then the sceptic faces a question. No matter how problematic a power libertarian freedom might be, many people have come to believe in its existence. But how has this belief arisen? The alleged conceptual impossibility of freedom libertarianly understood only deepens the problem. For it emphasizes the gap between the world as it exists and is revealed to us, and the beliefs about our freedom that we actually possess. If freedom is not just non-existent, but conceptually impossible, how could the world even appear to contain such a power? Where then did the idea of libertarian freedom come from? If our beliefs about human self-determination are mired in conceptual error, the sceptic needs to be able to explain how, in the world as the sceptic conceives it, such an error could ever arise.

The voluntariness-based model of action builds a theory of action on one specific causal power possessed by agents—or, more precisely, possessed by passive motivations within the agent. This is voluntariness—the power to act as we will or desire because we so will or desire. The popularity of the voluntariness-based model has led a number of modern philosophers to attempt to trace any conception we might have of self-determination back to nothing other than the experience of our own voluntariness.

On their view, the only power we ever actually experience ourselves as having over our action is voluntariness—the power of our motivations to cause us to act in a way that would satisfy them. And that is because action just is voluntariness. The exercise of the power of voluntariness constitutes the very essence of action, and so that is how we experience our own agency. The child wants to pick up that ball lying on the floor, and finds itself managing to pick the ball up exactly as it wanted to do. In managing to do what it wants, the child has had, if you like, its first experience of control. It is only from reflecting on this experience of being able to act as we want that we ever arrive at the idea of action as being something which we determine for ourselves.

Thus Galen Strawson:

A naturalistic explanation of this sense of self-determination would connect it tightly with our sense, massively and incessantly confirmed since earliest infancy, of our ability *to do what we want in order to (try to) get what we want,* by performing a vast variety of actions great and small, walking where we want, making ourselves understood, picking up this and putting down that. We pass our days in more or less continual and almost entirely successful self-directing intentional activity, and we know it. Even if we don't always achieve our aims, when we act, we almost always perform a movement of the kind we intended to perform, and in that vital sense (vital for the sense of self-determining self-control) we are almost entirely successful in our action.

This gives rise to a sense of freedom to act, of complete self-control, or responsibility in self-directedness, that is in itself compatibilistically unexceptionable, and is quite untouched by arguments against true responsibility based on the impossibility of self-determination. But it is precisely this compatibilistically speaking unexceptionable sense of freedom and efficacy that is one of the fundamental bases of the growth in us of the compatibilistically impermissible sense of true responsibility. To observe a child of two fully in control of its limbs, *doing what it wants to do with them, and to this extent fully free to act in the compatibilist sense of the phrase,* and to realise that it is precisely such unremitting experience of self-control that is the deepest foundation of our naturally incompatibilistic sense of true-responsibility-entailing self-determination, is to understand one of the most important facts about the genesis and power of our ordinary strong sense of freedom.[3]

And Bernard Williams likewise talks of our primitive conception of freedom as being nothing more than Hobbesian voluntariness, or 'action unimpeded' in the execution of one's will; a conception which stands as 'seed' to the 'plant' of any more developed or demanding conception of self-determination as libertarian freedom.[4]

---

[3] Galen Strawson, *Freedom and Belief,* pp. 110–11—my emphases.
[4] See 'Saint-Just's illusion', in Bernard Williams, *Making Sense of Humanity, and Other Philosophical Papers 1982–93* (Cambridge: Cambridge University Press, 1995), p. 136.

This approach would leave something like classical English-language compatibilism as our initial and primitive theory of our own freedom. On the classical compatibilist view, freedom is indeed supposed to exist as a genuine power of self-determination involving power over alternatives; but freedom comes nonetheless to nothing more than a complex case of voluntariness—to nothing more than the power to act as we desire or will. The sceptical account, however, is importantly different from classical compatibilism. It recognizes that our present concept of freedom is not equivalent to the concept of a simple power to act as we desire or will. But still the naturalistically acceptable concept of such a simple power is where all our thinking about self-determination began; it is the concept of a genuine, if metaphysically unadventurous form of control. And the idea of libertarian freedom can be traced back to it—as a plant to an original seed.

So we begin with a conception of freedom or control as nothing more than the causal power of our desires to move us successfully to do what would satisfy them. And if the story just given about how we experience our own agency is right, it is easy to see why we should begin with this understanding. It would be an understanding of freedom firmly based on the only power to determine action within us that experience can ever reveal. What is less obvious is how we would ever arrive, as we so naturally do, at a conception of freedom that is incompatibilist. But there is a possible extension of the story so far to explain this. Our belief in a power of self-determination conceived in terms of incompatibilist freedom would be a later development, and one that involved, beyond the experience of voluntariness, our adopting a further hypothesis. The hypothesis we adopt is that our actions, though causally influenced by our desires to act, are not in fact causally determined by them. This hypothesis is not itself based on experience. For experience, though it may not establish that our actions are outright causally predetermined, does nothing to establish that our actions are causally undetermined either—or so the story would claim. Experience simply reveals that our actions are voluntary effects of our desires, leaving it open whether our desires merely influence how we act, or have the power causally to determine outright the performance of a particular action.

Causal influence can, after all, come in degrees. Some causes determine that their effects must and will occur. But perhaps other causes may be less powerful. They may merely influence whether their effects occur, without determining that those effects *must* occur. There may be causes that leave some chance of their effects not occurring. Such causes that influence without determining are often called *probabilistic* causes. They merely give their effects some probability without actually ensuring that they occur. Perhaps, then, the desires that motivate our voluntary actions are no more than probabilistic. Our actions are at best influenced by our desires, and not causally determined by them. That, in effect, is the hypothesis that we adopt.

But if this hypothesis, though not contradicted by experience, goes beyond what experience supports, then it must have some origin outside or beyond experience. And so, according to the story, it does. The hypothesis comes instead from ethical theory.

In blaming people we assert that their wrong or faulty actions are their fault; that their actions are their responsibility. The generator of a belief in incompatibilist freedom might then turn out to be a theory of this moral responsibility, and one which ties blameworthiness not simply to voluntariness, but to a lack of causal predetermination as well. The theory might run thus: for what was done to be truly the agent's fault, it is not enough for the agent to have acted voluntarily. What he did could not have been the determined result of prior causes not of his own doing. In which case what incompatibilist freedom comes to, according to this account of the genesis of the idea, is just what this conception of moral responsibility requires: voluntariness combined with a lack of causal predetermination—a lack of causal predetermination that leaves it possible for the agent to act otherwise.

What of the psychologizing element in our conception of freedom—our belief that freedom of action depends on a prior freedom of will, with the belief in the existence of the actions of the will which that freedom of will presupposes? One obvious possibility is this. The psychologizing conception might grow out of our libertarianism—our belief in our actual possession of freedom incompatibilistically understood. For there is an obvious route from an incompatibilist conception of our freedom to belief in an agency and freedom of the will. We need only appeal to a central intuition about decisions and intentions: namely that they are motivations that, as causes, serve to determine—settle in advance—which voluntary actions we end up performing. At least in the absence of some subsequent change of information, the point of deciding and forming intentions about how one will act is causally to determine one's future voluntary action. This advance determination of how we will act is fundamental to why we bother forming intentions about what we shall do well before we actually do it. Taking decisions and forming intentions in advance enables us to coordinate our actions over time, so that the actions we shall be performing in the future can be rendered consistent with and suitable to those we are performing now. We decide in advance where we shall be going on holiday, so that we can make the right preparations now, secure in the knowledge of where we shall actually be going.[5] But this does require that, at least in the absence of change in the assumptions on which our decision was based, our decision about where to go does ensure—causally determine—that we go there as decided.

Suppose, then, that many of our voluntary actions are causally determined by prior decisions. Suppose, too, that those decisions are not free actions, but passive events outside our control. Then how in incompatibilist terms can the actions determined be within our control? According to incompatibilism, after all, the predetermination of action by uncontrolled causes not of our own doing is inconsistent with our having any control over the occurrence of the action determined. It seems, then, that

---

[5] This view of the function of decision and intention has been illuminatingly defended in Michael Bratman, *Intention, Plans and Practical Reason* (Cambridge, MA: Harvard University Press, 1987). It is certainly part of the truth about intention—though not the whole truth, as Chapter 10 will discuss.

a libertarian conception of our freedom might well encourage a conception of our action-determining decisions as being actions themselves, and of freedom as being dependent on the freedom of these actions in particular. Thanks to our ignorance of any determining causes that these decisions might in turn have, we identify them as a special class of undetermined motivation that counts as our own free doing—a type of motivation that we determine for ourselves. And so 'We tend to think we have a will (a power of decision) distinct from all our particular [passive] motives.'[6] And we believe this as the price for preserving the freedom of our agency as a whole.

6.4 Event-Causal Libertarianism

This genetic account of our natural belief in our actual possession of incompatibilist freedom looks to be a sceptical one. For according to this story, the widespread belief in the reality of incompatibilist freedom has no support from experience. Our belief in libertarian freedom and in the extension of that freedom to include the will rests instead on a kind of ethical faith—on a certain understanding of the moral signifi-cance of our agency, and one without any direct empirical support.

Could this same account of what incompatibilist freedom actually consists in—voluntariness plus lack of causal predetermination—be proposed non-sceptically, by libertarian philosophers who do believe that we actually are free in incompatibilist terms? I shall follow Randolph Clarke and call such a theory an *event-causal* libertarian theory of freedom.[7]

According to event-causal libertarianism, incompatibilist freedom consists in a variety of attitudes influencing and so permitting the agent voluntarily to act in a variety of ways, but without causally determining which way the agent will act. The term 'event-causal' reminds us that the causal power involved is just the causal power of certain occurrences, of events or states, within their lives—those agents' prior desires, the very desires that motivate their actions, and whose causal influence constitutes what the agent does voluntarily as a genuine case of action.

Event-causal libertarianism accepts that action is by its nature a voluntary effect of prior motivations, and requires that such motivations cause the occurrence of any free action. It is just that the causal influence of these motivations must not outright determine action. For that would remove the agent's freedom libertarianly under-stood. But provided this non-determination condition is met, event-causal libertar-ianism then takes the agent's freedom or control of how he acts to be exercised in and through the causal influence of these motivations:

When these conditions are satisfied, it is held, the agent exercises in performing his action a certain variety of active control (which is said to consist in the action's being caused by those

---

[6] Galen Strawson, *Freedom and Belief*, p. 113.
[7] See Randolph Clarke, *Libertarian Accounts of Free Will*, chapter 2.

agent-involving events), the action is performed for reasons, and there was a chance of the agent's not performing that action. It is thus said to have been open to the agent to do otherwise...[8]

So 'On event-causal libertarian accounts, as on rival compatibilist views, the agent's exercise of direct active control consists just in her action's being caused, in an appropriate way, by agent-involving mental events of certain kinds.'[9] David Wiggins has also suggested such an event-causal libertarianism.[10] In his view, libertarianism requires only that as voluntary agents our biographies unfold 'non-deterministically but intelligibly'—that our actions be made intelligible by attitudes that motivate but do not causally determine their occurrence. Another leading proponent of an event-causal libertarianism is Robert Kane. In his *The Significance of Free Will* he defends the view that free actions arise out of conflict between competing motivations, where these competing motivations do not of themselves determine which way the conflict is resolved.[11]

But as a libertarian theory, a theory that is not sceptical about the actual existence of incompatibilist freedom, the event-causal theory is surely not going to deliver.

Where in this theory is the power of incompatibilist or libertarian freedom to be found? In the causal power of prior desires? Clearly not—for this power threatens freedom, and so cannot be constitutive of it. Incompatibilist freedom is present only if this causal power is limited and fails to determine outright how the agent acts. In the action's simple lack of causal determination? Also evidently not, for that is merely an absence of power—mere chance or randomness. In the combination, then, of this causal power and its limitation by the element of mere chance? Again, clearly not. For how can the presence of one power be constituted by the mere limitation of another power that threatens it? Granted, the limitation of the threatening power may *permit* the presence of the power threatened and leave room for it. But it cannot of itself *constitute* that threatened power's presence.

Freedom surely is a power of control over which action we perform—a power to determine that action for ourselves. Now the event-causal libertarian may want to identify this action-determining power with the only power his account of freedom mentions—with the causal power of prior desires, provided of course this power is not outright action-determining but only action-influencing. But the identification is doubly wrong-headed. It is wrong-headed not only for the reason already given; that our power to determine action for ourselves is being implausibly identified with what is really a potential threat to it. It is wrong-headed also for a second and surely

---

[8] Randolph Clarke, 'Libertarian views: critical survey', in *The Oxford Handbook to Free Will*, ed. Robert Kane (Oxford: Oxford University Press 2002), p. 362.

[9] Randolph Clarke, *Libertarian Accounts of Free Will*, p. 151.

[10] See David Wiggins, 'Towards a reasonable libertarianism', in *Essays on Freedom of Action*, ed. Ted Honderich (London: Routledge, 1973), pp. 33–61.

[11] Robert Kane, *The Significance of Free Will* (Oxford: Oxford University Press, 1998).

decisive reason. The power of freedom, which is a power to *determine* action, is being identified with a causal power that is not itself action-determining, and which cannot be action-determining if incompatibilist freedom is to be possible. But how can a power that is action-determining be identical with another power that is not? As far as libertarianism or an incompatibilism that is non-sceptical goes, the event-causal theory is a clear non-starter.

We think that freedom or control, when complete—it need not be in some cases of course—is a power to determine, and not just influence which action we perform. But event-causal power in merely probabilistic terms is not such an event-determining power. It leaves actions merely influenced, not determined, which action occurs being left dependent to some degree on mere chance. But if we are in full control of what we do, it is not down to mere chance what we do, but fully up to us. We have, then, a power to determine how we act that a merely action-influencing event, a merely probabilistic cause, does not. But when the causal power of events is no longer merely influencing but is outright determining as our freedom can be determining, then, alas, libertarian freedom is no more. So where in event-causal power can be found a libertarian power of freedom to determine action?

6.5 The Impossibility of Libertarian Freedom?

It is important to emphasize that there really are two quite distinct problems facing libertarianism—problems that require quite different solutions, but which sceptics are apt to run together.

6.5.1 The randomness problem

The first problem facing the libertarian has to do with the threat of randomness—the operation of mere chance. Mere chance, randomness, as we have noted, is quite opposed to freedom. If an event or process is developing purely by chance, we cannot be exercising control over how it is developing. But, the sceptic alleges, freedom conceived in libertarian terms does threaten to come to nothing more than chance. For there really are only two alternatives. Either an action must be causally determined in advance, as by prior motivations—in which case the libertarian will deny that it really is free. Or to the extent that the action is causally undetermined, its occurrence must just depend on chance. By banishing causal predetermination libertarianism has tried to make room for what it regards as genuine freedom. But in the absence of causal predetermination all we really find is chance—which does not amount to genuine freedom at all. I shall call this problem which libertarians face the *randomness problem*.

And this of course is the very problem that event-causal libertarianism comes up against. All that the event-causal libertarian provides by way of freedom is a failure of prior motivating causes to determine. And that really comes to nothing more than chance.

How serious is the randomness problem? True, if whether an event occurs is causally undetermined, its occurrence must be chance. Chance is absence of causal determination. But that does not mean that such an event's occurrence need depend on chance alone. What is causally undetermined need not be random. For the randomness problem is based on one key assumption. The assumption is that the only alternatives are these— either the outcome is causally determined, or else it must depend on pure chance. But perhaps there is a third possibility—that there are some events which are neither causally determined, nor merely chance, because they occur under our control, as an exercise of our freedom. Now it is clear that critics of libertarianism want to exclude this as a genuine and third possibility. But it is not obvious why it should be excluded.

After all, one might very well suppose this. Some events are already causally determined and so were bound to happen anyway. These, the libertarian would insist, must be outside our control. Then there are other things which occur purely by chance. They are to a degree causally undetermined—and nothing more. As occurring by pure chance, these events also must be occurring without being controlled by us. These really are cases of genuine randomness. But other things are occurring under our control—in which case they are neither causally determined nor purely chance. When these events happen, more than chance is involved. Things aren't happening randomly. We are controlling whether and when they happen. Put like that, what could be more natural than to distinguish between these as three perfectly distinct and equally genuine possibilities (see Table 6.1)?

Table 6.1. Determination, randomness, and control

Causally Determined	Causally Undetermined and Uncontrolled (Chance and nothing more – so random)	Causally Undetermined and Controlled

One thing needs emphasizing. There seems nothing immediately incoherent about distinguishing these three possibilities. The terms by which they are specified seem consistent and intelligible enough. And as specified, the possibilities seem clearly distinct. To resolve the randomness problem there is therefore one thing we shall need to understand. We shall need to understand why so many philosophers take it almost for granted that there is no third possibility—that causal determination or mere chance are the only possibilities that there are.

One reason for this assumption has already emerged. According to the Williams–Strawson story of how the idea of self-determination first emerges, causal determinism and mere chance are the only alternatives that our experience of our own agency

FREEDOM AND SCEPTICISM: INCOMPATIBILISM 95

ever reveals. There is only the power of voluntariness or, failing voluntariness, nothing more than chance. Either our actions are causally determined by our own prior motivations; or to the extent that they are not, we must be acting randomly. Whether, on examination, this really is a plausible account of what our experience of our own agency reveals is an important question to which we must return.

6.5.2 The action problem

There is yet another problem which faces the libertarian. Is libertarian freedom something we could ever exercise, in the only way that freedom ever can be exercised—through what we deliberately do, in genuine and intelligible action? The worry is that it is not—that libertarian freedom is at odds with anything recognizable as genuine action. Libertarian freedom seems to reduce what we do to no more than blind, undirected motion—to the equivalent of jerks and spasms. And freedom—genuine control—is not something that could ever be exercised through mere jerks and spasms. I shall call this problem the *action problem*. Let me now explain exactly how the action problem arises.

Freedom, remember, is something which we exercise in and through intentional action or omission. That is what our own action is—the medium in and through which we exercise our control of what happens. Action is freedom's medium or vehicle. But this platitude has an important consequence, which I shall term the *action principle*. And the principle is this: if intentional action really is freedom's vehicle and medium, then what constitutes action as genuine action must not be a threat to freedom or in tension with it.

But what is an action? As we have seen, action is always something done for a purpose—in order to attain some goal. Every genuine action has a purpose—something which makes the action intelligible as a deliberate doing, and which allows us to explain why the action was performed. Actions are not blind reflexes. And where does the goal-direction of our action come from? The voluntariness-based model of action gives a simple answer. The purposes for which we act come from motivations distinct from the actions they explain—motivations that are passive desires. And these desires cause us voluntarily to act in the way that we do. My action counts as a genuine action by occurring, then, not through chance, or through some external cause, but as an effect of my desire to attain some goal by what I am doing. And the goal or purpose of my action comes from the 'object' of this motivating desire—from what it is that I desire to do. On the voluntariness-based model then, action occurs only as a voluntary effect of desires. And it is from these causes—from desires and from the objects of these desires—that actions get their purpose, and so too their identity as genuine deliberate actions.

It follows that, on the voluntariness-based model, action is by its very nature an effect of occurrences outside our control. That is the *only* form that action can ever take. Actions count as such, and acquire the goal-direction which is essential to action, only as effects of desires—desires that are passive occurrences which are not our doing, and so which we cannot control. In the absence of such causes nothing could count as an intelligible purposive action. It could be no more than a mere purposeless happening. And, as we have agreed, freedom, genuine control, can never be exercised through a mere purposeless happening.

The problem facing libertarianism now becomes clear. Libertarianism says that free action cannot be causally determined by occurrences outside our control—such as by prior desires. But the voluntariness-based model says that action only counts as an action at all if it is an effect of just such desires. And this detaches libertarian freedom from the very nature of action, and in a way that is deeply problematic.

Freedom is something that we are supposed to exercise in and through how we act—through our capacity for action. But on the voluntariness-based model, our capacity for action is identified with a kind of causal power. Our capacity for action is identified with a particular causal power of our desires—with their power to cause us to act as desired. That is what action comes to on the theory—managing to do what we want because we want to do it. But far from ever exercising libertarian freedom through this causal power, libertarian freedom is something which this causal power actually *threatens*. After all, in libertarian terms we are unfree if this causal power comes in a strong enough form—if our desires causally determine our action in advance. The causal power of prior desires to influence what we do—this causal power which, on the model, constitutes our very capacity for action—has to be limited if libertarian freedom is ever to be exercised.

It seems, then, that libertarian freedom is a kind of freedom which cannot be exercised through our capacity for action. Libertarian freedom is instead in conflict with, threatened by, that very capacity. But as a view of freedom, this is absurd. Any freedom which is genuinely possible for us—which is a freedom which we really could possess and exercise—must be exercisable through action. And so we have the action problem. Not only does libertarianism appear to confuse freedom with randomness. It also seems to leave freedom something that we cannot exercise through how we act. But real freedom, any freedom which we could possibly enjoy, must be exercisable through how we act.

At this point some philosophers might wonder whether there really is a problem. They are willing to suppose that all actions occur as effects of prior causes—as effects of desires. But having supposed this, they insist that we then need to remember a distinction that we have made already. What takes away our freedom of action is not the prior causation of our actions as such, but their causal *determination*. Causes need not determine their effects, however. They may be probabilistic rather than determining causes—causes that merely influence outcomes, rather than determining them outright. Our freedom is removed, not just by prior causes, but by prior causes which actually determine that their effects must occur—that leave no chance that we will act other than as they cause us to. If we make this distinction between different kinds of cause, determining and merely probabilistic, it will be argued, libertarian freedom can still turn out to be perfectly consistent with the voluntariness-based model of action. What action requires is that it be an effect of desires. But these desires need not actually determine how we act. They may merely be influences on which action we perform. As causes, they may be probabilistic rather than determining.

But the distinction between determining and probabilistic causes does not really help. The conflict between action and libertarian freedom is not so easily resolved. And it is fairly clear why. True, libertarian freedom is strictly consistent with actions having unfree causes—provided the influence of these causes is sufficiently weak, so that these causes merely influence how we act without actually determining what we do. But this causal influence, even if it does not actually remove libertarian freedom, is still a threat to it. Enough of an increase in this causal influence—the influence which is supposed to be exactly what makes an action our own deliberate doing—and you will remove libertarian freedom.

But this means that if we add more of what makes action genuine action—if we increase the causal influence of prior desires—then freedom is ended. And this is surely intolerable. It is intolerable that what actually makes action *action*, and so constitutes it as the very medium for our exercise of freedom, should at the same time be freedom-threatening. It is intolerable that what gives action its very identity should have to be limited if freedom is to be at all possible. Freedom is something which we exercise through how we act. It therefore cannot be something which is threatened by the very nature of action.

So the problem is not that free actions cannot have causes. Even libertarians admit that free action can have causes—provided these prior causes are not action-determining. The problem instead is that if, as many philosophers suppose, being an effect of prior causes is what makes action action, action's very identity comes from a kind of causal influence that is freedom-threatening—that has to be limited for freedom to be possible. Libertarian freedom is left something threatened by action's very nature. But such a threat to freedom is absurd. Freedom is something which our capacity for action allows us to exercise. So that same capacity cannot plausibly by its very nature threaten and conflict with freedom.

The libertarian might want to claim that the causal influence of motivations is not a threat to freedom at all. The libertarian might claim that motivations and their causal influence fall within the agent's control and not outside it—indeed that a free agent can only have control over how he acts if he also possesses control over his motivations. After all, do we not naturally believe in a dependence of freedom of action on freedom of will?—on, in other words, a freedom of motivation, a freedom of motivation that we suppose ourselves actually to possess?

Unfortunately for the libertarian, any such dependence threatens to be vicious—at least if action is understood in voluntariness-based terms. For on the voluntariness-based model, the motivations which explain our agency and in terms of which action is defined are not actions themselves, but are instead passive antecedents of action. Given that these motivations are passive states, an agent cannot be in direct control of whether he holds them. If the agent is to exercise control over these motivations, that presupposes yet further and prior actions which would cause or prevent them—actions by which the agent might control the motivations indirectly. But then the question of how the agent controls *these* actions arises, and we are back to where we started.

So of course the libertarian is right. We do believe in a dependence of freedom of action on a freedom of motivation or will. But this intuitive dependence is no help to solving the action problem, or so the sceptic will allege. The intuitive dependence is merely a product of that very problem, and is in fact viciously regressive. It is not just that, as we already noted, many actions are in fact often predetermined causally by motivations of decision and intention, making our free and active determination of those particular decisions and intentions a condition of incompatibilist freedom. The action problem reveals that the dependence of action control on a prior motivation control in incompatibilist terms goes deeper. Incompatibilism forces us to assume quite generally that if any of our actions are free at all, the causing motivations that give them their identity as actions must themselves be our doing.

It seems clear that libertarianism is left with an impossible dilemma. Either our motivations are uncontrolled by us and the exercise of freedom is absurdly threatened by the nature of intentional action and what constitutes it; or we are supposed to control our motivations, and freedom is turned into a viciously regressive phenomenon, involving an infinite causal chain of motivation-manipulative actions.

What I have called the action problem is, I think, more or less the same as the well-known sceptical problem for freedom raised by Galen Strawson in *Freedom and Belief* and in many other writings. Consider, for example, the following very typical exposition of the problem as Strawson sees it:

... then since intentional actions are necessarily a function of how we are, mentally, we must be truly responsible for how we are mentally, at least in certain vital respects. We must be genuine 'originators' of ourselves, and our natures, at least in certain vital respects. But the attempt to explain how we could possibly be true originators of ourselves in this way leads self-defeatingly to infinite regress (quite apart from being quite fantastically unrealistic): for even if one could somehow choose how to be, and then bring it about that one was that way, one would in order to do this already have to have existed prior to that choice, with a certain set of preferences about how to be, in the light of which one chose how to be. But then the question would arise: where did these preferences come from? Or were they just there, unchosen preferences for which one was not responsible? And so on.

This argument proceeds completely independently of any appeal to determinism or indeterminism, and if valid shows that true-desert-entailing freedom of will is provably impossible—impossible whether determinism is true or false.[12]

A number of points are left crucially obscure by this passage. First, it is left obscure by Strawson in what way action is a function of how we are mentally, and so why control

12   Galen Strawson, 'Consciousness, free will, and the unimportance of determinism', *Inquiry* 32, (1989): pp. 10–11.

of our actions presupposes control of and responsibility for mental characteristics. Secondly it is left obscure why this control of the mental should be so problematic and why, in particular, it should generate a vicious regress.

The answer to both questions is surely provided by the combination, with incompatibilism, of both the voluntariness-based model of action and also what I have called the action principle. The voluntariness-based model leaves the goal-directedness which is constitutive of action a function of prior motivational causes which, if the theory of action is not to be viciously regressive, must themselves be passive. The action principle then requires that this action-constitutive causal influence not be freedom-threatening—that it not be an influence which freedom requires be limited or reduced. But this in turn means, on an incompatibilist understanding of freedom, that those causing motivations must be controlled themselves. And finally the voluntariness-based model of action implies that, since the motivations are themselves passive, exercising such control presupposes the occurrence of yet prior motivation-generative action, so generating the vicious regress.

6.5.3 The randomness and action problems compared

Opponents of libertarianism say that it is an incoherent theory of freedom. But remember that there are really two distinct grounds for making this claim. Opponents of libertarianism could have the randomness problem in mind. They could be alleging that libertarianism turns freedom into nothing more than chance. Or they could have the action problem in mind. They could be claiming that libertarians are turning the exercise of freedom into something blind and unmotivated, by divorcing it from what makes what we do a genuinely purposive and intelligible action. And these are two quite distinct accusations. They are accusations which would need to be answered in very different ways.

To reply to the allegation that libertarianism confuses freedom with randomness, we would need to establish that libertarian freedom involves something more than mere chance—that it involves more than a mere lack of prior causal determination. To reply to the second accusation we would need to establish that there could be intelligible actions—genuinely goal-directed, deliberate doings—that were nevertheless uncaused. And, of course, we might manage to show one of these things without managing to establish the other.

But though the problems are distinct, they are not commonly clearly distinguished. Galen Strawson, for example, is apt to treat the demand that free actions be non-random as identical with the demand that they be intelligibly goal-directed—and so, as he understands it, products of our desires. He treats both demands as if they raised fundamentally the same problem for our naturally libertarian understanding of freedom:

We may grant that our having the non-self-determined desire to eat does not of itself determine that we do eat, and that whether or not we do also depends on our decision and choice; but then the decision or choice must itself be shown to be free if the ensuing action is to be. It is for the libertarian *ex hypothesi* not free if determined. But it is no good if it is merely undetermined or a chance occurrence. *[randomness problem—freedom must be distinguishable from chance]* The fundamental libertarian thought is (or ought to be) that it must, if it is to be our free choice, issue from us in such a way that we are truly self-determining in making it. But, surely, for this to be the case it must also be the case that we choose to eat because, all things considered, we want (or judge it best or right) so to choose. *[voluntariness-based model—self-determined action is constituted such by prior motivations]* But then this want (this judging right or best) must enter into the true rational explanation of why we choose as we do ... But then questions arise about this determinant, the same questions as before ... are we, the agents, self-determined with respect to it? *[action problem—which motivations, however, must not be uncontrolled threats to our freedom]*[13]

Any confusion between the two problems is very much a consequence of the voluntariness-based model of action. This is a model of action which is now so deeply taken for granted as to have become almost invisible and unremarked. It exerts its influence on most modern philosophers without their showing any real awareness of the fact—as witness the utterly casual and completely tacit nature of Galen Strawson's reliance on the model. Now, on that model, it is the same causal influence of prior motivations which ensures both that actions are not performed at random, and that actions possess goal-direction and so count as genuine actions. Remove this causal influence, and then, according to the model, we are left with randomness and directionlessness together.

Suppose, though, that we could abandon the voluntariness-based model. Suppose we could find a non-causal way of accounting for action's identity as action and, in particular, for its goal-direction, so that direction towards an end turns out to have no implication for whether the action is caused or not. Then the constitutive end-direction of our action would no longer threaten libertarian freedom. The action problem would disappear.

But the randomness problem would remain. We might be able to show that even entirely uncaused decisions could be genuine goal-directed actions. But that would still leave open the possibility that as uncaused, or at least as causally undetermined, these decisions were being taken randomly—that as undetermined their occurrence involved nothing more than chance. We should still have to explain how what libertarians call freedom is more than simple chance.

6.6 The Sceptic's Error Theory—and the Real Problem about Freedom

The sceptic says that libertarian or incompatibilist freedom is impossible. No such power of self-determination is represented to experience. At most, experience fails to

---

[13] Galen Strawson, *Freedom and Belief*, pp. 46–7—square brackets are my insertions.

represent the determination of our actions by past events. But it never represents any independent determination of our action by us. Talk of such libertarian determination is our invention, as Hobbes so famously claimed:

Commonly when we see and know the strength that moves us, we acknowledge necessity, but when we see not, or mark not the force that moves us, we then think there is none, and that it is not causes but liberty that produceth the action.[14]

Where, then, does our belief in incompatibilist freedom come from? The sceptic has proposed an error theory of it, that appeals to an alleged intrusion of ethics into psychology. An incompatibilist conception of freedom is supposed to develop out of an original conception of voluntariness, by the intrusion into psychology of an ethics of blame and moral responsibility committed to indeterminism. Our moral responsibility is supposed by us to depend on our actions not being causally determined by past occurrences outside our control—or so, as folk moralists, we believe. To meet the demands of moral responsibility so understood, we introduce a power of self-determination conceived in similarly incompatibilist terms.

But there are serious problems facing this error theory. First, there are problems about its story of a *development* from an original conception of self-determination as voluntariness. The development is supposed to involve adding an absence of causal determination to voluntariness. But it is by now apparent that libertarian freedom—the conception this error theory purports to explain—is radically different from voluntariness plus causal indetermination.

Not only do we see freedom as a freedom of will—as dependent on a freedom of motivation. We do so without viewing motivations as voluntary themselves, or even as the outcomes of prior voluntary actions. So freedom seems importantly detached from any form of voluntariness. And what freedom does involve seems very different from any mere lack of causal determination. For what it involves is a power to determine alternative outcomes—something very different from mere indeterminism, as the failure of event-causal libertarianism reminds us. Freedom does not leave our actions undetermined and down to chance, but leaves them determined by us. So rather than amounting to voluntariness with a lack of determination of the outcomes, our idea of freedom involves outright determination of the outcomes, and that through a power that may be exercised over the non-voluntary. There is nothing in the sceptic's error theory to explain where the idea of such a power might come from. It certainly seems to have nothing whatsoever to do with any experience we might have of simple voluntariness.

But there is a further question—about the very strategy of devising an ethical explanation for the beliefs we currently hold about our power of self-determination. We put an incompatibilist condition on self-determination, it is alleged, because we

---

[14] Thomas Hobbes in *The Questions Concerning Liberty, Necessity and Chance, clearly stated between Dr Bramhall Bishop of Derry, and Thomas Hobbes of Malmesbury* (London 1656), p. 217.

already have an incompatibilist conception of moral responsibility—and we need a psychology that supports moral responsibility so conceived. But it could of course be argued that things might well be the other way around. We start with an incompatibilist conception of self-determination. And then because moral responsibility depends on our having a power of self-determination, that incompatibilist conception of self-determination then imposes a similarly incompatibilist condition on moral responsibility.

It might be suggested that the direction of explanation must be the second way around—from psychology to ethics and not vice versa. This is because all that the ethics of blame and moral responsibility strictly requires is that we possess a power of self-determination—that we determine for ourselves what we do. Provided that we do determine for ourselves what we do, moral responsibility does not involve, as a further requirement distinct from this, that our actions also be causally undetermined by prior conditions outside our control. If moral responsibility does exclude the causal determination of our action by conditions beyond our control, this can only be because such an exclusion is anyway a consequence of what moral responsibility clearly and immediately depends on—self-determination.

For remember again what blaming people involves. It involves putting a fault in someone down to them as their fault. And that in turn requires that they have some capacity to determine for themselves what they do. The fault is their fault because they determined for themselves that the fault occurred; or because, though they had the power to prevent the fault's occurrence, they failed to exercise that power. Provided they possess the requisite power, then the fault really is their fault; they are to blame for it and morally responsible. It should not matter whether or not prior causes determined them to act as they did—unless such prior causes are to be supposed incompatible with our possession and exercise of the crucial power to determine things for ourselves. But that then depends on whether incompatibilism about self-determination is already true; and incompatibilism about self-determination is the very conception of self-determination that the sceptic was attempting to use our conception of moral responsibility to explain.

It is indeed central to common-sense ethics that there exist a distinctively moral responsibility for how we act. This responsibility is what is asserted in moral blame. And it is essential to blame that faults in the agent are put down to the agent as the agent's fault—and as the agent's fault because the agent can determine their occurrence or non-occurrence for himself. So there is a clear ethical commitment to the existence of a power of self-determination—a power on the part of agents to determine for themselves what they do. But that does not commit us to any form of incompatibilism—unless we already have an incompatibilist conception of the power. But such a conception must then come from outside ethics, and feed into our conception of moral responsibility; it is not itself generated by our conception of moral responsibility. Incompatibilism about moral responsibility need not be ethical in origin.

The next two chapters will take this line of thought further. We shall see that freedom as we ordinarily conceive it has many distinctive features besides incompatibilism; indeed, compared to these other features, incompatibilism is a relatively contentious and peripheral aspect of freedom. But not all these features of freedom as ordinarily understood are convincingly to be explained as the intrusion of ethics into psychology. These features of freedom shape our ethics because they have important implications for the moral responsibility that depends on freedom. But the understanding of freedom involved very clearly does not come from ethics.

These features of freedom have to do with its involvement of alternatives. And they radically distinguish freedom from ordinary causal power—especially from any causal power of the kind involved in voluntariness. For this reason, they make freedom the object of a powerful scepticism—a scepticism that is based not on incompatibilism but on metaphysical naturalism. It is this naturalist scepticism which is the more serious threat to belief in freedom as we currently understand it. Indeed, much scepticism supposedly to do with incompatibilism will turn out really to be based on metaphysical naturalism, and not on incompatibilism at all.

7

Freedom and Scepticism
Alternatives

7.1 Power

Self-determination is the power that bases our moral responsibility. It is our power to determine for ourselves what actions we perform. We have discovered two very different conceptions of what power self-determination might involve. There is English-language compatibilism, at least in its classical form. This takes the power to be voluntariness—the power of our motivations to cause the actions motivated. And then there is our ordinary understanding of self-determination as a freedom specifically of the will, a capacity to determine alternatives that is immediately exercised over motivations themselves—over decisions that are non-voluntary. Voluntariness and a capacity to determine non-voluntary alternatives at the point of motivation—these are clearly quite different kinds of power. Behind disputes about the nature of human action and responsibility lies a profound controversy about what kinds of power humans possess and exercise. We need then to consider the nature of power.

Competing theories of human self-determination involve very different conceptions of the power which that self-determination might involve. But how different can different cases of power really be? Many philosophers think or write as if power were a rather uniform phenomenon. We have seen it proposed that power is, by its very nature, a causal phenomenon:

In the first place, the notions of power or disposition are already causally laden notions and it can thus reasonably be argued that unless one already has a grasp of causation, one cannot have a grasp of power. Powers, indeed, are often called causal powers.[1]

But is power causal by its very nature? And must freedom, in particular, be a form of causal power?

Of course, as we have already observed, the claim that all power is causal could be so understood as to be trivial. 'Causation' could be used as no more than a general label to apply to whatever power turns out to be. But in the passage just cited the

---

[1] See again Mumford and Anjum, *Getting Causes from Powers*, p. 7.

claim that all power is causal is presented as a substantial thesis—as something that is not trivial, but to be 'reasonably argued'. In which case the idea might be to inform the theory of power by importing a definite and specific conception of causation. And this has certainly been a project of much metaphysics since Thomas Hobbes. One very intuitive case of power is the very familiar kind that appears to be involved in obvious cases of causation, and to be possessed and exercised, not by causes and effects indifferently, but specifically by causes. This is the power of stones to break windows or the power of fire to melt ice—the power that ordinary causes have to produce their effects. Is all power, then, power in this specific form? The project would then be to understand all forms of power in terms of this particular form of power—the power involved in ordinary causation. All genuine power is like the power of stones to break windows and of fire to melt ice.

At this point it is useful to step back, and raise the question why causation itself is so widely viewed as involving power—and, more specifically, a power possessed and exercised by causes over what they affect?

Power involves a kind of capacity. Causal power constitutes, after all, a capacity to produce effects. But, of course, it is not the mere presence in them of a capacity that makes it true that causes possess power. And that is because the idea of a capacity extends far wider than that of power. For example, there are capacities not to cause and affect, but to be affected. But the capacity to be affected hardly constitutes any kind of power over anything, and the process of being affected is hardly the exercise of power. The contrary is true: to be affected is to be subject to power that is possessed and exercised by something else. Contrast my view with Locke's. In *An Essay Concerning Human Understanding*, Locke divides power into active and passive.[2] Active is defined as the power to make a change, passive is the power to receive it. As an account of power this is certainly defective. For, of course, Locke ignores powers to prevent change from occurring. But more importantly, Locke's 'passive power' involves the opposite of any exercise of genuine power. It is a form of powerlessness—subjection to the power of another.

Power, then, is a very special capacity. And what, I conjecture, is common to power in all its forms is a capacity to produce or, at the upper limit, to outright determine the occurrence or non-occurrence of outcomes. It is this capacity to determine what happens that causes possess, but which their effects lack. Causes determine the occurrence of their effects, and not vice versa. Furthermore, linked to the general notion of determination, where power is concerned, is an equally general notion of responsibility. Whatever exercises a power to determine outcomes is in some corresponding way responsible for what that exercise of power determines. Causes possess power in so far as they can influence or determine an outcome.

[2] John Locke, *An Essay Concerning Human Understanding*, ed. P.H. Nidditch (Oxford: Clarendon Press, 1975), p. 234.

And in so determining that outcome they are responsible, causally responsible, for its happening. Causes are responsible for the occurrence of their effects, and not the other way round, just as anything that possesses power is correspondingly responsible for what that power's exercise determines.

The point that freedom, the up-to-usness of our action, if it exists at all, exists as a power—a capacity to determine—is, once made, hard to deny. But it has sometimes been blurred within English language philosophy. There has been a tendency to think of freedom in terms of a 'capacity to do otherwise', and to investigate the nature of freedom by analysing the conditions under which someone might be said to be able to do otherwise. Hence the classic debate within the twentieth century analytic free will literature about the conditions for such a capacity—a debate largely conducted as an exercise in the conceptual analysis of the locution 'could have done otherwise', and involving Moore, Austin, Aune, Lehrer, and many others. This analytic debate may have distorted the focus of inquiry, and led to a misunderstanding of its proper form. An enquiry into the nature of freedom is not an inquiry into the meaning and proper application of terms, but an inquiry into the nature of a power—which is a quite different form of enquiry, and which need not simply involve the analysis of concepts.

By concentrating on the analysis of 'could have done otherwise', the classical analytic debate importantly fudged the central concern with power. We see the fruits of this in the strange popularity of event-causal libertarianism, the appeal of which depends on ignoring the fact that freedom does not just involve a thin capacity to do otherwise, something that might be provided by a mere absence of causal predetermination, but requires the presence of a distinctive power to determine otherwise. For just as capacities in general need not amount to powers, capacities to do otherwise need not amount to powers either. In fact a capacity to do otherwise may reflect not the presence of any power but rather its diminishment or absence. The force resisted me and stopped me from entering, but it was weak enough that it could have done otherwise. The force was so weak that it might not have stopped me. Clearly, here it is not power but a lack of power that underlies the capacity to do otherwise. To understand freedom, then, we need to focus on the far more definite notion of power. Freedom is not a simple capacity to do otherwise. It is a power that allows us to determine for ourselves whether we do otherwise.[3]

So in discussing freedom, our subject undoubtedly is power. But how far, in discussing freedom, are we concerned with power in specifically causal form—the kind of power that is involved in stones breaking windows and in fire melting ice?

---

[3] For a recent discussion of the free will problem that wholly ignores freedom's identity as a power, and which addresses it simply as 'the ability to do otherwise' see Christian List, 'Free will, determinism, and the possibility of doing otherwise', Nous 48, (2014): pp. 156–78. I return to discuss List's view later in the chapter.

7.2 Powers Causal and Non-Causal

If a power is a capacity to determine, a causal power must be a capacity to determine causally. And that immediately suggests the possibility, at least at the conceptual level, of power that is not causal. A power that is not causal is going to be a power the exercise of which determines outcomes, but without determining them causally. And so understood, we certainly entertain ideas of other kinds of power besides the causal. We do deploy an understanding of capacities that determine outcomes without determining them causally.

There are, for example, various kinds of moral power, such as powers to impose or release from moral obligations. Consider promising, for example. Promisors have the power to impose an obligation on themselves—an obligation, owed to a promisee, to act as promised. And then promisees can release the promisors from the moral obligation of their promise by declaring them released. The promise determines or produces an obligation; and then the promisee's declaration determines the removal of the obligation and the promisor's release. But in neither case is the obligation or release from it produced as an effect, by virtue of some causal law. Rather the promise constitutes the imposition of the obligation and the promisee's declaration constitutes the promisor's release from it; and each does so by virtue of something very different from causal laws, namely the moral principles governing promising.

As with moral powers, so too there are legal powers. A creditor has the power to release his debtor from a debt—a power exercised through making some legally valid declaration of release. By making the declaration, such as by declaring 'I release you', the creditor determines that the debtor is released, and so is responsible for the occurrence of that release. But again the power here is not causal. Uttering the declaration does not cause the debtor to be released. Rather, thanks not to some causal law but to rules governing credit, the utterance constitutes that very event of release. The declaration determines the release, but does not determine it causally. But uttering the declaration is no less an exercise of a power or capacity to determine outcomes for that.

Then there are normative powers attaching not to agents, but to things that cannot be causes at all, to which we readily attribute capacities to move and to determine nonetheless. Suppose you entertain in thought a mathematical truth. That truth might determine or strongly incline you to assent. But what is it about the truth that moves you to assent? The everyday answer in such cases is clear: its evident nature—in other words you are moved to believe by the clear justification there is for believing the truth. Perhaps indeed you are not only led to believe the truth, but that there is justification for believing it. Either way, what leads you to form the mathematical belief, and possibly also the belief in the justification, is the truth and the justification for believing it. Now in this case what is described as moving you is not the sort of feature involved in ordinary causation. You are contemplating, not an entity with a location in time and space, but an object of thought—a mathematical truth. And if the object of your thought is true, its truth is plausibly necessary, and certainly not something that functions as an ordinary cause. For ordinary causes and effects are contingent. And what moves you to believe it is the evident nature of the truth, the clear justifiability of believing it. And this is a normative property attaching to the truth—something that, no matter if it moves or even determines your assent, is again not the sort of feature involved in ordinary causation.

As with mathematical truths, so too with desirable options by way of actions and outcomes. The evident goodness or desirability of a possible action might move you to form a desire for its performance or believe its performance desirable, and eventually even to decide on and intend its performance. What led you to want to perform that action or to believe performing it desirable and then to decide to do it? We have just given the answer: the evident desirability of doing it. And such an answer reveals you as rational animal, responsive to and moved by the good—just as you might also be moved, as rational animal, by the true. The action that is so desirable may never be performed, of course. What moves you is not some contingent event in the world, but, again, an object of your thought—such as the truth that a given kind of action is desirable. You may be moved by the justifiability of desiring and intending the action. But the desirability or justifiability of a given kind of action is again something normative, and not the sort of property involved in ordinary causation.

We readily use a vocabulary of power, influence, and determination to pick out normativity as well as causation. We talk of being moved by the *force* of an argument. And we use this vocabulary of force just because we think of normatively forceful arguments as really possessing the capacity to influence or move or even to determine our assent—and to move or determine it through the justifications they present. Our capacity for reason or rationality is a capacity to be moved by argument—and by the normative force of an argument in particular. So reason or rationality involves responsiveness to a kind of power—the power of good argument and genuine justification.

It is tempting to dismiss this talk of normative power as not literal, just because the power envisaged is not causal. At best we have here, it might be alleged, a manner of speaking or a metaphor. But there is an obvious difficulty with this move. Power follows from a genuine capacity to determine or move or influence. And surely we think it true that the very quality of an argument can be what moves people to assent to it. But for that to be true the quality of an argument must actually have a capacity to move. Good arguments must have genuine force—a power that is non-causal because located in the normativity attaching to objects of thought, but which is a genuine capacity to move nonetheless.

Again, consider the normative powers, not of objects of thought, but of agents themselves. Our talk of promisors and promisees as having the capacity to determine moral obligations—as imposing those obligations on themselves or releasing others from them—does not appear to be metaphorical. That is exactly how promising is understood: as an act by which moral obligations to promisees may be imposed, and from which obligations promisees may in turn generally provide release should they so choose. Whatever moral principles underlie these powers, we very clearly do understand them as genuine powers—genuine capacities, possessed by promisors and promisees, to determine outcomes. But the powers are not causal. For the powers are underpinned by moral principles and not by causal laws.

The idea of power in non-causal form is very controversial—a controversy that, as we shall see, was raised in especially sharp form in the seventeenth century by the work of Hobbes. But two different issues are involved that we must take great care to distinguish. One issue concerns our very concept of power, while the other concerns the metaphysics of power.

Some philosophers would insist that whatever we might ordinarily think or say, all genuine power is causal, at least regarding its fundamental constitution. No outcomes are determined without being determined causally. Now this claim is about metaphysics. It is about the true constitution of power, and the reality of its operation. And this metaphysical claim might turn out to be correct. But this is not the sort of claim proposed by Mumford and Anjum (see n.1), which is about our very concept of power. That claim is that our very concept of power is causal. To think of a power operating to determine an outcome just is to think of it as determining the outcome causally. But this conceptual claim is not obviously true; and it should not be assumed to be true just because of the metaphysical conviction that only power in causal form is real. We may have a concept of power that allows for power to take non-causal form, even if it indeed turns out that all the cases of power that do really exist are causal.

Take our psychology as it involves rationality or what we ordinarily take to be our receptiveness to justifications. The metaphysician who believes that all genuine power and determination is causal must claim that if my belief in a mathematical truth or in its justifiability really is produced or determined by anything, it cannot be determined by the normative properties of an object of thought. If anything really is determining me to believe in the truth or in the justifiability of assenting to it, this must be some genuine cause, and the determination must be causal. Perhaps, for example, the immediate cause of my belief in the mathematical truth is a prior psychological event—such as the event of entertaining that truth. It is this psycho-logical entertaining that is the immediate, and causal, determinant of my belief. To describe me as rational is just to describe my beliefs as susceptible to a particular kind of causal force—the causal force of those entertainings that present good justifica-tions for believing. Similarly with desires: what determines me to desire an outcome is not its desirability, but the psychological event of entertaining that outcome. Agents are rational if their desires are susceptible to the causal power of those entertainings of outcomes that are in fact desirable.

Now it might in the end prove true that causation is the only real case of power in nature. But if so, that is still not what we ordinarily assume. Take the prior entertaining of the object of thought. It is certainly not this event alone that we ordinarily think of as determining belief or desire. For we ordinarily take a rational agent's belief to be determined not simply by the fact that they have entertained a claim, but by the evidence for or clear justification for the truth of what is entertained. Similarly a rational agent's desire is motivated not by the mere fact that they have entertained a given option, but by the desirability of the option entertained. Rational or reasonable agents respond to justifications not because the event of entertaining them just happens to produce that effect, but because the justifications are good ones. The quality of these justifications really is what moves rational agents to respond as justified. That is rationality as ordinarily understood—not susceptibility to causal forces merely, but susceptibility to the force of justification.

Again, consider the moral powers we ordinarily ascribe to promisors and promisees. These are powers to produce moral obligations and remove them. And the principles that base these powers, as we have observed, are not causal laws but moral principles—the moral principles governing promising. These principles are, in particular, distinct from any psychological laws that might cover what we actually, whether rightly or wrongly, do. For moral principles are concerned not with what we actually do, but with what we are under an obligation to do. Now it might be that these moral powers and the obligations they are exercised to produce and remove do not really exist. It may be that moral principles transcending and normatively corrective of actual human practices are entirely imaginary; and so are the moral powers those principles supposedly constitute. But again this claim is highly controversial. If true, it will be made true by metaphysical reality, not by the fact that our concept of power is just a concept of causation. For our entertainment of various moral and normative powers—powers reflecting moral and normative principles, and not causal laws—seems to suggest that our concept of power is considerably broader than any concept of causation.

We need then to make an important distinction. One question is whether we think of some capacities to determine outcomes as determining those outcomes non-causally. And it seems that we do. It is then a further and importantly different question whether these non-causal powers really do exist and operate—as we so clearly assume them to. That is, we should distinguish analytic claims about our concept of power from metaphysical claims about what powers actually obtain. For it seems plain that whether or not moral and normative powers actually exist, we do at least suppose them to exist, and to operate non-causally.

What seems to distinguish cases of power that, real or not, are at least understood by us to be non-causal? There seems a range of possible differences from ordinary causation, from the breaking of windows by stones and the melting of ice by fire, not all of which need be exemplified together. There may be many different forms of non-causal determination.

In some cases, two things combine together to differentiate the power from ordinary causation. First there is the nature of the determining or moving entity, which is not an entity contingently located and operative in space and time as a stone must be, but an object of thought. And then secondly there is the mode of determination or influence, which is through properties that are normative—that are to do with the justifiability of responding to the object in certain ways, such as by forming a desire or a belief directed at it. It is these normative properties that move us so to respond. It is the evident truth or desirability of what we are thinking of that moves us to believe or want it to be true—or so we suppose. And not everyone is so moved, of course. Our rationality reflects our susceptibility to the power of justifications. We will be moved by justifications, but only to the extent that we are indeed susceptible to their normative power—only to the extent that we are indeed rational.

In other cases the outcome is certainly determined, just as in ordinary causation, by a specific entity located in time and space, such as by an agent doing something. What in these cases establishes the non-causal nature of the power is the mode of determination involved taken together with the nature of the outcomes immediately determined. In the case of moral and legal powers, determination of the outcome seems to involve the application not of some causal law, but of moral or legal principles to determine specifically moral and legal outcomes, such as obligations. Thanks to these principles, the utterance of certain words constitutes the incurring or removal of an obligation.

What of freedom? As a power freedom belongs not to truths or objects of thought, but to agents—and so to potential bearers also of power in causal form. Moreover, as with causation, the outcomes immediately determined need not be legal or moral, and are not determined according to specifically legal or moral principles. Which is no doubt why it is so especially tempting to assimilate freedom to some form of causation. But freedom may yet prove not to be a form of causal power. Though as agents we may also be bearers of causal power, and though the outcomes we control may be outcomes that could also be produced by us through mere causation, the way we determine those outcomes through exercising freedom may prove to be very unlike the way causes such as stones or events involving these would determine them. Free agents may determine outcomes, but quite differently from the way causes determine outcomes.

English-language philosophy has tended to suppose that the causal nature of power in general is somehow a conceptual truth, so that it is not only unproblematic but actually mandatory to assimilate the capacities to determine outcomes that we postulate in ordinary thinking to various cases of causal power. Freedom, especially, has been treated by philosophers in just this way. Even the sceptic has tended to assume that though our belief in freedom may be belief in a power that does not exist, it is still a belief in some non-existent form of causal power. But this approach to understanding the concept of freedom may be misconceived. Whether freedom exists or not, our conception of it cannot be assumed to be of some kind of power in causal form.

Thomas Hobbes pursued each of the two philosophical projects that tie power exclusively to causation—the metaphysical project of claiming that causation is the only power there is, and the analytic project of identifying the very concept of a power or capacity to determine outcomes with the concept of causation. We shall shortly be examining Hobbes' disbelief in the existence of freedom as a power involving alternatives. But Hobbes' attack on freedom was part of a wider scepticism. He denied the very intelligibility of any kind of power or determination beyond ordinary efficient causation. For example, Hobbes' scholastic Aristotelian opponent Bramhall was happy to talk of the desirability of the goal or object of an action as moving or determining the action's performance, but without doing so as an efficient cause. The source of the motivation involved an object of thought; and its mode of determination was characterized by Bramhall not as natural, as in efficient causation, but as normative or moral:

> Secondly, for the manner how the understanding doth determine the will, it is not naturally but morally. The will is moved by the understanding, not as by an efficient, having a causal influence into the effect, but only by proposing and representing the object.[4]

We can now see what Bramhall has in mind. The understanding moves us by presenting us with a claim or with an option. But to the extent that we are rational, what finally determines our belief or will is not the understanding, or some occurrence within it, operating merely as an efficient cause. What determines our belief is not simply the psychological event of entertaining the claim or option. What determines us to believe a claim or to decide on an option has to do with the object that the understanding presents and, specifically, its normativity—such as its evident truth or desirability.

The acknowledgement of powers or capacities to determine that are normative, and that do not simply involve ordinary causation, was a central feature of scholastic ethical theory—and a feature, in particular, of its theory of action and motivation. We have seen that motivation is naturally conceived by us often to involve our subjection to a form of power: something *moves* us to act as we do in pursuit of goals. Modern philosophers, taking it to be a conceptual truth that power is inherently causal, assume that any motivating power must be understood by us in causal terms. Those contemporary philosophers, therefore, who oppose Hobbes and Davidson, and who assume that motives are not causes, tend to write as if motivation, as ordinarily understood by us, had nothing to do with power at all.[5]

But Hobbes' scholastic opponents were quite different. They took motivation to involve a variety of kinds of power. One sort might be efficient causal, especially—as

---

[4] John Bramhall in *The Questions Concerning Liberty, Necessity and Chance, clearly stated between Dr Bramhall Bishop of Derry, and Thomas Hobbes of Malmesbury*, pp. 55–6.

[5] Thus in his *Teleological Realism* Scott Sehon, whose views we shall be discussing in Chapter 12, claims that the explanation of action by motivating psychological attitudes is teleological not causal. But, in his account of common-sense psychology, the only power involved is causal—as exercised not by our attitudes themselves, but by the physical states that underlie our attitudes. Our attitudes themselves and their objects appear not strictly to *move* us after all.

we shall see—where the motivation of voluntary actions by prior decisions and intentions so to act was concerned. Intending to do something would indeed move us to do it by causing us to do it. But motivation was provided not simply by attitudes, but also by the objects at which those attitudes were directed—a motivation that explained those attitudes themselves as well as the further voluntary actions that those attitudes caused. We could be moved to want something, as well as to decide on it and to pursue it as our goal, by its clear goodness and desirability. And here some form of determination was again involved—but a determination that was moral rather than efficient causal.

We have seen that there is a tension in the common-sense psychology of action between two kinds of power. There is the power involved in motivation—a power of motives to get us to perform actions. And then there is the power of self-determination—our power to determine actions for ourselves. The conflict between compatibilists and incompatibilists concerns, in particular, a tension between these two forms of power. Are some forms of motivating power incompatible with our power to determine for ourselves what we do?

Just because scholastic action theory allowed room for more than one kind of motivating power, so for this reason that there existed within the scholastic tradition more than one problem about the compatibility of freedom with prior determination, and with motivation in particular. There was of course a problem specifically about causation and causal power—about the compatibility of freedom with the determination of the agent by causes outside his control. But there was also a parallel problem to do with the compatibility of freedom with normative power. If evidences or proofs are sufficiently powerful, can they not outright determine the assent of any rational agent in a way that removes any freedom to believe otherwise? And similarly can there not be outcomes or objects so completely good as, once entertained, to determine the agent's choice in a way that removes the agent's freedom to decide otherwise? God, or the good in infinite and unqualified form, was conceived within the Thomist tradition as just such an object. That even now we readily describe proofs or evidence as *compelling* or *overwhelming* shows that we still allow for normative power in a form that can reduce or threaten freedom.

Hobbes, by clear contrast, caustically rejected all such appeals to powers other than ordinary causation: 'Moved not by an efficient, is nonsense.'[6] In Hobbes' view, any determination of anything, including any action, must be by an efficient cause. Hobbes therefore turns Bramhall's motivating object of thought into a prior psychological occurrence. Rather than being moved into a decision by a normative property—the desirability of an option—we are moved causally by a psychological event, such as a prior passion for or desire for that option, an occurrence located in

---

[6] Thomas Hobbes in *The Questions Concerning Liberty, Necessity and Chance, clearly stated between Dr Bramhall Bishop of Derry, and Thomas Hobbes of Malmesbury*, p. 59.

the world as is any efficient cause, and of the same metaphysical kind as the action it motivates and causes.

7.3 Freedom as Power over Alternatives

What I shall call the *causal theory of freedom* says that, whether freedom actually obtains or not, our concept of freedom is not only of a power, but of a causal power. It is a conceptual truth, the causal theory says, that to exercise freedom is to exercise power causally, so that any outcome determined through the exercise of freedom is determined causally. What we determine to happen through the exercise of our control occurs as an effect that we cause: 'The exercise of active control is essentially a causal phenomenon.'[7]

The causal theory is widely believed. But even if the Hobbesian metaphysical view, that all real power is causal, is true, the causal theory of freedom—an analytic theory of our concept of freedom—may still be false. It may still misrepresent our understanding of what freedom is.

We certainly understand causation as extending freedom. Given control of how I act, I can control what causally depends on my actions. If flicking the switch would cause the lights to go on or off, controlling whether I flick the switch will give me control over whether the lights go on or off. But the fact that freedom is causally extendible does not show freedom itself, as ordinarily conceived, to be a causal power. For other powers besides causation can extend our freedom too. Indeed, any powers attaching to my actions may further extend my freedom, what I have control over, provided I control those actions. If my actions have the power legally to determine a given outcome, such as your release from debt, then my control of how I act can give me further control over that outcome too; I gain control over whether you remain in debt to me. So the power of freedom is legally extendible. But freedom is not shown by this to be itself a legal power. No more does freedom's causal extendibility show it to be a causal power. All that has been established thus far is that freedom is a power that can be extended by a variety of other powers, whether causal or non-causal. What kind of power freedom itself amounts to remains quite open.

We have seen that freedom is understood by us to be a power to determine alternatives—a power of control over which actions we perform. Our conception of our power of self-determination is as up-to-usness—a conception of self-determination that immediately characterizes it as a power over more than option. Freedom is a power that leaves it up to us whether we do A or refrain; it is a power of *control* over which actions we perform. Central to the idea of freedom, then, is power over alternatives. This involvement of alternatives is picked out by the 'up to me whether'

---

[7] Randolph Clarke, *Libertarian Accounts of Free Will*, p. 151.

construction, which is completed by specification of alternatives by way of actions and outcomes within my power; freedom is the power to determine for ourselves which alternative occurs.

This constitution as power over alternatives seems to distinguish freedom from other forms of power, and from ordinary causal power in particular. The power under given circumstances to produce more than one outcome seems essential to the character of freedom. It is not obvious that there is anything left of our ordinary understanding of up-to-usness if we subtract this capacity to produce more than one outcome. That is just what the power is: control of how I act. So to have the power, at least in its complete form, there must be more than one outcome that I can determine. How can my action be within my control if I lack the power to refrain as well as to do? Our conception of causal power, on the other hand, is quite different. We have an understanding of causation as commonly a power to produce but one outcome. Heavy bricks hurled at fragile windows may have a causal power then to do but one thing—to break the window. We have no tendency to understand causal power as being always and by nature a power to produce alternatives.

There are other ways in which freedom differs from ordinary causation. One way is especially obvious, and has already been mentioned. Any exercise of the power of freedom has to occur through agency—and specifically through agency that is intentional or deliberate. If I am to exercise my power to determine for myself what happens, then I must do so either through deliberately and intentionally doing something or through intentionally refraining. If it is to be up to me whether the lights are on or off, there must be some action available to me—up to me to perform or not—such as flicking a switch, by which I can affect whether or not the lights are on or off. And actually to be exercising my power I must either be intentionally performing the action—intentionally flicking the switch—or be intentionally refraining from its performance. But ordinary causation carries no such tie to agency. I can produce many effects other than through doing or refraining. I can crush something just through my very weight, independently of any action I may perform or omit performing.

Furthermore, this power over alternatives by way of action seems to matter to moral responsibility as ordinary causation does not. I may, just through my weight and size and other features of me, produce many effects. But that I have produced effects does not come close to establishing any moral responsibility on my part for their occurrence, unless I had some control over what led to these effects—or so it is very natural to suppose. Whereas that it was up to me whether or not something occurred seems immediately relevant to the question of my moral responsibility for the occurrence.

We shall return to consider what might lie both behind freedom's peculiar tie to agency and its distinctive relevance to our moral responsibility. But for the moment I wish to concentrate just on freedom's essential character as involving power over alternatives.

Thomas Hobbes saw in freedom's involvement of a power over alternatives a central and very problematic difference between freedom and ordinary causation. The way in which freedom is supposed to involve alternatives violated, in Hobbes' view, central truths about causation. Since in his view causation was the only power in nature, Hobbes concluded that there could not be such a power as freedom. Hobbes was not even a compatibilist about freedom as a power. He denied its very existence outright. Freedom consisted not in a power over alternatives, but in something quite different: namely, in an absence of obstacles to the satisfaction of an ordinary one-way causal power—the power of a motivation to cause its satisfaction. Freedom consists, for example, in the absence of external constraints, such as chains, that might prevent my desires from causing movements by me that might satisfy them: 'Liberty is the absence of all impediments to action, that are not contained in the nature, and in the intrinsecal quality of the agent.'[8] Indeed Hobbes not only denied the existence of freedom as a power. He denied its very intelligibility. He claimed that we lacked even the concept of a power to determine things for ourselves. Talk of such a power was mere philosophers' jargon. He mounted his assault on the very intelligibility of self-determination as part of a radical programme to detach ethical and political theory from reliance on the notion. How did Hobbes propose to detach ethics from self-determination? Some of the time, as we have already seen, Hobbes did what Hume would do later as well—which is to treat moral blame as no more than negative evaluation:

[Why do we blame people?] I answer because they please us not. I might ask him, whether blaming be any thing else but saying the thing blamed is ill or imperfect ... I answer, they are to be blamed though their wills be not in their power. Is not good good and evill evill though they be not in our power? And shall I not call them so? And is that not praise and blame? But it seems that the Bishop takes blame not for the dispraise of a thing, but for a praetext and colour of malice and revenge against him that he blameth.[9]

In other contexts Hobbes seems to allow for a distinctive responsibility for how we act: 'The nature of sin consisteth in this, that the action done proceed from our will and be against the law.'[10] But the responsibility here involves a kind of legal responsibility—according to a view of that responsibility which avoids appeal to self-determination. Holding someone responsible, in Hobbes' view, seems to involve no more than holding them to sanction-backed directives on the voluntary— something that presupposes no more than their rational responsiveness to such directives. To be morally responsible, on this model, we have merely to be legally

---

[8] Thomas Hobbes in *The Questions Concerning Liberty, Necessity and Chance, clearly stated between Dr Bramhall Bishop of Derry, and Thomas Hobbes of Malmesbury*, p. 285.

[9] Hobbes in *The Questions Concerning Liberty, Necessity and Chance, clearly stated between Dr Bramhall Bishop of Derry, and Thomas Hobbes of Malmesbury*, p. 40.

[10] Hobbes in *The Questions Concerning Liberty, Necessity and Chance, clearly stated between Dr Bramhall Bishop of Derry, and Thomas Hobbes of Malmesbury*, p. 185.

governable. But, for Hobbes, that only requires that we be capable of performing or avoiding actions on the basis of a desire so to do, as a means to avoiding sanctions. And this presupposes nothing more than action in the form of Hobbesian voluntariness—something that Hobbes thought had nothing to do with self-determination.

Hobbes' opponent Bramhall was effectively a spokesman for the ethical and psychological theory of the late scholastic Francisco Suarez. And it is Suarez who is the ultimate target of much of Hobbes' writing in this area. In Suarez the idea of freedom really is the idea of a special kind of power—a power that, though still for Suarez a form of causation, is causation of a quite distinctive kind. Freedom is causal power in what he describes as *contingent* form.[11] As a free agent I am not a necessary cause as causes in wider nature are—a cause that under any given circumstances can operate in only one way. A massive brick that strikes a window can determine but one outcome—that the window breaks. Whereas, by contrast, I have a power, freedom, by which in one and the same set of circumstances I could equally well determine any one of a range of alternative outcomes. So under a given set of circumstances I have the power, say, to lower my hand or to raise it—and my nature as possessor of the power leaves it contingent how I will exercise it, and so which action I shall perform.

Hobbes denied that such a contingent power is possible, because it is unrecognizable as causal power. For Hobbes' scepticism about freedom is based on a clear view of the only form that power can take in nature. The only possible form that power, the capacity to produce or determine outcomes, can take, in Hobbes' view, is as ordinary causation—the kind of power that bricks, or motions involving them, possess and exercise to break windows. We shall see that Hobbes is right on one point at least. Whether or not the power of freedom is real, our conception of it radically distinguishes freedom and its operation from ordinary causation. In particular, freedom involves modes of determination not to be found in ordinary causation. In exercising freedom we exercise a power to determine that does not determine causally.

It is tempting to think that Hobbes' problem with freedom is mainly with what I have called *multi-wayness*. Freedom or control of what we do involves alternatives. To have control of whether one does A is to be capable of determining either that one does A or that one refrains. And it is very natural to view this control as a single power that could under given circumstances be employed in more than one way—hence multi-wayness—to produce either the outcome that I do A or the outcome that I refrain. That is the nature of control as a power: to leave it up to me which I do, and to be employable in doing either. Hobbes' case, on this reading of him, is simply that

---

[11] See Francisco Suarez, *Metaphysical Disputations*, disputation 19: *On causes that act necessarily and causes that act freely or contingently; also, on fate, fortune, and chance* in *Francisco Suarez S.J. on Efficient Causality*, ed. Alfred Freddoso (New Haven: Yale University Press, 1994).

there cannot be such a thing as a multi-way power—a power that can, under a given set of circumstances, be used in more than one way, to produce one of a variety of outcomes.

However, we should beware of this tempting assumption. It should not be assumed that freedom, understood as its being up to me to determine a range of alternatives, need involve multi-wayness as just defined—a single power employable in more than one way, to produce any one of these alternatives. Indeed, I shall suggest, even if freedom did not involve multi-wayness, it would still involve a form of power which Hobbes denied.

Moreover, it seems there could be cases of multi-way power that are not at all like freedom, but much more like (possibly slightly unusual) cases of ordinary causal power. True, much ordinary causation seems not to be multi-way—as the case of the brick hitting the window reminds us. Causation here seems to take one-way form. In a given set of circumstances, when the massive brick hits the window, the brick or its motion can exercise its power to produce but one effect—that the window breaks. But need this be true universally? Can there not be probabilistic causes with a power that could, under certain circumstances, operate in more than one way, to produce a range of outcomes? Perhaps the power of one particle to accelerate another could produce in the other particle, with some probability, one acceleration; or perhaps, with another probability, another slightly different acceleration instead. This would still be recognizable as ordinary causal power. And it would not involve the causing particle's possession of freedom. It would not be up to the particle which acceleration it produced; that would not be something that the particle 'determined for itself'.

Hobbes was, of course, a determinist. Probabilistic causation is not a possibility on his metaphysics of causation. He thought that a cause's power operates, under any given circumstances, to produce but one outcome. But the issue of multi-wayness— the possibility of a causal power's operating under given circumstances in more than one way, to produce more than one possible outcome—is not what was fundamental to Hobbes' scepticism about the very reality of freedom, or indeed of self-determination in any form at all. Hobbes' scepticism has more to do with something that can be detached from multi-wayness, and that radically distinguishes freedom from ordinary causation. I shall call this factor *contingency of determination*; and it has to do with how the possessor of a power, such as a cause, *determines* an outcome when it does.

In Hobbes' view, if an entity has the power to determine a specific outcome, and the conditions required for the successful exercise of the power are all met—then the power must be exercised. The determining entity's very presence, with its power, must necessitate the occurrence of the outcome it has the power then to determine. It follows on this view that an entity cannot really possess the power to determine, under one and the same set of circumstances, more than one alternative outcome. For an entity really to be capable of determining each outcome, Hobbes argues, it must simultaneously produce each outcome. Referring, abusively, to Suarez's contingent cause as an 'indetermination', Hobbes writes:

> But that the indetermination can make it happen or not happen is absurd; for indetermination maketh it equally to happen or not to happen; and therefore both; which is a contradiction. Therefore indetermination doth nothing, and whatsoever causes do, is necessary.[12]

Suarez was right about one thing. Contingent determination is part of our ordinary understanding of freedom, and distinguishes freedom from ordinary causation. In the case of freedom, the power-bearer may have the power to determine the occurrence of a particular outcome, and all the conditions required for the power's successful exercise may be met—without the power being exercised to produce that outcome. Freedom can involve the power to determine alternatives, only one of which can actually be produced, only because this is so.

Suppose by contrast an ordinary cause has under given circumstances the power to produce a range of possible effects. The cause is probabilistic: any one of these effects might with some probability occur, or it might not. In such a case the cause does not count as determining the effect that it produces. A probabilistic cause at most influences the occurrence of that effect, but without determining it in a way that removes all dependence of the final outcome on simple chance. Whereas we do think of the free agent as determining that he does what he does, but without the action's performance being guaranteed just by his presence as a free agent with the power then to determine it.[13]

Contingency of determination distinguishes a free agent from any cause—including a probabilistic cause. But so too does something else—something which involves not the power's relation to outcomes, but the agent's or power bearer's relation to the power.

Consider again ordinary causes. Either their operation is predetermined by the very nature of the power and the circumstances of its exercise: in those circumstances their power is to determine one particular outcome, an outcome which they will then produce. Or, as in the case of probabilistic causes, how the cause will operate is undetermined, that is, dependent on mere chance. But what seems importantly to distinguish freedom, as ordinarily conceived, is that this is not so. It is neither predetermined nor merely chance and undetermined which way a free agent exercises their power. The agent determines for himself how he exercises his power. And it seems impossible to characterize this relation that the agent has to the power without using the concept of freedom. If the agent can determine for himself how the

---

[12] Hobbes in *The Questions Concerning Liberty, Necessity and Chance, clearly stated between Dr Bramhall Bishop of Derry, and Thomas Hobbes of Malmesbury*, p. 184.

[13] I made this important distinction between freedom and ordinary causation, and discussed the problem it poses for a view of freedom as a straightforwardly agent-*causal* power in Thomas Pink, *Free Will: A Very Short Introduction* (Oxford: Oxford University Press, 2004), pp. 114–15. We shall return in Chapter 14 to the problems that face theories of freedom as a form of agent-causation.

power is exercised, it must be up to the agent whether he exercises his power to produce this outcome or that. If the power of freedom is indeed multi-way, a power employable in more than one way to produce more than one outcome, then in relation to that power there is what we might term a *freedom of specification*: it is up to the bearer which outcome the power is exercised to produce.

Hobbes was very well aware of this element to our conception of freedom as a power. The idea of the agent's determining his exercise of the power is arguably central to self-determination—to the very idea of determining outcomes *for oneself*. In Hobbes' view, this idea of a determination of how the power is exercised is viciously regressive. 'And if a man determine himself, the question will still remain what determined him to determine himself in that manner.'[14] So the very idea of self-determination, for Hobbes, is incoherent. And that is because it viciously involves the idea of an agent's power to determine, the exercise of which that same agent has first to determine.

But it is not obvious that Hobbes is right about the regress. The regress is vicious only if the way in which the exercise of the power is determined—to produce this outcome or that—involves a prior exercise of power distinct from the exercise of the power determined. But this is not obviously what we ordinarily suppose.

There is in the case of freedom a *conceptual* distinction between (a) the power's relation to outcomes—the power can operate to produce more than one outcome—and (b) the power's relation to me, namely that I determine for myself what way it operates. But we do not suppose there to be any corresponding *ontological* distinction between two distinct exercises of power—an exercise of power to produce outcomes, and then another and distinct exercise of power to determine the operation of that power to produce outcomes. Multi-wayness and determination of the mode of exercise by me are simply conceptually distinct features of a single exercise of control. In exercising control over outcomes I *ipso facto* determine for myself how the control is exercised. That is what control is—a power to produce outcomes the manner of exercise of which I determine for myself. In one and the same exercise of power I produce one outcome rather than another, and I determine how the power is exercised.

This freedom of specification does not involve, then, any exercise of power over and above that involved in the production of the outcome. But though there need be no vicious regress, we are clearly dealing with a kind of power that is not ordinary causation. In relation to this radically different kind of power the notion of freedom not only conveys a power over alternatives in relation to outcomes, but also the agent's distinctive relation to the power as its bearer.

We can separate contingency of determination and multi-wayness. First we might have multi-wayness but without contingency of determination. Probabilistic

---

[14] Hobbes in *The Questions Concerning Liberty, Necessity and Chance, clearly stated between Dr Bramhall Bishop of Derry, and Thomas Hobbes of Malmesbury*, p. 26.

causation seems to involve such a possibility, as we have just seen. A probabilistic cause might possess, as we have noted, a power to affect acceleration that could under given circumstances operate in more than one way, to produce acceleration at more than one rate. But this causal power involves no contingency of determination. Given that it is initially chancy how the power will operate, the effect is influenced by the cause but not determined by it.

But it is important that there might also be, as at least a conceptual possibility, contingency of determination without multi-wayness. That is, under any given set of circumstances the power can be exercised in only one way—to determine but one outcome. But though the power is outcome-determining, its exercise to produce that outcome is not ensured just by the presence, under the relevant circumstances, of the power's bearer. The agent could possess the power then to determine that outcome, and all the conditions required for that power's successful exercise could be met— and the agent just not exercise it. There could be a power involving contingency of determination that was not multi-way. This is a possibility to which we shall return, and which will be very important in the chapters that follow.

7.4 Scepticism about Freedom Revisited

Modern philosophical discussion of free will centres on a debate about causation between incompatibilists and compatibilists. This is a debate about the relation of freedom and causation—and specifically about the implications of causal determin-ism for the freedom to do otherwise. Is freedom as a power to do otherwise compatible with our being causally determined to do what we actually do? Contem-porary scepticism about the very possibility of freedom is mainly based, as we have already seen, on the supposed conceptual truth of incompatibilism and centres on the randomness problem. This is Hume's worry that if incompatibilism were true—if freedom did require causal indeterminism—that really would leave us, not with genuine freedom, but with mere chance: '...liberty, by removing necessity, removes also causes, and is the very same thing with chance.'[15] And that threatened indis-tinguishability of freedom from chance drives the incompatibilist sceptic into con-cluding that freedom, as anything more than randomness or mere chance, must be impossible.

But now we see that there is another scepticism about freedom, and one that also involves causation and the freedom to do otherwise, though in quite a different way. This form of scepticism objects to the very idea of freedom as a power over alternatives, on the grounds that causation is the only possible form of power—and that such a power over alternatives would be too radically unlike causation. This second form of scepticism is even more threatening to everyday belief. Incompatibilism is not universally believed,

---

[15] David Hume, *A Treatise of Human Nature*, p. 407.

even by ordinary people. Whereas freedom's identity as a capacity to determine more than one outcome seems far more basic. It seems central to our ordinary understanding of what freedom is like in itself.

We have begun to examine how freedom as a power over alternatives might differ from ordinary causation. And it has emerged that freedom seems to differ from ordinary causation in a number of ways. First, there is multi-wayness—a single power that might under given circumstances operate in more than one way, to produce more than one outcome. Now it is true, as we have discussed, that at least in some cases ordinary causal power could take multi-way form. What distinguishes freedom from causation, is that multi-wayness seems to be characteristic of the very kind of power that freedom is—control of how we act. Then, and as a presupposition of any power to determine alternatives, freedom involves contingency of determination—a radically different way of determining outcomes from that involved in causation. And then with multi-wayness comes, as equally essential to control, a freedom of specification. It is not mere chance and undetermined by anything how the power will operate. As control the operation of the power is determined by its possessor—the free agent.

The ideas of freedom that Hobbes attacks are not obviously incompatibilist in themselves. To say that a power involves contingency of determination, is not itself to say anything about the power's compatibility with causal determinism. All that contingency of determination expressly asserts, is that an agent might possess the power to determine an outcome in the circumstances—and yet still not exercise the power to produce that outcome. It is quite another question whether, compatibly with his possession of the power, the agent's exercising or failing to exercise it could itself be causally determined. And if contingency of determination is compatible with causal determinism, so too is multi-wayness. If it can be causally determined that I do not exercise a power then to determine one outcome, a power that I nevertheless possess, but instead exercise a power to determine another outcome, the power involved in relation to each outcome could perfectly well be one and the same. Is the power to produce one outcome distinct from the power to produce another? This question about the individuation of powers seems to have to do with their basis or constitution, not with their compatibility with causal determinism. And again the idea of a freedom of specification with respect to how control as a single multi-way power operates seems to add nothing to the case for an incompatibilist conception of freedom.

Nevertheless, English-language compatibilism has not been comfortable with this idea of freedom as a distinctive power to determine alternatives. English-language compatibilism has taken on board much of Hobbes' scepticism about freedom understood as such a power—though while still seeking to defend what Hobbes denied, namely the existence of freedom as some kind of power of self-determination. The strategy has been to reconceive freedom as a power in terms of ordinary causation, effectively denying that freedom, as a power, is genuinely a multi-way power to determine alternatives. Freedom is explained reductively as no more than a complex case of ordinary causal power in one-way form—as a combination of distinct powers of distinct, alternative motivations to cause the respective actions motivated. We shall be examining such reductive accounts and their implications in the next chapter. But though there has been this historical association between English-language compatibilism and scepticism about freedom as a multi-way power to determine alternatives, I shall argue that such scepticism is not obviously essential to compatibilism or the only respectable form for compatibilism to take.

Hobbes' scepticism about freedom as a power over alternatives is the expression of a kind of philosophical naturalism. This is the naturalism that refuses to allow that human nature and its capacities involve powers and capacities that are *sui generis*—that are qualitatively different from powers and capacities found in wider nature. And freedom is being attacked by Hobbes precisely as such a *sui generis* power. His is an especially penetrating attack, and a reminder that even prior to any incompatibilist theory of it, freedom as we ordinarily understand it is already vastly unlike ordinary causation. We may reject our ordinary belief in freedom because of its supposed incompatibilist commitment. But we may also reject freedom just because the kind of power envisaged, whether or not consistent with causal determinism, is too radically unlike any other power we are familiar with and, in particular, too unlike power in causal form. Hobbes' arguments serve to remind us of this radical dissimilarity.

Hobbes' scepticism raises a second issue too. How far are all the problems for freedom that are supposedly raised by incompatibilism really, on closer examination, incompatibilist in origin? Or do some arise as genuine problems, to the extent that they are genuine, from something else: from freedom's identity as a non-causal form of power—a power to determine that operates quite differently from ordinary causation?

Take the randomness problem—the threat that the operation of freedom is left indistinguishable from chance, so that to remove prior necessity is to leave the final outcome to a degree random or dependent on mere chance. Certainly with ordinary causes, if it is not determined in advance what effect a given cause will produce, the outcome must indeed depend, to a degree, on simple chance. If causation is the only power in play, take away prior necessity and you certainly are left with mere chance— chance and nothing else. So to the extent that a cause is merely probabilistic, what effect it will produce depends to a degree on mere chance. But to suppose that in all cases the alternative to necessity is mere chance is to assume that there can be no such power as freedom as we ordinarily understand it—a power involving contingency of determination. For even if the outcome is not already causally predetermined—so that it is initially chancy how the agent will act—freedom, as ordinarily understood, may prevent the final outcome from depending on simple chance. Freedom allows the outcome still to be determined—by the agent. It is arguable, then, that the real target of Hume's scepticism is not freedom conceived in incompatibilist terms, but freedom in a form that involves contingency of determination.

Where freedom is concerned, there are two forms of scepticism. There is scepticism from the supposed conceptual truth of incompatibilism. But there is also scepticism from freedom's basic identity as a power over alternatives distinct from ordinary causation. The second scepticism denies the very possibility of such a power, not because of any incompatibilist theory of it, but because as ordinarily understood, as a power over alternatives, freedom is too radically unlike the causation found in wider nature. It is this second form of scepticism that may prove the most serious. Indeed, it looks as though, as in Hume's case, some of the first kind of scepticism might really depend on the second. Freedom is indistinguishable from chance only if there can be no such thing as a power that is distinct from ordinary causation—a power to determine alternatives that can operate even in cases where the final outcome is undetermined causally.

7.5 Reason and Self-Determination

Freedom's supposed involvement of a power to determine alternatives has widely been taken to raise serious difficulties—either because the very idea of such a power is seen as problematic in itself, or through the role that freedom's nature as a power over alternatives supposedly plays in supporting incompatibilism. For this reason, many moralists have long tried to bypass or avoid the problematic involvement of alternatives by explaining self-determination in terms of another capacity that is not inherently alternative-involving. This is the capacity for reason or rationality—our capacity to respond to rational justifications.

Our capacity for reason seems at least necessary to our having a power of self-determination, as many philosophers have supposed and as I shall agree. But some philosophers have often been tempted to go further. They have straightforwardly identified self-determination with the capacity for reason. Such a doctrine constitutes *rationalism about self-determination.*

It is important to distinguish rationalism about self-determination from ethical rationalism. Ethical rationalism claims that ethical standards address and presuppose simply a capacity for reason. Rationalism about self-determination is importantly different—a doctrine not about ethical standards, but about the nature of the capacity for reason itself. Rationalism about self-determination states that that capacity for reason is what constitutes our power of self-determination. One could be an ethical rationalist in the mode of Scanlon without being a rationalist about self-determination. One would then deny that reason constitutes a capacity for self-determination, and maintain that in addressing our capacity for reason, ethical standards do not presuppose any capacity on our part to determine our actions for ourselves. And most ethical rationalists have indeed taken this position, detaching ethics from self-determination. Or one could be a rationalist about self-determination without being an ethical rationalist. One might then maintain that we possess in our capacity for reason a power of self-determination; but that ethical standards address other capacities besides the capacity for reason.

Rationalism about self-determination takes a variety of forms. A rationalist about self-determination might claim that the capacity for reason constitutes, just in itself, and under all circumstances, a power of self-determination. On this view, whenever we exercise our capacity for reason in forming a belief or a desire or other attitude, or to perform an action, we *ipso facto* determine for ourselves what we believe, desire, or do. But, on the other hand, the rationalist might make a more restrictive claim instead. The rationalist might claim instead that only certain forms taken by our capacity for reason constitute a power of self-determination, perhaps—for example— limiting self-determination to the exercise of reason in some form specific to action.

Again many, perhaps most, rationalists about self-determination claim that the power of self-determination constituted by our reason need not provide us with any power to determine alternatives. As constituted by reason, self-determination may be a one-way power—a power to determine for ourselves what we actually think or do, without leaving us with any capacity to determine otherwise. But some rationalists about self-determination still allow that reason may in at least some cases give us a power to determine otherwise. These are rationalists who are appealing to reason not so much to detach self-determination from the capacity to determine alternatives, but to explain how self-determination may sometimes involve such a capacity.

So rationalism about self-determination can be put to more than one use. Sometimes the doctrine is employed to support the view that self-determination extends more widely than action. But sometimes the principal concern is to bypass the idea of a power to determine alternatives—and to do so by using reason to show that self-determination does not, after all, necessarily involve alternatives. And sometimes the concern is very different: to explain in terms of reason how self-determination as involving alternatives is really possible.

7.5.1 Freedom and reason

It should be no surprise that rationalism about self-determination has had a wide appeal. For self-determination and reason seem to be intimately related. In particular, the power of freedom, as ordinarily understood, seems to depend on possession of a capacity for reason. This dependence has often been presented as one very important reason why there can be action apart from self-determination. For, it is often supposed, there can be beings who perform actions but who, just because they lack the capacity for reason, also lack the capacity to determine for themselves which actions they perform.

Consider the animals. At this stage we need not dogmatically claim that all non-human animals lack freedom. For example, it is a matter of dispute exactly how intelligent chimpanzees and dolphins really are—and perhaps they will turn out to be free agents too. I suspect, in fact, that chimpanzees and dolphins are not intelligent enough in the particular ways needed for freedom—but this is not the place to argue the matter. We may well not yet know enough about precisely how capable these higher animals really are. It does seem very plausible, though, that there other, much less sophisticated animals whose capacities clearly fall very far short of our own, and who do very plausibly lack freedom of action as a result.

Consider sharks, for example. Sharks seem to perform actions—actions that are at least very analogous to ours. For example, a feature common both to shark and human actions is purposiveness—the pursuit of an end or goal. We reach to the supermarket counter in order to get that loaf which we have just seen. The shark doubles back in order to get that fast-moving little fish which it has just spotted. Both shark and human are acting purposively, and both are trying to get something that they want.

With this purposiveness comes some sort of capacity for believing and desiring, even if, in sharks, these beliefs and desires may be fairly primitive. How better to explain why the shark doubles back to catch that fish, but by supposing that there is some goal that it wants—to eat the fish—and something that it has just perceived or come to believe—that the fish is now over *there*? Guided by its beliefs about where the fish is, the shark's desire for food moves it to turn this way and that, so that the shark is acting purposively: the shark's doubling back is directed at the goal of catching the fish.

A shark may hold beliefs and desires, and it may perform goal-directed actions as we do. Yet is a shark in control of its actions as we are? Does a shark determine for itself which actions it performs? Is a shark really free to act otherwise than it actually does?

It is very natural for us to suppose not. But why? If we do naturally incline to deny that sharks are free agents, this cannot simply be because we believe that the shark's actions are causally predetermined. For we cannot be sure that the shark's built-in desires and instincts do determine its actions in advance. In any case, the causal predetermination of a shark's actions is not the issue. Even if we did learn that the shark's movements were sometimes causally undetermined, we would not conclude that therefore they must be free. We would simply conclude, in this case, that it was sometimes just a matter of chance, or quite random, what movements the shark would make. And to be moving around at random, as we have already seen, is not the same as to be exercising control over how one acts.

One reason why sharks are so plausibly unfree is that sharks lack our capacity for rationality. We can act on the basis of informed reasoning about how we should act. But sharks lack any such capacity to reason about how to act. Their actions are guided by instinct and not by reason. And that is why it is not up to them which actions they perform.

Crucial here is that we can do something which sharks cannot. We have the capacity to understand and respond to practical problems as practical problems. We are able to think of ourselves as having a choice between a variety of possible actions. And so we can think of ourselves as faced with the question of which action it would be best for us to perform—a question to which there can be an argued and right answer. There is such a thing for us as a question of what to do, a question that we can understand as such—as a practical problem, a problem about how best to act.

So we really can reason about how to act. We can actually ask ourselves which action is most worth performing, and then look for justifications or reasons why we should perform this action rather than that. It is this ability to recognize a justification for performing a particular action as a justification, and to appeal to such justifications in wondering about which actions are most worth performing, that gives us our capacity for rationality. And it is this capacity that a shark lacks. Sharks plainly do not think about justifications for and against the actions they perform.

Why does it matter to freedom whether we can reason about how to act—whether we have this reflective understanding of practical problems as practical problems? The answer is simple. To be exercising control over something involves, at the very least, giving it deliberate guidance and direction. Our own actions, then, must in particular be things that as free agents we can deliberately guide and direct. But such deliberate guidance is impossible if we cannot even think of our own actions as needing guidance and direction. Yet that is what the lack of any understanding of justifications involves. It involves an inability to understand actions as requiring direction because some are more or less justified than others. Free agents have, then, to be able to think of there being more or less justified ways of acting, and to understand what is involved in arguing for the worth of doing this rather than that. Free agents need to be able to reason about their own practice—about how to act. They need a capacity for practical reason.

There is a further and often drawn connection between freedom and reason. Here the thought is not so much that freedom depends on reason, but that freedom is attained through reason. Augustine gave a very clear statement of this view, identifying freedom in its truest form with a state of complete rationality—with full conformity to reason's law: 'Now the only genuine freedom is that possessed by those who are happy and cleave to the eternal law.'[16] It is tempting to read Augustine as espousing here a form of rationalism about self-determination—as just identifying self-determination in its 'true' form with reason. But the 'genuine' or 'true' freedom described here, though related to our power of self-determination, is not obviously being identified by Augustine with that power. In fact, Augustine took the power of self-determination that bases our moral responsibility to be a power over alternatives that does not presuppose complete conformity to reason at all—that includes a power to act unreasonably as well reasonably. But he terms this power a *libertas minor* or lesser freedom. What Augustine refers to as 'genuine' or 'true' freedom is the greater freedom or *libertas maior* that we are to attain in heaven. And this greater freedom, far from being straightforwardly greater as a kind of power, actually involves,

---

[16] Augustine, *On Free Choice of the Will*, ed. Thomas Williams (Indianapolis: Hackett, 1993), p. 25.

through the perfection of our rationality, a loss of power—specifically the loss of the power to act unreasonably. In fact, the *libertas maior* of heaven is not obviously a form of power at all. *Libertas maior* is 'greater' as something quite different. It is a state of perfection, a goal at which agents with freedom as a power should aim—a condition of being that, once attained through the proper use of our power of self-determination, importantly constrains that same power. Augustine's theory of the 'true' or 'most perfect' form of freedom is less a theory of self-determination, and more a theory of liberation—a liberation that importantly involves the limitation of our own power to determine action for ourselves. For us to be liberated, we need to be liberated in particular from the capacity to misuse that power. Liberation involves the containment of self-determination within the bounds of reason.[17]

7.5.2 Rationalism about self-determination

So freedom as a power depends on the capacity for reason. And it may even be that, as Augustine supposed, the point or purpose of freedom as a power is to attain another kind of freedom—a state of liberation in which our exercise of freedom as a power is always in conformity with reason. But none of this shows that freedom or self-determination as a power is just the same thing as our capacity for reason.

Nevertheless, the rationalist about self-determination makes this very identification. Thus in her *Freedom within Reason*, Susan Wolf explores what she calls the Reason view that free will in relation to action just consists in 'the ability to act in accordance with Reason', so that to be a free and responsible being is to have 'the ability to act in accordance with the True and the Good'.[18]

Now rationality or the capacity for reason is very different from any power over alternatives. For reason has nothing essentially to do with alternatives. Rationality is a capacity to respond to reasons and to think or desire or act in those ways that are rationally justified. Alternatives need not be involved if there are no alternatives that are sufficiently justified—which there might well not be. For in many situations following reason may leave us with only one option. Any alternative, because unjustified, would be rationally excluded. In these cases rationality need not of itself involve the capacity to think or want or do in any way but one—the way that reason supports, in response to the fact that reason supports it. It is of course true that many agents with the capacity for reason are also capable of misusing it. Many agents equipped with rationality are perfectly capable of doing what is unreasonable too. But, nevertheless, an ability to do what is unreasonable is hardly essential to rationality. Indeed, it seems that the more rational or reasonable an agent is, the less capable they should of thinking or doing other than what reason supports. So to

---

[17] The relation between free will and liberation—between freedom as a power and as a desirable condition—is discussed further in *Normativity: The Ethics of Action, volume 2*. For a preliminary discussion, see also my 'Thomas Hobbes and the ethics of freedom'.

[18] Susan Wolf, *Freedom and Reason* (Oxford: Oxford University Press, 1990), pp. 68, 73.

identify freedom with reason is to deny that freedom, properly understood, is by its very nature a power over alternatives, the nature of which is always to leave it up to us which actions we perform—a power which makes alternatives available to us as rationality need not.

John McDowell seems in the following passage to be using *freedom* to refer to reason as just such a power of self-determination that need not involve alternatives:

Judging, making up one's mind what to think, is something for which we are, in principle, responsible—something we freely do, as opposed to something that merely happens in our lives .... This freedom, exemplified in responsible acts of judging, is essentially a matter of being answerable to criticism in the light of rationally relevant considerations. So the realm of freedom, at least the realm of freedom of judging, can be identified with the space of reasons.[19]

Though he uses the word *freedom*, McDowell is not here proposing, where belief is concerned, any kind of power to determine alternatives. He is not supposing that reason leaves us generally free to believe otherwise than we actually do. For it is all too evident that reason clearly does not do that, at least generally. Take the following everyday form of belief, for example. When I believe, as I do, that I am sitting in my study and am surrounded by tables, books, and chairs; that outside my study, and extending far beyond what I can presently hear or see, is a whole city with millions of people in it—all this is a perfectly good exercise of my capacity for rationality. These beliefs that I form are a fully reasonable response on my part both to the evidence of my present experience and to what I remember of the past. But I certainly do not have any control over whether I form these beliefs. It is not up to me whether I believe that there are chairs in my room and that there are millions of people outside, or else refrain from so believing, or even believe that the room is chair-less and the region without any population. If I do determine for myself that I believe what I do, this power of determination does look to be at best one-way in form. I certainly have no power to determine that I believe otherwise.

An opponent of McDowell might simply dig in. Self-determination just is a capacity to determine alternatives, as a matter of conceptual necessity. Since our capacity for reason does not generally serve to make alternatives available to us, it cannot be a capacity for true self-determination. But this may not be the right way to object to McDowell. It is not obviously conceptually true that a power of self-determination need extend to alternatives. We certainly seem to believe, at least in ordinary life, that the power of self-determination we actually possess involves alternatives—and we may be right to do so. But it may be conceptually possible, as we shall see in the next chapter, for self-determination to take other forms. If McDowell is involved in any conceptual error, it may lie not in supposing that

---

[19] John McDowell, 'Sellars on perceptual experience', in *Having the World in View: Essays on Kant, Hegel, and Sellars* (Harvard: Harvard University Press, 2009), p. 6.

self-determination can be a one-way power, but in supposing that our capacity for reason, in particular, can provide such a power.

For whatever form a power of self-determination may take, be it one-way or not, it seems it cannot take the form of reason. Rationality may be a condition of any genuine capacity for self-determination. But to exercise a capacity for self-determination is not simply to exercise rationality. And this is not because the very concept of a power of self-determination involves alternatives. The objection to a rationalist view of self-determination has instead to do with the nature of reason itself and the kind of capacity that reason involves.

Self-determination involves the agent's possession of power; it is a capacity of the agent to determine outcomes. But rationality does not obviously involve such a capacity on the rational agent's part at all. In fact rationality is a quite different kind of capacity. It is a second level capacity—a capacity exercised in relation to other capacities, such as for desire, belief, and action. Rationality is a capacity to exercise those capacities in a certain way—a way that is responsive to reasons or justifications. Now these capacities that are to be exercised rationally need not themselves involve their possessor in the exercise of power over anything. For me to form a belief or a desire need not involve any capacity on my part to determine any outcome. I have merely come to hold an attitude to an object of thought, and it is an open question what if anything may have determined me to hold that attitude. And the further involvement of reason, of a capacity to respond to justifications for the attitude, far from implying any exercise of power by me, seems, if anything, to imply some subjection on my part to power from without—and to power as much in normative as in causal form. For we have seen that we ordinarily conceive of rationality as involving a power of justifications to move the agent. In which case the exercise of rationality may be a mode, not of exercising power, but of being subject to it.

Take again my beliefs about my surroundings—that I am in a room in a great city, with streets, houses, and multitudes of people all about. I think of my very rationality as something that, through my senses and my memory and my other beliefs, imposes these beliefs upon me. My rationality imposes these beliefs on me as so obviously true that it simply is not within my control to think otherwise. The grounds for what I believe may even be described by me in terms suggestive of great force—as grounds that are *overwhelmingly compelling.*

A supporter of McDowell might reply that even if reason does involve the rational agent's subjection to various kinds of power, this does not rule out the concomitant operation of a power of self-determination on the agent's part. An agent's perceptual belief may, as the outcome of the exercise of reason, be determined by the justifications, but also by the agent too. The rationalist might propose a theory of the rational agent as having a power to determine his beliefs for himself, and also a compatibilist theory of the relation of this power to the power of justifications to move, or even to determine rational belief. And if the agent is not free to believe otherwise, that is not because he lacks the power to determine for himself what he believes, but because of the nature of that power. The power may take one-way form, and so fail to involve the capacity to determine an alternative.

The problem with this proposal is that reason's alleged status as a power on the agent's part to determine what he believes is doing no real work. It seems superfluous to understanding what, on any view, the capacity for reason clearly is—a capacity to respond to justifications. For example rationality has an obvious function in respect of an agent's beliefs about his surroundings. That function is to leave those beliefs determined by the evidence. For it is precisely to the extent that his belief is so determined by the evidence that the agent counts as rational. McDowell may claim that, compatibly with this, rationality also involves the agent's determination of his own belief. But it is not clear what this claim adds to our understanding of rationality in this case. The agent's rationality as a believer seems entirely a function of his responsiveness to evidence—not of any capacity to determine for himself what he believes.

It looks as though our general conception of the workings of rationality is in terms, not of a determination of beliefs or desires by us, but in terms of the operation of power, normative as well as causal, on us. Of course we do think we determine our action for ourselves, and through a power that involves alternatives. And we think that our receptiveness to the force of justifications does not generally remove this power. We may be moved by the desirability of an option towards deciding on it, but our final decision can still be down to us. Where action is concerned we possess a power to determine what we do—a power that we lack in the case of everyday rational belief. But if that is so, that is because in the case of rational action there is another element involved besides our capacity for rationality, that element being power over alternatives by way of action, a power the exercise of which is in turn subject to justification and guided by reason. So exercising rationality has nothing directly to do with exercising power—with determining as opposed to being determined—unless, of course, the particular justifications to which one is responsive are justifications for exercising a power. But if they are, then the power, such as the power of freedom in relation to our action, has to be supplied. It is a further and distinct element beyond any general capacity for rationality.

Rationality is not a capacity for self-determination. It is something very different. Reason is a second-order capacity: a capacity to exercise other capacities in a reason-responsive way. The function of rationality is certainly not to give the agent a determining role in relation to capacities, such as ordinary belief, where something other than the agent, i.e., the evidence, must anyway and already be playing the determining role. As for belief, so for action. Our capacity for rationality in action enables us to respond to justifications for action. But that capacity so to respond to justifications is not itself a power of self-determination. Any power to determine outcomes for ourselves is something over and above our capacity for reason. Though if we do have the power, our rationality will involve in particular the capacity to exercise that power in a way responsive to reason.

7.5.3 Practical reason and rationalism about power over alternatives

The rationalist might admit that in the case of action we do have a power of self-determination that is not involved in the exercise of reason generally. But an attempt might still be made to preserve some form of rationalism about self-determination. For it may be claimed that the source of this special power over our action is still our capacity for reason. Action is indeed determined by us as the generality of our belief is not—or so the rationalist now concedes; but the explanation for this lies in the peculiar nature of practical reason—the distinctive form taken by reason in the case of action. Indeed, the rationalist may also admit that our power to determine action for ourselves involves alternatives. The rationalist will simply seek to explain this involvement of alternatives in terms of the peculiar features of practical reason as it relates to those alternatives. We have a capacity to act otherwise as we do not generally have a capacity to believe otherwise, but this involvement of alternatives is to be understood in rationalist terms—as explained by the distinctive way in which reason guides action. Instead of seeking to displace alternatives from self-determination, where action is concerned the rationalist might seek to accommodate the involvement of alternatives and to explain it.

In medieval philosophy, freedom as a power—the *libertas minor* of this life—was generally understood to involve a power to determine alternatives by way of action. According to Peter Lombard 'liberum arbitrium' or 'free will' is 'free with respect to alternatives, since it can be freely moved to this option or that.'[20] There was, however, a lively debate about how far this power over alternatives could be explained in terms of reason. Aquinas and his Thomist followers sought to construct a rationalist theory of freedom's involvement of such power. To explain this, they appealed to a supposedly distinctive form taken by reason in the practical sphere. Practical reason affords us with a variety of options by way of the good, none of which is unqualifiedly or wholly good. That multiplicity of options constitutes, given our capacity for rationality, a freedom to determine for ourselves which such option we decide on.

Other scholastic philosophers, such as Francisco Suarez, resisted this rationalist project. As a power over alternatives, freedom may presuppose our capacity for rationality. But freedom, Suarez insisted, is still quite distinct from that capacity. Without freedom, it might be that there would be no point to deliberating how to act. But the capacity to reason how to act does not itself provide us with freedom. The power of freedom is a further and distinct capacity. Indeed, Suarez proposed an important view of how we acquire knowledge of this further capacity for self-determination—a view we shall be returning to consider later. He thought that the existence of this further capacity for self-determination is revealed only in our experience—as something phenomenologically given.

---

[20] Peter Lombard, *Sententiae in IV libris distinctae*, (Grottaferrata: St Bonaventure, 1971) vol. 1, p. 461.

Second we can prove the matter from experience. For it is evident to us from experience that it is within our power to do a given thing or to refrain from doing it; and we use reason, discourse, and deliberation in order to incline ourselves towards the one rather than the other. That is why choice is placed in our control. Otherwise as Damascene correctly observed in the place cited above, this ability to ponder and deliberate would have been given to us in vain.[21]

It looks as though the Thomist view must be wrong. The problem is obvious, and we have already raised it as the fundamental problem facing rationalism about self-determination. Reason is not a capacity on the rational agent's part to determine outcomes. It is something quite different, which is a capacity to respond to justifications. So the capacity is second order—a capacity to exercise other capacities governed by those justifications, and in a way responsive to those justifications. These first-order capacities need not in themselves involve the exercise by the agent of any power. And if power is involved in responding to justifications, the bearer of the power seems to be the justifications, not the agent. For responsiveness to justifications involves being moved by those justifications, and so being subject to their determination or at least their influence.

The Thomist adverts to a multiplicity of options—objects of thought—each of which in being good has some normative power to move the agent to decide on that option. So a variety of options are left as at last minimally intelligible objects of choice or decision. But that at best leaves room for freedom. It does not constitute freedom. For the power that these options involve is a power to influence and move the agent. But freedom is not a power to which the agent is subject. It is instead a power that he exercises for himself. And this power has entirely been left out of the story.

There is in fact a clear parallel between the Thomist theory of freedom as a multi-way power and event-causal libertarian theories of freedom. The Thomist multiplicity of distinct options by way of the good parallels, at the level of a normative conception of power, the modern event-causal theorist's multiplicity of desires each possessing some causal power to move the agent. In each case we find a similar attempt to construct a theory of a power of the agent over alternatives out of the power, causal or normative, over the agent held by other action-guiding or moving entities. In each case the method of construction is to appeal to a similar limitation in that relevant power over the agent. The power is divided between competing options, so that no single case of the power is capable of removing the agent's freedom to do otherwise by determining the agent to pick that particular option. No single option is solely and perfectly good, or the only option desired. The agent is not determined in one direction only, because there are multiple and competing bearers of the power to move him, no one of which is in a position to determine what he does. The existence of this variety of distinct options each with some power to move the agent is supposed to give the agent the power to determine things for himself. But how can

---

[21] Francisco Suarez, *Metaphysical Disputations*, p. 291.

a power exercised by other entities over the agent of itself constitute a power on the agent's part to determine anything? At best we have a multiplicity of non-determining influences on the agent, and not a power of the agent to determine things for himself. Such a multiplicity of non-determining influences on the agent may leave room for freedom; but it is not enough to constitute freedom.

Christian List has similarly tried to use the theory of rational choice to make sense of freedom. He claims that rational choice theory is committed to some conception of free will understood as involving alternatives, and furthermore that rational choice theory explains in what this freedom consists.

Rational choice theory makes use of the notion of an action- or strategy-set—a set of options by way of action. The agent's choice is determined by preferences or subjective utilities attaching to the members of this action-set—the mode of deter-mination being settled by some decision rule. There may be actions outside this set which possess a higher level of utility, or which are preferred to any in the set. But as outside the action-set, these actions will not be chosen by the agent. The agent might prefer making everyone in the world happy to doing anything else. But if the agent has no idea how to make everyone in the world happy, that action will not be within the agent's action-set, and the agent will not be moved by his preference into deciding on and attempting that action.

It is tempting to put this in terms of the language of freedom: the agent is 'free' to perform actions within the action-set, but not 'free' to perform actions outside it, no matter that he might prefer to do so. And List falls for just this temptation:

Just as folk psychology ascribes free will to people, in that people are assumed to be able to choose from more than one course of action, so our more sophisticated theories of agency are committed to free will, at least when they are interpreted literally. A central concept of any version of decision or game theory, whether we take the original versions of von Neumann and Morgenstern, Nash, and Savage or their latest, psychologically more advanced incarnations, is an agent's set of possible actions or strategies. The decision-theoretic or game-theoretic explanation of many social phenomena relies crucially on the assumption that the agents' action-or-strategy sets contain more than one option. Sometimes the addition or removal of options can make a significant difference to what the agents are predicted to do even if these options are not ultimately chosen. Unless we accept that there is at least a thin, technical sense in which such options could have been chosen, it is hard to make sense of those effects.[22]

And again, in a footnote, List refers to 'rational choice theory's implicit commit-ment to free will'.[23]

But this is to misunderstand the significance of an action- or strategy-set. Mem-bership of such a set is simply a condition that has to be met if a preference or utility attaching to an action is to help guide the agent's decision. In particular, only if the

---

[22] Christian List, 'Free will, determinism, and the possibility of doing otherwise'—at the end of section 5.
[23] In footnote 40.

action is in the set can a decision rule ever apply to support the action's performance. In that sense, only if an action is in an action-set is it true that the agent 'could have performed it'. But we must not confuse an agent's mere 'ability to do otherwise' with a genuine power on the agent's part—a capacity on the agent's part to determine otherwise. The only power presupposed by the notions of an action-set and a decision rule is a power—standardly understood as causal—possessed by the agent's preferences to move the agent to perform one of those actions in his action-set. The ideas of a decision rule and action-set have nothing to do with any power of the agent to determine actions for himself. Modern rational choice theory no more assumes the existence of freedom as a genuine power to determine action than Hobbes did.

8

Moral Responsibility and Reduction

8.1 Moral Responsibility and the Irrelevance of Freedom

Moral responsibility depends on a freedom to do otherwise, or so it is very natural to suppose. But moralists have long been found who doubted this, and who saw the basis of moral responsibility as lying elsewhere. One motive for such doubt is something we have already discussed—sheer scepticism about freedom as a power to do otherwise, or disbelief in its reality. But another motive is very different—and this is the supposed irrelevance of freedom. On this view, even if a freedom to do otherwise were a power we actually possessed, that would have no relevance whatsoever to our moral responsibility for anything we do.

We find accounts of moral responsibility that were initially based on scepticism taking on a new guise, as they come increasingly to reflect the more novel view—that real or not, the freedom to do otherwise has nothing whatsoever to do with responsibility. And what is the source of the novel view? As we shall see, the fundamental source of belief in freedom's irrelevance to moral responsibility is the failure to take seriously the multi-way nature of freedom—a nature that is fundamental, not to the very idea of freedom as leaving alternatives up to us (as we shall see that idea can be understood in other ways), but to its ethical significance.

One sceptic about our actual possession of freedom was John Calvin. He did allow that freedom, the power of controlling how we act, was a perfectly possible and genuine power of self-determination—a power by which, if we possessed it, we could determine for ourselves which actions we performed. So freedom would be a perfectly adequate basis of moral responsibility—were freedom something we were still really capable of. But—or so John Calvin claimed—our freedom has been unfortunately lost through the Fall and a resultant corruption of our human nature. Now we are all predetermined by prior necessity to do wrong, and lack any freedom to do right. As far as doing right and avoiding wrong is concerned, our actions are no longer within our control. So any moral responsibility we actually have for what we do cannot depend on freedom. Our moral responsibility for what we do, if we possess it, must have some other basis.

Calvin did not doubt that even in the absence of a freedom to do right, we can still be morally responsible for our inevitable wrongdoing. And that is because our wrongdoing is done voluntarily, out of a preference for or will towards doing it:

> The chief point of this distinction, then, must be that man, as he was corrupted by the Fall, sinned willingly, not unwillingly or by compulsion; by the most eager inclination of his heart, not by forced compulsion; by the prompting of his own lust, not by compulsion from without... he who sins of necessity sins no less voluntarily.[1]

So for Calvin we remain morally responsible because we still determine our actions for ourselves through the exercise not of freedom but of a very different power which, despite the Fall, we still retain—the power of voluntariness.

Let us consider further what voluntariness involves as a way of understanding, not just action and purposiveness, but self-determination. For voluntariness to constitute a mode of self-determination the agent must be identified with his will—with his own decisions, or with the balance of his desires or preferences. Self-determination, then, consists in that will determining and causing its own content, what is willed, to be executed. We might not be free to act otherwise than as we do. But our actions can still be our responsibility because in them we are doing what we ourselves will. We are acting as we ourselves decide or prefer.

Voluntariness does resemble freedom in being a power to determine that looks as though it might be agency-specific. To exercise the power of voluntariness just is to exercise a capacity to do things on the basis of a pro attitude towards doing them. And is that not to perform an action? Indeed we have seen that the dominant modern model of action and its purposiveness straightforwardly identifies action and voluntariness. We arrive then at the project, already mentioned in Chapter 2 as characteristic of modern action theory, of using a model of action and the purposiveness it involves also to provide a model of self-determination. A model of how action comes to be goal-directed—of action's relation to an object—now furnishes a model of the agent's relation to the actions he determines.

Unlike freedom, voluntariness is very clearly consistent with one possibility—that one's action result from predetermining causes not of one's own doing. After all, voluntary actions can be determined through the effect on our actions of prior occurrences—of our prior motivations, motivations that could perfectly well be caused and determined in their turn. Hence basing moral responsibility on voluntariness can be part of a compatibilist theory—this time not of freedom, but of moral responsibility alone. Our actions may result from predetermining causes not of our own doing. But we can still be morally responsible for how we act because in acting as we do we are acting voluntarily. So we can establish the compatibility of our moral responsibility with the determination of our actions by prior causes not of our own

---

[1] John Calvin, *Institutes of the Christian Religion*, ed. John T. McNeill (Philadelphia: Westminster Press, 1960) vol. 1, pp. 296 and 317.

doing—but without having to defend the compatibility of freedom with such causal determination. Since moral responsibility does not depend on freedom, the relation of freedom to the operation of such determining causes can be left open. Indeed Calvin himself remained an incompatibilist in his conception of freedom. We lack the freedom to do otherwise, in his view, precisely because our actions are necessitated by predetermining causes.[2]

In our day, Harry Frankfurt's positive account of moral responsibility is really a variation of Calvin. It is enough for moral responsibility that:

> ...a person has done what he wanted to do, that he did it because he wanted to do it, and that the will by which he was moved when he did it was his will because it was the will he wanted.[3]

There is of course one complexity to Frankfurt's account. Frankfurt appeals not only to the action's being performed because it is willed, but also to the action's being so willed because the agent wants it to be so willed. And by this Frankfurt means that the action should not only be performed because the agent wants to perform it; but that these desires to perform it should be motivating the agent into action because the agent wants to be motivated by them. We shall return to consider this further element in the story, and why Frankfurt adds it. But this complexity does not materially distance Frankfurt's positive account from that of Calvin.

For just like Calvin, Frankfurt is seeking to demonstrate that moral responsibility would be fully consistent with prior events causing and determining what we do. And he is similarly doing so by displacing freedom as the self-determination on which our moral responsibility is based. Moral responsibility is compatible with action resulting from predetermining causes, because our moral responsibility is based on voluntariness not freedom.

There is, however, one difference between Frankfurt and Calvin; and this difference is crucial, revealing something peculiarly modern about Frankfurt's position. Calvin does not deny that were we free, our freedom would certainly make us fully responsible for our actions. Frankfurt's view, on the other hand, is quite different. Unlike Calvin, Frankfurt is happy to leave open the possibility that we might actually be free to act otherwise. For Frankfurt, what prevents our moral responsibility being based on freedom, is not any lack of freedom, but its sheer irrelevance. Even if we were free to act otherwise, that would not matter to our moral responsibility. Freedom is just not something on which moral responsibility can ever be based:

---

[2]   *Semi-compatibilism* is the doctrine that though freedom requires that prior events not be causing and determining how we act, the operation of such causes is still compatible with moral responsibility. Calvin was a clear semi-compatibilist.

[3]   Harry Frankfurt, 'Freedom of the will and the concept of a person', in *The Importance of What We Care About* (Cambridge: Cambridge University Press, 1988), p. 24.

It is a vexed question just how 'he could have done otherwise' is to be understood in contexts such as this one. But although this question is important to the theory of freedom, it has no bearing on the theory of moral responsibility.[4]

This is a highly counter-intuitive, even an astonishing claim. If it really is up to me whether or not I do A, doesn't that make whether I do A my responsibility? After all, I am in control. No wonder that Calvin assumed that freedom would indeed base moral responsibility were it present. That assumption seems evidently true.

Frankfurt goes on to suggest why he denies the relevance of freedom to moral responsibility:

When a person acts for reasons of his own, and is guided entirely by his own beliefs and preferences, the question of whether he could have done something else instead is quite irrelevant to the assessment of his moral responsibility. Analyses purporting to show that agents do invariably have alternatives are simply not to the point, when there is no reason to suppose that having those alternatives affects the decision or conduct of the agents in any way.[5]

The line of thought is now a little clearer. Freedom, by its very nature, is an ability to do otherwise; it involves some alternative, non-actual possibility by way of action. Yet moral responsibility has to do with what the agent actually does, and why he actually did it—not with some unrealized possibility regarding what the agent might have done but did not do. So, even if it is present, the freedom to do otherwise is irrelevant to moral responsibility.

In Frankfurt's case, as I have already observed, this novel form of attack on the idea that moral responsibility depends on freedom goes along with the traditional appeal to voluntariness as a rival conception of moral responsibility. In basing moral responsibility on voluntariness, Frankfurt is still part of a very old project, going back at least as far as Calvin, of thereby reconciling moral responsibility with the causal determination of human action.

But not all those who accept that freedom is irrelevant to moral responsibility follow Frankfurt in pursuing his compatibilism about moral responsibility. Not all agree with him that moral responsibility for how we act is compatible with the operation of predetermining causes not of our own doing. Some, such as Martha Klein and Eleonore Stump, are opposed to this reconciling project, and remain avowed incompatibilists about moral responsibility.[6]

[4] Harry Frankfurt, 'Freedom of the will and the concept of a person', p. 24.

[5] Harry Frankfurt, 'Some thoughts concerning the principle of alternate possibilities', in *Moral Responsibility and Alternative Possibilities*, eds David Widerker and Michael McKenna, p. 340.

[6] See for example, Martha Klein, *Determinism, Blameworthiness and Deprivation* (Oxford: Oxford University Press, 1990); Eleonore Stump, 'Libertarian freedom and the principle of alternate possibilities', in *Faith, Freedom and Rationality*, eds Daniel Howard-Snyder and Jeff Jordan (Lanham: Rowman and Littlefield, 1996), pp. 73–88; Eleonore Stump, 'Moral responsibility without alternative possibilities', in *Moral Responsibility and Alternative Possibilities*, eds David Widerker and Michael McKenna, pp. 139–59.

Moral responsibility, according to these philosophers, does depend on an agent's actions not being caused by determining conditions not of the agent's doing and for which the agent is not responsible. But this dependence has nothing to do with any further dependence of moral responsibility on a freedom to do otherwise. Frankfurt is wrong in his compatibilism about moral responsibility and so too in his supposition that voluntariness is a sufficient basis of self-determination; but he is still right about the irrelevance of freedom to moral responsibility.

Morally responsible action excludes the causation of action by determinants other than us. But this incompatibilist condition on self-determination has entirely to do with the actual causal genesis of what we do; not with the unactualized possibilities which the freedom to do otherwise involves. The incompatibilist condition on moral responsibility is, to quote Martha Klein, an Undetermination or U-condition, not a Could-have-done-otherwise or C-condition.[7] What really matters to moral responsibility is that our actions must not be caused by predetermining factors not of our doing; not that in addition to this we be free to act otherwise. If morally responsible actions are typically accompanied by a freedom to do otherwise, this is only because, as a matter of contingent fact, those agents whose actions do not result from external predetermination are, in general, also free to act otherwise. Moral responsibility is not however directly dependent on such a freedom, which taken in itself is irrelevant and which might under certain conditions be absent. At least in principle, the U-condition might be met without the C-condition being met too.

By way of illustration, Klein asks us to consider the case of a hypothetical agent whose every action resulted from some prior determining cause, so that, on a libertarian view of freedom at least, he was never free to act otherwise.[8] His actions could still be his own responsibility, Klein suggests, if what was causing and predetermining his every action was, not some factor external to him, but some previous action of the agent's own. Were such an agent possible—and Klein certainly grants the difficulty of imagining such a agent—then moral responsibility could still be preserved in such a case since, even without the freedom to do otherwise, the agent's every action would be self-determined rather than determined from without. Given that the U-condition was met, the failure to meet a C-condition would be immaterial.

There are three issues, then, which we should distinguish: the possibility of moral responsibility without freedom; the relevance of freedom to moral responsibility when freedom is present; and the compatibility of moral responsibility with causal determinism. And philosophers have managed to combine a variety of opinions about each of these issues (Table 8.1).

---

[7] See *Determinism, Blameworthiness and Deprivation*, introduction, p. 2.

[8] See *Determinism, Blameworthiness and Deprivation*, pp. 56–65.

Table 8.1. Moral responsibility and freedom

	Does moral responsibility depend on freedom?	Is freedom irrelevant to moral responsibility?	Compatibilism about moral responsibility?
Calvin	No	No	Yes
Frankfurt	No	Yes	Yes
Klein, Stump	No	Yes	No

Consider again the distinctively modern claim that Calvin did not make and Frankfurt does—that, real or not, freedom is wholly irrelevant to moral responsibility. On the view of Frankfurt and his allies, what matters to an agent's moral responsibility for his action is what has or has not actually given rise to it—not some unrealized alternative possibility to it that the freedom to do otherwise involves. It is worth examining this doctrine more closely.

Agents are morally responsible through having the capacity to determine actions for themselves. So their responsibility must depend on factors that can actually play a role in the determination of how they act. Why, then, are freedom and the unactualized alternative possibilities which freedom involves irrelevant? The thought might be this. Unactualized possibilities play no actual role in the determination of anything—precisely because they are unactualized. They haven't happened. Only those possibilities that are actualized—what has actually been the case—can help give rise to or determine other things that happen. Since unactualized possibilities play no role in the determination of any action, the freedom to do otherwise must be irrelevant to any agent's moral responsibility for what he does.

But if this is Frankfurt's argument, there is an obvious objection to it. We naturally treat freedom as a condition of moral responsibility. But in so doing, we are not identifying freedom with some unactualized alternative possibility that cannot plausibly play a role in the determination of what the agent does. Rather, if it exists at all, freedom is a fully actual power—a power that is there and fully capable of being exercised, and that leaves it up to the agent how he acts. It is this power that is supposed to play a role in the agent's action, not any unactualized alternative possibility. Of course, the availability of an unactualized alternative matters too—but only because its availability is guaranteed by the power of freedom which, by its very nature, must make alternatives available to its possessor. If the alternative were not available, the power could not be present, let alone be exercised.

Unactualized alternatives may not themselves determine anything. But what can make a difference is the power of freedom that guarantees their availability. If such a power is ever real, it can perfectly well be as decisive to determining what we do—to the genesis of our action—and so as relevant to our moral responsibility for what we do as anything might be. Its nature is to be, after all, a power to determine which action we perform. Frankfurt and his allies might indeed continue to claim that a complete account of what determines or gives rise to our actions must always omit any power of freedom and mention only other factors—such as the passive causes to be found in our own prior desires and wants. But then this amounts to a denial of the very existence of freedom as an action-determining power—and we are back with the first line of attack on freedom as a basis for moral responsibility, Calvin's attack, which begins with scepticism about the very reality of freedom, and not with scepticism about freedom's relevance to moral responsibility even if real.

So is the doctrine that by its very nature freedom is irrelevant to moral responsibility based on a simple confusion—between unactualized possibilities that play no role in determining anything, and a power that makes such possibilities available and which, if real, could perfectly well be used by us to determine what we do? Some such confusion may well have helped attract many believers to the doctrine. After all, as we have already noted, there has been a strong tendency within recent English-language philosophy to blur the true nature of freedom. Freedom, if it exists at all, does so as a power. But it is often spoken of simply as a capacity to do otherwise.[9] And of course the idea of a capacity is far more general and far less specific than that of a power. As we have seen, a power is a very specific capacity—a capacity to produce outcomes or even to determine them. But capacities to do otherwise can perfectly well exist in some form without amounting to any power—and so without constituting any capacity to determine what is done. The capacity to do otherwise could come to nothing more than the mere chance of something being done otherwise. In other words it could indeed, on occasion, consist in nothing more than a mere unactualized chance possibility. So the more philosophers cease identifying freedom clearly and definitely as a power, the greater the temptation dogmatically to exclude it as a possible basis of moral responsibility.

But in fact this confusion of power with mere capacity is not the full story. There is a deeper reason why Frankfurt in particular assumes that freedom must be irrelevant to moral responsibility. As we shall see, he has also inherited from English-language compatibilism a particular way of thinking of freedom as a power—one which has made freedom, even conceived of as a power, clearly irrelevant to moral responsibility, and irrelevant in just the way that Frankfurt supposes. It is this distinctive and very modern conception of the power that freedom involves which separates Frankfurt from a predecessor such as Calvin, and which leads him to view the presence or absence of freedom as a side issue.

Before we turn to this very modern conception of the kind of power which freedom involves, there is one obvious worry about voluntariness to be faced. Not all action that is voluntary is plausibly self-determined. Not everything we do because we want to is really our responsibility. Desires might be compulsive, or imposed from without, or in some other way alien to the agent. To be motivated into action by such

---

[9] Note again Klein's characterization of freedom as no more than a 'Could-have done-otherwise condition' on moral responsibility.

desires is not to be self-determining. Accounts of self-determination that rely on voluntariness will therefore need to beef the notion up. We may need to isolate those desires and other motivations which are properly the agent's—with which the agent really can be identified: self-determination must involve acting voluntarily on the basis of these motivations in particular.

And this, clearly, was part of the intention behind Harry Frankfurt's appeal to our wanting to be moved by the desires that move us. Remember Frankfurt's character-ization of the kind of voluntariness that bases moral responsibility. It is a kind of voluntariness that involves higher order desires. Moral responsibility is based on the fact that:

> ...a person has done what he wanted to do, that he did it because he wanted to do it, and that the will by which he was moved when he did it was his will because it was the will he wanted.[10]

If we are acting on certain desires because we want them to motivate us, then perhaps those desires are ones with which we can be identified—so making the action which they motivate one which is genuinely self-determined.

Frankfurt's theory faces two objections. First, it is most implausible to suppose that such reinforcing desires are very commonly held. Consider the voluntary actions with which I am normally concerned—such as whether I get to the station in time, or pay my bills. What motivates me to perform them? Certainly not a desire to act out of any particular motivation. I want to get to the station on time simply in order to get to work. I want to pay my bills simply in order to retain my credit. The desires which generally motivate actions such as these—what appear to be perfectly good, morally responsible, and fully self-determined actions—are entirely unreinforced by any desires to act out of certain desires rather than others. Frankfurt's theory is wholly implausible in the concerns which it foists on morally responsible agents.

Secondly—and this is a very familiar objection to Frankfurt—the theory also threatens to be viciously regressive, since it only raises the further question of our identification with the reinforcing motivations—with the desires to act out of other desires. What if these reinforcing motivations are not relevantly 'ours'? It seems that to be ours, these further motivations would in turn have to be reinforced by further motivations to act out of them. In which case a vicious regress is bound to ensue.

Clearly the theory of what it is to identify with one's motivations is going to need some finessing. We may well need somehow to avoid Frankfurt's baroque theory of it as involving desires being reinforced by further desires to act out of those desires. But behind this problem is another, more fundamental one. For there is an obvious difficulty with basing moral responsibility for action on voluntariness rather than freedom. Whatever its initial appeal, voluntariness does not, on reflection, look quite so convincing a form of self-determination as its rival. In the case of freedom, as we

---

[10] 'Freedom of the will and the concept of a person', p. 24.

have already noted, it is indisputably the agent himself who determines his action. It is the agent himself who is exercising control over how he acts. While in the case of voluntariness, strictly speaking it is not the agent himself who is determining his actions, but something distinct from the agent—that is, his motivating attitudes, of which the voluntary action is an effect. So where we hoped to find self-determination we find its contrary—determination by something other than the agent himself. To act voluntarily, it seems, is precisely for one's action not to be determined by oneself.

The obvious reply is that, as we have been discussing, the agent is supposed somehow to be identified with these motivating attitudes. But why should this reply not be rejected out of hand? After all, not only are these attitudes distinct from the agent, but they are presupposed by and so exist prior to any exercise of the agent's capacity for self-determination. So these attitudes are things which just happen to the agent. They are certainly not in any interesting sense the agent's responsibility. So why *should* we identify the agent with them? We shall return to this problem later in the chapter, and to the basic adequacy of voluntariness as a candidate form of self-determination.

8.2 Freedom as Voluntariness

I have presented voluntariness as an alternative to freedom—as a quite different and clearly opposed way of understanding self-determination. But the way in which philosophers have conceived the relation between voluntariness and freedom is more complex. For, as we have already seen, voluntariness can also be used as a way of understanding freedom. It provided the basis for much compatibilism about freedom within the English-language tradition—what I have called English-language compatibilism in its *classical* form.

Freedom, we have seen, involves a power over alternatives—power to determine or produce more than one outcome—as ordinary causal power does not. But we may still be able to model freedom in causal terms—as a form of one-way causal power, but in complex form. According to this classical compatibilism, freedom is consti-tuted by a complex case of voluntariness. To have control over whether one does A is for it to be true both that one would do A if one wanted to, and that one would refrain from doing A if one wanted to. Freedom, then, is a power to act however one wants to act and as an effect of one's wanting so to act. Such a conception of freedom of action is plainly compatibilist. It is fully consistent with one's actions being entirely deter-mined, via one's desires, by conditions outside one's control.

This conception of freedom as a complex form of voluntariness is very important in a number of ways. First, it has been historically widely held, particularly within the English-language philosophical tradition from Locke to Moore, down to Davidson and Frankfurt in our own day. Secondly, it is one embodiment of a very important theoretical ambition—a fundamentally naturalistic ambition that has had even wider appeal, an appeal going beyond compatibilism to include, as we have seen, many modern libertarians as well. This is the ambition to give an account of freedom that is *naturalistically reductive*. The ambition is to characterize all that freedom involves in terms of capacities and powers, such as ordinary causation, that apply more widely in nature—that are not peculiar to human nature or free agency.

Remember that neither compatibilism nor incompatibilism is directly committed to a reductive account of freedom. Each doctrine is about a quite different issue—freedom's compatibility or otherwise with other powers that might be acting on an agent. But, particularly within the English-language tradition, compatibilism especially has become associated with a naturalistic approach to human psychology and action. And that is because naturalism offers to vindicate compatibilism. Accounting for freedom in terms of causation as a power found generally through nature promises to deliver compatibilism as a conceptual consequence—a conceptual truth that will certainly follow if freedom can be reduced to causal powers of a kind operative in a deterministic system. This naturalistic approach reinforces, in turn, the view that the free will problem is an entirely conceptual problem—a problem that can be solved just by giving an analysis of what is implied in our very concept of freedom.

Classical compatibilism's account of freedom as a complex case of voluntariness is a very clear example of this naturalistically reductive programme. Control is being explained by appeal to a combination of distinct one-way causal powers, each of which can be possessed and exercised alone. Freedom is being identified as a special and complex case of causal power—a power of desires to cause us successfully to do whatever would satisfy them.

This classical compatibilism has proved thoroughly subversive of freedom's place in moral theory. In particular, classical compatibilism further explains why Frankfurt so readily assumes the irrelevance of freedom to moral responsibility. Defining freedom in terms of voluntariness profoundly changes our view of what is going on when an agent exercises freedom—and in a way that immediately renders freedom quite irrelevant to moral responsibility.

The distinctive feature of freedom or control is its involvement of alternatives. To be free is to be free to do A or not—to have control over whether one does A or not. And it is natural to understand this involvement of alternatives in terms of multi-wayness—a single power that could in the same circumstances be used to produce more than one outcome. One and the same power could be exercised either to do A, or to refrain. To do A through exercising this power is to do A through the exercise of a power to do otherwise—a power, control of which action one performs, that could equally have been used to omit doing A. To possess that power of control with respect to an action's performance is, equally, to possess it with respect to the action's omission.

Whereas voluntariness is obviously quite different. To do A voluntarily is to do A because one decides or wants to. But this capacity to do A on the basis of wanting to do it would in no way be involved in refraining from doing A. Voluntarily to refrain from doing A would involve the quite distinct power to refrain from doing A on the basis of wanting to refrain. And the powers really are distinct, in that each power is a power of a quite distinct motivation, and can be present without the other. To use Locke's example: I can be exercising a power to stay in my room on the basis of wanting to; but, unbeknown to me, the door may be locked, and I altogether lack the power to leave should I so want.[11] Moreover, as distinct, the two powers are exercised quite separately: each of these two powers is exercised without any exercise of the other—we obviously cannot at one and the same time both be doing A on the basis of the power voluntarily to do A, and refraining from doing A on the basis of the power voluntarily to refrain.

Voluntariness can only be used to provide an account of freedom, then, by appealing to an agent's possession of both these two distinct voluntary powers—both a power to do A voluntarily and also a power voluntarily to refrain; and by then claiming that the agent is exercising his freedom whenever he is exercising one of these powers. Instead of a single power that is inherently multi-way, we have a combination of two distinct one-way powers. But if freedom is indeed nothing but a combination of two distinct powers for voluntariness, then freedom will surely drop out as a distinct condition on moral responsibility. And that is because, on this classic reductive account of freedom, the only power of self-determination we ever exercise is voluntariness. Freedom as a power to do otherwise is left a power that is never exercised at all.

On the classical English-language compatibilist reduction, whenever I do A, the power of self-determination which I am exercising is the power to do A voluntarily. But this, very evidently, is not a power to act otherwise. Any power to act otherwise—to refrain—that I may possess is quite distinct. It is the power voluntarily to refrain from doing A. And even if this power does happen to be possessed, it is certainly not being exercised. It is quite inert. Its absence would make no difference to the power I am actually exercising, since the two powers are distinct and independent of each other. In which case, the presence or absence of this unexercised power to act otherwise must be irrelevant to my moral responsibility for what I do. How can moral responsibility ever depend on a kind of power that is never actually exercised to determine what we do? But that, on this reductive account of freedom, is precisely what the power to do otherwise becomes.

Our moral responsibility for action depends on the fact that we ourselves determine how we act. The question then is what kind of self-determining power we really exercise. For that will provide the true basis of our moral responsibility. Is it that we are exercising a power to act otherwise? Or is that we are acting as we will and because we so will? Which matters—control or voluntariness? The idea of freedom as a complex case of voluntariness is an attempt to combine both conceptions. But it is a

---

[11] John Locke, *An Essay Concerning Human Understanding*, p. 238.

deeply unstable compromise, and control is surely going to be the loser. And this is because the power to act otherwise is never actually being exercised to determine action—only a power to act as one wills. The power to act otherwise is present, but as a dummy that plays no active role at all. Why make moral responsibility depend on it, if it is irrelevant to any power that the agent actually exercises over how he acts?

We have seen that Frankfurt supposes that the freedom to do otherwise is irrelevant to moral responsibility. For he says that: 'Analyses purporting to show that agents do invariably have alternatives are simply not to the point, when there is no reason to suppose that having those alternatives affects the decision or conduct of the agents in any way.' And it did seem initially puzzling why Frankfurt should say this. Suppose the power I exercise over how I act, and that bases my moral responsibility for how I act, is an inherently multi-way power of freedom that could equally be used to do A or to refrain. Then surely the presence or absence of alternatives to whichever I actually do, which is the presence or absence of the power to perform that alternative, would make a difference to my actual decision or conduct in one crucial respect. It will betoken the very presence or absence of a power on my part to determine what I do. But that this could be a possibility is not something that Frankfurt shows much sign of realizing. For he does not even begin to imagine that freedom might be a single inherently multi-way power.

Frankfurt is claiming to show that moral responsibility is independent of the freedom to do otherwise—and he is claiming to do so while not assuming compatibilism about the nature of freedom. For he wishes to establish a compatibility of moral responsibility with causal determinism, but to do so independently of the traditional free will debate about the compatibility with causal determinism of a freedom to do otherwise. But in fact Frankfurt's intuitions are profoundly shaped by a central element of English-language compatibilism about freedom—a compatibilism that (though compatibilism need not do this) has taken reductive form. The power of freedom is no longer a single multi-way power, but a complex of distinct one-way powers—and a complex that is never exercised as a unit to determine anything.

So we see the basis for Frankfurt's doctrine that freedom is irrelevant to moral responsibility. It lies in an unargued assumption that control of whether we do A— what appears to be a power that only ever occurs in multi-way form, as just such control—is really exercised as distinct cases of power in one-way form. Control of whether we do A is exercised either as the power to do A or else as a distinct power to refrain, where each of these powers can be possessed and exercised without the other. This one-way power that is used to construct and compose freedom and that, in effect, replaces it, is supposed to be recognizably a power of self-determination, sufficient to base the agent's moral responsibility for what he does. And when we exercise our power to determine our actions for ourselves, it is only ever this one-way power that we exercise. There really is no inherently multi-way power of self-determination that could be exercised instead. Granted this account of self-determination, the presence or absence of a freedom to act otherwise would make no difference to the power being exercised by the agent over what he does—and so it would indeed be of no relevance to the agent's moral responsibility for what he does.

Of course it is far from obvious that the power of freedom really is decomposable in anything like this way. Whether we are incompatibilists or compatibilists, why not suppose that freedom is what it appears to be—a power that only ever occurs in multi-way form, the nature of which is to leave it up to us, within our control, which action we perform? And in fact our conviction that freedom is of immediate relevance to moral responsibility suggests that our understanding of freedom is of such a multi-way power. As far as intuition is concerned, its being up to me which action I perform provides immediate support for how I act being my responsibility; and my lacking control over which action I perform provides equally intuitive support for my not being responsible. And that suggests that our ordinary conception of freedom does not allow for its reduction into distinct cases of one-way power.

Frankfurt's project is to exclude freedom from the theory of moral responsibility, thereby reconciling moral responsibility with causal predetermination. We now see that this project is by no means as neutral about the nature of freedom as it initially appeared. Freedom is supposed to be irrelevant to moral responsibility; it is voluntariness that is to matter instead. But freedom will only be irrelevant if it really is reducible to some power, such as ordinary causation, that can be possessed and exercised in one-way form. So, whether Frankfurt is fully aware of this or not, his case for the irrelevance of freedom is really based on an account of what freedom is that is profoundly shaped by a very particular and debatable form of compatibilism—one which combines compatibilism with a reductionist account of freedom in terms of ordinary causal power.

It was natural, even inevitable, given its inherent logic, that the classical English-language compatibilist account of freedom as a complex form of voluntariness would eventually lead many philosophers to abandon any interest in freedom as such. Indeed, for many modern compatibilists, freedom is no longer properly recognized as a distinctive conception of self-determination in its own right. Freedom has begun to disappear as a clear alternative notion to voluntariness. The terms 'free' and 'control' are now applied to the exercise of mere voluntariness, as if there was nothing else that they really could mean. Davidson gives clear expression to just this shift:

It is natural to suppose that an action one is free to perform is an action that one is also free *not* to perform...isn't it an empty pretence to say a man is free to perform an action if he is not also free not to perform it? Surely, freedom means the existence of alternatives.

The difficulty (recently brought to the fore by Harry Frankfurt) is that if we say a man is free to do x only if his doing x depends on whether or not the attitudinal condition holds (he chooses to do x, decides to, wills it, has rationalising attitudes), then we find counter instances in cases of overdetermination. What a man does of his own free will—an action done by choice and with intent, caused by his own wants and beliefs—may be something he would have been caused to do in another way if the choice or motives had been lacking.

Two intuitions seem at war...The intuitions are, on the one hand, the view that we cannot be free to do what we would be causally determined to do in any case, and on the other hand, the feeling that if we choose to do something and do it because we chose it, then the action is free no matter what would have happened if we *hadn't* chosen.[12]

Davidson wants to hold on to the term 'freedom' to express the self-determination which action distinctively involves. But, at the same time, the self-determination that really attracts him is voluntariness—*doing something because we choose to do it*, as Davidson puts it. That surely provides all the self-determination that we could ever want—and, of course, it is a self-determination which we can perfectly well exercise even if we lack the freedom to act otherwise: '...it is an error to suppose we add anything to the analysis of freedom when we say an agent is free to do something if he can do it *or not*, as he pleases (chooses, etc.)'.[13] Notice, though, how keen Davidson is to disguise his abandonment of freedom. Freedom is a highly intuitive conception of the self-determination underlying moral responsibility—far too intuitive to be abandoned openly. The language of freedom cannot be given up entirely, but is reapplied. Terms such as 'freely' are retained, but are used now to pick out voluntariness, not freedom. Davidson hijacks the terminology of freedom to pick out voluntariness—and he can get away with this because compatibilism had already allowed freedom to evaporate to not much more than voluntariness anyway. And here we see a further fundamental difference between Davidson and Frankfurt and their predecessor Calvin.

Calvin was fully aware that freedom and voluntariness are quite different notions. In fact he was engaged in an ideological battle that was only worth fighting at all if that difference was deep and real. The scholastic accounts of moral responsibility which Calvin confronted and opposed appealed to a human freedom to act otherwise. And that made them, in Calvin's eyes, the dangerous intellectual constructions of a false religion. Calvin saw himself as battling against a Pelagianizing version of Christianity— a version of Christianity which misguidedly sought to turn the exercise of moral responsibility into a human achievement that was independent of God's work, and which used the alleged continuing reality, even after the Fall, of a human freedom to act otherwise to assert this independence. Calvin was not concerned to reinterpret this theory of a continuing human freedom, but to identify its error clearly and to reject it. For Calvin, belief in human freedom was a dangerous myth—a myth to be denounced, not accommodated. So Calvin condemned as a dangerous fudge any attempt to redefine 'freedom' to mean the same as voluntariness. Such redefinition simply clouded the issue, leaving room for the continuation of Pelagian error:

Man will then be spoken of as having this sort of free decision, not because he has a free choice equally of good and evil, but because he acts wickedly by will, not by compulsion. Well put, indeed, but what purpose is served by labeling with a proud name such a slight thing? A noble

---

[12] Donald Davidson, 'Freedom to act', in *Essays on Actions and Events*, pp. 74–5.
[13] 'Freedom to act', p. 75.

freedom, indeed—for man not to be forced to serve sin, yet to be such a willing slave that his will is bound by the fetters of sin! Indeed, I abhor contentions about words, with which the church is harassed to no purpose. But I have scrupulously resolved to avoid those words which signify something absurd, especially where pernicious error is involved. How few men are there, I ask, who when they hear free will attributed to man do not immediately conceive him to be master of both his mind and will, able of his own power to turn himself toward either good or evil?[14]

Whereas the modern attempt to rebuild moral responsibility on the foundation of voluntariness has arisen in a very different way. Davidson and Frankfurt are working within, not against, an already existing and well-established tradition of thinking about freedom—in their case, the tradition which is English-language compatibilism in its classical reductive form. This tradition was originally not about rejecting freedom, but was instead about redefining freedom in terms of a complex case of voluntariness. The move into explaining responsibility simply in terms of voluntariness alone is really an inevitable end-stage of this compatibilist tradition—a stage in which, as far as the theory of moral responsibility is concerned, we are passing, very softly but ineluctably, from the steady conceptual dilution of freedom into its final and complete abandonment. And so the language of freedom and control can continue to be used—but now to pick out voluntariness, and not freedom proper at all. Though we entirely lack the freedom to do otherwise, as voluntary agents we are still said to do A 'freely'. The language of freedom and control has effectively been stolen, and misapplied to voluntariness—without, it seems, even the appropriators themselves being fully aware of what they are really doing.

There is also another factor in play—a factor that lulls us into accepting what is really an outright theft of terms such as 'free' and 'control'. Even in ordinary usage, where someone, through exercising freedom, through doing something that they were genuinely free not to do, brings about an outcome which in fact would have happened anyway, we still talk of that outcome as something they bring about *freely*—as occurring through an exercise of their control. And this despite the fact that the occurrence would have occurred anyway, and so is outside their control. Thus, to return to Locke's example, we might describe someone as freely staying in a room that was, unbeknown to them locked, despite the fact that they lack control over whether they stay or go. But we describe them as staying freely because their staying is the result of their decision to stay; and this decision was within their control.

But this simply shows that we can be morally responsible not only for how we exercise our freedom, but also for the consequences of that exercise. It may indeed be true that had we exercised our freedom otherwise, those consequences would have arisen anyway, being produced in some other way. Nevertheless, in actual fact it is

[14] John Calvin, *Institutes of the Christian Religion*, vol. 1, p. 264.

through the exercise of our freedom, as effects of something we were free not to do, that the consequences have resulted; and so they have arisen as our responsibility, and we are said to have brought them about freely. In other words, terms such as 'freely' are being used here to track what is still a thoroughly freedom-dependent responsibility. There is nothing here that legitimizes Davidson's complete detachment of terms such as 'freely' or 'control' from genuine freedom or control. And certainly nothing here shows that freedom is not essential to human self-determination and responsibility.

8.3 'Frankfurt-cases'

Harry Frankfurt has of course claimed to *prove* that in itself the presence or absence of freedom makes no difference to moral responsibility. In his 'Moral responsibility and alternate possibilities' he asks us to consider cases where, he argues, an agent Jones is deprived of the freedom not to perform some action A, not by anyone else actually intervening to make him do A, but by the mere possibility of their so intervening. Someone immensely powerful and knowledgeable, Black, is monitoring Jones to check that he really is going to do A. Should Jones show any sign of acting otherwise Black would certainly act to ensure that Jones did indeed still do A. Hence, thanks just to Black's potent but inactive presence, Jones lacks the freedom not to do A. But Black does not have to intervene, since Jones goes ahead and does A 'off his own back' and independently. In fact he does A in just the same way that he would have done had Black not been present, so that he remained free not to do A. Jones does A anyway, independently of Black. Since Black's presence and the concomitant lack of a freedom to do otherwise make no difference to what Jones does and why he does it—'Indeed everything happened just as it would have happened without Black's presence in the situation and without his readiness to intrude into it'[15]—they can make no difference to Jones' moral responsibility. The presence or absence of freedom must in itself be irrelevant. Jones must be morally responsible whether or not he is free to act otherwise.

Frankfurt's original example has inspired a whole range of similar 'Frankfurt-cases'.[16] These all follow the same general pattern. An agent, let us again call him Jones, lacks the freedom to do otherwise because of some feature in his surrounding circumstances—though without that feature actually affecting what he does and why he does it. In fact Jones acts just as independently of the feature as would any agent with the freedom to act otherwise. The conclusion is supposed to follow: since the agent acts independently of the feature, that feature may remove his freedom, but it

---

[15] Harry Frankfurt, 'Alternate possibilities and moral responsibility', in *The Importance of What We Care About*, p. 7.

[16] As discussed by Widerker and McKenna in the introduction to *Moral Responsibility and Alternative Possibilities*.

cannot affect his moral responsibility. So, again, the freedom to do otherwise must be irrelevant to moral responsibility. In itself, the presence or absence of such a freedom makes no difference.

Let us suppose that in these cases, just as Frankfurt hypothesizes, Jones does lack the freedom to do otherwise. Do these Frankfurt-cases actually show that even in the absence of a freedom to act otherwise, Jones can still be morally responsible? If so, how?

Perhaps, it might be thought, Frankfurt-cases are ones where it is just obvious that Jones is morally responsible. So once it is clear that in them the freedom to do otherwise is lacking, Frankfurt's conclusion that moral responsibility has nothing to do with freedom will just follow. But why is it obvious that Jones is morally responsible? Perhaps it is enough that when Jones acts, he does so without in any way being caused to act by whatever has removed his freedom to do otherwise. In other words, Jones is responsible because he is acting 'off his own back'.

But that is not enough to establish Jones's moral responsibility. For the fact of Jones' action alone is not enough to establish moral responsibility—even if we add that the action is not imposed on the agent from without. Jones' responsibility for the action must be based, as we have seen, on some power he has over what he does. There must be some power of self-determination possessed by Jones that bases his moral responsibility for performing the action. And, for Frankfurt's project to succeed, this power must be exercisable apart from any freedom to do otherwise— as a one-way power. So if Jones' moral responsibility in Frankfurt-cases is supposed to be obvious, it must be obvious that in those cases there really is a one-way power of self-determination that Jones can exercise, and on the basis of which he is morally responsible.

But if this is obvious, why not establish the point as Calvin tried to establish it— without super-complicated thought experiments, and simply by specifying what the one-way power is, and claiming that the exercise of such a power, when its nature is properly considered, is clearly sufficient to constitute the exercise of self-determination, and so to base moral responsibility? For if such a power does not anyway look on inspection as a convincing basis of moral responsibility, it will not help to provide yet more entirely hypothetical cases where the same power operates, but with the further detail of an actual lack of any freedom to act otherwise. Only those already convinced that we have in this one-way power a sufficient basis of moral responsibility will read these further cases too as cases where the agent really is morally responsible.

But perhaps this is to misunderstand the point of the Frankfurt-cases. Their point is really to take cases where his opponents would already admit an agent's moral responsibility—and show those opponents that the moral responsibility that they admit cannot after all depend on any freedom to act otherwise. That is, Frankfurt takes cases where his opponents would already accept that the agent is morally responsible—which *ex hypothesi* are cases where the agent is free to act otherwise;

and hopes to show that these cases can be transformed into examples where the agent is not free to act otherwise, but without change in any features of the case that might be relevant to the agent's moral responsibility. The removal of the agent's freedom to act otherwise must make no difference to how the agent acts and to the power deployed by him to determine how he acts. That's why Frankfurt is so keen to emphasize that, with the removal of Jones' freedom, 'Indeed everything happened just as it would have happened without Black's presence in the situation and without his readiness to intrude into it.'[17] If Black's potent but inert presence does indeed make no difference, someone who believes in Jones' moral responsibility given his freedom to do otherwise and Black's concomitant absence, will remain committed to admitting Jones' moral responsibility even given Black's presence—and even given the consequent lack of any freedom to act otherwise. Having admitted Jones' moral responsibility initially, they must go on admitting it even when Black is introduced into the story.

But this strategy will only work if the removal of a freedom to act otherwise does make no difference to how the agent acts and to the power deployed by him to determine how he acts. And that will only be true if agents can determine how they act by exercising power in one-way form, and not in a form that is inherently multi-way. The problem for Frankfurt is that those who believe that moral responsibility does depend on a freedom to do otherwise should not accept his view that human self-determination is exercised as a one-way power. They are committed to an opposing position—that self-determination is only ever exercised by us through a power of freedom that is multi-way. Why else would moral responsibility depend on the freedom to do otherwise? For if self-determination were exercised as a one-way power, then the irrelevance of a freedom to do otherwise to moral responsibility would follow immediately—as we have already seen, and without having to appeal to complicated Frankfurtian thought-experiments.

Frankfurt's opponents cannot be expected to admit that the presence or absence even of a Black who does not actually intervene is irrelevant to Jones' moral responsibility. For in so far as the presence of Black, willing and able to intervene, and with consequent control over Jones' action, did imply the absence in Jones of any power to act otherwise, Black's presence would—in their view—also imply that Jones lacked any power to determine for himself how he would act. And lacking that power, Jones would lack moral responsibility for his actions. Thanks to what Black's intentions and ability to determine Jones imply for Jones' own powers, Jones simply cannot be determining his action as he might in a world where Black were absent.[18]

---

[17] Harry Frankfurt, 'Alternate possibilities and moral responsibility', p. 7.

[18] Robert Kane endorses what he calls 'a powerful intuition':

> we feel that if a Frankfurt-controller [such as Black] never actually intervened throughout an agent's entire lifetime, so that the agent always acted on his or her own, then the *mere presence* of the controller should not make any difference to the agent's ultimate responsibility. *The Significance of Free Will*, p. 143.

The work is all done, then, by Frankfurt's assumption that self-determination is exercised as a one-way power. And the Frankfurt-cases are irrelevant to the argument. They do no actual work themselves. For once we grant that self-determination is exercised as a one-way power, then, as we have seen, Frankfurt's claim of the irrelevance of freedom to moral responsibility follows immediately, and without the need to appeal to complex Frankfurt-cases. On the other hand, without this assumption, the Frankfurt-cases cannot be used to prove freedom's irrelevance anyway. For Black's presence or absence can no longer be assumed to imply no difference in Jones' power to determine for himself what he does. When Frankfurt expressly asserts, 'Indeed *everything* happened just as it would have happened without Black's presence in the situation and without his readiness to intrude into it', that claim can only be true if the power exercised over Jones' action to determine what he does is not inherently multi-way. And that is just the point at issue.

So appealing to Frankfurt-cases has, in reality, done nothing to advance the debate. In fact the cases have proved a dangerous philosophical distraction. What purport to be proof cases are simply situations described in terms that frankly assume the view of self-determination that Frankfurt has to prove—that self-determination can be exercised in one-way and not multi-way form. And so the cases have only clouded the issue. They have discouraged philosophers from attending critically to that central question—what form the power of self-determination really takes.

The supposed irrelevance of freedom to moral responsibility really does hang on the assumption that self-determination can be exercised as a one-way power. It is this assumption that has to be proved; and it is this assumption, once proved, that delivers the supposed conclusion. So defenders of Frankfurt's programme do need to make this assumption good. They should clearly state the assumption and defend it. For it is far from self-evidently true. In fact, to the extent that we naturally think of self-determination as involving alternatives, as its being up to us which actions we perform, there might even be a presumption against the possibility of self-determination taking one-way form.

The need to deliver the assumption seems not sufficiently appreciated by Frankfurt's supporters. Consider again Martha Klein's fantasy of the self-determining but unfree agent—the agent whose every action resulted from prior causal determination, but through his own prior action. Suppose we grant that because this agent's every action is causally predetermined, he must lack the freedom to do otherwise.[19] That still leaves a crucial question—a question to which Klein in fact never gives any

---

But what is crucial is the implications of that presence for the agent's power. If Black is not only intent on preventing the agent from acting otherwise, but is fully able to prevent him from so acting, and if (as is supposed) Black's presence equipped with such an intention and such a power over the agent is enough to imply the agent lacks all power to act otherwise, then that may be very relevant to the agent's ultimate responsibility. It will be relevant if the agent can determine his actions for himself only through exercising a multi-way power to act otherwise.

[19] In fact I shall later suggest, in Chapter 15, that even libertarians should not grant this.

answer: why, in the absence of this power, should we so blithely assume that the agent's actions could still be self-determined and so his responsibility? Granted, each action performed by the agent would be caused and determined by another action performed by the very same agent. But the self-determined quality of the determining action is no more obvious than that of the determined. The agent is clearly performing actions. And these actions are not being caused by any factor outside the agent. But, in the absence of a freedom to do otherwise, can the agent still be determining for himself that he acts as he does?

Obviously, our actions' *self*-determined quality cannot be exhausted by the fact that they happen to be uncaused by certain kinds of prior event. Non-actions such as beliefs and desires can be thus uncaused too without our *ipso facto* being morally responsible for them. Mere chanciness or mere lack of certain kinds of causation from without is not a source of responsibility. If we are distinctively responsible for how we act that is because we have some genuine power to determine for ourselves what happens—a power which we exercise over and through how we act. And such power cannot plausibly be constituted by the mere fact that our actions are unaffected by certain kinds of prior event. That is simply to report the non-involvement of one kind of power, not the involvement of another.

8.4 One-Way Self-Determination—How Not to Understand It

Anyone who wants to deny the dependence of moral responsibility on a freedom to do otherwise must explain how the self-determination that moral responsibility requires can take one-way form. Self-determination must be shown to be explicable in terms of some form of one-way power.

So any supposed one-way power of self-determination that is to take freedom's place had better really be what it pretends. It really must be a genuine case of power—a capacity exercised by us to determine our actions and their consequences. It must not be some more general mere capacity that does not involve the exercise of power by us. And of course if the power is supposed to base a moral responsibility that is specifically for action, that power must likewise be specific to action. Otherwise it will do nothing to explain why it should be specifically for our agency that we are responsible.[20] But these are conditions not met by some current proposals for what self-determination in one-way form might consist in. Not only do these proposals not pick out a power that is specific to agency. They fail to pick out a genuine capacity to determine—a genuine power at all.

[20] None of the writers discussed—Fischer, Ravizza, Wolf, Klein, Frankfurt, Stump—doubts that it is agency for which we are responsible. None follows Scanlon and Adams in severing the tie of moral responsibility to being for action and omission. The question arises whether, if we do not appeal to freedom to explain moral responsibility, this tie of moral responsibility to being for agency can be preserved.

Thus, in their *Responsibility and Control*, John Martin Fischer and Mark Ravizza deny any dependence of moral responsibility on a freedom to do otherwise. They maintain that we can be morally responsible for how we act even in the absence of such a freedom. But they agree that there is still a requirement that the responsible agent's actions be self-determined—that they be performed 'freely'. Moral responsibility is still supposed to depend on a kind of agency-specific 'control'—but not the control that constitutes multi-way freedom.

> When we are morally responsible for our actions, we do possess a kind of control. So the traditional assumption of the association of moral responsibility with control is quite correct. But the relevant sort of control need not involve alternative possibilities.[21]

They call the control that does involve the freedom to do otherwise 'regulative control'. This regulative control is supposed in turn to involve the complex com-presence of two distinct one-way powers—the power to do A and the power to refrain. And the one-way power in question is called 'guidance-control'. It is really on this one-way guidance control that, in their view, our moral responsibility depends. But what is this 'guidance-control'? It turns out to consist in the fact that our actions are the products of a psychological mechanism that is sufficiently responsive to justifications for and against.[22] That does not mean that the agent is actually free not to perform the action. It's just that the process which gives rise to the action is one which would tend to be activated by justifications for the action's performance, and tend not to be activated by justifications against. Multi-way freedom is being replaced in the theory of moral responsibility by reason-responsiveness—by the capacity for reason.

But if 'guidance-control' is just a form of reason-responsiveness, then, despite Fischer and Ravizza's terminological pretensions to the contrary, we do not have here a form of self-determination in one-way form. And it is clear why. We do not have here a conception of self-determination at all, let alone one that is agency-specific as freedom is. We simply have a capacity to exercise reason—a capacity that extends beyond action to our attitudes generally, and that is not a capacity on our part to determine anything. The capacity for reason is, as we have seen, a second-order capacity to exercise other capacities in a way responsive to justifications, and that generically involves, if anything, our subjection to power rather than our exercise of it. In which case how does the appeal to 'guidance-control' explain how we have a distinctively moral responsibility for anything, let alone why it should be for action in particular that we are so responsible? How is action self-determined as reasoned and reason-responsive beliefs and desires are not?

---

[21] John Martin Fischer and Mark Ravizza, *Responsibility and Control* (Cambridge: Cambridge University Press, 1998), pp. 32–3.
[22] See *Responsibility and Control*, pp. 28–55.

We cannot appeal to mere reason-responsiveness in order to explain moral responsibility—or we cannot if we want to preserve the tie of moral responsibility to self-determination. Identifying the exercise of moral responsibility with the exercise of rationality is exactly how a philosopher such as Scanlon seeks to *detach* moral responsibility from any substantial conception of self-determination and so too from any tie to agency.

Susan Wolf faces similar difficulties. As we have already seen, in her *Freedom and Reason* Wolf too has argued for the view that moral responsibility need not involve a capacity to act otherwise. Moral responsibility depends on a capacity to act rightly or rationally, which is sufficiently provided in the case of a rational and right-acting agent by the fact that on the basis of their rationality they actually have so acted. It is only the wrongdoers or the irrational whose moral responsibility, in depending on a capacity to act rightly, depends on a capacity to act otherwise. But the problem with Wolf's general view is clear. Moral responsibility involves, on the face of it, the same idea in all cases. When we hold people morally responsible for what they do, we are in all cases putting the plus or the minus, the admirability or the fault in their action, down to them as their responsibility—which is a further claim beyond the initial observation that there was something admirable or criticizable about what they did. And this same moral responsibility presupposes some power to determine for themselves what they did—a power that is exercised over how they act.

What does this power amount to? If Wolf's programme of detaching moral responsibility from the freedom to do otherwise is to work, the power must be exercisable in one-way form. But it is not enough for Wolf just to appeal to the capacity to conform to reason. For, again, that is not a power on our part to determine anything, but a mere capacity involving, to a degree, some subjection on our part to power, and one which we anyway possess in relation to non-actions as well as actions. Nothing in that idea explains why we have a distinctively moral responsibility for anything at all, let alone why it is for our actions that we are peculiarly so responsible. Nor, to meet the latter problem, will it do to appeal to the idea of a more specific capacity to conform to reason *in respect of how we act*. That specifies no distinctive kind of power that peculiarly determines agency, but simply labels one case of a more general capacity we have in relation to action and non-action alike. Granted the agent who acts well may have conformed to reason. But in what way has she determined for herself that she shall so conform, so that she is responsible for that conformity? If not by exercising control or a power to act otherwise, in what way? Wolf provides no answer. The answer needed is an alternative conception of self-determination—and one that does not appeal simply to the idea of rationality, but to something recognizable as a power to determine things for oneself.

What of the appeal to voluntariness? The suggestion, going back at least as far as Calvin, and supported today by Frankfurt, is that it is enough for agents to be determining for themselves what they do that they be acting voluntarily, as an effect of a desire so to act. By contrast to reason, this appeal to voluntariness certainly involves a power, and moreover a power that is very plausibly agency-specific. To act voluntarily, motivated by a pro attitude towards so doing, is to perform an action. But we have already mentioned an obvious criticism of this proposal. It involves a problematic displacement of the self from self-determination. Self-determination involves determination by the self. But voluntariness, the power supposed to explain and constitute this power of self-determination, is a power not immediately of the self, but of an entity distinct from the self—a passive motivation for which the self is not responsible.

This raises two related difficulties. The first is that a compatibilist conception of moral responsibility is being built into the theory from the outset. Self-determination is being explained in terms of the determination of action by some entity that is distinct from the agent, and that, as prior to what the agent is responsible for, is not itself the agent's responsibility. But this obviously presupposes that the self-determined character of action must be compatible with the action's determination by factors for which the agent is not responsible. The problem is clear. Apparently conceptually very competent philosophers, and non-philosophers too, disagree about whether compatibilism about moral responsibility is true. But that makes it implausible that compatibilism about moral responsibility, even if it proves to be true, should follow immediately and trivially from the very concept of the power that leaves us responsible.

The worry is reinforced, and in a way that does not involve the issue of incompatibilism, by the distinctive nature of moral blame—the criticism that asserts moral responsibility. Ordinary rational criticism operates, as we have seen, at just one level. It criticizes the person by reference to some deficiency in a state or occurrence in the life of that person. We criticize someone as irrational because they hold or are disposed to hold attitudes that are irrational. The criticism is of defective states and of the person just as possessing those defective states. Blame, on the other hand, does not simply criticize someone for deficiencies in their attitudes or other states but puts their possession of such states down to them as their fault. This supposes something more—a problem not simply with events and states in the agent's life, but with the agent as determiner of those events and states. But explaining such determination in terms of voluntariness removes this distinctive element. The supposed problem with the agent as determiner is turned back into a problem that primarily involves an event or state within their life, such as a motivation, and the agent just as possessor of the event or state. In which case, what is left of the idea that the agent is especially responsible, in a way that goes beyond ordinary criticizability?

Neither reason nor voluntariness looks like providing an adequate conception of self-determination in one-way form. Indeed it might be thought that there can be no such conception, and that it is a conceptual truth that self-determination must take the form of multi-way freedom. But that may not be true. Self-determination in one-way form may indeed be possible, though perhaps only conceptually so. For one-way self-determination may involve a kind of power that, though conceptually possible, is not actually part of human nature, and is not a capacity that humans actually possess and exercise.

8.5 One-Way Self-Determination—How to Understand It

Frankfurt's attempt to divorce moral responsibility from a freedom to do otherwise is part of a broadly naturalistic theory of self-determination. Central to the project is an exercise in naturalistic reductionism in the tradition of classical English-language compatibilism. Our power to determine action for ourselves is identified with causal power of a kind found in wider nature—one-way causal power attaching to occurrences. But self-determination is not obviously susceptible of such a naturalistic interpretation—as Thomas Hobbes fully realized, rejecting the very possibility of self-determination outright.

Our ordinary conception of self-determination takes it to occur only as a multi-way power—only as a power to produce more than one outcome—and this multi-wayness is important to its ethical significance. It is this multi-wayness that leaves moral responsibility dependent on a freedom to act otherwise. Take away the power to do otherwise, and you take away the power of self-determination altogether. But multi-wayness is clearly not what distinguishes self-determination from ordinary causal power. For we saw in the last chapter that probabilistic causation could involve multi-way causal power: one and the same power could operate, under a given set of circumstances, to produce a variety of possible outcomes. Even the thought, essential to self-determination, that the bearer of the power must be the self, the agent, and not a mere occurrence, does not obviously differentiate self-determination from ordinary causation. Ordinary causal power has often been understood to be a power not, or not simply, of occurrences, but a power of substances too. The cause of the window's breaking may be understood to be not just the event of the brick's hitting it, but the brick itself, when it hits the window.

What is most distinctive of self-determination as a power, and most sharply distinguishes it from ordinary causal power? What is distinctive flows from the basic thought that in exercising the power the agent must really be determining outcomes *for himself*. The agent is the determiner of what he does, and in a way that does not subordinate his role either to prior determining factors for which he is not responsible or to simple chance. The alternative to the action's determination by factors for which the agent is not responsible is not, as Hume alleged, the operation of mere chance, but determination of the action by the agent. It is this aspect of self-determination that makes incompatibilism about the power, and about the moral responsibility that rests upon it, at least an initial theoretical possibility, and so—as it clearly is—a matter for real debate, rather than something ruled out immediately, just by our very concept of what the power amounts to.

This is missing from ordinary causation. To the extent that an ordinary cause determines an outcome, this involves prior factors, the circumstances under which it finds itself and its possession, under those circumstances, of a power to determine that outcome, ensuring that it operates to produce that very outcome. How the cause will operate is predetermined, and not left to the cause. If the cause's operation is not so predetermined—if that or how it operates is not already settled by its powers and circumstances—then the cause can at most influence and not determine what will happen. Its operation to produce a given outcome will be random to some degree, and the outcome will depend on mere chance.

What prevents this being true where self-determination is concerned? We have seen that two factors are crucial. First, contingency of determination, which leaves it open whether an agent with the power to determine a given outcome will so exercise his power. The agent's exercise of his power to produce a given outcome is not, as in the case of a determining cause, guaranteed by factors for which he need not be responsible—by his circumstances and by the very nature of his power. But nor, as in the case of a probabilistic cause, is the outcome simply left open by the limited nature of the power, so that the outcome depends on mere chance. The agent has the power to determine that the outcome happens; but the outcome's occurrence is contingent on whether the agent actually exercises this power—something not guaranteed by the agent's mere possession of it. This seems essential to its being true that the agent determines the outcome *for himself.*

The second factor is freedom—not in relation to outcomes, but in relation to the agent's very exercise of power. The agent's exercise of power is not undetermined, but up to the agent, so that the agent determines that exercise for himself. Self-determination involves the operation of the power being determined by the self—by the bearer. In the case of a multi-way power that can operate in more than one way, to produce any one of a range of possible outcomes, the bearer determines for himself how the power is exercised, to produce this outcome or that. The concept of freedom applies—not to pick out the way the power relates to outcomes, but to pick out the bearer's relation to the power. It is up to the bearer or within his control how he exercises his power. This involvement of the agent as determinant of his own exercise of power is what Hobbes most objected to in his attack on the very idea of self-determination.

But we can detach both contingency of determination and freedom in relation to the power from multi-wayness—from the identity of freedom as a power to produce more than one outcome.

It is possible, at least conceptually, for a power to determine to be one-way, and still involve contingency of determination. Contingency of determination means that an agent can be present with the power then to determine that he does A, along with all the conditions required for the power's successful exercise—and not exercise it. But the possibility of not exercising one's power to determine one outcome does not amount to the power to determine another. An agent who failed to determine that he did A might perfectly well lack the power to determine that he refrains, and indeed might do A in any case—though other than through having himself determined that he does so. In such a case it could perhaps be that, as Frankfurt imagined, were the agent not to exercise his power to determine that he did A, something else would operate to determine that he did A anyway.

Similarly there could be a one-way power the exercise of which was up to the agent. Obviously if the power were one-way—under given circumstances there is only one outcome its exercise can produce—it could not be up to us *how* we exercised it, to produce this outcome or that. In relation to a one-way power, there could be no room for what we have termed a freedom of *specification*. But it could still be up to us whether we exercised the power at all. There is room, then, for our possession, even in relation to a one-way power, of a *freedom of exercise*—a freedom to use the power or not. Self-determination could involve the exercise of a power to determine but one outcome, where it was up to the agent, not which outcome he determined—that is fixed by the one-way nature of the power—but whether he exercised the power at all.

We can then have a power to determine outcomes involving contingency of determination and freedom in relation to the power—but a power that is one-way. And that would surely amount to a capacity for self-determination. The agent can have the power to determine what he does, without his mere possession of the power necessitating its exercise. Instead whether he exercises the power is up to him. If then he does exercise his power to determine that he does A, he determines this *for himself*. And he can have such a power without *ipso facto* having any power to determine otherwise. There can be self-determination without multi-wayness.

Of course we ordinarily conceive of self-determination as involving power or control over alternatives—as involving freedom, not merely in relation to the power, but in relation to outcomes. But notice that we could even have this freedom in relation to outcomes without multi-wayness. Though if we did possess such a freedom in relation to outcomes without multi-wayness, it would be in a form that deprived that freedom of its ordinary ethical significance. Freedom in that form would still involve alternative actions or outcomes being up to us. But it would no longer involve the exercise of a power to determine otherwise.

How could a power of self-determination in one-way form give us freedom as involving control over outcomes? How could it leave it up to us whether we do A or whether we refrain? For the outcomes to be left up to the agent it might be enough that the agent should possess a power to determine that he does A and a distinct power to determine that he refrains—each one-way power involving contingency of determination, with a freedom of exercise in relation to each of these powers. That would leave it up to the agent which power he exercised and so whether he did A or not—just as freedom requires. But no multi-way power would be involved in the determination of action; no power to do otherwise—to determine alternative actions or outcomes—would ever be exercised by the agent in the determination of what he actually does. In which case the power to do or determine otherwise would remain an inert extra. It might be lacking without making any difference to what the agent is actually doing, or to the power actually exercised by him to determine what he does. In which case the power or freedom to do otherwise, in relation to outcomes, would be irrelevant to moral responsibility, just as Frankfurt supposes. So if we did possess control over outcomes in this form, it would be control deprived of its ordinary ethical significance. Freedom could still involve alternative actions or outcomes being up to us. But freedom, even in that form, would no longer involve the exercise of any power to determine otherwise.

Such an account of freedom as power over alternatives by way of action would be *ontologically* reductive. Freedom would no longer be characterized as a multi-way power—a single power to determine more than one outcome. It would be decomposed into a combination of distinct one-way powers. But the theory of freedom would no longer be naturalistic. As involving contingency of determination and freedom of exercise, the one-way power constitutive of freedom would no longer be ordinary causation.

So this account of one-way self-determination is wholly detached from any naturalistic programme. There is no attempt to identify self-determination with a kind of power, such as causation, of a kind found in wider nature. Just because of this, the power involved is plainly a form of self-determination adequate to base moral responsibility. The bearer of the one-way power is the agent, and not some other entity for which the agent has no responsibility; and it is genuinely up to the agent whether he exercises the power. So the power of self-determination involved is plainly sufficient, on any reasonable view, to base moral blame as ordinarily understood. This is a coherent and fully substantial conception of self-determination sufficient to base moral responsibility. So it looks as though one central position agreed on by all of Calvin, Frankfurt, Stump, and Klein alike, is true. There is no conceptual dependence of moral responsibility on a freedom of alternatives at the point of action. It is conceptually perfectly open that an agent be morally responsible for what they do, without possessing a freedom to determine otherwise at the point of outcomes. On that specific issue, Frankfurt seems to be right.

Frankfurt supposes, though, that from the conceptual possibility of moral responsibility without the freedom to do otherwise, it follows that our moral responsibility is actually independent of the freedom to do otherwise. But that does not follow. Our moral responsibility may still depend on a freedom to do otherwise, but without this following from the very concepts of moral responsibility and self-determination. For it might be a non-conceptual or a contingent truth, but a truth nonetheless, that as humans are, the power that we actually possess and exercise to determine how we act occurs only as a multi-way power. In the absence of this power, as human nature is actually constructed we would be simply incapable of self-determination in any form. In the absence of a freedom to do otherwise, we would not be morally responsible at all. There is nothing in Frankfurt's arguments to rule out the possibility that we are actually capable of self-determination only in this multi-way form. Indeed, as we have seen, Frankfurt's arguments entirely beg the question against multi-wayness.

Our belief in freedom does seem to be a belief in our possession of a multi-way power to determine alternatives. But because it is at least conceptually open that we could be morally responsible without such a power, this speaks against one hypothesis about the possible origin of our belief in multi-way freedom. The hypothesis, a sceptical one, is one that we raised in Chapter 6—the error theory of our belief in freedom that appealed to ethics. According to this theory, our belief in multi-way freedom is not based on anything genuinely in human nature, or even on the way that human nature and human action is represented in experience to us. Instead it comes from an intrusion of ethics into psychology. We postulate the power only because forced into it by our belief in our moral responsibility and by our practice of blaming people, and putting their faults down to them as their fault.

This hypothesis is put in doubt because it now appears that we could intelligibly hold people morally responsible for what they do without any belief in freedom as a multi-way power. We have just established that we could operate a theory of moral blame and moral responsibility that justifiably puts faults in the agent down to the agent as their fault, and even left room for an incompatibilist conception of that responsibility and the power that based it, but which did not involve a conception of that power as occurring only in multi-way form, and that consequently did not treat the agent's responsibility as depending on the power to do otherwise. Belief in the multi-wayness of self-determination and in a freedom of specification in relation to that power seems strictly inessential to our ordinary understanding of moral blame. That belief in the multi-wayness of self-determination must surely come from outside ethics—perhaps from what human nature contains in itself, or, at least, from the way that human nature and human action is represented to us.

8.6 Freedom in Relation to the Power

Frankurt's discussion of moral responsibility only ever considered freedom in relation to outcomes—as a freedom to determine otherwise. But now we see that freedom can be considered in another way—as a freedom not in relation to the outcomes determined by a power, but in relation to the very exercise of that power itself. The concept of freedom is employed in thinking not just about our relation to the outcomes we determine for ourselves, but also about our relation to our own power to determine them. Indeed, freedom considered in this last way seems essential to self-determination. How can I determine for myself that I do A, if it is in no way up to me whether I so exercise my power?

Frankfurt's neglect of freedom in relation to power itself is hardly surprising. It is a neglect built into the naturalism inherited by him from compatibilism in its classical English-language form. That tradition is wholly committed to accounting for freedom in terms of causation as that power operates through wider nature. And we simply do not allow for freedom in relation to the exercise of causal power in nature. It is not up to any ordinary cause whether or how it exercises its causal power. From a naturalistic viewpoint, then, assimilating self-determination to ordinary causation, one would never consider whether moral responsibility might depend on an agent's having control, not over alternative outcomes, but over his own power to determine outcomes.

But as soon as we consider our conception of self-determination fairly, and seek to examine its content free of naturalistic assumptions about what is metaphysically the case—as soon as we distinguish the analytic problem from the metaphysical—the question of freedom in relation to the power arises immediately. When we determine for ourselves what we do, the exercise by us of the power to determine is not dictated by the very nature of the power; our operation to determine that we do something is not necessitated like that of an ordinary cause. Rather that or how we exercise our power is up to us.

Inheriting the assumptions of a metaphysical naturalism that was, by his time, long entrenched, Frankfurt easily ignored this element of our conception of self-determination. But for Hobbes, who was that naturalism's pioneer rather its inheritor, things were different. He might officially proclaim that we have no real understanding of a power of self-determination, or of any power beyond efficient causation. But he was still highly sensitive to the content of that understanding nonetheless. As we have seen, Hobbes was very well aware that self-determination involves the idea of a freedom in relation to the power, and condemned that idea as incoherent because viciously regressive. It would imply a further exercise of power distinct from the exercise of power determined—a prior exercise of power by the agent to determine how, or whether, his power was exercised.

What, then, does freedom in relation to the power really involve? We saw that Hobbes' objection to its very possibility might not be decisive, because it seems to get the content of our conception of self-determination crucially wrong. The agent's control over his power, as ordinarily understood, does not involve a further exercise of power distinct from the exercise of the power controlled. The agent controls the power just in exercising it. That is how we understand freedom as a multi-way power over alternatives. In exercising control over outcomes I *ipso facto* determine for myself how the control is exercised. This is just what control over outcomes comes to—a power to produce outcomes the manner of exercise of which I determine for myself. In one and the same exercise of power I produce one outcome rather than another, and I determine how the power is exercised.

As it is for self-determination in multi-way form, so too for one-way self-determination: in exercising his power to determine the outcome, the agent *ipso facto* controls whether he exercises it. But this control does not involve some prior exercise of power to determine or prevent exercise of the outcome-determining power. It is simply that if the agent does exercise his outcome-determining power, he does so controlling whether or not it is exercised. Control of the power is just a feature of the exercise of the power controlled.

But how might control of a power be just a feature of the power controlled? How can it arise without involving some prior exercise of power to determine the power controlled? There is one very natural answer. Control of the power is as much a feature of the power controlled as the way that power determines outcomes. For where self-determination is concerned, control of the power is just the same feature as that power's mode of operation—contingency of determination. Control of the power and contingency of determination are one and the same phenomenon. In other words, in thinking of the agent as controlling how they exercise the power, we are simply thinking of what contingency of determination implies, not for the power's relation to outcomes, but for the agent's relation to the power.

It certainly looks as though freedom in relation to the power requires and implies contingency of determination; mere possession of the power in determining form must not guarantee its exercise. Suppose that contingency of determination did not apply, and that my mere possession of a power to determine a given outcome did necessitate that I so exercise it. It seems very hard to see how my so exercising that power could still be up to me. But nor do we allow for contingency of determination in any case where we do not also suppose that the operation of a power is up to its possessor. This shows up in the way we think about chance and what chance implies for power. Chance is the absence of causal determination. But what chance implies for power depends very much on the nature of the power and on whether its bearer controls the power.

Take a cause which determines that a particle accelerates, but which might produce more than one possible rate of acceleration. Either that cause might produce an acceleration of rate A or it might produce an acceleration of rate B, but it is not determined which. Perhaps, given the cause, the chance of rate A being produced is 0.6, that B is produced is 0.4. The nature of the cause's power leaves its operation open. Where causation is concerned, we understand the chance nature of the outcome as reflecting simply a limitation in the cause's power. The cause determines that the particle will accelerate, but it does not determine the precise rate. The cause influences that rate, but the final rate depends on mere chance.

Suppose, though, that while the chances of the outcomes given the cause remained the same, the cause could determine how it exercised its power: it was up to the cause whether it exercised its power in a way that produced rate A or in a way that produced rate B. The cause would then have the power to determine the rate of acceleration, and the significance of chance for how the cause would operate would be quite different. It would reflect just a lack of prior determination of how that power would be exercised, and not a limitation in the power. The cause would be like a self-determining agent who has the power under given circumstances contingently to determine more than one outcome—and who has this power in circumstances where it is causally undetermined, and so chance, how he will exercise it.

Of course we do not actually understand probabilistic causes as capable of determining for themselves how they exercise their power. But nor do we think of them as determining outcomes, though contingently, either. We think of chance in their case as no more than randomness—as chance and nothing more. Since it is not up to a cause whether or how it exercises its power, chance can only do one job, which is to mark the limited nature of the cause's power—a limitation that leaves the outcome dependent on mere chance.

If, on the other hand, the operation of a power really is up to its bearer, the chance nature of the outcome need not arise from a limitation in the power. It may have instead to do with the bearer—with a lack of causal determination of how the bearer will exercise control over what, nevertheless, may yet be a power on their part to determine. Once we think of the operation of the power as being up to its bearer there is, then, another role for chance to play. The chance nature of the outcome may reflect, as a factor distinct from any limitation in the power, a lack of determination of the bearer who controls the power. The power may still be a power to determine. But its exercise is up to the bearer—and it is not determined causally whether or how the bearer will exercise this control.

Contingency of determination and freedom in relation to the power are, then, one and the same phenomenon. It is possible for a power to determine an outcome contingently when and only when the chance nature of the outcome need not reflect some limitation in the power to produce it. And that will be so when the outcome depends not just on the extent of the power to produce it, but on control by that power's possessor of its operation. Where such control is present, the outcome can be chance, not because of some limitation in the power to produce it, but simply because of a lack of causal determination of how the agent will exercise that control. Where such control of the power is lacking, as with ordinary causation, then by contrast chance reflects a limitation in the power. With causes, outcomes are determined whenever the power exists then to determine them, and they will be chance only where that power is lacking.

So a power can determine outcomes contingently, in a way consistent with the outcomes still being chance, only if its bearer controls its operation. If it is contingent that the bearer exercises his power to determine at all, we have a freedom of exercise; it is up to the bearer to exercise the power or not. If it is contingent how the bearer exercises a multi-way power—in the circumstances the bearer could exercise one and the same power to determine more than one outcome—we have a freedom of specification; it is up to the bearer how he exercises his power.

8.7 Conclusion

Once we examine in more detail what one-way self-determination might involve, it becomes clear how complex the idea of self-determination really is. For the involvement of freedom in our conception of self-determination is not primarily in respect of the actions or outcomes that our power determines, but, it seems, in respect of our relation to the power itself. When we determine outcomes for ourselves, those outcomes do not depend simply on the nature of our power. The outcomes also depend on us as power-bearers capable of freely determining whether or how we exercise our power.

The kind of freedom that has principally concerned Frankfurt and his followers was not this freedom, but the freedom to act otherwise—freedom with respect to outcomes. Does moral responsibility ever depend on this freedom? Now where this dependence of moral responsibility on freedom was concerned, Frankfurt and his followers ignored a crucial possibility, that our power to determine our own actions might take multi-way form. And this is strange, since multi-wayness seems to be a possible feature even of ordinary causal power. But their principal omission is to have neglected to examine where freedom may really matter—linked to contingency of determination, as a feature of the self-determining agent's relation to his power. In this they have shown themselves far less perspicacious than Thomas Hobbes, who fully realized the importance to self-determination of contingency of determination and freedom in relation to the power itself, and, disbelieving in their coherence, denied the possibility of self-determination altogether.

Frankfurt was clearly wrong to suppose it a conceptual truth that the freedom to do otherwise must always be irrelevant to moral responsibility. Frankfurt's arguments for this conclusion are wholly question-begging. But it is equally a mistake to suppose that any dependence of moral responsibility on a freedom over alternatives must be conceptual too. The dependence, if it holds at all, rests on something that, it seems, could have been otherwise—which is the multi-way form that our power of self-determination actually happens to take. It may be that other aspects of moral responsibility and the self-determination that bases it will prove to be conceptually open too—such as the very debate between compatibilist and incompatibilist conceptions of that power. And this is a possibility to which we shall return.

What does seem clear is that certain reductive accounts of self-determination as something one-way are implausible from the start, on conceptual grounds alone. We cannot see self-determination as provided by the agent's capacity for rationality—and so by his capacity to act rightly. For we have seen that the capacity for rationality is not a power on the agent's part, but rather a capacity to exercise other capacities, some being powers or capacities to determine, some not, in a way sensitive to justifications. And voluntariness—a capacity to do as one wills—does not constitute a power of self-determination either, since the power it involves attaches not to the agent immediately, but to a passive attitude within him.

But there is of course a further obstacle to explaining self-determination in terms of voluntariness. The power of voluntariness will not serve to explain our moral responsibility for, in particular, actions of the will—for the actions of decision and intention-formation that we ordinarily see as our own doing. For these decisions are not voluntary; yet, as we are now about to see, they really are as much actions, and intuitively self-determinable actions, as are the voluntary actions they motivate and explain.

9

The Practical Reason-Based Model and Its Past

9.1 Volitionism

So far we have been looking at the voluntariness-based model of action which dominates contemporary philosophy. On this model's approach, if our decisions themselves are to be actions, that can only be because those decisions are further cases of voluntariness, to be understood on the model of the actions decided upon which those decisions motivate and explain. So to be actions themselves, decisions too must be motivated by pro attitudes towards taking them, such as by decisions or desires to decide. But decisions do not appear to be taken voluntarily in this way; which is why, from Hobbes through Ryle to Bernard Williams and Galen Strawson in our own day, there has been so much scepticism about whether action really does occur in the will.

If decisions or intention-formations are actions, it seems that we need quite another model of action. There must be something about decisions that makes them actions that has nothing to do with pro attitudes towards so deciding, but rather has to do with their character as a distinctive kind of attitude or attitude-formation in their own right.

But then we face a problem. It may well be that this model of the agency of decisions, a model that has to do with the peculiar nature of decisions as attitude-formations, cannot in turn apply, at least directly, to the actions decided upon. A story that has to do with the special character of decisions as non-voluntary attitude-formations is unlikely to fit, or so it might be thought, the voluntary actions those decisions motivate—actions that in general appear not to be attitude-formations, but which include ordinary bodily actions, such as crossing the road and the like. What, then, makes those further actions decided upon actions too?

Perhaps simply the fact that these further voluntary actions occur as effects of actions of the will that aim at their occurrence. There are, on this view, two kinds of action. Action in its primary form occurs as an event within the mind—as a decision or the formation of an intention—and involves capacities that are psychological, the peculiar nature of which explains why decisions or intention-formations count as actions. These actions have as their goal the performance of further actions—the voluntary actions intended—involving quite different capacities, such as capacities for moving one's limbs and the like. These voluntary actions then count as actions themselves not because they share the same action-constitutive properties that belong to actions of the will, but simply because they occur through being willed. Voluntary actions count as actions just as intended effects of prior action, and take on the goals or purposes of the actions directed at their occurrence.

And so we arrive at a form of *volitionism*. According to volitionism, decisions form the primary case of action. Decisions and intention-formations count as intentional or deliberate actions of ours as distinctively practical or action-constitutive kinds of attitude-formation—by virtue of some psychological property or properties applying to these actions of the will alone. The rest of what we do, the voluntary actions willed that these decisions and intention-formations then motivate, count as our intentional doing too—but only indirectly, as intended effects of these prior decisions of the will. The core of any volitionist approach to action, then, is its account of what makes decisions actions in the first place—a story which applies to decisions and intention-formations alone. And the story told on this point may vary. So volitionism covers a family of accounts of agency—a family sharing a structure in common, while allowing for important differences in their central account of what makes volition action.

In the middle ages, scholastic philosophers such as Aquinas and Scotus proposed theories of action which clearly had this volitionist structure. When fully deliberate or intentional our voluntary actions are supposed *always* to result from prior actions of the will—from inner mental actions of decision or choice by which we decide to perform this voluntary action or that.[1]

Let us take the example of a simple voluntary action—walking to the bank. When we perform an action such as this, according to scholastic action theory, we perform it in the following way. First, we *will*, we decide or choose, to walk to the bank. This decision or choice is a goal-directed psychological event, and possesses its goal-direction or purpose, that we walk to the bank, through its own content. Then this decision has the appropriate effects—the very effects that we have decided or chosen to occur. The decision causes us to exercise the capacities involved in actually crossing the road. And so we perform a further action—the action of deliberately crossing the road. In scholastic action theory, these further voluntary actions that the will generates and explains were termed *actus imperati*—imperated or commanded actions, the will being understood on the analogy of a faculty commanding and directing the operation of other capacities or faculties. By contrast, the actions of the will itself were termed *actus eliciti* or elicited actions—actions elicited from the will itself rather than performed by some other capacity at the will's command. And elicited action was very clearly held to be the primary and direct case of human

---

[1] For more detailed historical discussion, see Thomas Pink, 'Suarez, Hobbes and the scholastic tradition in action theory'.

action. Using *praxis* as his term for intentional action, Scotus, for example, made the entirely derivative nature of imperated action very clear:

> Since an imperated action has the character of *praxis* or intentional action only because some elicited action possesses such, because it is the elicited action that can come first, it follows that only the will's own elicited action is primarily *praxis*. And because the formal meaning of *praxis* is to be found primarily in an action of the will, all other actions are *praxis* only in virtue of some action of the will.[2]

We find a shared framework common to Aristotelian scholasticism and Hobbes alike. This framework concerns motivation and voluntary action, and treats these as ontologically quite distinct. Motivation consists in psychological attitudes that cause the performance of voluntary action; and voluntary action, as in itself without content, has to derive its goals from without—from the contents of its motivating causes (Table 9.1).

Table 9.1. Scholasticism and Hobbes: the shared framework

Motivation	causes	Voluntary action
content-bearing		contentless

The debate between Hobbes and his opponents, then, was about where in this shared framework action itself was to be found. Was the primary case of action to be as a form of motivation, or instead as a contentless effect, such as a bodily movement?

Volitionism and the voluntariness-based model are mirror or reverse images of each other. The voluntariness-based model takes human action to occur only in the voluntary, tying action to arising as a voluntary effect of a prior pro attitude to its performance. An agency of decision-making is denied; or only admitted by the device of treating decisions as voluntary or quasi-voluntary actions—anticipatory copies, whether complete or only qualified, of the genuine voluntariness which they explain.

Whereas, by contrast, volitionism implies just the opposite. Voluntary actions counts as action only indirectly, as the intended effect of prior actions of the will. Such voluntariness is not the form in which action primarily occurs. That primary form is restricted to the will. All we do directly is take decisions and form intentions. The rest thereafter is up to nature—to the effects which our immediate will activity happens to have. And so we arrive at a very distinctive view of human freedom. According to volitionist theory, what we control immediately is just our decisions and intention-formations. Since voluntary actions count as action only as effects of will action directed at their occurrence, our control of voluntary action is indirect, exercised only through our control of our decisions and intentions and through the effects these have on our voluntary action.

---

[2] *Duns Scotus on the Will and Morality*, ed. Allan Wolter (Washington: CUA Press, 1986), pp. 128–9.

But volitionism seems very implausible. When I take a decision to cross the road, my immediate involvement in agency is not limited to some action performed entirely within my mind, detached from any actual crossing of the road. The rest is not left up to nature, as it might be when a thrown stone leaves my hand. For when I actually cross the road, my crossing of it is not something I am simply impelled into through the effects of a prior decision to cross. My voluntary crossing of the road is as much and as directly a case of agency as is any decision to cross. And that is connected with the fact that my control over whether I cross the road is not exercised only indirectly, through a prior decision, but is being exercised directly by me as I cross. This means that the bodily action is not some mere effect of prior action performed entirely inside my head. It is a further and direct involvement on my part in agency—something over which I am exercising direct control as I do it.

If the voluntariness-based model finds it difficult to make sense of the intuitive agency of our decisions, volitionism has the opposite problem—but one no less serious. Volitionism is utterly failing to make sense of the intuitive agency of our voluntary actions.

It might seem that we have but two choices. One is to understand action as something based on and motivated by pro attitudes to its performance. But that seems to exclude the idea of decisions themselves as actions. The other is to do what volitionism once did and take decisions to be the primary form of action, and voluntary actions as actions only indirectly, just as effects of prior actions performed entirely within the mind. Indeed, belief that decisions themselves are actions has come to be associated in the minds of many philosophers with volitionist accounts of agency. And so suspicion of volitionism has tended only further to discredit the very idea of decisions as actions. Since volitionism seems so clearly a mistake, belief in actions of the will is treated simply as an occasion for applying some kind of error theory. And modern philosophy is not short of theories that purport to explain through what kinds of fundamental mistake belief in decisions as actions arose.

On one error theory, the belief comes from dualism—a dualism that attempts to locate the self and its immediate action outside the physical world. We find this metaphysical error theory in Gilbert Ryle. What else but some dualist prejudice, some urge to divorce the mind and its action from matter, could lead us to find intentional agency in willings or decisions? As Ryle put it:

Volitions have been postulated as special acts, or operations, 'in the mind', by means of which a mind gets its ideas translated into facts...It will be clear why I reject this story. It is just an inevitable extension of the myth of the ghost in the machine.[3]

The plausibility of Ryle's diagnosis is increased when we consider that scholastics such as Aquinas and Scotus did indeed locate the actions of the will in an immaterial faculty. Deliberate or intentional agency was for them primarily an immaterial

---

[3] Gilbert Ryle, *The Concept of Mind*, chapter 3, 'The will', p. 62.

phenomenon, located as it was in a faculty, the will, that was supposed to operate independently of any bodily organ.

Another error theory is one that we have already discussed in relation to self-determination. Belief in actions of the will is supposed to result from an attempt to moralize the theory of action—to reconstruct human action so as to support certain kinds of misguided but metaphysically demanding ethical theory. Just as erroneous theories of blame are supposed to have encouraged us to believe in some implausible power of self-determination, so too those same erroneous theories are supposed to have led us to believe in actions of the will through which that power of self-determination could be exercised. Belief in the will as a locus of agency can only be the creation of false moral theory—a theory which treats moral responsibility as something incompatible with the causal determination of human action, and which ties that responsibility to a supposedly over-optimistic conception of what human self-determination can come to, such as we find in libertarian freedom.[4]

However, such error theories, whether metaphysical or ethical, are based on a misunderstanding of why we do regard decisions as actions. They also misunderstand the fundamental conception behind medieval action theory. It is true that dualism, in particular, played a role in giving scholastic action theory its volitionist character. But the scholastic belief in an agency of the will had roots that were nothing to do with dualism, or with incompatibilism, or any theory of morals or of moral responsibility. These roots lay in a conception of action that, in itself, is not volitionist at all—indeed that, understood rightly, is quite inconsistent with volitionism.

To understand this conception we have to go beyond the choice with which we began—identifying agency exclusively with voluntary actions or with decisions. Agency is something that can equally well occur in each form.

Once this is understood, we are free to question another, further assumption that has been made, not just by volitionists, but by their Hobbesian opponents too. This is the assumption that motivation, be it conceived as the primary form of action, or else as a passive antecedent of action, is an entirely 'inner' or wholly mental phenomenon, and quite distinct from the voluntary actions motivated. This view of motivation as wholly inner is what makes volitionism so unattractive, locating action proper as understood by volitionists entirely within the mind. But the conception of motivation involved is not just a feature of volitionism. It is deeply part of the voluntariness-based model of action too. To avoid this view of motivation as wholly internal to the mind, we need to abandon not only volitionism itself as an account of how action is constituted, but also the voluntariness-based model, its Hobbesian mirror image.

---

[4] See, for example, Bernard Williams' *Shame and Necessity* and 'Nietzsche's minimalist moral psychology' in *Making Sense of Humanity*.

9.2 The Puzzle of Action in Common-Sense Psychology

The difficulty facing the philosophy of action is clear. In Chapter 5 we saw that decisions or intention-formations and the voluntary actions which they explain appear to be importantly dissimilar kinds of event. Decisions are events of attitude-formation which count as goal-directed actions in their own right. And that is because decisions derive an immediate goal-direction, towards performance of the action decided upon, internally, from their very own content. Whereas voluntary actions appear very different. Voluntary actions are events which depend on the contents of pro attitudes to their performance for their goal-direction and so too for their status as actions. Is there, then, a unifying conception of agency that can apply equally to two such apparently different cases, and explain how they are equally good cases of action?

How to avoid both errors, of volitionism, privileging actions of the will, and of the voluntariness-based model, privileging the case of actions that are willed? How to do equal justice to intentional agency in both its forms, non-voluntary and voluntary alike? We need some factor X which is to be found, just as directly and just as fully, in each of these two cases of action, and which is plainly action-constitutive. Any event with the factor will count as an intentional action. Decisions or intention-formations are actions, it seems, independently of being motivated by pro attitudes to their being taken. So the factor must be found in decisions independently of their being so motivated. On the other hand voluntary action counts as action only because it is done voluntarily, on the basis of pro attitudes towards doing it. So the factor must be found in voluntary actions because they are based on such pro attitudes. What might this factor be?

We might simply appeal, without further ado, to something that we have agreed is fundamental to agency—namely goal-directedness. An action is a goal-directed event—an event in which the agent is making a change as a means to an end. What makes decisions and the voluntary actions which decisions explain all cases of action is just this—that they are all goal-directed events.

But appealing to goal-directedness is not enough. For one thing, we want to know more about what makes a decision a goal-directed event. After all, goal-directedness in voluntary actions comes from their being motivated by pro attitudes to their performance. If decisions are by nature not so motivated, how can decisions generally be goal-directed too? We need to show that we can explain goal-directedness in terms of some feature other than voluntariness—some feature which is common to non-voluntary decisions and voluntary actions alike.

But there is another problem too. Decisions and intention-formations are not just goal-directed actions. They are goal-directed actions which are deliberate or per-formed intentionally, and essentially so. And in this they are again importantly different from actions in voluntary form. For I might take your money intentionally; but I might also take it unintentionally, without meaning to. On the other hand if

I decide to take your money, my taking that decision cannot have been unintentional. I surely cannot take a specific decision inadvertently, without meaning to take that very decision. Taking a specific decision to act, it seems, is not something we ever do unintentionally.

The inherent intentionality or deliberateness of decisions might be thought to follow simply from their inherent purposiveness or goal-directedness. That is, I cannot take a decision to do A without taking that particular decision intentionally, on this line of thought, precisely because I must have taken that very decision as a means to an end, and for one purpose in particular—that through taking that specific decision I end up doing A. Whereas I might take your money without having had the purpose or goal of so acting.

But in fact the point goes deeper. For, as we are now about to see, actions can be performed, and performed for a purpose, without being intentionally performed for that purpose. Purposiveness does not of itself guarantee deliberateness or intentionality. As examples will soon show, there can be actions that are purposive without being in any way deliberate. These are actions which are sub-intentional—wholly inadvertent but still purposive. But if some actions can be purposive without being in any way deliberate, decisions seem different. Not only does my decision to do A seem inherently purposive but, at least as taken for the purpose of acting as decided, it also seems inherently intentional. That I decide on one action rather than another does seem by its very nature something that I must be doing deliberately, not by complete inadvertence; and this is a further feature of decisions additional to any inherent purposiveness.

But why should purposive decisions be inherently intentional, if other kinds of purposive action need not be? As an action, making a decision is clearly very distinctive. Not only is a decision an action that can get its basic goal-direction from its own content, as no voluntary action seems to do; but taken for that purpose—as a decision to do *that*—it seems to count by its very nature as something done intentionally.

To take the matter further, we need to look further at intentionality in action and at its relation to decision and intention. And that means looking more closely at the phenomenon of action in sub-intentional form.

9.3 Intentional Action and Intention

As Brian O'Shaughnessy has pointed out, not all action is intentional. It is not just that what we do intentionally always has some characteristics and effects which are unintentional—characteristics and effects which we did not mean or perhaps did not even suspect would arise. O'Shaughnessy's point goes further. There can be actions which are wholly unintentional—which are not deliberate or intentional in any respect at all.[5] People can perform actions—do things goal-directedly, as a means

---

[5] See Brian O'Shaughnessy, *The Will* (Cambridge: Cambridge University Press, 1980) vol. 2, chapter 10, 'The sub-intentional act'.

to ends, on the basis of some sort of desire so to act—but without in any way meaning to. They can be absent-mindedly scratching in order to remove an unwanted itch, or absent-mindedly picking their nose in order to remove a disliked blockage. What they are doing is goal-directed, but is being done by them quite unintentionally. They may remain quite unaware throughout that they are doing it. O'Shaughnessy calls this phenomenon *sub-intentional action*.

Sub-intentional actions—actions of wholly unintentional scratching and the like— are goal-directed actions which bypass our power of control. And that is because we can only be exercising control over what we do if we are doing it, or refraining from it, deliberately or intentionally. To do things wholly unintentionally, in an absence of mind as it were, is precisely not to be exercising control over what we are doing. We may of course possess the control—and if so we may well start to exercise it once we realize what we have been doing. We may then exercise our control intentionally to stop doing, or even intentionally to continue doing, what we were previously doing wholly unintentionally. But for as long as we are acting wholly unintentionally our power to control what we are doing will be disengaged.

It also seems that actions which are sub-intentional bypass our practical rationality. That is, these wholly inadvertent, unmeant actions bypass our capacity to respond to justifications for and against performing them. What shows this is that we can often find ourselves performing actions sub-intentionally despite the fact that we are in circumstances, such as appearing publicly at a meeting and the like, which we perfectly well know leave the actions a clearly bad idea. At the meeting, in full view of the audience, I suddenly realize that I am scratching myself *there*. The fact that I knew that kind of action to be a bad idea seems not to have prevented me from performing it—until I finally realize what I am doing and stop. For I do stop the embarrassing scratching as soon as I realize what I have been doing. And I stop because my practical rationality is re-engaged. When I realize what I have been doing, my conception of what it is desirable and justified to do, a conception which I have had all along and which rules that particular kind of action out, finally begins again to govern how I act.

Action which is intentional or deliberate looks, then, as though it is action which involves and is based on our capacity for practical rationality. What we do intentionally is sensitive to our overall view of what we have reason to do, as what we do sub-intentionally is not. But there is more to intentionality in action than that. Action which is fully intentional also seems to be action which involves a distinctive psychological state—the motivating pro attitude that is intention.

Our very language links intentionality in action with the attitude of intention. The term 'intention' for the pro attitude is a component of the term 'intentional' for deliberateness in action. Now 'intentional' does not imply that when X is done intentionally, the doing of X is *ipso facto* intended. For the unintended outcomes of what we do intentionally may themselves be described as outcomes produced by us intentionally—in some cases at least where those outcomes are foreseen by us. If

I intentionally throw a brick fully aware that it will break a window, then even if the window's breaking was not intended by me—it was not my goal—I may be described as having broken the window intentionally or deliberately.[6]

But intentionality in action does seem to imply some involvement of intention nevertheless. Action is purposive, and when we act intentionally, there will be goals which we are intentionally or deliberately pursuing—goals that, in the case of voluntary action, depend on the pro attitudes motivating the action. In the case of voluntary action that is intentional, those goals can be reported by referring to the intentions motivating the action—the intentions with which the action is being performed. If crossing the road is something that I am doing intentionally, and I am intentionally and deliberately doing it in order to get to the other side, then I can always be said to be acting with the intention of getting to the other side. To perform a voluntary action intentionally, and to do it intentionally as a means of attaining E, is to do it with the intention of attaining E. In which case, it seems, the intentionality of voluntary action must imply some motivation by intention. Voluntary action which is intentionally being performed in order to attain certain ends must be motivated by intentions to attain those ends.

But does the intentionality of voluntary action really imply its motivation by intention? The matter is controversial. There are some views of intention that tie it to occurring as an attitude of 'pure intending' that occurs in advance of the action intended. The intending is 'pure' because in intending to act the agent is not yet acting as intended. These views are especially associated with views of intention as involved in the advance planning of action.[7] Intentions are attitudes we form before acting as intended so as to be able efficiently to plan and coordinate for the future. But it is not obvious that intentional action need involve such a prior attitude of 'pure intending'. Suddenly presented by my family with a surprise, I might without warning be asked to close my eyes—and I immediately do so, quite deliberately, with the intention of taking part in the surprise. It seems that my purpose for shutting my eyes involves intention. At least that is how we naturally describe it. But there is no prior planning involved. Far from having been formed in advance, my intention of participating in the surprise by closing my eyes seems to be held by me just as I carry it out—as I deliberately close my eyes. As Davidson observes: '. . . often intentional action is not preceded by intention.'[8] What if ordinary language is not misleading, and voluntary action which is intentional really must be motivated by intention? Then there must be another way of understanding intention than as a 'pure' attitude involved in the planning of action in advance—a theory of intention

---

[6] See Michael Bratman, *Intention Plans and Practical Reason*, chapter 8, and Richard Holton *Willing, Wanting, Waiting* (Oxford: Oxford University Press, 2009), chapter 1.

[7] We shall consider these views, associated with the work of Michael Bratman, in the next chapter.

[8] Donald Davidson, 'Intending', in *Essays on Actions and Events*, p. 88.

that explains why intentionality in action implies motivation by intention. And perhaps there is such a theory.

Intentional action, we have already seen, is action which is based on our capacity for practical rationality. If intentional action must also involve intention, that may be because intention is the motivation in and through which we apply practical reason. Intention may be the motivation by which we respond to justifications for action. On this view, voluntary action which is intentional requires motivation by intention because only then will it be what genuinely intentional action must be—responsive to the relevant practical justifications for and against its performance, at least as we conceive these to be.

Intention, on this view, is that action-motivating pro attitude through which we respond to justifications for action—through which we apply practical reason. And this is a very natural view of intention. It makes sense of the way in which common sense links justifications for intention to justifications for subsequently acting as intended. The rationality of forming an intention to do A, we ordinarily think, guarantees the rationality of doing A thereafter. And this is because the primary function of forming an intention to do A is precisely to respond to and apply practical reason as it concerns the voluntary—to ensure that we end up performing those voluntary actions which are rational rather than otherwise.

Intentional action, then, is action based on our capacity to apply practical reason. And it is so based because the motivation which it involves is intention—and intention is that motivation in and through which we respond to practical justifications. But of course, we do not see intention merely as a reason-responsive motivation. Decision-making or intention-formation is viewed by us as itself an action which is as deliberate and intentional as the voluntary actions intended. For, to repeat, while voluntary action may be unintentional, the taking of a particular decision never is.

Why then should intention-formation itself be an intentional action? Perhaps because the connection between intentional action and the exercise of practical reason is even closer than I have suggested. It is not just that to act intentionally requires that one's action be based on a capacity to respond to practical justifications. An exercise of one's capacity to respond to such justifications may be exactly what an intentional action is. Intentional action, in other words, may be constituted as a distinctive mode of responding to reason—a mode of responding to reason that is practice-constitutive. This mode of responding to reason occurs when we exercise our capacity to apply and conform to justifications that are practical and action-governing; and it occurs as much in intention-formation as in voluntary action motivated by intention. And so we arrive at the practical reason-based model of intentional action.

The practical reason-based model promises to tell us just what this X-factor is which unites all cases of intentional action, whether they be non-voluntary decisions and intention-formations, or actions in voluntary form. The uniting factor is a distinctive mode of exercising reason—a mode that is fully practical in the sense of being practice- or action-constitutive. According to the model, events are intentional actions when they occur as an exercise of our capacity to respond to and apply reason in its practical or action-governing form. Intentional action consists, not in any kind of effect, as on the voluntariness-based model—but in a distinctive mode of exercising reason.

9.4 The Practical Reason-Based Model—an Initial Outline

As we saw in Chapter 3, practical reason must govern and address our motivations as well as our voluntary actions. Justifications for doing voluntary A move us only by being justifications for becoming motivated to do A. They move us by providing the same support for deciding or forming an intention to do A that they provide for actually doing A.

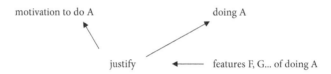

Figure 9.1. The structure of practical justification.

We respond to justifications for voluntary action, then, in our decisions and intention-formations, and not just in our performance of the actions thereby intended. We exercise our capacity to respond to practical reason in our non-voluntary motivations, and not just in our voluntary actions.

This means, as we saw in Chapter 5, that for the voluntariness-based model of action the exercise of this capacity to respond to practical reason cannot be an inherently action-constitutive phenomenon. The response to practical justifications that we make when we form motivations to act must, as a response that is non-voluntary, be made passively and precede the performance of action itself.

The practical reason-based model is quite different. According to the practical reason-based model, the exercise of the capacity for reason that occurs when we form an intention to act serves to explain and constitute the very nature of action in intentional form. The exercise of our capacity to respond to practical reason no longer straddles the passive–active divide, but is itself fully practical. It is the exercise of reason in a form that is action-constitutive.

Notice, of course, that intentional action so conceived, as a specifically practical or action-constitutive exercise of reason, need not always be performed rationally. Intentional action may occur as an exercise of one's reason—of one's capacity for rationality. But that capacity can still perfectly well be exercised defectively as well as competently. It is, after all, the very fact that we can be incompetent in our exercise of reason that allows our attitudes and our actions to count, not simply as a- or non-rational, but as genuinely irrational—as constituting a genuine misuse of reason.[9]

9.5 The Practical Reason-Based Model and Scholastic Action Theory

The practical reason-based model was once widely believed. In particular, it was really allegiance to the practical reason-based model that underlay the surface volitionism of scholastic action theory.[10]

Aquinas, for example, refers to the general category of intentional agency as the *voluntarium*—a term normally translated nowadays as 'the voluntary'. But for Aquinas the *voluntarium* does not mean voluntariness as I have defined it, and as it has commonly been understood in the voluntariness-based tradition that comes to us from Hobbes. The *voluntarium* is not what is done on the basis of a will or intention to do it. For Aquinas the *voluntarium* consists, in its primary form, in the exercise of *voluntas* or the will itself.

By *voluntas* or will Aquinas meant our capacity for decision and intention. And he termed this capacity an *appetitus rationalis* or rational appetite. He used the term *appetite* to mark the fact that our capacity for decision-making and intention-formation is a motivational capacity; and he used the term *rational*, because he saw the capacity as fully responsive to reason. The will, then, is that motivational capacity which responds to and applies our prior deliberation about how we should act by leaving us disposed and motivated to act as we have deliberated that we should. And the will's exercise is what constitutes intentional action: 'However the *voluntarium* signifies an exercise of the appetitive power, which power presupposes a cognition of the understanding, in that an understanding of the good is what moves the appetite.'[11] Our understanding presents us with possible goals or objects of decision. And the will is a capacity to respond to such goals or objects, and to respond to them as good, and so as justifying such a response to them. So the exercise of the will constitutes a case of action—because it is the exercise of a capacity to respond to

---

[9] For a, typically forceful, expression of Hobbes' failure to understand this point, see: 'The Definition of the *Will*, given commonly by the Schooles, that it is a *Rationall Appetite*, is not good. For if it were, then there could be no Voluntary Act against Reason.' (*Leviathan*, ed. Noel Malcolm, (Oxford: Clarendon Press, 2012), vol. 2, p. 92.)

[10] In fact the model of action as an action-constitutive mode of exercising reason runs from ancient Stoicism through medieval and early modern scholasticism, and was still being assumed, with some important qualifications, by Kant. But it was the scholastics who developed the model in greatest detail, and it is scholastic versions of the model that I shall mainly consider. For more detailed historical discussion, see again my 'Suarez, Hobbes and the scholastic tradition in action theory'.

[11] Thomas Aquinas, *In decem libros Ethicorum Aristotelis ad Nicomachum expositio* (Turin: Marietti, 1964), p. 112.

and apply practical reason. Hence intentional action is characterized by Aquinas as an *operatio rationalis* or an exercise of reason.[12]

We also find an equally clear statement of the practical reason-based model in Duns Scotus. Scotus had an importantly different conception of the will's relation to the intellect from Aquinas. Aquinas conceived the exercise of the will in intellectualist terms, as a function of the exercise of the practical intellect, decisions being identified with judgements about how we should act. The freedom of the will was, therefore, for Aquinas a freedom of the intellect too—something that was closely linked to Aquinas's rationalist conception of freedom, as given by the way options are presented to us by practical reason. Whereas Scotus conceived the exercise of the will in voluntarist terms, as strictly distinct from any exercise of the intellect. According to Scotus, one can take decisions apart from, even against one's judgements about how to act. Even though such decisions might be irrational—a misuse of the will and in contravention of its proper function—they are still possible. So for Scotus the will's freedom is peculiar to it, and is not to be linked with any concomitant freedom of belief or of the intellect.

This different conception of the will's precise relation to the intellect should not prevent us from seeing that Scotus still exactly shared Aquinas's conception of action. For so he did. Though there was disagreement in their theories of freedom and self-determination, their conception of action and of purposiveness was the same. Scotus conceived intentional agency in the very same practical reason-based terms as did Aquinas. Scotus also saw the will as a rational motivational capacity. He also saw its proper function as to respond to and apply prior deliberation about how to act. And, for Scotus as for Aquinas, that left the exercise of the will in intention-formation an intentional action.

In a passage that was quoted approvingly by many later commentators[13] in his tradition, Scotus claimed:

> Also note that *praxis* or intentional action is an act of some capacity other than intellect, that naturally follows an act of knowledge or intellection, and is suited by nature to be elicited in accord with correct knowledge if it is to be right.[14]

This passage in Scotus identifies *praxis* or intentional agency with the exercise of a certain kind of capacity for rational responsiveness. The capacity exercised, though rational or reason-responsive, is not simply the intellect itself. The capacity for rationality is practical rather than theoretical—it is motivation-involving rather than simply cognitive. It is a motivational capacity to respond to prior judgement or knowledge about what to do. Again we find intentional action being conceived as

---

[12] Thomas Aquinas, *Summa Theologiae*, 1a 2ae q6 a1, sed contra (Turin: Marietti, 1950), p. 38.

[13] For an example over three hundred years later, see Francisco Suarez, *Commentaria una cum quaestionibus in libros Aristotelis De Anima* (Madrid: Sociedad de Estudios y Publicaciones, 1991) vol. 3, p. 250.

[14] *Duns Scotus on the Will and Morality*, pp. 126–8.

the exercise of a capacity to apply practical reason—to respond motivationally to justifications for action. And the locus of this capacity is again, in Scotus's view, the will—our capacity for decision-making and intention-formation.

Intention is the psychological attitude which takes central stage in scholastic accounts of intentional action. To act intentionally is either to be forming intentions, or to be acting voluntarily on the basis of intentions already formed. And that is because intention is taken by the scholastics to be that motivation in and through which we respond to and apply practical reason—and because, in their view, intentional action occurs as or through such response to and application of reason in practical form.

Desires are quite different attitudes from intentions, according to scholastic psychology. And that is because desire is taken not to be an attitude which is responsive to practical reason in the way that intention is. Decision and intention—*electio* and *intentio*—are located in the will as a rational motivating power or appetite, as motivation in fully reason-responsive form. Whereas desire is taken to be a form of motivation common to us and non-rational animals, located not in the will but in a motivating power or appetite that is 'sensitive' rather than 'rational'. This view of desire is highly problematic, as we shall see, but it is crucial to the scholastic theory of action. For the scholastics shared the common sense intuition that while decision and intention-formation is an action, something that we deliberately and intentionally do, desire-formation is a passion—something that happens to us. And they sought to explain this distinction in practical reason-based terms—by viewing intention-formation as the exercise of a capacity to respond to reason as it governs action, while denying that desire-formation is the exercise of such a capacity.

We have seen that the scholastics counted intention-formation as an intentional action, and why. But what of intentional actions in voluntary form—actions that involve capacities outside the will itself and which we perform on the basis of having intended or willed their performance? We have seen that a volitionist approach was taken to these actions. But why was this?

The answer is clear enough. The key notion, on the practical reason-based model, is the notion of a practice- or action-constitutive mode of exercising reason. It is this notion which picks out those events or changes that count as actions. Actions are those events which involve the exercise of reason in that distinctively action-constitutive form. The scholastics committed themselves to volitionism by restricting the application of this key notion to the will. Only decisions and intention-formations counted as exercises of reason in its practice-constitutive form. The agent's response to practical reason was supposed to occur in the will—and in the will alone. Voluntary actions involving capacities outside the will itself, actions of raising one's hand and the like, were mere effects of such exercises of reason. They did not count as action-constitutive exercises of reason in their own right. Their status as actions then had to be explained derivatively, as intended or willed effects of these prior actions of the will.

Why did scholastic action theory take this volitionist form? The explanation is not hard to find. Intentional action was being understood by the scholastics, rightly, in practical reason-based terms as a mode of exercising reason—an event in which the agent exercised a capacity to respond to practical or action-governing justifications. But Aquinas and Scotus and others in their tradition had a profoundly dualist attitude to reason and rationality. They were developing the practical reason-based model within a complex faculty psychology. And the world view within which this psychology was being developed included a metaphysical hierarchy—a hierarchy in which reason had a higher dignity than matter. This dignity was then understood in a very distinctive way—as severing the exercise of reason from material embodiment. Any exercise of a capacity to respond to justifications had to occur in immaterial faculties of intellect or will and apart from any bodily organ. The agent's immediate involvement in intentional agency must, then, as an exercise of reason, always occur wholly within the immaterial faculty of will. It could never occur outside the will, in the corporeal capacities for limb motion and the like which voluntary action can involve. And so that was why voluntary action that was intentional had always to occur derivatively or indirectly, as an intended effect of a prior action of the will.

Scholastic volitionism was the product, then, of a particular understanding of a metaphysical hierarchy, of reason over matter. This understanding taught a detachment of reason from material processes. Reason could not be exercised through the operation of a bodily organ. It was this exclusion of reason from the material that gave volitionist form to the practical reason-based model of action. Yet the practical reason-based model is not inherently volitionist. Far from it, in fact. For properly understood, the practical reason-based model actually opposes volitionism. Once we abandon this particular medieval detachment of reason from matter, I shall argue, there is no obstacle at all to including voluntary actions as practical exercises of rationality in their own right, and so as perfectly good cases of agency.

9.6 Hobbes' Critique of the Model

Scholastic models of action met the fierce opposition of Hobbes. And it is not hard for modern philosophers to share Hobbes' disbelief. How can intentional action be an essentially immaterial phenomenon, located entirely within a purely mental faculty of will? We are left with an objectionably volitionist theory—wrapped in a dualism which is especially implausible.

But Hobbes' opposition was not simply to dualist volitionism. He clearly saw through this surface to the practical reason-based model that lay beneath. And it was against this underlying model of action as a mode of exercising reason that Hobbes directed his most searching criticism. Hobbes exposed a fundamental problem—a problem which faces the practical reason-based model in all its forms. This is the problem of explaining more precisely what it is to exercise reason in practice-constitutive form; and of explaining this key notion in a way which allows intention-formation to constitute a convincing instance of the phenomenon as desire-formation is not.

Suppose an agent is made a tempting offer. As soon as he hears the offer, and before he makes any decision about it, the agent may immediately form a strong desire to accept. But that the agent forms this desire is not his intentional doing; still less, therefore, is it anything within his direct control. The desire can simply come over him; he just finds himself forming it. The first thing that counts as genuinely the agent's own doing, then, is what he actually decides—his formation of an intention, be it to accept the offer or reject it.

Or so we may want to say. But the problem which faces us is an obvious one. Forming a desire is not a deliberate or intentional action; but, according to the practical reason-based model, forming an intention is. So what makes intention-formation an action as desire-formation is not? Obviously, the practical reason-based model has a preliminary answer to this question. This is that intention-formation occurs as a response to and application of practical reason as desire-formation does not. Intention is a reason-responsive attitude as desire is not. The problem is making sense of this answer. How is intention responsive to practical reason as desire is not? And this was what practical reason-based theorists never really managed to explain.

Kant sometimes suggests, at least by his terminology, a radical account of the difference between intention and desire. According to this story, desire is simply not a rational or reason-responsive attitude at all. It is instead a mere 'pathological feeling'.[15] Far from being an attitude which is responsive to reason, desire serves merely as a felt obstacle to such responsiveness.

But this is a clearly false view of desire. There can be justifications for wanting to do something (it might be fun or interesting or just or courageous to do it) just as much as there can be justifications for actually doing or intending to do it; and we can, as rational beings, perfectly well form desires in response to such justifications. Desire is a reason-responsive attitude too. Consider again that tempting offer. The agent finds himself feeling a desire to accept it—and he may be feeling the desire precisely because the offer has features which make accepting it highly desirable, and which therefore justify a strong desire to accept. The response of forming the desire may be passive; but it can still be a response which the agent is making as rational animal.

The scholastic tradition already recognized this. This tradition was inclined to allow that desire, at least as experienced by humans, is responsive to reason—but to claim that this responsiveness is imperfect. This imperfect responsiveness was often explained in terms of a restriction in the conceptions of objects and of the good which desire is sensitive to. Intentions, as intellectual motivations which only rational

---

[15] Thus, in so far as motivations can be determined by reason, Kant regards them as by that very fact included within the faculty of will or of choice and decision—see *Metaphysics of Morals*, Introduction, II, 6.213, in *The Cambridge Edition of the Works of Immanuel Kant: Practical Philosophy*, ed. Mary Gregor (Cambridge: Cambridge University Press, 1996), p. 375.

humans possessed, are sensitive to a fully intellectual conception of objects and of the justifiability of obtaining them. Whereas desire, a motivation shared with non-rational animals, is sensitive only to intellectually less developed conceptions—to thoughts of this sensorily presented good or that which do not involve an intellectually developed conception of them and of their good.[16]

But this again is not right. In adult humans, at any rate, wants and desires can be responsive to the same fully intellectual conceptions of goods that guide our decisions and intentions. Suppose I develop an understanding, as mature and explicit as you like, of how writing an informative account of Kant's transcendental deduction of the categories is something inherently good. That conception can guide me into deciding to write such an account. But beforehand, as my enthusiasm is wakened, that same deeply intellectual conception can guide me into forming an initial desire to embark on such an account. Any possible object of intention is a possible object of desire. Any feature of a voluntary action which finally moves me to decide to perform it can first have moved me, just as effectively and just as rationally, merely to desire to perform it. So what could be the difference between desires and intentions? How are intentions reason-involving as desires are not?

It seems that when I hear the tempting offer, then, as far as the theory of rationality is concerned there is no fundamental difference between intention and desire. In each case, both when I form a desire to accept the offer and when I decide or form an intention to accept it, I am exercising the same kind of capacity for responding to reason. In both cases I am forming pro attitudes which are equally responsive to and governed by the very same kinds of justification—justifications which depend on the desirability of their object, the voluntary action of accepting the offer. But then I am responding to practical reason in both cases. For in both cases I am exercising my capacity to respond motivationally to justifications for action. It is just that in one case I am merely forming an initial inclination to act; in the other case the pro attitude is one which determines outright how I am disposed to act. Granted, the outcome of forming these two pro attitudes is different. In the one case we are forming a mere inclination; in the other an outright disposition. But the way reason is being exercised in forming the two pro attitudes seems fundamentally the same. We have found in the theory of their rationality no convincing basis for a distinction between a mere passion and a deliberate action.

It is a fundamental tenet of the practical reason-based model that intention-formation engages our capacity for rationality—and does so distinctively, in a fundamentally different way from desire-formation. Intention is supposed to be responsive to justifications for action as desire is not. That is what allows the exercise of rationality that occurs in intention-formation to be practical or action-constitutive

<hr/>

[16] Thus Aquinas regards love of or motivation towards a purely intellectual object such as wisdom, as by that very fact not a passion or ordinary desire, but a motivation of the rational appetite or will. See *Summa Theologiae*, 1.2ae, q26, a. 1 resp ad primum (Turin: Marietti, 1950), p. 127.

as desire-formation is not. But no satisfactory account was ever given of how intention might engage our capacity for rationality in a way substantially different from desire. Reason seems to be exercised in a fundamentally similar way in each case. Each attitude seems to be responsive to the same justifications in the same way.

So Hobbes could convincingly deny that the differences in rationality between intention and desire are substantial enough to leave intentions active and desires passive. Each attitude seems as intellectual or reason-involving a motivation as the other, and the rationality of each is related to the desirability of its object in broadly the same way. Both desires and intentions are non-voluntary motivations; and, as we have seen, they are both non-voluntary for the same reason, because they are both responses to their objects as desirable or good. There seems no scope, therefore, for supposing that the exercise of reason in intention-formation is materially different from its exercise in desire-formation—that it is so different as to make intention-formation a deliberate action when desire-formation is not. For Hobbes, there is no distinctively rational appetite—but only a general motivational capacity that as much includes the mere yen to eat something as it does an actual decision to eat it. And there is no distinctive form of normative guidance given by reason that is specific to the will, but only a general capacity on our part to respond motivationally to goods presented by the senses or the imagination:

For I do not fear it will be thought too hot for my fingers, to shew the vanity of words such as these, Intellectual appetite, conformity of the appetite to the object, rational will, elective power of the rational will;...I understand how objects, and the conveniences and inconveniences of them, may be represented to a man by the help of his senses; but how reason representeth anything to the will, I [do not] understand...[17]

And so '...nor can a man more determine his will than any other appetite; that is, more than he can determine when he shall be hungry and when not'.[18] The effect of Hobbes' assault has proved profound. Its main legacy is that the idea of identifying action as a mode of exercising reason has largely disappeared from modern English-language action theory. Our capacity to respond to justifications for action was supposed to be inherently practice- or action-constitutive. Exercising it was supposed to constitute the performance of intentional action. But this capacity seems not to be inherently action-constitutive after all. For we seem to respond to justifications for action as much by desire-formation as by intention-formation. Yet desire-formation is passive. It is not an action.

The voluntariness-based model claims that responding to practical reason is not something action-constitutive—that the application of practical reason straddles the divide between action and passion. And it seems that on this crucial issue the

[17] Hobbes in *The Questions Concerning Liberty, Necessity and Chance, clearly stated between Dr Bramhall Bishop of Derry, and Thomas Hobbes of Malmesbury*, pp. 35–6.
[18] Hobbes in *The Questions Concerning Liberty, Necessity and Chance, clearly stated between Dr Bramhall Bishop of Derry, and Thomas Hobbes of Malmesbury*, p. 25.

voluntariness-based model is right. There seems to be no mode of exercising reason that is distinctive in its own right and which can then be used to specify what an intentional action is.

9.7 Replying to Hobbes

The practical reason-based model identifies intentional action as a distinctive mode of exercising reason. Its key idea is that there is indeed a mode of exercising reason that is distinctive in just this way—that is practical and agency-constitutive. It was the discrediting of this key idea by Hobbes which led to the eventual disappearance of the model. So this is the idea that we now have to explain and rehabilitate if the model is to be restored.

Hobbes' attack on the practical reason-based model raises the question whether intention really is the *locus* of a distinctive mode of exercising reason—and whether intentional action really does occur as the exercise of reason in this form. The attitude at the centre of the dispute between the two competing models of human action is, then, intention. To understand intentional action we shall need to understand what intention is, and its relation to action that is intentional.

Our reply to Hobbes' attack will therefore be based on an account of intention and intention-formation—an account, to be given over the chapters that follow, which will vindicate the practical reason-based model at every point. The defence will proceed in three steps.

First, in the next chapter, we shall show that voluntary action which is intentional has to be based on a motivation that engages the agent's practical reason—that serves to respond to and apply reason as it governs the voluntary; and that this motivation really is intention rather than desire. Exactly as common sense supposes, intention is the motivation behind all voluntary action which is intentional. And that is because it is through intention, not desire, that we respond to reason in its action-governing form.

Then in the following chapter we shall show that, in contrast to desire, the formation of an intention is an exercise of rationality which is fully practical or action-constitutive. Decision-making or intention-formation is an intentional action—just because it engages the agent's capacity for practical rationality as desire-formation does not.

Thirdly, we shall show that, provided it is motivated by intention, voluntary action can be as much and as directly a practice-constitutive mode of exercising reason as any decision. Far from being volitionist, properly understood the practical reason-based model is wholly inconsistent with volitionism in any form. The model will do exactly what we want a model of action to do—to explain how events so apparently different in kind as decisions and voluntary actions can count as intentional actions, and count as such on exactly the same terms.

10

Intention and Practical Reason

10.1 What Is Intention?

One recently popular account of intention, associated particularly with the work of Michael Bratman, is the planning theory.[1] We need to plan our voluntary action over time, so that what we do in the present coordinates with what we do in the future. Intention allows us to fix or determine voluntary action in advance, so that we can use our knowledge of what we intend for the future to base our action in the present. For example, I need to settle in advance whether this summer I shall be going to Spain or to Germany on holiday. Only if the matter is settled now can I make the appropriate advance preparations. What can settle the matter is my present intention. If I form an intention to go to Spain, I am left able safely to prepare for a Spanish holiday, buying guide books to Spain rather than Germany, booking Spanish and not German hotels, and so forth—all the while secure in the knowledge that, thanks to my intention, my efforts won't be wasted, since it really is Spain and not Germany where I shall be holidaying.

Intention, on this view, has a planning function, enabling us to settle and determine our voluntary action in advance. We deliberate about how to act well in advance of our actual performance of any voluntary action; and then having concluded in favour of a particular act, in lieu of its present performance, a performance which obviously can only occur in the future, we now form an intention to perform the action—the intention serving to fix and determine in the present that it is that particular action which we shall be performing in the future. Which means that as attitudes with a planning function, intentions are gap-fillers. They fill a temporal gap between advance deliberation about how to act later, and the eventual performance of a given voluntary action on the basis of that earlier deliberation.

This planning theory of intention is clearly on the right track. It is part of the truth—but not the whole truth. For the theory does not explain why intention should also occur in cases where our voluntary actions are not planned in advance. Suppose I do something right now, quite deliberately—such as just closing my eyes—but I do

---

[1] See especially Michael Bratman, *Intention, Plans and Practical Reason*. I relied on this planning theory in a previous book, *The Psychology of Freedom* (Cambridge: Cambridge University Press, 1996). But as this chapter explains, while the planning theory covers a very important aspect of intention, I now think it is not sufficient on its own. The planning theory does not provide a complete theory of intention.

it spontaneously, without having in any way planned my action beforehand. It seems that in acting intentionally in this way, in closing my eyes deliberately and for the sake of closing them, what is motivating me is my intention to close them. But if so, how, on the planning theory, is this possible? Since there is no question of action being planned in advance of its performance, so it seems that there is no gap-filling, advance coordinative work for an intention to do.[2]

Some theorists of intention might be willing to allow that voluntary action can be intentional without being motivated by intention. But as we have already noted, common sense seems to suppose otherwise. Those goals of voluntary action that are pursued deliberately or intentionally count as intended. Voluntary action that is deliberately done in order that E is performed with the intention that E. So if the intentionality of voluntary action does presuppose motivation by intention, there must be more to intention than facilitating planning. We have to go beyond the planning theory. There must be a more general role which intention plays—a role of which the planning and coordination of action through time is only one part. We must now examine what this role is, and how intentions fulfil it.

10.2 Intention, Intentionality, and the Engagement of Practical Reason

All voluntary action requires some sort of motivation. Moreover, as we have seen, an agent's capacity to respond to justifications for and against the voluntary is exercised in and through motivation. What an agent capable of rationality in respect of the voluntary requires, then, is a form of motivation which serves to respond to the full range of justifications for and against a given voluntary action, at least as the agent takes these to be—and which then serves to determine, in the light of all the relevant justifications, and in a way rationally integrated with the rest of what the agent does, whether that voluntary action is performed.

Motivation in this form would engage the agent's capacity for practical rationality in his performance of voluntary action. Action that is intentional or deliberate, I suggest, is action in which the agent's capacity for practical rationality is so exercised and engaged. And it is intention that provides the practical rationality-engaging form of motivation—which is why intentional action involves motivation of the voluntary by intention.

10.2.1 Sub-intentional action again

Action, in all its forms, involves both motivation and the pursuit of goals through that motivation. Take, then, some simple goal-directed action, such as scratching in

---

[2] Bratman concedes that since, in these cases, there is no planning work for intention to do, there is a question on his theory about why such spontaneous intentional actions should be motivated by intention. See *Intention, Plans and Practical Reason*, p. 126.

order to remove an itch. Here one is doing something, scratching, that is directed at a goal which one wants or is motivated to attain—getting rid of the itch. And this goal-direction makes the scratching as clear a case of action as any.

But the scratching, though a perfectly good goal-directed action, might still be wholly unintentional. And we have already seen how. First, one might be entirely unaware of one's scratching. Indeed, one might be quite surprised to discover oneself doing it. The scratching might be something one simply finds oneself doing. Secondly, as soon as one does notice what one is doing, one might well become very embarrassed, and immediately stop doing it. Scratching *there* at this rather public moment—in an important meeting, say—may be a particularly bad idea, as one can have been perfectly aware all along. But, unfortunately, at least until one does become aware of what one is doing, one's unimpeachable grasp of the scratching's overall practical unwisdom has had no effect whatsoever. One has been scratching on regardless.

Action that is sub-intentional, then, has a number of salient characteristics. First, sub-intentional action is detached from one's inbuilt capacity directly to monitor what one does as one does it. But this is a capacity which definitely does apply to any voluntary action that is intentional. If I do something voluntary intentionally, I am generally aware that I am doing it—or at least that I am trying to do it—as I do it; and I am aware of what I am doing directly, without having to look at or otherwise sensorily attend to what I am doing.[3] By contrast, unintentional voluntary action is action which I can *find* myself doing.

Notice, of course, that one's awareness of what one is intentionally doing as one does it need not be conscious. As I intentionally post the letter through the letter box, I need not be consciously entertaining thoughts about what I am doing. I might be consciously thinking about something quite different. The awareness of what I am doing need come to no more than an unentertained belief—but still a belief that is not dependent on my having to look to see what I am doing. The belief is enough to make it true that were you to ask me, I could tell you immediately that I was posting a letter, or at least that I was trying to; and I could tell you this without having to look or otherwise sensorily attend to what I am doing.

That my sub-intentional scratching is not rationally integrated with the rest of what I am doing is owing, at least in part, to the action's being unmonitored. Given the lack of monitoring, any motivation that drives me to perform the action can exert its influence unchecked by awareness on my own part of what it is leading me to do; and since I am unaware of the sub-intentional action, the rest of what I do cannot be adapted to suit the fact that I am performing it. Which is why sub-intentional actions and the rest of what one is doing intentionally can so easily conflict: at the intentional

---

[3] See G.E.M. Anscombe, *Intention* (Oxford: Blackwell, 1957).

level one may be seeking to perform effectively at a public meeting; but at the sub-intentional level, one is scratching oneself *there*.

Then, besides being unmonitored, sub-intentional action generally occurs as a response to a rather local need or desideratum—such as the need to get rid of an itch. And, very importantly, the motivation behind sub-intentional action is responsive only to this single feature of the action. One's performance of the action can therefore occur in complete disregard of what else one believes about the action or one's other needs and interests.

And that is also why what one is doing sub-intentionally may not match one's needs and interests overall, not even one's needs and interests as one believes them to be. Hence the way in which one can find oneself doing things that one knows perfectly well would be embarrassing or silly, such as scratching at an important meeting.

In sub-intentional action, what is very clearly motivating one is some sort of desire—a desire which is getting one to perform a goal-directed action; but the desire is doing so in a way that is detached from the generality of one's beliefs, and so from one's capacity to deliberate, on the basis of those beliefs, about how to act. The desire does nothing to ensure that in acting as motivated, one is acting in a way that is good overall, or at least not undesirable or bad. One's reason is disengaged from one's action.

Much sub-intentional action takes forms, such as scratching, that are in general low risk or trivial in their effects—which is why it can make sense to perform such actions sub-intentionally, without bothering to engage one's reason. But just because one's capacity for practical reason is not engaged, one may continue to perform the actions when they are no longer appropriate—even though, as a rational agent, one is perfectly well aware of the problems performing such actions would cause.

What then is required for my voluntary A-ing to be intentional? I must be motivated by an attitude towards doing A which

- is rationally governed by and responsive to the desirability overall or on balance of thereafter doing A—and so to my general belief about what doing A would involve;
- functions to determine my voluntary action on the basis of that responsiveness;
- leads me to suppose, without my having to look, that I am or shall be doing A, or at least that I may well do so, allowing me to adapt my remaining voluntary agency to the fact of my doing A.

But any such motivating attitude just is an intention. For intention has a special reason-applying function, serving to apply reason as it governs the voluntary—a function which desires do not have. And this function, which is peculiar to intentions, means that though intentions are like desires in being non-voluntary motivations, they differ crucially from desires in their mode of rationality. Let us now go through in detail what distinguishes intentions from desires.

10.2.2 Intentions function to determine voluntary action

The first point to be made about intentions is that they are always intentions to act or refrain from acting. Whatever the object of an intention might be, the intention is always an intention to attain that object through one's own voluntary agency. By contrast, one can quite easily want something to happen independently of one's own agency. Intentions are tied to being directed at subsequent voluntary action or omission as desires are not.

And this is because intentions have the function of determining voluntary action by ensuring that we act as intended. The point of taking decisions and forming intentions is to settle how one will act. This action-determining function is what distinguishes intentions from desires, and the rationality of intending from the rationality of desiring.

The action-determining function of intention means that an intention, once formed, should be retained—unless, of course, it becomes clear that the intention was based on mistake or ignorance. It is irrational to take decisions and then abandon them capriciously, for no good reason; and that is because such capriciousness defeats the whole point of decision-making, which is precisely to settle how we shall be acting thereafter. And because intention serves to determine our voluntary action, for as long as we retain an intention we must be genuinely disposed or ready to act as intended. We cannot lack the disposition because the intention is being overridden by a motivation to do something else.

Contrast desires. There seems nothing irrational in desire change as such. Some things can be just a matter of taste, and tastes can just change. And even if a desire is a desire specifically to act, it can be held while still being overridden; we can genuinely want to do A—but be disposed to do B instead because some other motivation, a desire or an intention, is overriding our desire to do A.

10.2.3 The rationality of intentions depends on the overall desirability of their objects

Intentions have the function of disposing us to act as intended, and of doing so in a way that ensures the rationality of our subsequent voluntary action. That means that the rationality of intentions, unlike that of desires, depends on the desirability overall or on balance of their voluntary objects.

Suppose I learn that an action I previously wanted very much to perform carries a cost—a cost which makes its performance, on balance, something bad. That need not remove my desire to perform the action or lessen its strength; but it should remove any intention I had to perform it. A rational intention cannot be based merely on the desirability or goodness of an action in some particular respect. The intention, after all, is supposed to be the final determinant of whether we perform the action or not.

By contrast, a rational desire can perfectly well be based on the goodness of its object in one respect only. The rationality of a desire does not depend on whether its object is good or bad on balance. Which is why we can quite rationally both want and want not to perform a given action, as in our desires we respond to both the good and the bad features of one and the same deed. A desire can rationally persist even if, balancing good against bad, its object is, on balance, undesirable. And that is because desires are not action-determining attitudes. A mere desire to perform an action does not have the function of ensuring that we actually perform it.

Of course at a given time a particular desire may perfectly well reflect the overall character of its object as the agent then believes it to be. Having taken everything into account known by him to date, on balance an agent may presently want to do A rather than B—because doing A will be more profitable and involve less effort. For the moment, then, this desire to do A rather than B constitutes an overall preference. It is this desire that reflects the present balance of all the relevant considerations known to the agent. But this desire is still different from any intention. For unlike an intention, the desire may rationally persist even if further information comes in to suggest that, overall, doing B is a better idea than doing A. Suppose that the agent learns that doing B, though less profitable and involving more effort, will win him far more friends. And suppose that on balance this makes doing B the best option. Then his desire to do A rather than B—the desire which reflects the greater ease and profitability of doing A—need not just vanish or even lessen. The greater profitability and ease of doing A may perfectly well leave the agent, as before, still very much wanting to do A and not B. It is just that this desire is now overridden, by another, differently based desire to do B rather than A—a desire which reflects the fact that, as he now knows, and despite any cost and effort involved, doing B will win him valuable friends.

Intentions should be sensitive to the generality of our beliefs about the actions which they motivate. And in this intentions differ from desires. It is, of course, possible for an intention to be formed acratically, in disregard of some of what we believe about the action intended and despite our judging that the action is overall bad. But the intention will still be formed *in spite of* those beliefs and that judgement; and the intention so formed will be open to rational criticism. Whereas the desires that motivate sub-intentional action are not similarly rationally tied to being guided by all that the agent believes about their objects.

It is the function of intention to respond to the overall value of its voluntary object. But this is a function which desire lacks. And this means that, though the existence of sufficient justification for intending to do A guarantees that doing A thereafter is good overall or on balance, the analogous guarantee does not apply to desires. That one has sufficient justification for wanting to do A guarantees no more than that doing A is good in some respect—not that doing A is good overall or on balance. Even the existence of justification for holding a very strong desire to do A does not guarantee that doing A is good overall. All that is guaranteed is that there is some respect in which doing A would be very desirable or good—which is neither necessary nor sufficient for the doing of A being good on balance.

In intention-formation we are responding to and applying practical reason—and so, in particular, we are applying reason as it concerns the voluntary. Which is why, as Chapter 4 argued, the rationality of forming an intention to do A must guarantee the rationality of voluntarily doing A thereafter. There is no analogue of this principle for desire. The rationality of desiring to do A does not similarly guarantee the rationality of actually doing A. And this shows that, by contrast, desire is not a reason-applying attitude in the same way. To form a desire is not to apply reason as it governs action. For the rationality of wanting to do something is not similarly tied to the rationality of actually doing it. The rationality of forming a desire in no way guarantees the rationality of acting as desired.[4]

10.2.4 Intentions as increasing the expectation that one will act as intended

Because intending to do A is apt to lead us to do A as intended, intentions generally increase our expectation that we will act as intended. This increased expectation—which, as I discuss below, may or may not reach the level of outright belief—results from the intention itself, so that when we are being motivated into voluntary action by our intentions we do not have to attend sensorily to our own behaviour to find out what we are being motivated and led to do. It is plausibly a condition on an intention's being held that it have some such effect on our expectations. But desires need not do this, since desires anyway lack the function of determining how we act.

The effect of intention on our expectations is linked to the action-integrating role played by intentions. Since by forming an intention to do something I generally leave myself knowing that I shall act as intended, or at least suspecting that I may do so, intending serves to integrate my voluntary action as a whole. I can base my remaining voluntary action on my knowledge that I am or may be doing what I intend to do, ensuring that the rest of what I do fits rationally with the intended action.

That makes intention the attitude which can impose a rational unity on our voluntary agency, enabling us to integrate the rest of what we do with the voluntary action which it motivates. Intention is the attitude that serves to ensure that our voluntary agency, when taken as a whole, is desirable, or at least not undesirable, rather than otherwise.

The effect of intentions on our expectations is central to how we plan and coordinate voluntary actions through time. Intentions, as we have seen, facilitate planning by determining our action in advance and at the same time informing us

---

[4] Hence, when an agent acts sub-intentionally, a desire can be rationally held but still motivate an agent to act in a way for which he has no rational justification. The failure in the agent's rationality comes not from the desire's being held at all, but from the fact that this mere desire alone is moving the agent to act. The failure of rationality lies not in the desire alone, but in its motivational effect—an effect which bypasses the agent's intentions, and so his capacity to exercise and apply practical reason. The agent's capacity for practical rationality is being bypassed, not misused. And so the agent's total motivational state—his being left disposed to perform the act desired—and the voluntary action that results is not so much irrational as non-rational.

beforehand of how we shall be acting. But remember that this planning function is only one part of intentions' role. The planning theory is only part of the truth. Intentions have a wider reason-applying role to play—a role that they play even in the motivation of action that is spontaneous and unplanned. Even if I am becoming motivated, quite spontaneously and without any advance planning, simply to do something right now, there can still be a need for my motivation to be responsive to the overall desirability of its voluntary object, at least as that object appears to me, and to inform me of what I am doing as I do it. And it is this motivation and information that intentions distinctively serve to provide.[5]

10.3 Intentions as Beliefs?

Harman and Velleman have both claimed that intentions are beliefs that one will do what is intended.[6] Such a view of intention is quite contrary to the theory of intention as a practical reason-applying motivation which is defended here.

Granted, as motivations that serve to apply practical reason, intentions need to affect the agent's beliefs about what he will do. When intending to do A increases the likelihood that the agent will do A, the intention's presence must ensure that this is reflected in an increased expectation on the agent's part that he will do A. But this increased expectation is an effect of the intention's presence, and not the intention itself. And the increased expectation need not be an outright belief.

For intentions may not be sure or even very likely to lead to the successful performance of the action intended—and nor need intenders suppose otherwise. True, when we believe that we will do what we intend, we commonly convey the intention to others simply by expressing our belief that we will perform the act intended: 'We will be going to Paris next week'. The context generally makes it clear that the issue depends on what we now intend; and so, simply by asserting that we will indeed be acting in a given way, we thereby convey the maximum of information with economy. We communicate our present intention, as well as the future occurrence of the act intended.

But this way of conveying our intentions provides no support for identifying intentions to do A as a kind of belief that we will do A. For there is another and concomitant way of reporting intentions which neatly undermines this identification. Suppose, in the same context, instead of expressing belief that we will do something,

---

[5] It is worth noting that the account given of intention is broadly consistent with that given by Alfred Mele in his *Springs of Action* (Oxford: Oxford University Press, 1992), p. 140. There he claims that intentions (1) motivate intentional actions, (2) guide and monitor behaviour, (3) facilitate action coordination, and (4) motivate and terminate practical reasoning. What the account of intention adds here is a more fundamental characterization of what is special about both intentional action and intention: in my view, the occurrence of agency and agency-motivation in reason-applying form. Intention is that attitude that serves to apply practical reason.

[6] See Gilbert Harman, 'Practical reasoning', *Review of Metaphysics* 29, (1976): pp. 431–63, and David Velleman, *Practical Reflection* (Princeton: Princeton University Press, 1989).

we report merely that we intend to do it. Given the way intentions are normally conveyed, this reticence about what we will actually do clearly warns our hearer that though we hold the intention, we do not yet believe that we will manage to carry it out. 'Are you going to Paris next week?' 'Well, that's what we *intend*'—which is enough to warn the hearer that we ourselves do not yet assume that we will actually get there. Our linguistic practice clearly shows that intentions can coexist with doubt that we will do what is intended. Which is what one would expect if the goals deliberately aimed at in voluntary action are, *ipso facto*, goals which are intended. We can perfectly well be deliberately and intentionally pursuing a goal—acting with the intention of attaining it—while being doubtful or even pessimistic of actually attaining it.

It is notable that this modern identification of intentions with a kind of belief that one will act as intended was quite absent from scholastic theories of intention. And this reflects the governing scholastic conception of intention as the reason-applying motivation involved in all goal-directed action that is fully intentional. To form intentions is just to direct oneself at goals, but on the basis of one's capacity for practical rationality. And one can perfectly well do that while being thoroughly doubtful that one will manage to attain the goals so aimed at and intended.

10.4 Summary: Intentions as Engaging Practical Reason

Intention, then, is that motivating attitude which engages our capacity to exercise and apply practical reason. Intention is that motivation which has the function of determining our voluntary action—and of determining it so as to ensure that our voluntary action is, taken overall and on balance, desirable and good or, at any rate, not undesirable or bad. Intention plays this role by informing us of what we are doing as we do it and by being responsive to the overall value of its object. The rationality of an intention is tied to that overall value as the rationality of a desire is not.

As we already observed in the last chapter, the scholastics sometimes misperceived this difference between intention and desire. They often supposed that intentions are responsive to the good in its most general form, including any goods that are intellectual—and so to the full range of ends that can justify action; whereas desire or mere passion is responsive only to those goods to which we can have a non-intellectual or sensory access. Desire is limited in its objects as intentions are not. But this, we saw, misstates the distinction. The objects of our intentions can also occur as objects of our desires, and both states can be formed in response to the full range of the good. The difference between intention and desire is rather the way that the two states respond to the good. Intention has a peculiar tie to the goodness or desirability of its object overall, while desire has not.

The scholastic misperception is easy to understand. For where desire alone is what is motivating an action—where the agent acts sub-intentionally—we are often dealing with a simple action performed on the basis of some immediate sensory pleasurability or relief from discomfort, such as doodling, scratching, stretching, and the like. Such actions can in general be safely performed in detachment from any consideration of their overall value. The gain from performing them is immediate and obvious, the loss generally—except, say, at important meetings—negligible. Passion as usurping the motivational place of intention is, not always, but often, passion as directed at some good in non-intellectual or sensory form.

We have now explained why, as common sense and the practical reason-based model both maintain, voluntary action that is intentional must be motivated by intention. Action that is intentional must engage our capacity for practical reason. And so it must involve a specific motivation—a motivation whose function is to be fully responsive to reason as it governs the voluntary, and then, on the basis of that responsiveness, to determine what we do voluntarily; and that motivation is intention. To form intentions, then, is to acquire a motivation in the exercise of one's capacity for practical reason. We shall now see how the exercise of practical reason in intention-formation itself constitutes intentional action.

11

The Action-Constitutive Exercise of Reason

11.1 Applying Reason Practically

Action which is intentional is action that engages the capacity for practical reason. And essential to the engagement of this capacity, I have argued, is the attitude of intention. Which is why intentional action—action based on our capacity for practical reason—must, as its name suggests, be action which involves intention.

Now one could admit all this, while still remaining within the framework of a theory of action that is voluntariness-based. One could admit that, if action is to be intentional, the agent's capacity for practical reason must be engaged, and that therefore the agent's motivation must come from intention. But one could nevertheless continue to deny that intentional action itself consists in any mode of exercising rationality. Intentional agency may presuppose the exercise of practical reason, but its own nature is distinct, and consists in voluntariness. On this view, and just as the voluntariness-based model teaches, action remains constituted such by being an effect or expression of a pro attitude to its performance. It's just that for the action to be intentional, the motivating pro attitude must be one which is distinctively reason-involving. The motivating pro attitude must be intention.

To arrive at a model of intentional action that is practical reason-based, we need to establish something more: that intentional action not only presupposes, but itself occurs as the application of practical reason. Intentional actions, I shall now argue, are precisely those events, whether they be intention-formations or voluntariness motivated by intentions, in which our capacity to respond to and apply practical justifications is being exercised. In intentional action our capacity for practical reason is being exercised practically, as action. And what makes this true is a link between the exercise of practical reason and a characteristic feature of agency—goal-directedness.

As we have seen, goal-directedness does not just involve an event's having some function—that of producing a certain outcome or effect. The agent must be employing that event as a means, being motivated to do so by the end at which that means is being directed. But something more than employing means towards an end is involved—for, as we have seen, we can employ means to ends sub-intentionally, when we act voluntarily on the basis of a mere desire. To act intentionally then involves a further element. As the last chapter showed, it involves pursuing a goal on the basis of intention—in and through the exercise of our capacity for reason.

In fact, I shall now show, when an agent acts intentionally, she is not just pursuing a goal, and she is not just exercising a capacity for rationality. In pursuing the goal the means she is using is that very exercise of her own rationality—and she is being motivated to do so by the very goal which that exercise of rationality is being used to attain. And, as I shall here argue, we exercise reason in this goal-directed way whenever we apply reason in its practical or action-governing form.

There are two importantly different ways of exercising reason practically, as action—non-voluntarily, in intention-formation, and voluntarily, in acting as intended. So I shall consider the non-voluntary case of intention-formation first. Then we can consider the voluntary case—to which it is important that the practical reason-based model also equally applies.

11.2 The Action-Constitutive Exercise of Reason: The Case of Intention-Formation

We are responding to practical reason when we form intentions to act. But when we form these intentions, we are not only responding to practical reason. We are exercising reason practically—as action. And what shows this is the relation between a decision or intention-formation and its object.

This object is provided by the content, not of any other motivation, but of the decision itself. Decisions and the states of intention that they initiate are content-bearing occurrences in their own right. They involve a certain mode of direction at an object—an object provided by their very own content. It is this mode of direction that makes decisions exercises of rationality that are goal-directed—and so intentional actions—with their object as the goal being aimed at. And what reveals this mode of direction is the very nature of decision rationality—the way that decisions and the intentions they form are governed by reason. Decisions and intention-formations are events which reason treats as goal-directed doings, as actions. And if it is reason itself which treats decisions as actions, then actions are what decisions must really be.

The theory of rationality that reveals decisions to be actions will equally show that desires are passive attitudes. Desires and the events of coming to hold them are not goal-directed—with the consequence that coming to hold a desire is not an action. So Hobbes' challenge, to show how intention-formation is an action as desire-formation is not, can be met.

11.2.1 Decisions and desire-formations

Let us examine decision rationality in more detail, comparing it with the rationality of desire-formation as we go. If a decision or intention-formation is an action, it must have some goal or end. For any action, we have agreed, must be directed at attaining some goal. In the case of a decision one such goal is obvious. A decision's goal must surely be the attainment of what has been decided. If deciding that E is an action, its goal or end must be the attainment of E. In which case the correct model for the rationality of a decision that E must be the rationality of an action whose goal or end is E's attainment. And that, we shall now see, is exactly how the rationality of a decision should be modelled.

As much as desire, action occurs as a response to what is good or desirable. In argument to persuade someone into acting in order to attain an end E, you need, by way of justification, to argue or assume that what E involves is indeed good—exactly what you would have to argue to get someone to want E. But of course to provide a sufficient justification for action, as opposed to a justification for merely wanting to act, the goodness of E must be a goodness on balance or overall, and not merely in a particular respect.

And this is what we have already found with decisions. The point of taking decisions about how to act is, as we have observed, to ensure that we end up performing the right voluntary actions, or at least avoid performing the wrong ones. So a decision's rationality must depend on the goodness or desirability overall of its object—the subsequent performance of the voluntary action decided upon. That action must be on balance desirable, or at least not undesirable. Decisions must occur as responses that are appropriate to the goodness on balance or overall of their objects.

But for a decision or intention that E be justified, the sufficient goodness or desirability of E is not enough. Since action directed at attaining E is about, precisely, *attaining* E, the action must also be sufficiently likely to bring that end about. And so it is with a decision that E. The function of decision and intention is to ensure that we perform the action decided upon and intended. And the rationality of decision and intention reflects this function. Taking a decision or forming an intention is justified only if this action-determining function is likely to be fulfilled—only if the object decided on and intended is likely enough to be attained through deciding on it. Deciding to attain E is only justified if taking that decision is likely enough to bring E about. Which is why sensible people don't take decisions about matters their decisions clearly can't affect; since the function of decisions is to lead to their fulfilment, that a decision has no chance of doing this is a conclusive argument against taking it. I may, quite rationally, very much want and hope to spend my old age doing useful and interesting things, rather than in idleness. But there's no point my now deciding or intending to spend my old age being useful if that intention will have no effect—if, for example, given the long time yet to pass, no intention I formed now would make any difference to my motivations in old age.

Desire-formations are non-actions. And that is because they are not goal-directed events. They are not formed as means to attaining what is desired. This shows up in the rationality of desire-formation. There is nothing irrational about coming to want something to happen while being very sure that if it happens, it will happen other than because one wants it to happen. We have and report such wants and desires all the time, and no one criticizes their rationality. Who do I want to win the cup? It's England that I want to win the cup—simply because, from my point of view, England's winning would be highly desirable. Perhaps England is my national team; or perhaps it's just that England's winning would put my boss in a good mood. Such considerations are quite enough to leave an England win a perfectly sensible thing for me to want. I need not also suppose, what is obviously false, that my wanting England to win will actually help England to win. What I happen to want will most certainly have no effect at all on England's chances of winning. But that does not matter. Since my desire for England to win is not something I am actually forming in order to get England to win, the fact that the actual outcome will be quite unaffected by the desire is quite irrelevant to the rationality of my forming it.

Sometimes it's not just that I want something to happen which will happen, if it does, independently of my wanting it to. Its happening independently can be part of what I want, and very much matter to the desirability of what I desire. Parents, for example, might reasonably want their grown up children to do the right thing—but to do the right thing for themselves, and quite independently of the fact that their parents want them to do it. Suppose a parent is indeed sure that her grown-up children's actions are by now entirely beyond parental influence. What the children end up doing is sure to be causally independent of that parent's wants and attitudes. Given this belief, it is still both rational and natural for the parent very much to want her children to do the right thing—all the more so as this, if the child does it, will be its independent achievement. What, under the circumstances, the parent cannot rationally do is *decide* or form an *intention* that her children will do the right thing. And that is because reason governs the decision as a goal-directed action—as an exercise of rationality with a goal, namely ensuring the doing of the decision's object, what has been decided. For it is always and obviously irrational to employ an action as means towards an end when one is sure the means employed will have no effect on the attainment of that end.

Notice that the following does not appear to be a possibility: that though there be a perfectly good justification for taking a decision to do A—a justification that lies in the fact both that doing A would be very desirable, and also that deciding to do A would ensure that A was done; nevertheless the decision is still taken irrationally since, despite being taken, it is not in fact taken as a means to doing A—to that particular object's attainment. Such a failure when taking a decision to use it as a means to acting as decided is something we never allow for in appraising the rationality of someone's decision.

That is surely because by the very nature of decisions that possibility never occurs. To take a decision to do A just is to exercise one's will with the aim of ensuring that one does A. Whenever an agent takes a decision, she must in taking it be performing a goal-directed action; and at least one goal motivating the decision is written into it by the decision's very nature—which is the object specified in the decision's content. And we always appraise the rationality of the decision on this assumption.

An event is an intentional action if it is rationally appraisable—an exercise of reason—and has an object; and if its rationality depends not only on that object being sufficiently desirable, but also on the object being sufficiently likely to be attained through the event's occurrence. In other words, an event's status as an action comes from reason treating its object as its goal. Decisions fit this model. So decisions are actions. Desire-formation does not fit this model. Which is why desire-formation is passive.

11.2.2 Exercising reason, as action and otherwise

Two notions here are key. First, there is the notion of an event. For an action is not distinguished just by its having goal direction. Persisting states too can have goal-direction. I can remain very still, and do so for a purpose—to remain unseen and unsuspected by you. Despite its having this goal, my remaining very still is not an action, but rather a deliberate omission of action. What is lacking is change—the occurrence of a definite event. Action is goal-directedness in change. As for voluntary agency, so too for agency in its non-voluntary form: for action we need a definite event. Something must actually happen. So it is content-bearing events of decision or intention-formation, events of psychological change, that constitute action, and not the persisting states of intention thereby formed—even though in both cases we have the same mode of direction at a content-provided object, and so the same phenomenon of goal-direction.

The second key notion is, of course, goal-direction. And this notion is a very specific one. It involves some attitudes—but not attitudes generally. Now this may not be obvious. For attitudes generally are often said to have aims. Beliefs are said to 'aim' at truth, desires and intentions to 'aim' at the good. In which case, it seems, all such attitudes and the events of forming them will turn out to be goal-directed. Does this mean that, contrary to what I have so far been arguing, on my theory any attitude-formation whatsoever is an action?[1]

Not so. This talk of attitudes as having aims does not imply genuine goal-direction. It does not mean that attitudes or attitude-formations in general have goals as actions do, but something much weaker. It is simply that each such attitude has a function. And this function is given by a concept—be it a concept of truth or of goodness or of something else—which helps define the proper object of the attitude, and so what it is for the attitude to be rationally formed. Thus beliefs are rationally formed only if their objects are likely to be true; desires and intentions only if their objects are likely to be sufficiently good or desirable. But this does not make belief- or desire-formations or attitude-formations generally all goal-directed actions. For in this sense of 'aim', intentional actions as goal-directed events 'aim', that is, are properly directed, at something very special: not truth, nor simply the good—but the attainment of the

---

[1] My thanks to David Gauthier for putting this objection to me.

Table 11.1. Modes of rationality

Mode in which rationality exercised	Cognitive	Desiderative	Practical
attitude formed	belief	desire	intention
object responded to	as true	as good	as a good end to be attained by intending it
justification for response	likelihood of object's truth	likely goodness of object in some respect	likelihood of intention's attaining object and the object's overall goodness as so attained

good through the action. An action is rationally performed only if its object is both likely enough to be good, and likely enough to be attained through the action. That is what makes the object of an action a genuine goal—an end which the action is being used as means to attain (Table 11.1).

Compare the case of genuine action with belief. Belief may 'aim' at truth. But belief-formation is not, just by its very nature as a cognition that aims at truth, a goal-directed action. And this is because in aiming at truth, the rationality of forming a belief that p depends, not on the likelihood of some good's being attained through forming the belief, but simply on the likelihood that the belief's object is true. So, for example, arriving at the truth about whether p may be desirable or good; but also—if the truth is unpleasant or trivial—it may not. Either way, in general the issue is irrelevant to the rationality of forming a belief that p—which depends simply on whether p is likely enough to be true.[2]

Crucial to whether an attitude-formation is by its very nature an action is the exact nature of its relation to its object—to what the agent is coming to believe, desire, or intend. That object must stand to the attitude-formation as the object of an action stands to it—as a goal to be brought about. And among attitude-formations, by this criterion, only decisions and intention-formations count by their very nature as actions. For only in their case does the rationality of the attitude-formation depend both on its object's goodness and on the likelihood of the object's being attained through the attitude-formation.

---

[2] Particular cases of belief-formation might still count as actions. In forming some beliefs it might be that we are responding both to some claim as true, and to some outcome as a desirable goal to be attained through the belief-formation. I do not wish to rule out this possibility. My point is simply that belief-formation is not a goal-directed action considered just as a cognition—considered just as a response to an object of thought as true.

For a preliminary discussion of issues concerning a possible agency of belief, see Thomas Pink, 'Law and the normativity of obligation'. We shall return to the case of a possible agency of belief and to its normative implications in *Normativity: The Ethics of Action, volume 2*.

An intention-formation is therefore justified practically—by the goodness of its object, but also by the intention's efficacy at ensuring that object's attainment. That tie to the goodness or desirability of its object, the act intended, makes intention as non-voluntary as is desire; but an intention's distinctive practical role—its serving and being justified as a means to its object's attainment—makes intention-formations intentional actions nonetheless.

11.2.3 Intentional action without decision-making

It is important not to over-intellectualize what an action of intention-formation involves. Though for simplicity I often talk as if intention-formation and decision-making were the same, the action of forming an intention can fall short of explicit choice. It need not occur as the full-blown taking of a decision. Decisions, properly speaking, are those cases of intention-formation—of starting to intend—which occur given, if not actual deliberation, at least some explicit entertainment of alternatives to the action finally intended. But much of what we do intentionally or deliberately, at both the non-voluntary and voluntary levels, does not involve actual prior deliberation, or even the entertainment of alternatives.

For example, when you ask me something and I reply, I am certainly acting intentionally or deliberately. I am acting with the intention of replying—an intention which I immediately formed on hearing your question, and which is motivating my reply. But I needn't count as having taken a decision to reply, because I probably won't even have entertained and considered the alternative of not replying, let alone deliberated about that alternative. And that will be because it was so obvious that replying was the only sensible thing to do. The alternatives were not worth considering. Contrast a hostile interrogation, where my every reply may have been preceded by a careful decision whether to respond at all.

The practical reason-based model need not claim that all actions of intention-formation have to occur as decisions. The model of agency can still apply, even in the absence of my intention-formation counting as a full-blown decision or choice. The reason is clear. The model identifies intentional agency with an exercise of one's capacity for practical reason. And even if I haven't actually entertained alternative options, my intention-formation can still constitute such an exercise of my capacity for reason. For it may be a measure of my rationality that, without having even to rehearse alternatives, I can so readily form an intention to do what is, after all, the obviously right thing—replying to you. I do not have to rehearse the alternatives to myself just because my reason is engaged—because the right thing is, to me, as a practically rational being, so obviously right.

So when I form an intention to reply, but without having to make a choice or decision, the formation of that intention is still a deliberate and intentional action—as much as is the reply that results. Both in forming the intention and in carrying it out, I am deliberately aiming at a goal—responding to you. In both cases my action is no less deliberate because I have not expressly considered an alternative.

Intentionality or deliberateness in what I do may depend on my being able to entertain alternatives and deliberate about them. There is this link between deliberateness in action and the capacity for deliberation. But my capacity for deliberation need not actually be exercised in every case of intentional action. I need not even consciously consider alternatives. Still less need I deliberate and entertain alternatives when I have no reason to bother, precisely because it is all too obvious to me or to anyone sensible what I should do.

11.3 The Action-Constitutive Exercise of Reason: The Case of Voluntary Action

We have arrived at a model of intentional agency that, as promised, is practical reason-, and not voluntariness-based. The practical reason-based model characterizes intentional action, not as the voluntary product of a passive motivation, but as a practice- or action-constitutive mode of exercising reason. To perform an intentional action is to exercise one's reason purposively, in pursuit of a goal.

It is important that this model of intentional action can apply not only to intention-formations, but also to the voluntary actions intended. We do not want a theory of action which is volitionist—which leaves actions of the will, of decision and intention-formation, the only actions to which the model can directly apply. The model must also apply to intentional action in its voluntary form. Intentional action in voluntary form had better not turn out to be what it was treated as being in scholastic action theory—no more than an intended effect of a prior action of the will.

But it looks as though the practical reason-based model can directly apply to what we do voluntarily, and not just to actions of the will. First, just as much as intention-formation, voluntary action can perfectly well occur as a mode of exercising reason. What is it, after all, to exercise reason? It is to do something for which there can be justifications *pro* or *contra*—and to do it on the basis of one's capacity to be guided by such justifications. But that is exactly what happens when one performs a voluntary action on the basis of an intention to perform it.

As I have already argued in Chapter 3, voluntary action is certainly something for which there can be justifications *pro* or *contra*. Moreover, when it is motivated by intention, a voluntary action is being performed on the basis of one's capacity to be guided by such justifications. And that is because, as the last chapter showed, intention is that motivating pro attitude which serves to apply reason as it governs the voluntary. Intentions are exactly the pro attitudes which are sensitive to all the justifications for and against their voluntary objects, and which serve to determine voluntary actions on the basis of those justifications.

So just as with intention-formation itself, when one acts voluntarily on the basis of an intention one is doing something reason-governed on the basis of one's capacity to be guided by justifications for and against doing it. One is exercising one's capacity for rationality—one's reason. And this exercise of one's reason counts as action because its object stands to it as its goal—as an object which the exercise of reason, the voluntary action, is being motivated by and which it is directed to attaining. What shows that the object is a goal? As with intention-formation, what shows this is the way the voluntary action's rationality depends on this object at which it is being directed. The mode of dependence is that appropriate to something done in order to attain the object. For the action to be performed rationally, that object must be sufficiently desirable, and the action must also be sufficiently likely to attain the object.

Remember that we needed to explain how intentional action can occur in two apparently very different forms. It can occur as intention-formation—and here its occurrence seems to be non-voluntary. It seems to be independent of any motivating pro attitude towards forming that intention. But intentional action can also occur in voluntary form, based on a pro attitude to performing it—and here its occurrence is very much dependent on the occurrence of that motivating attitude. To account for intentional agency, then, we needed a common factor—some action-constitutive phenomenon which can arise equally well in each of these two rather different forms: in a form independent of a further attitude motivating us so to act, and a form very much dependent on such motivation.

The practical exercise of reason is the factor that we have been seeking—a factor to unite intentional action in each of its two forms. In each case of action, both the non-voluntary case and the voluntary, we are exercising reason purposively—we are making a rationally appraisable response to an object as goal, and on the basis of our capacity to be guided by justifications for and against making it. And in each case both the object responded to and the capacity to be guided by reason is provided by intention. But in the non-voluntary case, the response is the formation of the intention itself—and so the response's object, the goal of the action, is provided by a content which the response has just as that intention-formation. In the voluntary case, the response is made on the basis of and as the object of an intention so to act. And here the object of the response, and also the capacity to be guided by justifications for and against making it, is provided by that motivating intention. In the one case the action—the action-constitutive exercise of reason—occurs in a form independent of motivation by an intention so to act. In the other case motivation by such an intention is presupposed. But each case is still a perfectly good case of the action-constitutive exercise of reason—a perfectly good case of intentional action.

There is of course one important way in which decisions or actions of the will do differ from actions in voluntary form—a way that we have already mentioned. As actions, decisions are inherently intentional. If I take a decision to do A rather than a decision to do B, I cannot do so inadvertently or unintentionally. But, as O'Shaughnessy reminded us, one can perform voluntary actions that, though goal-directed and purposive, are in no way intentional. The explanation for this difference between the inherent intentionality of decisions and the possible sub-intentionality of voluntary actions is by now obvious.

Agency in intentional form has not only to be goal-directed. It must also engage, through intention, the agent's capacity for practical reason. The difference between non-voluntary intention-formation and voluntary action is simply this. Action in voluntary form can occur independently of intention, being motivated by simple desire, and so a way that is not reason-applying at all. So in the case of the voluntary action, goal-directedness can be found quite detached from deliberateness or intentionality. But of course this is not true if the action is the formation of an intention. For the attitude formed is just that attitude which not only guarantees purposiveness, but which is reason-applying—which engages our capacity for practical reason.

I have argued that the practical reason-based model is not overtly volitionist. Given that a voluntary action is motivated by an intention so to act, it constitutes a purposive exercise of reason in pursuit of a goal. So the practical reason-based model does apply to voluntary actions as well. The model does not apply just to decisions and intention-formations—to actions of the will. But, it might be objected, this is not really enough to detach the practical reason-based model from volitionism. After all, the practical reason-based model only applies to voluntary action as motivated by intention. So it looks as though what we do voluntarily still only counts as our intentional doing as an effect and expression of something else—an attitude of intention—that is itself formed through our own deliberate agency, and that counts as our own intentional doing in a far more immediate way, just as the kind of attitude-formation it is. We seem, then, stuck after all with something very like volitionism. There is intentional action in its immediate or primary form—inner actions of the will itself, deliberate actions of decision and intention-formation that count as our doing immediately; and then there is the rest of our deliberate action, our voluntary action, which occurs only as an intended effect of intentional action in its primary form.

But this objection makes some debatable assumptions. First, it assumes that intentions always arise through actions of intention-formation. But that is not obviously true. An intention may be held, and may be motivating an agent to act as intended; but there may have been no definite event, and so no action, of forming it. As far as the practical reason-based model is concerned, what matters to intentional agency at the point of the voluntary is that the voluntary action be motivated by the reason-responsive attitude of intention, not that that intention is in turn formed by some action of the will. Whether or not such an action of the will occurred plays no role in the account of the intentionality of the voluntary action.

Secondly, the objection assumes that when there is an action of decision or intention-formation, the voluntary action motivated occurs as nothing more than an intended effect of the decision. It is assumed that actions of the will are wholly inner occurrences that are ontologically quite distinct from the voluntary actions they motivate and explain, so that there can be the contrast that lies at the heart of volitionism—between action in its immediate form, a wholly inner action of the will, and voluntary action, as a supposedly quite different and derivative form of action that only occurs as a willed or intended effect of actions of the will.

But there is nothing in the practical reason-based model that commits us to this view of decisions and their relation to the voluntary. As we shall see in the next chapter, once we think through the implications of the practical reason-based model, we need no longer make a rigid ontological distinction between the non-voluntary attitudes of decision and intention and the voluntary actions they motivate and explain. Decisions and the actions decided upon may occur as aspects, respectively non-voluntary and voluntary, of one and the same intentional action. Not only does the practical reason-based model tell the same rationality-involving story about voluntary action that it tells about non-voluntary action. It allows, in many cases, for an identification of these two forms of action. We shall return in the next chapter to examine further the relation between voluntary actions and the attitudes that motivate them. Once we properly understand the relationship between motivating attitudes and voluntary actions, the suspicion that the practical reason-based model is in any way a volitionist theory can finally be removed.

11.4 Animal Action

It seems that many, at least, of the lower animals lack our capacity for reason. They do not share our capacity to consider and respond to justifications. If so, then the practical reason-based model of action cannot apply to them. But is this not an objection to the model? For surely it is just obvious that animals perform actions as we do. At least Hobbes' appeal to voluntariness allowed for action to take the same form in human and animal alike. And indeed the Hobbesian tradition takes this to be an especial advantage of their model—that it provides a general account of action that can unproblematically apply to rational humans and non-rational animals alike.

But this objection misrepresents the practical reason-based model and what it implies. The model does not deny that animals can perform actions, or do things as a means to ends. All that follows from the model is that animals do not perform actions that are deliberate or intentional as human actions can be deliberate and intentional. It does not follow that animal action involving purposiveness is impossible. For we have already seen that there can be human action that by-passes our capacity for practical reason too. This is action that occurs in sub-intentional form—which occurs as voluntary action motivated by desire.

Moreover, although the scholastic tradition tended to deny that non-rational animals are in any way capable of decision-making, this view may require some qualification. For just as there are versions of belief, desire, and other attitudes in the lower, non-rational animals, so too there may be versions of decision. Consider beliefs in us. Beliefs occur in humans as attitudes responsive to various kinds of theoretical justification for and against their objects. In lower animals incapable of reason, belief will certainly not occur in that form. But it does not follow that animals lack a capacity for cognition altogether. It need not follow that there are no truth-directed attitudes in these animals. They may still possess cognitive attitudes that, without being responsive to anything understood by the animals as justifications, still resemble our beliefs in other respects, such as in their sensitivity to sensory or perceptual states that represent their truth, or in the way these cognitive attitudes interact with motivations to give rise to action in voluntary form. Similarly for desires, which may in animals function similarly to desires in us, though without being formable on the basis of thoughts about what is good or desirable as our desires can be.

Just as there may be analogues in lower animals of our belief or desire, but as attitudes that are non-rational, so too among the motivations of lower animals there might be analogues of our decision and intention. These attitudes might not be sensitive to anything understood by the animal as a justification for deciding. They might not be sensitive to thoughts about the goodness or desirability of their objects overall, or about the likelihood of the attitudes helping attain those objects. But these motivations might still serve to determine what the animal voluntarily does as mere desires need not; and again, unlike mere desires, but like decisions and intentions, the motivations may do so in a way sensitive to the full range of the animal's cognition regarding the motivation's object and its possible consequences. These motivations would then be non-rational analogues of decision and intention as these occur in us, just as beliefs and desires in animals are non-rational analogues of beliefs and desires in us. Animal decisions might be non-rational attitudes; but just as animal beliefs could still be directed at their objects as true and animal desires still be directed at their objects as desirable, so these animal decisions could still be directed at their objects as goals to be attained.

So not only can voluntary action occur in animals. There may also be actions of animal decision—animal action in non-voluntary form. In neither case would the animal performing the actions be acting intentionally or deliberately as we do. In neither case would any capacity for genuine reason be engaged. But in each case there would be purposiveness or the use of means in pursuit of ends.

11.5 Action without Passion

English-language philosophers may disagree about whether actions occur as effects of motivations to perform them. But on the whole they do mostly agree that for action to occur some motivation is required that is distinct from the action motivated—motivation of which the action is at least the expression, if not the effect. This motivation will be directed at the action's goal. And, since otherwise their theory would be viciously regressive, this motivation must itself be passive. In this sense it will be some kind of desire—a desire to do what the action aims at doing. On causal theories the action is caused by the desire. But the doctrine may take non-causal form too. Action may be seen as by its very nature performed, not as an effect of, but nevertheless 'in the light of' some prior desire.[3] Again, the motivation could on some views be cognitive—a 'besire' or belief that is also a desire. It might, for example, be a belief that attaining the goal aimed at would be good or desirable, where the very possession of this belief is supposed to motivate. Or the motivation might be some non-cognitive mere 'passion'. But some such motivating attitude must always precede and motivate our action.

This assumption is one that the practical reason-based model denies. Decision- or intention-formation counts as an intentional action—but on terms that have nothing to do with motivation by prior desires. This story told of why decisions are actions is entirely independent of such desires. For a decision's goal-direction is not, as on the voluntariness-based model, provided by the content of some passive motivation. It is instead a function of the decision's own content and of the mode of direction which the decision constitutes towards that content. Decisions are content-bearing attitude-formations—startings to intend—whose occurrence, just as much as with belief-formations or desire-formations, constitutes a distinctive exercise, competent or defective, of the agent's capacity for reason. Just as the truth-directedness of a belief or belief-formation is internal to it, and comes from the very nature of belief as cognitive in relation to its content, so too the goal-directedness of a decision is internal to it, and comes from its very nature as practical in relation to *its* content.

Nor should this be a strange idea. After all, as we noted from the very beginning, actions are said to have objects—as much so as beliefs and desires. Just as we can talk of the object of a belief, we can talk of the object of an action—an object which is the action's goal. And at least some goal-directed actions may come to possess their objects in the same way as do events of belief- and desire-formation; not through being expressions or effects of prior attitudes directed at the same object, but through their possession of a content of their own. In other words decisions may count as actions through being events of attitude-formation in their own right—attitude-formations whose contents specify what object it is at which they are directed, and

---

[3] Thus Hugh McCann denies that actions are effects of prior desires, but still claims that: '...like all intentional behavior, decisions demand reasons...' McCann, 'The formation of intention' in *The Works of Agency*, p. 164.

By 'reasons' McCann means here motivations—motivations which are provided by prior action-explanatory attitudes such as desires. And all actions, decisions included, presuppose such prior motivations, without which they would have no genuine goal direction:

> Just as I cannot intentionally take my son to Swensen's if I have no reason for taking him there, so I cannot intentionally decide to take my son to Swensen's if I have no reason so to decide. Otherwise, my decision would be a non-rational act, a forming of a purpose *without a purpose*. McCann, 'The formation of intention', *The Works of Agency*, p. 164—my emphasis.

According to McCann, the decision is taken, not as an effect of, but 'in the light of' these prior motivations.

Table 11.2. Voluntariness-based model

Passive motivation		Intentional action
motivation to do A		doing A
(counts as passive because motivating attitude that is non-voluntary)		(counts as active only because done voluntarily, on basis of motivations)
object determined by content	*provides*	object *qua* goal
passive rationality	*determines*	rationality of action

Table 11.3. Practical reason-based model

Intentional action in non-voluntary form		Intentional action in voluntary form
forming intention to do A		doing A
(intentional as practical exercise of rationality in non-voluntary intention-formation)		(intentional as practical exercise of rationality, in that done voluntarily on basis of intention)
object determined by content is also object *qua goal*	*provides*	object *qua* goal

whose kind determines in what way they are directed at that object. And this is a central feature of the practical reason-based model of agency.

So the status of decisions as actions comes from their character as the kind of content-bearing events that they are. But that means that their status as actions is not derived from prior attitudes—just as the character of other events of attitude-formation is derived, not from prior attitudes but from their own internal constitution.

On the voluntariness-based model, we saw, the systematic differences between non-voluntary pro attitudes and voluntary actions are turned into differences between passion and action (Table 11.2).

So the formation of pro attitudes may constitute a response to and application of practical reason—but it is an exercise of rationality which is passive, not active; and the goal-direction of our action is given to us, determined by motivations that are passive and not our own doing.

But with the practical reason-based model this is not so. The exercise of practical reason is inherently active; and the goal-direction of our agency can now be our own direct doing—entirely determined by what we ourselves do (Table 11.3).

For on the practical reason-based model the goal-direction and rationality of what we do intentionally depend on a pro attitude, the attitude of intention, the forming of which can itself be an intentional action, and over which we can have direct control. The goal-direction and rationality of our agency can now be determined by actions of intention-formation by which we as agents intentionally motivate ourselves towards this goal rather than that. The objects *qua* goals of our voluntary actions are the contents, not of a passion, but of a motivation that is practical—that can itself be formed by goal-directed action. And that leaves action something that can occur quite independently of prior passions or passive motivations—something which, on the voluntariness-based model, is quite impossible.

Kant developed his ethical theory within the framework of a practical reason-based model of agency.[4] Notice how for Kant, a free agent's goals may be freely adopted by him as an initial exercise of his capacity for agency, and are certainly not imposed on him by 'nature'—by passive motivations:

> An *end* is an *object* of free choice, the representation of which determines it to an action (by which the object is brought about). Every action, therefore, has its end; and since no one can have an end without *himself* making the object of his choice into an end, to have any end of action whatsoever is an act of *freedom* on the part of the acting subject, not an effect of *nature*.[5]

On the practical reason-based model, free agency can indeed involve the initial free adoption, through intention-formation, of an end; and it can be through the effects of this free end-adoption that 'the object is brought about'—that voluntary action occurs, sharing the goal of the initial decision to perform it. Whereas on the voluntariness-based model, the ends of action are always 'effects of nature'; they are always supplied by content-bearing causes of action that are passive, causes that count as 'nature' in that they are not our own doing.

Notice that I do not deny the very obvious truth that end-directed actions can, as a matter of contingent fact, be motivated by prior passive motivations—such as desires which are directed at the very same objects. If I decide to attain E, or otherwise direct my action at attaining E, it is certainly possible, perhaps even quite usual for me to have been moved to do so by, for example, some prior desire or yen for attaining E. My point is not to deny this possibility, but simply to urge that my intentional action of deciding to attain E is not something dependent for its identity and nature on such a passive influence. Deciding to attain E is something that, in principle at least, I can do without being moved to do so by some prior and passive desire so to act.

Many English-language philosophers write as if it were just obvious that all action occurs as the expression of desire—of motivations which are passive. But this is not obvious. Sometimes the first and only ground we have for supposing that we are motivated to do something is that we actually have performed an action directed at

---

[4] This claim, like many claims about Kantian moral psychology, has to be qualified to take into account his peculiar metaphysics. For in important respects as an action-theorist Kant is also a Hobbesian thinker. His view of action *qua phenomenon* owes much to the voluntariness-based model, and in ways that affect his conception of agency as a whole. This is a matter I discuss later on when we consider what kind of knowledge we have of our own freedom.

[5] Immanuel Kant, *Metaphysics of Morals*, Ak 6:384–5, in *The Cambridge Edition of the Works of Immanuel Kant: Practical Philosophy*, p. 516.

doing just that thing. Our first and only ground may be that that thing is something which we actually have decided to do.

Here is an example. Suppose that one afternoon, having paused to rest during a stroll, I decide to stand up to continue my walk, rather than stay sitting by the river or start to go home. This decision to continue my walk is my very own decision—a decision that I quite deliberately take. The decision then is my very own doing—an action of mine. But just because it is my own action the decision need not appear to be motivated or caused in any way by some prior desire. For until the moment of that decision there need have been no detectable desire on my part whatsoever to go on with my walk. Prior to the decision there need have been no evidence or hint of a passion or other inclination that was somehow moving me towards deciding on that particular option. And that, I suspect, is because there need have been no such prior desire. On the face of it, sometimes we can just decide to do things, without any desire or other passive motivation having moved us so to decide.

What decisions we take and how we decide is indeed our own doing. A decision is not some passive event which comes over us like a feeling. That is something of which in everyday life we are deeply convinced. But this conviction certainly does not rest on any belief that we are moved to decide as we do by desires. Suppose I do just decide to do something, and it appears that I take that decision without any prior desire having motivated me so to decide. At any rate there is no independent evidence of any such desire. Cannot my taking that particular decision still have been my own deliberate and intentional doing? Should the apparent lack of any prior desire inclining me towards taking that or any decision lead me to doubt whether the decision really is my own doing—my own quite deliberately taken decision? A doubt so grounded seems absurd. The presence of such a desire seems quite inessential to my belief that my own decisions are indeed my very own doing. My own decisions are my own doing simply because they are decisions of mine—and not because of any prior motivations they might have. And now we can see exactly why. What makes the decision my own action is not any prior pro attitude, but the kind of content-bearing event which the decision itself is—the kind of attitude to its content which it initiates and constitutes.

There is an objection to this sort of example that is always raised. In the case of the stroll and in all like cases, how do we know there is not some hidden desire that is motivating the decision? The contents of the mind are not transparent. There may be many things motivating us of which we have no awareness. Action has not actually been shown to occur apart from passion.

And of course we do not know that motivating passions are not present. But this misses the point of the example, which is certainly not to rule out the possibility of such hidden motivations. What matters in such cases is that we have no particular reason to suppose such prior motivations to be present; and that our belief that our decisions are our own doing plainly does not depend on any hypothesis that such desires must be present. Doubt about the existence of such desires does not lead us to doubt that we took the decisions of ourselves, deliberately and intentionally. Nor should it, as there is another story to be told about what makes decisions actions that is independent of such desires—the story that has just been told.

11.6 Purposes and Representations

Jay Wallace has also proposed a view of decisions as actions that appeals to the special character of decisions as content-bearing attitudes. So his view is related to mine, but is also significantly different from it.[6] My view of how decisions are actions is practical reason-based, whereas Wallace's view is content-based; and the two views are not the same.

In Wallace's view, the reasons for someone's decision to do A are represented as its goals by the decision's own content. For we do not decide simply to perform some action A. We always decide to do A in order that E. That is, the content of the decision will always represent a goal—attaining E—as the purposed end of doing A, the reason why A is to be done. It follows from this representation of purposiveness that the decision and the action which it explains have a motivation or reason. They are aimed at attaining E.[7]

Alfred Mele makes two objections to Wallace's doctrine.[8] First, the reason for a decision cannot always be represented in its content as a purpose which the action decided upon is intended to serve. For unless action is ultimately to be based on decisions that are taken for no reason, which would undermine the overall intentionality and motivation of an agent's action, Wallace's view would generate a viciously regressive infinite complexity in intention contents. For we can ask after the agent's reason for deciding to do A in order to attain E. Unless this decision is to be unmotivated, the decision to do A in order to attain E would in turn have to be a decision to attain E in order to attain F. But then we need to know the motivation for that decision. And so the process would go on ad infinitum. Secondly, Wallace's view involves an implausibly explicit grasp of their motivations on agents' parts, the purposes for which they act all being represented as those purposes in the contents of their decisions.

---

[6] R. Jay Wallace, 'Three conceptions of rational agency', in *Normativity and the Will* (Oxford: Oxford University Press, 2006).

[7] See 'Three conceptions of rational agency':

> the contents of the intentions that are expressed in our actions are specified by maxims. These may be thought of as having, potentially, the following, schematic form: 'I shall do x, in circumstances C, in order to y/ as a way of y-ing'. By filling in the slots in this schematic representation of a maxim, we provide information about what agents take themselves to be up to in acting as they do . . . A person is guided by their conception of their reasons when that conception is reflected in the content of the intention on which they act; in that case, one will be able to understand what the agent is doing only by grasping what speaks in favour of so acting, from the agent's own point of view. *Normativity and the Will*, p .60.

[8] See Alfred Mele, *Motivation and Agency*, pp. 42–5.

Part of Mele's response is based on a simple confusion. A decision to do A can still have a motivation even if it is not directed at any end beyond doing A. The decision will still be motivated in that it has a goal—the doing of A. And there is nothing wrong with pursuing an end for its own sake, without its serving some further purpose. Some ends just have to be ultimate—ends pursued for their own sake. Nor, to repeat, is the intelligibility of the pursuit of these ultimate ends one which increased by seeing it as the effect of a passive motivation directed at the same object.

But if Mele's regress argument fails, his worry about the explicit representation of complex purposes is legitimate. It simply is not plausible that agents generally represent to themselves, in their decisions or in their other attitudes, such as their beliefs, all the purposes for which they are acting. Let me show how my view differs from Wallace's and is not vulnerable to the same objection.

Wallace's view disagrees with my own in one important respect. He supposes that all the goals at which our decisions are directed have to be represented in the contents of those decisions, and represented as purposes for performing the action decided upon. The content of an intention is that a given voluntary action be performed as a means to a specific end—and so for a certain purpose.

But this brings me to the first important difference between us. Purposes in my view are not subject to the will or voluntary—and so are not in general themselves intended. It is outcomes alone that are intended, not the purposes for which those outcomes are to be produced. I intend to cross the road; and I may do so because I also intend to get to the chip shop on the other side. That leaves me crossing the road for the purpose of getting to the chip shop. But that I cross the road for that purpose is not itself something I intend. This means that, on my doctrine, an agent can and will hold intentions without having to deploy in so doing the concept of a purpose.

The point is one of substance. It is crucial to my view that purpose or goal-direction is to be found not as part of the content of an intention, but in the mode of direction of the intention to its content—in just the way the practical reason-based model of action explains. The status of an intention's immediate object as its purposed goal comes not from the fact that it is represented *as a purpose*, but from the fact that the rationality of the intention directed at that object depends on the likelihood of attaining it—as with any goal-directed action. And that is connected with my fundamental approach to understanding intentional agency—which is to characterize action as consisting in a certain distinctive mode of rationality, one which involves not some distinctive content, but rather a distinctive mode of direction at that content.

Indeed, it is a little mysterious on what grounds Wallace takes decisions to be actions at all. It cannot simply be that the contents of decisions specify the actions decided upon as performed for this or that purpose. For one might come to hold a passive desire with the very same content—a desire to perform an action for a given purpose. The desire's formation would not by virtue just of that content constitute an action. Crucial must be, not the contents of decisions, but their peculiar mode of direction at those contents. Our theory needs to appeal to a distinctively purposive mode of exercising reason, not to a supposedly action-constitutive form of content.

Moreover, not all the goals at which an intention or decision is directed need come from its own content. For the following seems an evident truth. If my pursuit of one goal A is motivated by my belief that doing A would help attain a further goal E, and by my already holding a pro attitude towards the attainment of that further goal, then, surely, my pursuit of A can have a further purpose—the attainment of E. As for goal-directed agency in general, so for decisions and intention-formations in particular: when I decide to do A, my decision may have the attainment of E as its further goal, not through its own content, but thanks to prior attitudes that have motivated the decision. It may be that the decision is motivated by a belief that doing A would attain E and by a prior decision to attain E. Or the motivating pro attitude could even be passive—not a decision to attain E but a desire.

Only part then of a decision or intention's goal-direction need come from its own content. Part may come from without, from the content of a prior motivation that already existed. The purposes for which an agent acts may then perfectly well depend to a significant degree on the relation of his action to earlier motivations, and in ways which that agent may not be aware of or even be fully capable of representing to himself. Which is, I think, just what we ordinarily suppose.

11.7 Action and the Agent

To perform an intentional action is, then, to make a certain kind of rationally appraisable object-directed change—a change which is goal-directed, being directed at its object as a goal which that change is being used to attain. The change may be made voluntarily—on the basis of a prior intention that it occur. Or it may be made non-voluntarily—as in the initial taking of that decision.

Has something been left out of our account of intentional action? It might appear to some that something has been left out. For actions, it might be objected, are not merely goal-directed events. They are not merely events used to attain the objects at which they are directed. Actions also have a special relationship to their agent—a relationship which allows the agent to play a special role in generating or producing the action's performance, as something the agent *does*. And nothing so far has been said by the practical reason-based model to relate actions in that special way to their agents.[9] The practical reason-based model merely says that to act intentionally is to exercise reason purposively, in an action-constitutive way. But what distinguishes this mode of exercising reason from any other? Not, it seems, any special relation to its agent as doer and producer of the action. What distinguishes this practical mode

[9] My thanks to Michael Bratman for putting this objection to me.

of exercising reason from other object-directed exercises of rationality is the special way in which it is related to its object—as to a goal—and not any special way of being related to its agent.

But the objection does not make it clear what the agent's supposedly distinctive involvement in *doing* amounts to. If it amounts to purposiveness, the making of a change as means to ends, then that is certainly distinctive, and essential to agency—but has entirely to do with the distinctiveness of the change's relation to its object, as a goal to be attained. The practical reason-based model certainly does not ignore this relation, but provides an account of it as it occurs in intentional form, and so of what it is for an event in an agent's life to count as something done deliberately as a means to an end. Perhaps then the objector must be pointing not to anything that matters to the action's purposiveness in itself, but to some further distinctive relation between the agent and the purposive doing. And of course there is such a relation, and one where the agent is indeed involved in producing or generating the action. As agents we have the capacity to determine our actions for ourselves. But that capacity and the agent–action relation it involves is the business of a theory of self-determination to explain—a theory which the practical reason-based model does not claim to provide.

Remember that goal-directedness and self-determination, even when both are present, are two quite separate features of agency. The first involves a relation between an action and its object, and second between an action and its agent. These relations are obviously very different in that they relate the action to two quite distinct things. It is simply not obvious why the story which we tell about goal-directedness, a relation which any action has to the object at which it is directed, should also involve a story about self-determination and the special relation which agents can but need not have to their actions as things they determine.

The voluntariness-based model does of course explain purposiveness in terms that involve a relationship between action and the agent as its producer. Action is supposedly goal-directed through being caused to occur by its agent's willing, wanting, or deciding that it occur. Actions are events which are determined to occur by their agent's own will understood as a passive antecedent of action. But we have seen that this model simply does not apply to much of what we consider to be genuine action. Voluntariness fails as a general model for purposiveness. And of course it also fails as a model of self-determination too, for reasons we have already discussed: voluntariness involves determination, but by motivations and not by the self. We should abandon the project of explaining purposiveness in terms of some distinctive relation of production or determination held by agents towards their actions.

12

Action and Its Motivation

12.1 Motivation

Hobbes took the motivation for an action always to come from some attitude or attitudes distinct from the action motivated, and to involve causation of the action by the motivating attitudes. And this view has been central to much recent discussion of motivation in English-language action theory.

Suppose we assume that motivation has to do with a relation between distinct occurrences—between motivating attitudes, on the one hand, and actions understood as further events distinct from the attitudes that motivate them. Then we shall face the question of what links the attitudes that motivate an action to the action that they motivate. And causation is often defended as essential to motivation because it provides the required link.

The need for some such connecting link is made more pressing by the fact that where prior attitudes do motivate some subsequent action, their motivating role is not fixed by the contents of the attitudes themselves. As Davidson reminded us, there can be cases where someone might hold attitudes that support or favour an action's performance, and might also perform that action—but without the action being motivated by those attitudes.[1] I might want to make my friend happy; and I might also want to reward the best work. Awarding my friend a prize would, I believe, produce both outcomes. But that those two wants each favour the action's performance—each rationalize it, to use Davidson's phrase—does not settle the action's true motivation. I could want to make my friend happy without that desire actually moving me to award the prize. I might award my friend the prize—but simply in order to reward the best work. The attitudes themselves and their contents do not settle on their own how the action is motivated. Something else is needed that provides a genuine link between the true motives and the action. That link, Davidson has argued, is causation. The motivating desires are the desires that actually cause the agent to act as desired; in this case it is my desire to reward the best work that causes my action, and not my desire to make my friend happy.

Causation, then, is often brought into the theory of motivation as if it were simply needed to settle the question—underdetermined by the content of the attitudes

---

[1] See Davidson, 'Actions, reasons, and causes', in *Essays on Actions and Events*, p. 9.

themselves—of which among an agent's attitudes count as motivating his perform-ance of a given action. But of course, if the rationale for appealing to causation were simply to answer that question, there might be perfectly good non-causal alterna-tives. The modern opposition to Davidson has generally retained the assumption that motivation comes to an action from attitudes as occurrences distinct from it, and then cast about for some other way of linking those attitudes to the action motivated—one that does not involve a causal relation between them.

For example, in his *Teleological Realism* Scott Sehon agrees that something associated with causation does link motivating attitudes and action—namely the truth of certain subjunctive conditionals. Where attitudes motivate an action, it will be true that if those attitudes had not been held, the agent would have acted differently. If my prize-giving is motivated by my desire to reward the best work but not by my desire to make my friend happy, then even if I had not wanted to make my friend happy, or I had not believed giving him the prize would make him happy, I would still have awarded him the prize. Whereas I would not have awarded him the prize had I not believed his work to be the best. Sehon denies, though, that the motivating attitudes need be causes of the action motivated. The conditionals that explain motivation can obtain without a direct causal link between motivation and the action motivated. The true causes of action are located in the realm of material states, such as brain states, not in psychological attitudes such as motivations—and common-sense psychology is alleged not to suppose otherwise. On this view, explan-ation by appeal to causes is one thing, and explanation by prior motivations is always quite another. On Sehon's view, common-sense psychology treats explanation of action by prior motivations as a *sui generis* mode of teleological or purposive explanation—a teleological explanation that involves no direct appeal to causes. The view that motivation implies causation in this case is a philosophical importation and not part of our common-sense understanding of the mind.[2]

Another strategy is to allow, as Hobbes did not, that some actions take the form of decisions with contents of their own. These contents are then used to provide a non-causal connection between the action and the prior attitudes that motivate it. Consider a proposal that has been made by Timothy O'Connor.[3] On O'Connor's view, a desire to do A might be thought to motivate a decision by virtue of such a desire's being specified in the decision's content. The decision is a decision to satisfy a desire to do A—and, even in the absence of any causal connection between the desire

---

[2] Thus Sehon:

> In physical science, explanations are typically causal explanations: We explain an event by giving its antecedent cause...Most philosophers of mind assume that CSP [common-sense psychological] explanations are causal too; thus when CSP says, 'Vera went to the kitchen because she wanted tea,' this is construed as making the claim that Vera's desire for tea caused her going to the kitchen...I claim that CSP explanations are not causal; instead I claim they are teleological. *Teleological Realism*, pp. 12–13.

[3] Timothy O'Connor, *Persons and Causes: The Metaphysics of Free Will*, p. 86.

and the decision, that fact about the decision's content is supposed to leave the decision counting as explained and motivated by the desire.

But this debate between Davidson and his opponents may be misconceived. For if our only concern were to relate the attitudes that actually motivate actions to the actions that they motivate, it is unclear why anything need be brought into the picture besides the bare fact of motivation. Why not rest content with the view that, of the attitudes that favour an action's performance, some may actually motivate it, whereas others may not? Nothing more need be said about the attitudes that do motivate, than that is what they do. If it is objected that we need to say in other terms what the motivating relationship involves, we might simply deny that any such account need be given. The objection, it might be claimed, is assuming that a theory of motivation has to be conceptually reductive; that it has to specify the relation between the attitudes that motivate an action and that action other than in terms simply of motivation. But why should this reductive assumption be granted?

It would, however, be a mistake to suppose that causation enters the theory of motivation only as a way of reductively specifying, in other terms, how, as distinct occurrences, motivating attitudes and actions motivated are linked. Causation enters the picture because, as I have already suggested, our ordinary understanding of motivation importantly involves the agent actually being *moved*—subjected to some form of power. And the role played by motivating power in common-sense psychology is not simply to link an action to prior attitudes. The idea of motivation— of being moved by something to act as one does—extends far more widely, as we have seen. It also includes the idea of being moved, not by an attitude, but by the object of an attitude—by the desirability of an outcome, as well as by a desire for that outcome. And the power involved in motivation may therefore be normative as well as causal.

Moreover, we have seen that the practical reason-based model of action in any case challenges the assumption that is fundamental to much modern discussion, and that is shared by Davidson and many of his opponents—that the motivation for an action must always come via attitudes understood as occurrences distinct from the action that they motivate. The motivation for an action can be internal to it—from an object at which the action is directed through its own content, as an attitude itself. Indeed, as we shall see, this may even be true for voluntary actions themselves, as well as for the decisions and intention-formations that motivate them.

12.2 Motivation and Power

An action's motivation need not always involve some form of power. Essential to motivation, and to action's very intelligibility as action, is goal-direction. But goal-direction need not on its own involve the agent's subjection to any motivating power. Nothing need have moved the agent to pursue that particular goal—neither the desirability of the goal itself, nor any further attitude towards that goal, such as a desire for its attainment or a belief in its desirability. Someone might decide, say, to continue a stroll by going left—rather than going right, or staying put, or ending the stroll by going back. But though the decision is an action with a goal, there need be nothing that moved the agent to take that particular decision and aim at that particular goal. The question is entirely open whether anything or anyone moved the agent so to decide.

Motivating power comes into the story with the thought that something did in fact move or determine the agent to aim at—decide on—that particular goal. Power is involved if beyond the occurrence of goal-direction in itself, something moves, that is, determines or influences, the agent to act towards that particular goal. But it is important to note that power does not come into the story just because of the need for some link, causal or otherwise, between the action and prior attitudes that count as its motives. For as far as common-sense psychology is concerned, the power could be importantly normative, and relate not to a prior attitude, but to an object of thought. I may be moved to decide to go left by the clear desirability of so doing.

But of course motivation could also come from some prior attitude, perhaps itself already formed in response to the desirability of going left, such as a strong desire to go left, or a belief that going left would be the most sensible thing to do. And where what moves us to pursue a goal is a prior attitude, it does seem that power is again involved. Motivating attitudes, in particular, are understood as moving us because they influence how we act. Take away that influence, and what is left of the thought that the attitudes actually *move* us? And where attitudes are concerned, the power in question seems to be causal.

Sehon denies that common-sense psychology views motives as causes. But ordinary thinking about motivation constantly appeals to notions of what very much appears to be causal power. Our desires and motivations are said to incline us and, if strong enough, they sometimes seem even to drive or compel us. We think of desires and emotions as exercising a force on us, and describe ourselves as feeling their force.

This force seems not to be normative. Desires, emotions, and other motivating attitudes are very different from the objects of thought that move us in so far as we are rational, and which do so by the force of justification. Like other causes, desires and other attitudes are contingent occurrences with spatio-temporal location, and their force is not tied to justification. I can be driven to act by overwhelming anger even if that anger is quite irrational. The anger's overwhelming power seems, then, to be understood by us as causal rather than normative. Likewise the power of will to move us to act as decided on and intended. A strong will is a will that resists the force of conflicting desires to ensure our eventual performance of the actions decided upon. And this force of will is again causal rather than normative; it is not tied to the justifiability of sticking to one's decision. Causation comes in also at the point of the voluntary, as relating our attitudes, and in particular our decisions and intentions, to the outcomes decided upon. Suppose the limb motions that take me across a road are not effects of any decision or intention of mine, but occur quite by chance, or as the effect of quite other causes, such as a landslip. Why, then, should we think that my motion across the road was my own intentional doing, and done on the basis of my decision so to act?

The practical reason-based model of action changes this debate between Davidson and his opponents in two ways. First, as we have already noted, it challenges the view that frames the debate—that motivation, by its very nature, involves a relation between two entities, an action and an attitude distinct from it. For the object of an action need not come from a prior attitude. The object may be internal to the action as an attitude in its own right. To render an action intelligible as action, in terms of its goal-direction, need not be to refer to any other event, cause or otherwise. Reference to the action's own content may be enough. Explaining an action in this way need no more involve detecting causes than need interpreting an utterance. In both cases it may be content that we are uncovering, not causation. So the practical reason-based model detaches goal-direction as such from causation.

But besides any goal-direction internal to the action itself, goal-direction can also come from attitudes that are indeed distinct from the action itself, and that may considerably precede the action in time. And a central case involves the use of decisions and intentions to plan and coordinate action in advance. As we saw in our discussion of Jay Wallace's content-based theory of action, decisions to adopt means, and the actions of employing those means, can be motivated by and acquire goal-direction from earlier decisions to pursue ends. Here part of the decision's goal-direction comes from without—from ends previously decided upon, and the prior decisions directed at those ends. The use of decisions and intentions in the advance planning and coordination of action establishes that much motivation for action does arise out of mental states that precede and are distinct from the further action that they motivate.

The practical reason-based model requires us to understand the motivating role of decisions and intentions, in particular, in causal terms. Contrary to Sehon's claim that common sense does not accord a causal role to motivating attitudes, common-sense psychology seems deeply committed to decisions and intentions causing the successful performance of the actions intended. For our ordinary understanding of decisions and intentions is precisely as directed, like any goal-directed action, at ensuring the attainment of their objects; and this understanding is fundamental to our conception of decision and intention rationality. But this use of decisions as means involves causation.

Actions are performed as means to attaining goals or ends. And where the goal aimed at involves outcomes distinct from mere performance of the action itself, the action provides the means only thanks to its power to influence or determine the relevant further outcomes. If we can be sure that the action has no power to influence those outcomes, or that those outcomes depend entirely on power exercised by something else, there is no point to using the action as a means.

Now the powers involved need not in all cases be causal. An action might be performed to attain a legal or moral outcome, as in the creation of a legal or moral obligation; and here the power exercised might well be normative or legal. In this case the action's performance constitutes, in virtue of moral or legal principles, the creation of the obligation determined. But in many cases no legal or normative power need be involved. The power to produce or determine outcomes employed in using the action as a means may just be ordinary causation. Such an action does not constitute the attainment of the outcomes aimed at by virtue of moral or legal principles, but rather increases their chances as would an ordinary cause.

Decisions and intention-formations are no exception. If they are employed as means, they must exercise some form of outcome-influencing or determining power. And certainly in their case the power generally exercised seems, as ordinarily conceived, to be no different from ordinary causation. Decisions to act in the future do not themselves constitute performance of those future actions, and certainly not just by virtue of some normative or moral principle. Instead, like any ordinary cause, they are occurrences which by their presence raise the chances of those actions being performed, ideally so as to determine the occurrence of those actions, at least on the supposition that circumstances do not change. The determination involved is that associated with causation, not the contingent determination involved in freedom. A decision or intention has the power to determine the action intended only if the decision's very occurrence, under the circumstances, ensures the subsequent performance of that action.

It is thanks to this capacity to determine causally that we can use our knowledge of people's present decisions and intentions as a guide to what they will do. Once we know what a person has decided, and that their decisions are powerful determiners of future action, we can rely on their eventually acting as decided—at least provided circumstances do not change. As to what power to produce future action actually attaches to a particular decision, this is something we may investigate just as we might investigate the powers of other causes. We can refer to like cases. For example, we might examine whether similar decisions have tended to produce the requisite persisting intentions in this agent or like agents in the past. Decisions seem to be conceived by us as exercising power over further outcomes as would any probabilifying or determining cause. This point holds not just for decisions to act in the future. It holds as much for decisions to act now. A decision to do A now also has the doing of A as its goal, a goal it may or may not attain, but which will be attained, if it is, through the decision's affecting the chance of the outcomes necessary to successfully doing A. My decision to cross the road now had better have the power to determine that my legs actually move in the required ways, or at least to raise the chances of their so doing. Otherwise there is no point to taking the decision with the goal of getting me to cross.

Where I am sure that whether I eventually do A is causally independent of what I now decide—no decision I now took would affect the chance of my doing A—then, as we have already seen, it simply is not sensible for me to bother deciding about whether to do A. The function of decisions and intentions, then, is to cause successful performance of the voluntary actions they explain. Decisions and intentions exercise causal power either to move us to act voluntarily at some later time, or, where action in the present is concerned, to produce the outcomes necessary to its successful performance now. This is a basic feature of our ordinary understanding of the will and of the status of decisions as goal-directed actions—and as directed in particular at bringing about the successful performance, whether now or in the future, of the action decided on.

Consider again O'Connor's account of decision motivation in terms of a non-causal relation between decisions and prior desires. O'Connor sees the connection between the prior desires and the decision as provided through the decision's own content: the decision is a decision to act as a means to satisfying the relevant desires. But motivation of decisions by desires can surely occur in the absence of such content. Decisions can surely be motivated by desires without those decisions actually being directed at desire satisfaction—as Joseph Butler long ago reminded us.[4] I may decide to help you, and be moved by a desire for your good. But my decision is for your good, not to satisfy my own desire. If prior desires do play a role, they can do so like any prior attitude, by exercising a degree of causal influence, inclining the agent towards acting as desired. It need not be part of the content of the agent's decision that the motivating desire be satisfied.

But suppose a decision actually is aimed at desire-satisfaction as O'Connor suggests it might be; suppose I do decide to perform some action as a means to satisfying my desires. Then, on O'Connor's own account, desire enters the motivation of the decision in quite another way—as part of the decision's object, or the goal at which that decision is aimed. But this is simply goal-direction that is internal to the decision. The decision is directed at the goal of desire satisfaction, but just thanks to its own content. As with such content-provided goal-direction generally, it is left open what, if anything, moved the agent to aim at this particular goal. If the desires themselves moved the agent, then those desires must have played a further role beyond merely figuring in the decision's content. They must themselves have moved or inclined—causally influenced—the agent to aim at their satisfaction. Without this influence, O'Connor is certainly providing a case of non-causal motivation—but just as goal-direction internal to a decision through its content, not as motivation from prior attitudes for deciding on that goal.

12.3 Actions as Attitudes—Two Aristotelianisms

We have seen that, as theories of action, volitionism and the voluntariness-based model are mirror images of each other. They each make the same kind of distortion, discriminating improperly between action in its voluntary and its non-voluntary

---

[4] See Joseph Butler, *Fifteen Sermons Preached at the Rolls Chapel* (London 1729).

forms—though discriminating in opposed directions. And they have historically shared a certain conception of motivation and its relation to the voluntary.

On this shared view, which we find common property both to Hobbes and to the medieval scholasticism that he opposed, voluntary actions are inherently objectless and have to derive their goals from without, from the contents of attitudes that motivate them—attitudes from which the voluntary actions themselves are distinct. The debate between Hobbes and his scholastic opponents, then, was not about this way of relating motivation and voluntariness in itself, but about where within this shared framework action itself was to be found. Was the primary case of action to be as a form of inner motivation, or instead as a contentless effect, such as a bodily movement?

Why should we separate the mental element in action, as something supposedly wholly internal to the mind, from its voluntary expression? Some philosophers would detect here a deep and misguided metaphysical division between mind and world—the same questionable mind–world metaphysical division of which Cartesian substance dualism is another, particularly dramatic and worked through version. And certainly scholastic action theory did see voluntariness as contentless because of its own form of dualism—reason dualism. Intellectual content of the sort involved in the exercise of reason could not occur outside the immaterial faculties of intellect and will. It certainly could not occur in the corporeal organs and capacities where much of the voluntary action in execution of decisions of the will took place. Voluntary action would therefore have to acquire its goal-direction from without—from the prior motivations on which that voluntary action was based.

In his *Life and Action*, Michael Thompson has recently challenged the separation of mentality and voluntariness.[5] The paradigm of action should indeed, in his view, be voluntary action, but not as voluntary action is viewed within the scholastic and Hobbesian traditions—as an effect of mental will. Rather, voluntary action, and action generally, is to be understood as one form of what Thompson calls an imperfective process.

We can report the goal at which a voluntary action is directed other than by referring to some mental state that is motivating the action. We can describe the goal instead by the use of a continuous tense, as an outcome that the agent is producing or bringing about. We can report someone as acting with the aim of crossing the road by the locution 'She is crossing the road'—a claim that applies, as does the goal-direction reported, whether or not the agent actually manages to cross.

But voluntary actions are not the only processes that we can report in this way. Such processes abound in nature. We can report that a seed is ripening whether or not it ever ripens, that a bridge is collapsing even if, at the last minute, the collapse is prevented. An imperfective process is a temporally extended process oriented

---

[5] Michael Thompson, *Life and Action: Elementary Structures of Practice and Practical Thought* (Cambridge, MA: Harvard University Press, 2008).

towards an end or outcome—a process that may be blocked or interrupted, but which, while it continues, can be described using continuous tenses as the occurring of that outcome, even if the outcome does not finally occur. In the case of human action, of course, the orientation towards an end involves a mental element—the agent's motivation or intention. But this motivation is not provided by some ante-cedent mental state. For Thompson, goal-direction is internal to a given action in the same way that orientation towards a particular end or outcome is internal to a given kind of process, such as seed ripening, in wider nature. So though an action's motivating object-direction is a psychological phenomenon, it is not external to the action as something provided by a mental cause. The motivation occurs within the action, as itself part of what the agent does, and as constitutive of the action's imperfective aspect.

Thus in contrast to a 'sophisticated' mode of action explanation, that sees purposes as provided by wants conceived as mental causes, Thompson prefers to see purposes as internal to action as an imperfective process:

Such thoughts are the mark of what I will call a sophisticated philosophy of action, which finds in every genuine straightforward rationalization a movement from inner to outer, from mind to world, from spirit to nature, from 'desire' to 'action'. One of my principal theses will thus have to be this, that a sophisticated position cannot be defended, that the linguistic appear-ances ought to be saved, and that the role played by wanting, in the one sort of case, really is taken up, in the other, by what we might call the progress of the deed itself.[6]

The view that action is an imperfective process is contrasted with a theory that takes as its paradigm of action a completed event—something immediately done rather than an interruptible process extended through time. That Thompson's view might appear strange, he observes

is in part a consequence of received conceptions of intentional action itself, above all, of the tendency of students of practical philosophy to view individual human actions as discrete or atomic or pointlike or eye-blink-like units that might as well be instantaneous for all that it matters to the theory.[7]

But it is not just a Cartesian separation of mind and world that encourages the distinction between motivation and voluntary action. Support for this distinction lies just as much with the voluntariness-based model of action itself—a model that Thompson does not challenge. Hobbes was, after all, a thorough materialist. But he still distinguished motivating attitudes from actions. He did this, not because of any dualism, but because motivation is inherently non-voluntary and so correspondingly, on a voluntariness-based model, inherently passive. Since motivation is something passive it cannot, on the voluntariness-based model, be part of what the agent does. To report an action's motivating object or purpose must, on Hobbes' theory, be to

---

[6] *Life and Action*, p. 90.   [7] *Life and Action*, p. 91.

relate the action to something that as passive is distinct from that action—something that, as inherently non-voluntary, must happen to the agent rather than count as his own doing.

To explain how motivation can arise as directly and fully part of what the agent does we need therefore to oppose the exclusive identification of action with voluntariness. And Thompson's theory of action as a temporally extended imperfective process cannot be the right approach to distinguishing action from voluntariness. For a clear case of motivation occurring as the agent's own doing—the action of taking a decision—does not occur as an imperfective process. Decisions may indeed be oriented towards the occurrence of such processes as their goals. And deliberation and making up one's mind may itself be a process extending through time. But the actual taking of a specific decision, which need not be preceded by such extended deliberation, is not itself, considered just as a decision, a temporally extended process. It is a very definite point of change in which one moves, by one's own action, from lacking a particular intention to holding it. The decision is an action completed at a moment of its taking—the moment of decision.

Decisions need not immediately give rise to continuing action. They may simply produce instead a persisting intention—not a continuing action, but a state, formed through action, of remaining motivated to act. And this is why we do not use continuous tenses to report decisions as we do uncompleted voluntary actions. An agent who decides to cross the road does something with road crossing as its goal. But he does not *ipso facto* count as already crossing the road—and of course this is not simply because, though the decision is taken, the road is not yet crossed; for exactly as Thompson notes, an agent certainly can be crossing a road—acting voluntarily with crossing as his goal—before that road is yet crossed. Rather, just in deciding to cross the road the agent is not yet involved in any imperfective process with road crossing as its outcome; he may be merely intending such a process. But an action with road crossing as its goal has been performed nonetheless.

Thompson presents his view as a form of Aristotelianism.[8] Instead of appealing to efficient causation by inner mental phenomena, the teleological aspect of action is to be related to a similar orientation to ends found in temporally extended processes found in wider nature. But it is not clear that the parallel holds, as the end-direction involved in human action seems importantly unlike that involved in an imperfective process. For it involves a distinctive mode of responding to reason that, as in the case of taking a decision, need not be temporally extended. Scholastic Aristotelianism took a different approach by locating the goal-direction involved in action as a specifically psychological form of object-direction. Key to understanding action and its goal-direction was not a theory of temporally extended processes, but a theory of attitudes and their content.

---

[8] See *Life and Action*, pp. 10–11.

It is the practical reason-based model, not the theory of action as an imperfective process, which explains how action can take non-voluntary form, as decision-making, so that the motivation for a voluntary action could be as much what the agent does as is the voluntary production of outcomes. And the model actually supports the possibility that voluntary actions too occur as distinctively purposive attitudes.

Once we detach the practical reason-based model of action from reason dualism, voluntary action can count as an action in the same way as does a decision. In both cases the agent is involved in change directed at an object of thought—change that occurs as a distinctively practical mode of exercising reason. The change is directed at the object as its goal. But if voluntary actions are just as much actions as the decisions to perform them, may not part at least of their goal-direction arise in just the same way as the goal-direction of decisions—through content internal to the action itself? So part, at least, of a voluntary action's goal-direction could be internal to it. The practical reason-based model leaves this possibility open, precisely because it does not view the non-voluntariness inherent in motivating attitudes with content as implying passivity. The non-voluntariness characteristic of motivation is now consistent with its occurrence as part of what the agent does.

On this view, the intention with which a voluntary action is performed need not be an occurrence distinct from the action intended. The motivating intention could be an aspect of the action itself, and not its cause. The content internal to the action would involve intention in so far as the attitude directed at the action's goal was formed as an exercise of the agent's capacity for reason. As such it would count as an action in its own right—as an active but non-voluntary direction of oneself at that object as a goal to be attained. But it could count as a voluntary action too—as the voluntary exercise of capacities to act as willed.

Deciding to do something need not yet involve actually doing it. Decisions can be decisions simply to act in the future, and as such they immediately produce, not the outcomes involved in carrying the decision out, but rather a persisting intention to act. But one can also decide or form an intention to act *now*—a decision that does immediately produce the outcomes involved in successfully so acting. And such decisions and intention-formations could perfectly well be identical with the actions decided upon and intended. In causing the outcomes required for A to be done, the action of deciding to do A now could also be the doing of A, or at least its initial stage. The decision to act now can be, not the mere formation of a persisting intention, but the voluntary action itself.

One and the same action can be non-voluntary in some respects and voluntary in others. As an intention-formation, the action is non-voluntary, being responsive not to the desirability of so intending, but to the desirability of the intention's object, the action intended. But when also (through its effects) the performance of what is intended, the action is voluntary, responsive as it is to the desirability of that intended performance. Once we abandon both reason dualism and the voluntariness-based model of action as well, we can see intentional action as uniformly involving a distinctively purposive attitude—either that attitude alone, or the production of outcomes through the attitude.

12.4 The Action Problem Resolved

Many philosophers who deny that motivating attitudes need be causes are libertarians about free will. But they are not driven to this denial by libertarianism alone. They also retain, without much debate or reflection, that central element of Hobbesian action theory—the doctrine that actions, by their very nature, occur as expressions of motivations that are passive.[9] It is within the framework of this assumption that, as we have already seen, the link between motivation and causation becomes a problem for libertarian freedom. For if actions are taken to express passive motivations as their effects, we arrive at the Hobbesian theory that action is constituted as action by being an effect of passive causes—and so is constituted as action by the very causal power that threatens libertarian freedom. The action problem arises, as we saw, because, on the Hobbesian view, action is given its goal-direction, and so constituted as genuine action, by the operation of a power that threatens the very freedom that action is supposed to enable us to exercise. If libertarians retain the Hobbesian dogma that action occurs as an expression of prior attitudes that are passive, their only hope of avoiding the action problem is desperately to search for an entirely non-causal link between those passive attitudes and the actions they motivate—no matter how artificial and irrelevant to genuine motivation the link turns out to be.

It looks as though the practical reason-based model removes this problem. Since purposiveness can occur as a distinctively practical mode of exercising reason and as a distinctive attitude, we now have a new category of action—action in non-voluntary form. Actions can possess their goal-direction as a feature internal to them, coming from their own content, and the object which that content provides. And this leaves goal-directed agency a phenomenon which is strictly independent of prior attitudes that are passive. We no longer need appeal to the causal power of uncontrolled desires to find objects for our actions. Those objects can now be provided by intentions—by attitudes over which we can have direct control and in forming which we can be acting freely. And so the goal-direction of an agent's action can now be determined by the agent's own free action. It can be true that, as Kant said:

---

[9] Recall that the libertarian Hugh McCann (*The Works of Agency*, p. 165) supposes that a decision, as an intentional action, must be an expression of prior desire. The purpose of a decision to do A, that A be done, must be provided, according to McCann, not simply by the decision's own content, but by the content of some prior and distinct desire to do A. But there is an obvious question for McCann: why does the decision's direction at the goal of doing A not come just from its own content, which is after all to do A? A further passive motivation with just exactly the same content may or may not be present, but can hardly be needed to establish the decision's basic goal-direction.

'...to have an end of action is an act of *freedom* on the part of the acting subject, not an effect of *nature*.' Kant's conception of our freedom as a freedom of ends is often presented by Galen Strawson and others as evidently incoherent—as a mere fantasy, according agents powers of free self-constitution that are impossible a priori. And, certainly, such a general control over our end-direction must indeed be impossible on the voluntariness-based model. For on that model our goals and ends are provided by motivations that are inherently passive. So our goals or ends can only be within our control if these passive motivations are within our control. But since these motivations are themselves passive, they can only fall within our control indirectly, as effects of prior voluntary action—which action would in turn require a passive motivation of its own, which to be within our control would itself have to be an effect of yet prior voluntary action, and so on ad infinitum.

But there is no such vicious regress on the practical reason-based model, in that an agent's goals or ends may be determined by active motivations, not passive—by decisions and intentions, not desires. Intentions are the attitudes that determine the goals which we pursue intentionally, and intention-formation is itself an action over which we can exercise direct control. To take a decision or form an intention is itself to perform an intentional action—an action whose immediate goal-direction comes from its own content, and is internal to it. We are no longer characterizing the goal-direction of action in terms that would offend the libertarian—as given by some merely passive force that is not the agent's doing. The ends towards which an agent acts are not imposed on her passively from without, and in a way that therefore threatens her own freedom. The goals towards which an agent acts can arise as her very own free doing.

Libertarians certainly need not claim that action must be *wholly* independent of the passive. Libertarianism is not committed to any overheated fantasy of free agents as total self-creators—as responsible not only for their particular free actions, but for the very conditions of their free agency. Our performance of any particular free action must, on any sane view, depend on our prior possession of the very capacity for free action. And this is a capacity that must be given, and that cannot be our own doing. Nor need libertarians suppose otherwise.

This capacity for free action involves, in particular, a conceptual grasp or understanding of various possible goals—an understanding that, again, must at least at the outset be a passive given, and that is not the free agent's own doing. It is only once this understanding of possible goals is in place that an agent's freedom can then begin. This freedom consists, at least immediately, in control over which of these possible goals the agent then aims at and intends—for example, over whether she decides to go on with a walk or, alternatively, to stay where she is.

It is action as the medium for exercising this freedom—action as constituting a decision to do one thing rather than another—that must and can be characterized without appeal to passive causation. If libertarianism is to prove coherent, an agent must be able to decide for rather than against a given option without having to be caused so to decide by any prior desire for that option. The very identity of her action—the particular goal at which it is directed, what the decision is a decision to do—must not derive from a causal influence that, in libertarian terms, tends to remove her freedom to act otherwise. The identity of the action must be wholly the agent's own doing—wholly a function of how she exercises her capacity for agency, and not determined by some passive impulsion on the agent from without. This is surely the conception of human action and choice which libertarian freedom requires; and this is the conception which the practical reason-based model delivers.

A worry might arise at this point. The worry is that the practical reason-based model does not so much solve the action problem, as reintroduce it in a new form. True, intentional action is no longer being characterized as an effect of brute desire. Intentional action is being characterized instead as a practical mode of exercising reason. But action so understood must nevertheless be sensitive to the desirability of its object as a goal. And does this not still involve the agent in subjection to power, and in a way that might threaten libertarian freedom? This could be the causal power of beliefs about the action's object, or even a normative power attaching to that object itself. The worry is obvious—that the practical reason-based model is just a normative predecessor of Hobbes' causal theory of action. And as such, the model merely introduces its own earlier version of the action problem. As a mode of exercising rationality, action still occurs as something determined by some power besides that of the agent himself—if not by the causal power of a passion, then by the power exercised over the agent by an object of thought, or by beliefs about that object.

The worry is misconceived. The practical reason-based model is really quite different from Hobbes' causal theory. And we have already seen why. Goal-direction does not, according to the practical reason-based model, *ipso facto* involve the agent's subjection to some kind of power. Some such motivating power may be operative in some cases. But by contrast to Hobbes' theory, the exercise of such power is not what constitutes the very occurrence of goal-direction.

The practical reason-based model certainly characterizes action as consisting in the exercise of a capacity to respond to reason purposively. And of course the exercise of such a capacity may in specific cases involve the agent's subjection to various forms of causal or normative power. But this power is not what is directly constitutive of action in its own right. All that is required is the agent's direction at an object of thought as a goal. And that can occur, and rationally, without the action's object or beliefs about it determining or even influencing the action's occurrence. As we have noted, I can perform action aimed at a goal without anything having moved me to pursue that goal in particular. Indeed, there may easily be no specific rational grounding for such motivation. There need be no particular justification for pursuing that specific goal. What leaves the decision counting as an action directed to its object as a goal is simply the decision's content, and the way the decision's rationality depends on the object presented by that content—namely on the desirability or otherwise of that object and the likelihood of that object's being attained through the decision. The decision counts as goal-directed because it would be irrational if its object were undesirable, or if, though not undesirable, the object were insufficiently likely to be attained through the decision. The actual operation of some power to determine or influence the decision's occurrence plays no part in the story. Decisions can be directed at their objects as goals whether or not anything moved or caused those decisions to be taken.

Practical reason can perfectly well leave it open how we act or decide—or whether we act or decide at all. Take again that ordinary stroll. Nothing about the option of continuing my walk, or in my beliefs about that option, need influence me to decide on it, rather than on the alternatives of staying where I am or going home. And that is because it might be rationally perfectly indifferent which of these I do. Though the rationality and nature of any decision requires that it be sensitive to the desirability of its object, since there is nothing to differentiate the options, there is nothing remotely irrational about either these objects or my beliefs about them pushing me in any particular direction. It is perfectly consistent with my rationality that if I do decide to continue my walk, I do so without having been influenced to decide on that particular option by anything else. Why cannot I, as a perfectly rational decision maker, just decide on that particular option for no further reason, undetermined by anything besides myself?

It might still be objected that the action problem has not yet really been solved.[10] For this example, it might be objected, is just an example of a decision taken for no reason. But freedom requires action performed or decisions taken for a reason. The vehicle or medium of freedom is not decision or action as such, but decision or action for reasons. And then we have to reckon with the agent's subjection to motivating power, be it causal or normative—and the action problem returns.

But the objection is mistaken. True, all free action needs to be 'done for a reason'. But being done for a reason need have nothing to do with being subject to any form of motivating power. It is simply a matter of something being done as a means to some end—including an action being performed or decided on just for its own sake. And on the practical reason-based model such goal-direction simply requires the presence of an object, and the decision's rationality appropriately depending on the character of that object. The only power behind the occurrence of the decision may have been the agent's, to determine for himself that he so decide.

Someone might intentionally tap their finger on a glass, this deed being decided on and deliberately done simply for its own sake, and without having any further end in view. The reason for the action's performance is just this. It was done simply for its own sake. The agent's goal was simply to tap their finger on the glass. Now ensuring that one's finger taps a glass may not be a very interesting reason for acting. The goal aimed at may be whimsical, with nothing desirable about it in particular. But

---

[10] My thanks to Randolph Clarke for pressing me to address the objection.

sometimes people do just intentionally pursue goals out of whim, just for their own sake. And they can still perfectly well be acting freely in so doing. Intentional goal-direction is what freedom strictly requires, and no more than that.

The decision so to act has been taken for a reason in the only sense that matters. It is done for the sake of some goal—in this case for the sake of the goal presented by its content. The decision was taken in order that the glass be tapped on. Not that this is any news. For where decisions are concerned, one particular goal lies in their very nature—that determined by their content. So as soon as we report what the agent's decision specifically was—that it was a decision to tap on a glass—we *ipso facto* give one reason why the decision was taken. We report one specific goal at which the decision was directed, namely the goal of ensuring that the glass is tapped on. That reason having already being given in the decision's very description, when we go on to ask for a reason why the agent took this decision, we are always asking for a *further* reason for the agent's adopting tapping on the glass as his goal.

But the important point is that there need not be any further reason. Ultimately our pursuit of goals just has to start. Decisions to do things for their own sake are perfectly clear cases of intentional and goal-directed action. And that is enough to make them possible vehicles of the agent's freedom. All that the exercise of freedom strictly requires by way of medium or vehicle—and on this point we should insist—is the occurrence of goal-directed agency in intentional form. Provided what the agent is doing is at least minimally intelligible as something intentional and goal-directed, the agent can still be exercising control in doing it. The practical reason-based model of action detaches goal-direction or purposiveness from subjection to power, as Hobbes' voluntariness-based model does not. The action problem really has been solved.

12.5 Varieties of Motivation and Motivating Power

The view of motivation that we are arriving at is of some complexity—but one that makes more intelligible the variety of very different competing theories on the subject.

Some views tie an action's goal-direction to its causation by prior attitudes, goal-direction coming to the action from without, from the contents of those motivating attitudes. Scholastic action theory took this view for *actus imperati*—for specifically voluntary actions; and Hobbes and his followers extended this view to action in general. We have certainly rejected this causal view of goal-direction as applying to every case. Even voluntary action may possess goal-direction in a form that is internal to it, and that does not depend on the action's causation by prior attitudes. But nevertheless much goal-direction can come to an action through being caused by prior attitudes. This is central in particular to the use of decisions and intentions to coordinate actions through time. Decisions are taken to attain ends; and the goal-direction of those decisions will feed though to the further actions they motivate as means to those ends, and to the decisions to perform those actions. We may be moved to pursue a goal by prior attitudes; and when we are so moved, then the motivating power involved is indeed causal.

Other views go to the other extreme and altogether detach goal-direction from an agent's subjection to any form of motivating power. This approach has especially been encouraged by libertarian anxieties about freedom, and about the threat to freedom posed by causal power in particular. Again, such theories go too far. Actions can perfectly well be aimed at goals because something moved the agent to aim at those very goals. It could be the clear desirability of attaining the goals, as too beliefs about that desirability, or simply desires—not to forget prior decisions to attain those goals and thereby perhaps further ends as well. The idea of being moved to pursue goals is very plainly an idea of being *moved*—of being subjected to power. And the involvement of power is basic, in particular, to the practical reason-based model itself, as being implicit in the very idea of employing decisions and intentions as means to ends, determining the occurrence of the various actions and outcomes those ends involve.

Still, at the same time, the practical reason-based model does also leave open the possibility of goal-direction in a form detached from the agent's subjection to some form of motivating power. For I can decide on a whim, and here goal-direction, the decision on a particular option, does seem detached from the operation of any power, be it causal or otherwise, to determine or influence me towards that option in particular. I just decide I shall do that; and the only power to determine what I do could be my own—my freedom to determine for myself that I shall decide on and do that. Nothing else need push me to that option in particular—be it the object's particular desirability or a prior desire or other attitude causing me to decide on that option in particular. On the practical reason-based model, the object that establishes a decision's basic goal-direction can come with the decision's own content. So understood, the object does not imply the operation of any freedom-threatening power, such as that attaching to a prior attitude, to which the agent must be subject.

13

Voluntariness and Freedom of the Will

13.1 Freedom and Freedom of Will

Our conception of freedom involves a powerful intuition—that freedom generally, and so freedom at the point of the voluntary, depends on a freedom of motivation or will, and so on freedom at the point of the non-voluntary.

Not only do we have control over what we decide and intend. Without that control over our decisions and intentions, it is very natural for us to suppose, we would not have control over anything else. Take the question of whether I stay in or go out this afternoon. Which of these I do is up to me—but only because I can first decide which I shall do, and it is entirely up to me what I decide. More generally, it is up to me what actions I perform only because I have a capacity to decide for myself how I shall act, and it is up to me which such decisions I take—what I decide to do.

A condition of having action control at all, then, is that we have a capacity to take decisions and form intentions; and that we have control over what intentions we form. Freedom of action depends on a freedom of non-voluntary motivation or will. And I have termed this ordinary conception of our freedom of action a *psychologizing* one. Our voluntary action control is being made to depend on our having a control over a specific action-motivating psychological attitude—the pro attitude of intention that motivates much of what we do voluntarily.

Why should freedom of action depend on freedom of will? We have already come across some doctrines that would generate such a dependence, but which do so in the wrong way.

There was volitionism for example. Volitionism is the doctrine that voluntary action is controlled only indirectly, occurring only as an effect of prior, directly controlled decisions and intention-formations. From which it certainly follows that our action is free only to the degree that our will is free. But volitionism is not the explanation we want. For volitionism is false—and has been shown to be false by the same practical reason-based model of action that explains how will action is possible. For the model applies to voluntary actions—not to decisions and intention-formations alone, to the exclusion of voluntary actions. Our voluntary actions are perfectly good cases of action in their own right. Indeed voluntary actions may be actions of decision themselves.

Incompatibilism also suggested an explanation for why there should be a dependence of freedom of action, even freedom of voluntary action, on a prior freedom of will. If voluntary actions are causally determined by prior decisions, and those decisions are outside our control, how in incompatibilist terms can the actions determined be within our control? But this particular incompatibilist explanation is not quite the one we need either.

The intuitive dependence of freedom on freedom of will, a dependence of the kind which we naturally believe, does not arise simply because voluntary actions are *de facto* determined by prior decisions. The dependence of freedom of action on freedom of will does not arise only on the assumption that we already have a will or decision-making capacity which determines how we act voluntarily. Remember what our intuition really is. It is up to us how we act only because we have a capacity to decide how we shall act—and it is up to us which actions we decide to perform. So the dependence surely arises not just when our actions are actually predetermined through the will, but because our freedom also depends on our having a will, a decision-making capacity, in the first place.

To give a complete account of this conception of our freedom, we therefore need to explain this dependence—why freedom should depend on our having a decision-making capacity at all, and then on a free one at that. And one such explanation can be given. It is given by the practical reason-based model of action—the same theory of action which explained how decision-making, though non-voluntary, nevertheless occurs as an intentional action.

We have seen that our control of anything else derives from our control of how we intentionally act. Any control that we possess over other capacities and processes is exercised in and through our control of one capacity in particular—our capacity for intentional agency. And the practical reason-based model tells us exactly what this capacity for intentional agency really is. It is nothing other than our capacity for exercising reason purposively, in pursuit of this goal or that. It is our control of this capacity for exercising reason purposively, then, which is the source of our control over the operation of any other capacity, including capacities for limb motion and the like.

So as free agents we have control over the purposive, action-constitutive exercise of our reason—over how we use reason to pursue goals—and that is our control in its basic and original form. Any control exercised over the operation of other capacities must derive from and depend on this fundamental form of control.

Consider, then, this purposive exercise of reason—this use of our reason to pursue goals. As we have seen, it can take two forms, and both involve intention. It can occur non-voluntarily, as the simple direction of the self towards a goal, without any further capacities necessarily being exercised on its basis. It can occur, in other words, as a mere action of the will or of simple decision and intention-formation—as, say, the formation of an intention to raise one's arm. Or else the exercise of reason can occur as voluntary action. In which case we are still exercising reason purposively. But we are not exercising reason alone. In and through the practical exercise of reason, we are also exercising other capacities, such as capacities for limb motion and the like. Rather than simply forming an intention to raise one's arm, one intentionally raises it.

Intention, then, is the attitude involved in any purposive exercise of reason—in all action which is intentional. Insofar, then, as freedom must be exercised in and through intentional agency, the possession of freedom depends on a capacity for intention and intention-formation—on a decision-making capacity. Freedom depends on our possessing a will. But why does this will itself have to be free?

Consider the two ways of exercising reason purposively—alone, or in a way that involves other capacities as well. And suppose that, as the psychologizing conception of freedom teaches, freedom of action does depend on a freedom specifically of decision-making or will. If so, then this means that to have control over the purposive exercise of reason in its second form, the form which involves the exercise of control over other capacities, we must have control over it in its first form, which involves the purposive exercise of reason alone. But surely this follows from the principle that the basic form of control is over the purposive exercise of reason, all control over other capacities deriving therefrom.

Compare simply deciding or forming an intention to raise one's arm with actually and intendedly raising it. Both are intentional actions. Both are action-constitutive exercises of reason with raising one's arm as their goal. The difference between them is that the second involves a further limb-motive capacity which one might or might not also possess—the ability actually to move one's arm. Whereas the first purposive exercise of reason is merely that. It does not depend on and does not directly involve the further capacity for motion. Now if all my control is exercised in and through the purposive exercise of reason, I can hardly have less control over actions involving that capacity for rationality alone than I have over actions which differ only in involving other, entirely derivatively controlled capacities as well. For otherwise, control over the purposive exercise of my reason would not be the source of my control over those other capacities.

And that is why action control implies and depends on decision control in particular—why I cannot have less control over whether I merely decide and intend to raise my arm than I have over whether I actually manage to raise it. All freedom is exercised in and through our capacity for intentional agency—that is, through our capacity for exercising reason purposively; and extends to other capacities only as controlled through the purposive exercise of reason. We cannot, then, have more control over actions which also involve those further capacities than we have over otherwise similar actions which involve the purposive exercise of reason alone. There is no freedom without freedom of will.

13.2 The Freedom and Non-Voluntariness of the Will

If freedom depends on freedom of will, one thing follows immediately. Freedom, if we have it at all, must apply to motivations that are non-voluntary—to decisions and intention-formations. And we must have at least as much control over our non-voluntary decisions to act as we have over the voluntary actions decided upon. It follows that freedom can neither consist in nor imply a corresponding degree of voluntariness. Freedom cannot be a voluntary power.

But if this is so, we need to explain why so many philosophers have wanted to link freedom with voluntariness. The confusion of freedom or control with the power to do things voluntarily, on the basis of a will to do them, is general through the literature, as this very representative passage from the libertarian Robert Kane shows. Kane says that control, even over acts of the will itself, is exercised at will as 'voluntary control':

> The agents have plural voluntary control over a set of options (e.g. choosing morally or prudentially, or vice versa) when they are able to do whichever of the options they will to do, when they will to do it…These conditions can be summed up by saying, as people sometimes do, that agents can choose either way *at will*. Or, alternatively, when these conditions for plural voluntary control are satisfied, one can say that it is 'up to the agents' what they do when they act.[1]

It is very commonly held, then, that freedom implies voluntariness—that to have control over an action or outcome implies that the action or outcome controlled must depend on one's will.

We find this view, very obviously, in those who attempt simply to reduce freedom to some form of voluntariness. But actually the view extends far more widely, to include philosophers who would reject any such reductive account of freedom, just as they would reject the voluntariness-based model of action with which that reductive view of freedom has been so closely associated. As we are about to see, even Aquinas thought that to have control over something implies being able to do it at will, according as we decide. Things that are not so subject to our will must be outside our control. But if this linkage of freedom to voluntariness is a mistake, why is the mistake so intuitively appealing, and how does the strong tendency to make it arise?

To take discussion further, we need to distinguish two kinds of voluntariness—two cases of a power that attaches to prior motivations and that causes us to act voluntarily as motivated. There is what I shall call an *active* voluntariness attaching to decisions and intention-formations, where these are conceived as actions of the will. This is voluntariness as a power of actions of the will to move us to act as willed. Then there is a *passive* voluntariness attaching to motivations that are passive attitudes or passions. This is a power of passive desires to move us to act as desired.

Nowadays, theories of freedom often link freedom to passive voluntariness. Freedom is taken to be or to involve a causal power of desires to move us to act as desired. And the immediate source of this view of freedom is clear enough. It lies in the voluntariness-based model of action, which ties the very occurrence of action to the exercise of passive voluntariness—to doing as we want. Action by its nature occurs as

---

[1] Robert Kane, *The Significance of Free Will*, p. 143—my emphasis.

an effect of motivations that are passive. Hence insofar as freedom is always exercised in action, so the exercise of freedom must at least imply, even if it does not altogether consist in, the exercise of passive voluntariness. Thus, thanks to the dominance of the voluntariness-based model, even modern libertarians often share the view of their compatibilist opponents that the exercise of freedom has passive voluntariness as, at any rate, a component. This, remember, was the view of event-causal libertarianism—the libertarianism of Wiggins and Kane which strove, unsuccessfully, to account for freedom as constituted by some form of passive voluntariness in non-determining, merely probabilistic causal form.

But we also find an association of freedom with voluntariness—though in active rather than passive form—in many scholastic thinkers who understood action in practical reason-based terms. These scholastic thinkers denied that there was any necessary link between the occurrence of action and the exercise of passive voluntariness. Action conceived as the practical exercise of reason could perfectly well occur independently of any passion, or even in opposition to the agent's own desires. But they still saw freedom in terms that closely linked it to voluntariness in active form. Many scholastic thinkers did maintain that possessing and exercising control over an action implied at least the *possibility* of performing that action voluntarily, on the basis of an active decision to perform it. If we really do have control over whether we do something, then it must be possible for us to do it or not at will, according as we decide. To have control over X implies that X's occurrence must always be correspondingly subject to our will.

Although a philosopher such as Aquinas conceived of intentional agency as an exercise of rationality in purposive or action-constitutive form, he still failed clearly to perceive the non-voluntariness of agency so conceived. Just because decisions and intentions fall within our control, Aquinas thought that decisions and intentions must themselves be subject to the will, and as much so as the voluntary actions which decisions and intentions explain. It must be possible for us to take specific decisions on the basis of deciding to do so. If his conception of action itself was not voluntariness-*based*, his conception of action's freedom was certainly still voluntariness-*tied*.

What reasoning might lead one to believe that freedom implies voluntariness? Consider an important discussion by Aquinas of our control of the will—one to be found in the *Summa Theologiae*, 1a2ae, q17 a.5.[2] Aquinas begins with an intuitive and common enough thought—the very thought which we have just seen to follow from the psychologizing conception which we have of our freedom. We must have at least as much control over whether we decide to do A as we have over whether we actually do A. What we decide or intend must be at least as much within our control as whether we manage to perform the voluntary actions intended.

---

[2] See *Summa Theologiae* (Turin: Marietti), p. 83.

But—Aquinas argued—how can we have at least as much control over our decisions, if we can't take decisions at will?[3] For surely those actions that are voluntary—that we can perform at will—must be more within our control than those actions that we can't perform at will? Non-voluntariness in decisions would be a major limitation on our control over what we decide. If we are to have as much control over our decisions as we have over the voluntary actions which they explain, then our decisions must be voluntary too.

However, the non-voluntariness of decisions is not some limitation on our freedom of will. It does not in any way restrict the control we have over the will and how we exercise it. For consider what the will is. Our will is a capacity for deliberately and actively directing ourselves at goals. That is what the will enables us to do—deliberately to adopt and aim at one goal rather than another. It follows that any limitation to our freedom of will would have to reduce or remove our control over which goals we deliberately aimed at. It would have to restrict our freedom to direct ourselves at one goal rather than another. But the essential non-voluntariness of decisions is no restriction on this freedom at all.

In fact, the non-voluntariness of our decisions is mirrored at the level of the actions that we perform voluntarily. For in both cases there is one aspect of our agency that is always non-voluntary. And that is the purposiveness of our agency—the particular goals towards which it is being directed. Whatever we are doing, whether taking a decision, or doing something voluntarily on the basis of a decision, something has to be true if what we are doing is to count as directed at a given end E. We must hold a motivating pro attitude towards attaining E. No one can genuinely be aiming at an outcome if he in no way favours its attainment. Now such a pro attitude is in no way voluntary. It is a non-voluntary attitude justified, not by its own desirability, but by the desirability of its object E; and it is to the desirability of that outcome rather than its own desirability that, by its nature, the attitude must be responsive.

That we are acting in order to attain *this* specific end rather than *that* is not, therefore, an aspect of our agency that is voluntary—that we can deliver at will, on the basis of the general desirability of so acting. And that is simply because, to count as acting in order to attain a given goal, it must be to that goal that one is responding, and in a way appropriate to the desirability of attaining it. The object of one's action is, after all, that goal; not the state of having that goal as one's object. So the action must be performed in a way that is sensitive to that goal and its desirability, not to the

---

[3] More precisely, in *Summa Theologiae* 1ae2ae, q17, a.5, Aquinas makes our control or power over the will depend on its being subject to the *imperium* or command of our reason—and so also to the acts of the will itself which such commands of reason presuppose, and by virtue of which they motivate what is both willed and commanded:

> ... everything in our power is subject to our command. But acts of the will are more within our power than anything else: for all our acts are said to be within our power in so far as they are will-involving. Therefore acts of the will are themselves commanded by us.

desirability of aiming at the goal. If goals are attained voluntarily, in a way responsive to the desirability of attaining them, our aiming at their attainment cannot be voluntary too.

The non-voluntariness of intention does not limit our control of the will or of the purposes which the will's exercise determines. It is no limitation on our freedom to employ the will to aim at this or that goal or outcome. Instead, it is simply the requirement that when one does finally exercise the will in order to attain a specific goal A, one be doing just that.

After all, decisions are actions which have their basic goal-direction built in, through their content. To take a decision to do A is, by its very nature, to be acting in order that A be done. A decision to do A is just an action of the will that has through its content the doing of A as its goal—and so which is responsive to the desirability of doing A and of the further ends which doing A might help attain. If the decision were responsive not to these ends but to something else—such as to the simple desirability of its own occurrence—it could not, whatever it was, count as a decision to do A. In principle at least, one is perfectly free to use the will to attain any voluntary goal—to decide to perform any given voluntary action. But one cannot count as deciding to do A unless the real goal of the exercise of one's will is the attainment of A. One is not free to decide to do A without doing just that—deciding *to do A*.

It is of course true, exactly as Aquinas held, that we must have as much control over our decisions as we have over our voluntary actions. At any given time we can never have more control over whether we voluntarily do A than we have over whether we then intend to do A. But that guarantee is built into the structure of human freedom and the nature of the intentional agency which is its basis. Control is exercised in and through our capacity for intentional agency—for exercising reason in purposive or action-constitutive form. It extends to other capacities only as controlled through the purposive exercise of reason. We cannot, then, have more control over actions involving those further derivatively controlled capacities than we have over actions involving the purposive exercise of reason alone. The guarantee of our having no less control over our decisions than over our voluntary actions holds good for that structural reason alone. This being the case, the guarantee doesn't require the impossibility that, in addition, our decisions be voluntary.

13.3 Why Freedom Appears to Imply Voluntariness

We need a theory to explain the common philosophical view that freedom implies voluntariness. But we need the right theory. We have already come across the wrong one. For if there is an association between voluntariness and freedom or self-determination, this cannot be for the reason that we saw Bernard Williams and Galen Strawson to allege—that our experience of our own agency is an experience of voluntariness in passive form, and that therefore passive voluntariness is the original basis of any conception of self-determination that we might have. If we do have a conception of self-determination as freedom, a freedom exercisable over and through the will, and we plainly do, there are no grounds for taking passive voluntariness to be a more primitive version of it.

The reason why is obvious by now. There is no obvious way of turning voluntariness into freedom. And that is because freedom in the one form in which it must be possessed—as a freedom specifically of the will or control of what one intends—takes a form which *excludes* any kind of voluntariness, be it active or passive. Decisions and intention-formations cannot be voluntary as are the actions intended which they explain. But the greatest extent of our control is precisely over what we decide or intend. This we naturally believe. And, very importantly, we naturally believe this, at least in ordinary life, as non-philosophers, without in any way 'voluntarizing' decisions—without viewing decisions as being at the same time themselves voluntary or subject to the will. We do not ordinarily think of ourselves as taking specific decisions in the same way as we perform voluntary actions—at will, on the basis of having decided to take those decisions in particular.

Our natural conception of freedom sharply distinguishes it, then, from any kind of voluntariness, and attaches to a form of agency that we never ordinarily experience or seriously conceive as voluntary. It is quite mysterious, then, how we could have arrived at the conception of such a power of self-determination just from the experience of the power of our passive wants or appetites moving us to act as wanted.

Yet if freedom is a non-voluntary power, why does the exercise of voluntariness, at least in the form of acting as we decide, seem to so many philosophers so much like the essence of self-determination? Here we need to go back to the distinction between active and passive voluntariness. In my view, any intuitive link between self-determination and voluntariness is entirely with active voluntariness. In fact I think that in our ordinary thinking there is no association whatever of self-determination with passive voluntariness. We do not ordinarily think of self-determination as involving our action being determined by desires or appetites not of our own making. The very reverse. We incline to see that kind of determination of our actions as potentially threatening to self-determination—for reasons that I shall examine in Chapter 15.

There is, though, a very strong natural association between the exercise of freedom and active voluntariness—between exercising control over what we do and acting as we have decided. It is this association that led philosophers, even those such as Aquinas who accepted the practical reason-based model and did not crudely identify action with voluntariness in any form, still to misconceive freedom as being some kind of voluntary power. They misrepresented control of what we do as involving at least the possibility of doing it at will. Their theories then opened the way for later theories—theories that once the practical reason-based model was abandoned, and the will was turned into a passive motivational faculty, transformed the tie of freedom with active voluntariness into one with passive voluntariness. The association of freedom with passive voluntariness, then, is nothing primitive, and has no place in our ordinary thinking, but is the product of philosophical theorizing over centuries, and theorizing of a misguided and quite complex kind at that.

To see how this all happened, we must consider what is a quite fundamental source of tension within action theory. Going by what is strictly essential to their occurrence, each of freedom and intentional action is quite independent of voluntariness. Indeed, as we have seen, freedom can even be exercised and action performed in a form which definitely excludes voluntariness. Free action can occur as non-voluntary attitude-formation. On the other hand, if we go by what gives our exercise of freedom and agency its point, what we aim at when we act and what we deliberate about doing when we deliberate practically, then in every case we find voluntariness, and voluntariness of the active kind—managing to do something on the basis of having decided or intended to do it. The voluntary is the guise under which our agency principally concerns and matters to us, and under which it principally enters our awareness.

The fundamental tension in action theory, then, is this. The aspect of agency, including free agency, which is most salient—which is teleologically and deliberatively primary—is voluntariness. Yet it is precisely this aspect of free agency which is quite inessential to its occurrence. What is most salient about our action is fundamentally misleading as to what the essence of free action really is.

Consider the teleology of action—the goal of our agency as a whole. The goal of our agency as a whole is always the successful performance of the voluntary. Decisions are entirely aimed at producing voluntary actions and outcomes. And that means that Galen Strawson is right to see our experience of successful voluntariness as central to our appreciation of ourselves as free. As he put it, an explanation

> ... of this sense of self-determination would connect it tightly with our sense, massively and incessantly confirmed since earliest infancy, of our ability *to do what we want in order to (try to) get what we want*, by performing a vast variety of actions great and small, walking where we want, making ourselves understood, picking up this and putting down that.[4]

Strawson is right to this important degree: since the whole point of exercising freedom in action lies in the successful performance of the voluntary, successful voluntariness—*active* voluntariness, managing to act as we decide or intend—is central to one's freedom being at all effective, and so to its being of the slightest worth, and so is central to freedom as we ordinarily value it.

We must reaffirm, against Strawson, that our conception of self-determination is very definitely a conception of freedom. It is not, even in origin, a conception of voluntariness, let alone of passive voluntariness. But nevertheless, it is equally true that our freedom only begins to matter to us as a freedom of the voluntary. Freedom is at all valuable only insofar as it does extend into voluntariness of an active kind—only to the extent that through freedom we do manage to do what we decide.

---

[4] Galen Strawson, *Freedom and Belief*, pp. 110–11—my emphasis.

Epictetus the Stoic is famous for having envisaged a kind of freedom that was entirely divorced from control of the voluntary. Epictetus claimed that our freedom is wholly limited to *prohairesis*—to our capacity for decision-making and intention-formation alone.

As was fitting, therefore, the gods have put under our control only the most excellent faculty of all [*prohairesis*] ... The tyrant says 'But I will fetter you'. 'What is that you say, man? fetter me? My leg you will fetter, but my *prohairesis* not even Zeus will overcome.'[5]

Epictetus even celebrates this minimal freedom as the only freedom worth having. But in this he is surely wildly wrong. If we did possess no more than a purely Epictetan freedom, it would hardly be a freedom to *enjoy*. Because he is a Stoic, Epictetus completely fails to acknowledge the teleological primacy of the voluntary. For a Stoic, the real goal of the will's exercise lies in itself—in a wisdom and virtue which that exercise alone is supposed sufficient to attain. But the truth is quite different. The real point and goal of the will's exercise is always to be found beyond mere willing or deciding—in the free attainment, through the will, of voluntary ends. Which is why the experience of a purely Epictetan freedom would be so dismal. It would be freedom in a form so limited as to be either redundant—things intended by us would turn out to be bound to happen anyway—or subject to frustration in its every goal. The possessors of such a limited form of freedom would experience its exercise as impotence or imprisonment.

Connected with the teleological primacy of the voluntary is its deliberative salience. As we have already seen, we do not generally deliberate about action in its non-voluntary form—about which decision to take or which intention to form. The actions between which we do deliberate—those actions therefore which, as deliberators, we naturally explicitly consider as being 'the options that are up to us'—are almost always actions which are voluntary. And that is just because it is the successful performance of these voluntary actions that is the goal of our agency as a whole. The point of decisions, after all, is to ensure that we act as decided—that we attempt and attain the voluntary outcome intended. And we can normally take for granted the efficacy of our decisions as means to getting us at least to make the attempt. So once we have deliberated about which is the best voluntary action to perform or attempt performing, we have effectively settled which decision to take. There is absolutely no need to go on to deliberate further about what to decide.[6]

---

[5] Epictetus, *Discourses* (Cambridge, MA: Loeb Classical Library, 1925), vol. 1, p. 9.

[6] That is the typical case. But sometimes we cannot take the efficacy of our decisions for granted. Doing or at least attempting A in the future might be the best course of action; but a present decision so to act might be abandoned by us before we ever even attempted to carry it out—with consequences that could be very bad for the coordination of our action through time. Some decisions we might now take might not be reliable motivators and causes of subsequent actions and attempts—and we might know this. In these cases the questions whether it is best to do or attempt A in the future, and whether it is best now to decide to do A, are not the same. In these cases we may have to deliberate specifically about what to decide. I discuss

The options we normally deliberate between, then, are cases of action in its voluntary form. This is action which does only ever count as our own deliberate doing insofar as it occurs on the basis of our own intention that it should. The very voluntariness of such action really is a condition of its being performed intentionally, and so too of its performance ever constituting an exercise of freedom.

Practical deliberation, then, characteristically presents us with action in a form whose freedom does depend on its voluntariness. So we may conceptualize action as an exercise of practical rationality; and we may regard our moral responsibility as depending on freedom. But our natural picture of free action *qua* subject matter of our own practical deliberation is still going to be a picture of it as voluntary. Which is partly why, historically, even philosophical proponents of the practical reason-based model—philosophers such as Aquinas, for whom freedom, not voluntariness, was fundamental to moral responsibility—were still so apt to tie our control over our actions to a capacity to perform them voluntarily. They simply generalized from the case of those actions that are deliberatively salient to the case of deliberate action in general.

It is extremely difficult for a theory of action to do clear-headed justice to the relation within our agency between the two elements of voluntariness and non-voluntariness. It is voluntariness which hogs the limelight. Voluntariness is the aspect of what we do which matters to us, and which is salient to us as deliberators. It follows that, when we start to philosophize about action and its freedom, voluntariness is apt to colour our picture of agency as a whole. So, historically, even within the practical reason-based tradition, freedom was still taken to involve the possibility of voluntariness as at least a necessary condition.

Then, in early modern Europe, with the coming of Thomas Hobbes, the terms in which common sense understands intentional action—as a purposive exercise of reason—ceased to admit of ready philosophical defence and development. The will ceased to be seen as a distinctive locus of agency, and became a passive antecedent of action. Freedom came to be understood reductively, as nothing more than a mode of voluntariness—though this time voluntariness conceived in passive form, the will now being viewed as a passive cause of action and no longer as a locus of action in its own right. Where before freedom had been seen as requiring the possibility of doing as we actively decide, it was now seen as involving nothing more than doing as we want.

Proponents of self-determination as freedom have no trouble, therefore, in explaining the philosophical appeal of voluntariness as at least a condition on freedom and self-determination—and even its appeal to philosophers as a *prima facie* alternative conception of what constitutes self-determination itself. That explanation has just been given. But, as we have seen, proponents of self-determination as passive voluntariness are not correspondingly well placed to explain the appeal of freedom. There seems no intelligible route from an initial conception of self-determination as passive

---

such atypical cases in Thomas Pink, 'Reason and agency', *Aristotelian Society Proceedings* 97, (1997): pp. 263–80, and in *The Psychology of Freedom*, Chapter 8.

voluntariness to a conception of it as the quite different and non-voluntary power of freedom.

Theories of human self-determination as nothing more than voluntariness are not what Bernard Williams and Galen Strawson present them as being—the recovery of some psychological *Urbegriff*. They are, instead, philosophical distortions of what is really our original conception of self-determination—a conception of self-determination as freedom. The very prevalence of these theoretical distortions is, as we have seen, something which the practical reason-based model can explain. They have arisen from the very common failure of philosophers to understand the full implications of two closely related phenomena.

The first thing not properly understood is decisions' status as actions with an intrinsic goal-direction, towards the voluntary object that is given by their content—a goal-direction that makes decisions non-voluntary themselves, though without in any way compromising our control of the will or limiting our freedom to direct it to the attainment of any goal. And secondly, there is the consequent centrality of attaining that voluntary goal or object, both to the value of the freedom that we exercise so non-voluntarily in decision-making, and to our awareness of its exercise. The whole point of the agency which is exercised by us in decision-making is to bring about the successful performance of voluntariness. Which is why, whenever we are engaged in that action, though we are exercising freedom non-voluntarily, our attention is so entirely concentrated on the voluntary—this profound everyday salience of voluntariness being apt to distort any philosophical theory of action and self-determination.

It is supposed, wrongly, that ___ is reduced to mere chance.

14

Freedom and Causation

14.1 Freedom, Randomness, and Causal Power

We have already encountered the randomness problem—a problem that supposedly arises for freedom as understood by libertarians, and that has been raised since the days of David Hume. According to the sceptic, freedom understood in incompatibilist terms can come to no more than randomness. For if incompatibilism is true, there are only two alternatives. Either an action is causally predetermined—which excludes freedom. Or, to the extent that the action is not causally predetermined it must be occurring by pure chance. In which case, genuine freedom is again ruled out. There is no middle way.

The randomness problem is supposed to arise the instant that it is accepted, on incompatibilist grounds, that free action cannot be causally determined. Once we agree that freedom implies a lack of causal determination, it is supposed, freedom is immediately reduced to no more than chance.[1] But does an absence of causal determination necessarily leave us with nothing more than chance? The assumption that it must comes with the dogma that power in general, and the power of freedom in particular, must be causal, so that what is causally undetermined must be undetermined by any power.

We have seen that most modern philosophers take freedom to be a causal power. They assume that any exercise of freedom must consist in a certain mode of causation—in the production of an effect. So what occurs through one's exercise of control, occurs as an effect which one has produced. Without causation, many philosophers wonder, how could there be any control?

The exercise of active control is essentially a causal phenomenon.[2]

In which case

The view that free actions have uncaused volitions at their core is prima facie puzzling. If it is uncaused, if it is no sense determined to occur by anything at all, then it is not determined to occur by me in particular. And if I don't determine it, then it's not under my control.[3]

---

[1] Many philosophers have asserted this myth to me as a supposedly evident truth, both in communications and in conversation, including two Oxford University Press readers, one for this book and one for a previous publication, my *Free Will: A Very Short Introduction*.

[2] Randolph Clarke, *Libertarian Accounts of Free Will*, p. 151.

[3] Timothy O'Connor, *Persons and Causes*, p. 25.

Exercise/freedom is a non-causal power.

Table 14.1. Determination, randomness, and control

Causally Determined	Causally Undetermined and Uncontrolled (Randomness or mere chance)	Causally Undetermined and Controlled

But we have already asked why we should assume that if an action is not causally determined, it is not determined at all. It could be that there is a further possibility: that though causally undetermined, the action is not occurring randomly or purely by chance, and this because the action is still determined—non-causally, through the exercise of freedom as a non-causal power.

If chance is the absence of causal determination, pure chance or randomness is that absence of causal determination and *nothing more*. So there will be some events that are genuinely random in that their occurrence is purely a matter of chance. Obviously in the case of these events any involvement of freedom in their occurrence is excluded. But then there are those events that are undetermined causally but still controlled. Here we do not have mere chance or randomness because something more is involved than an absence of causal determination; and that something more is the exercise of freedom. The agent is controlling whether or not the event occurs (Table 14.1).

The randomness problem arises, then, only if we assume that all power is causal. But the very idea of self-determination is of a power involving contingency of determination—a power to determine even those outcomes that are not already determined causally. If it is not already determined what effect a mere cause will produce, that cause can at best operate probabilistically, influencing the outcome but not determining it, and leaving it dependent on mere chance. An agent capable of self-determination, by contrast, can determine outcomes without their occurrence being already guaranteed just by his presence with the power then to determine them. This essential feature of self-determination differentiates it from causation, allowing for outcomes to be determined without being determined causally. This contingency of determination is not tied to a libertarian or incompatibilist view of self-determination. It applies whether or not incompatibilism is true.

But just because freedom is so generally understood as a causal power, even libertarians have generally ignored the last possibility—of action that is causally undetermined, but still controlled. They have tried to defend the reality of incompatibilist freedom while still assuming the governing dogma, that the only alternative to causal determination is mere chance. So modern libertarians seek to defend incompatibilism by denying that incompatibilistically free action need be causally undetermined. Incompatibilism, they maintain, only implies the absence of a certain kind of causal determination—by prior causes outside the agent's control. Free action is not random—but only because it is causally determined in another way, by the agent himself, operating as free cause of his own actions. But obviously this ignores the possibility that freedom might be a capacity to determine, a capacity that excludes randomness, but which is non-causal; that in exercising freedom we might be determining how we act, but non-causally—and so in quite a different way from the way in which, say, a thrown stone determines that a window is broken.

We have already discussed why freedom might not be a causal power. This chapter will now add to the case by appealing to the practical reason-based model of action. The practical reason-based model of action considerably strengthens the case for distinguishing between freedom and causal power, and in ways that assume no specifically incompatibilist or libertarian view of freedom. I shall argue, in particular, that the project of modelling freedom as a causal power is not only very much responsible for generating the randomness problem in the first place, but is notably inadequate in supporting any solution to it.

We shall consider the two main causal theories of freedom in turn. First we shall consider the causal theory favoured by compatibilists—though also, and confusedly, by event-causal libertarians. This is the theory of freedom as a causal power of occurrences—of events and states. Then we shall consider the rival causal theory favoured by many libertarians—the theory I have just mentioned. This is the theory of freedom as a causal power of agents themselves.

2nd

14.2 Freedom as a Causal Power of Events and States?

Compatibilists say that freedom of action is compatible with the determination of one's actions by causes outside one's control. And those compatibilists who identify freedom as a causal power have generally maintained that it is a causal power of events or states—a causal power exercised, as freedom is, to determine how we act. The exercise of control consists in certain events or states prior to our action—occurrences which must, therefore, be inherently passive and not themselves doings by us—producing effects on how we act.

In the causal power of what occurrences might freedom lie? Clearly the occurrences must be ones that cause the actions over which the power of freedom is immediately exercised. There is one obvious candidate—our desires or passive motivations. Our freedom consists in the power of such passive motivations causally to determine or at least influence how we act. Such a theory in its simplest form gives us classical compatibilism:

> Freedom is our motivations' capacity to cause us to act in whatever way those motivations would favour. So we have control over whether we do A just in case were we passively motivated to do A, we would do A as a result, and were we passively motivated not to do A, we would refrain as a result.

Libertarians, of course, should never define freedom as a causal power of desires or other prior occurrences to determine how we act. And we have already seen why, in the criticisms already made of event-causal libertarianism. Such a causal power is something which, in action-determining form, would remove libertarian freedom. And so if this causal power is ever present in any form consistent with libertarian freedom, it cannot itself be a power that is action-determining. There is no event-causal power, therefore, with which libertarians can coherently identify freedom; not if freedom is ever to be what we ordinarily suppose it can be—an action-determining power, a power by which we settle outright how we act.

We have already raised a number of objections to regarding freedom as an event-causal power. The first objection is that the theory completely mislocates the bearer of the power. Our understanding of freedom takes it to be a power of the agent. It is the agent, after all, who is supposed to be in control. But on the event-causal theory, the immediate bearers of the causal power used to explain freedom are not the agent, but passive desires and other passions—occurrences within the agent's life which are none of his own doing. And that makes it impossible to do justice to moral blame—the criticism that presupposes freedom or some such power of self-determination. Blame is not simply a criticism of the agent for faulty occurrences in his life, such as for faulty motivations, but of the agent as determiner of those occurrences. The faults in the agent are his fault.

In any case, identifying freedom with a causal power of motivations reduces multi-way freedom to a complex case of one-way causal power. And that makes it impossible to explain how our moral responsibility for what we do could ever be based, as we suppose it to be based, on a power to do otherwise. For the power to do otherwise becomes a power that is never exercised, and which never actually determines what the agent does. It becomes a dummy, attaching unexercised to some hypothetical motivation other than that which is actually moving the agent, and so quite distinct from the power that is actually determining how the agent acts. To the extent that common sense treats the freedom to do otherwise as, when present, clearly relevant to the agent's moral responsibility for what he does, such a freedom cannot be decomposed into two distinct one-way powers.

Why might compatibilists, or anyone, regard freedom as a causal power of motivations to influence how we act? The answer is simple—out of allegiance to the voluntariness-based model of action.

Freedom can only be exercised through how we act. Anything that blocks or removes our capacity for action, then, is freedom-threatening. It blocks or removes a capacity essential to freedom's exercise. But, on the voluntariness-based model, essential to our capacity for action is the causal power of our desires or passive motivations to influence how we act. For that, on the voluntariness-based model, is just what action is—doing what one wants to do because one wants to do it. Remove that causal power of desires to effect their satisfaction, and you remove any possibility of action—and the exercise of freedom is precluded. On the voluntariness-based model, then, any block to desire-satisfaction is inherently freedom-threatening. It prevents the action through which alone freedom can be exercised.

It is very tempting, then, for supporters of the voluntariness-based model to define freedom as consisting, entirely or at least in part, in a causal power of desires to determine how we act. Even if the theory turns out to be more complex than classical compatibilism—so that freedom involves more than just a simple power of our passions to cause us to act however they motivate us to—such a power may still be seen as essential to freedom and partially constitutive of it.

While the voluntariness-based model of action gives some support to an event-causal theory of freedom, so our new theory of action as practical reason-based further undermines it. Intentional action now occurs, not as a voluntary effect, or indeed as an effect at all, but as a mode of exercising rationality—one that can perfectly well occur uncaused. The practical reason-based model locates agency, not in the voluntary alone, but in certain of our motivations too—our decisions and intention-formations. And as actions these decisions and intention-formations are goal-directed events in their own right; they do not depend for all their goal-direction on the contents of prior desires. Actions have no a priori dependence on prior motivations that are passive, or indeed on any other cause.

So there is no longer anything in the nature of action to tie it to desire-satisfaction. Action is left a desire-independent phenomenon, a phenomenon that can occur independently of what we want. In fact, since action is a desire-independent phenomenon, there is nothing in principle to stop us from deliberately deciding and acting in ways that opposed our own desires (if we disapproved of them) and ensured their frustration. What is essential to agency conceived in voluntariness-based terms—desires causing their own satisfaction—becomes, once the nature of action is divorced from the occurrence of desire-satisfaction, something which action can perfectly well prevent.

We have already come across the earlier traditions in action theory that shared just this view of action. These traditions grant that action may well often be causally influenced by prior desires. But, these theories insist, the presence and extent of such an influence is a contingency. It does not follow from the very nature of action. In the scholastic philosophy of the middle ages and in Kant we find action being treated in just this way, as occurring in decisions of the will which have an active nature and identity that is strictly desire-independent. Action can oppose passion and frustrate it.

This desire-independent nature of action opens up an important conceptual possibility—that the power to determine action for ourselves be desire-independent too. After all, if we can use our own action to oppose and frustrate desires as well as satisfy them, and we can determine for ourselves how we act, why can we not determine for ourselves and control which if any of our desires are to be satisfied? In which case freedom is a power which can limit desire-satisfaction, or even prevent it. Not only need freedom not consist in acting as we want. Freedom may even be used to prevent ourselves from acting as we want.

It is conceptually open, then, that freedom and the causal power of our passive motivations to determine how we act are two quite different kinds of power, which are not only distinct but may even be mutually opposing. Or so the practical reason-based model suggests. A block to the satisfaction of our desires need no longer be a freedom-threatening obstacle to our own action. For what might prevent the satisfaction of our desires could be nothing other than our very own deliberate decision—such as, for example, our decision just not to perform the low action that all our desires and appetites are inclining and tempting us towards. The block to the satisfaction of our desires could lie in our very own action. We could be deliberately frustrating our desires by the contrary exercise of our own will. But if it is, not some external obstacle, but our very own deliberate action which is frustrating our desires, what would be inherently freedom-threatening about that? The intentional exercise of this power to frustrate our desires rather than satisfy them—this is simply a restriction of desire through our own deliberate action, and not a restriction of our capacity for action. One's capacity for action is being deliberately used, not curbed. So why should such a deliberate use of our power to act preclude our still being in control of what we do?

There is another reason why freedom as ordinarily understood cannot be a causal power of desires to determine. Such a power cannot be found in a form that applies to our decisions—which we definitely do think we can control—while not equally applying to our desires, which we think of as passive and outside our direct control. For to the extent that our decisions can be determined by desires, so too plainly can desires themselves. My decision to do A might possibly be the determined effect of prior desires for certain ends and beliefs that doing A would attain those ends. But my desire to do A might equally well be the determined effect of just such desires too. In the latter case the determining causal power of my desires does not give me control of the desire determined. Why, then, should the same causal power give me control of the decision determined?

There is, of course, a mode of determination by prior desire that does seem more plausibly specific to action, and that does not apply to desires themselves. This is where desires determine us to do something voluntarily, on the basis of a desire or pro attitude specifically towards doing it. But then, as we have seen, this mode of determination by prior desire does not apply to decisions themselves, or certainly not to the same degree that it applies to unqualifiedly voluntary actions. Yet we think we control our decisions just as much as we control our voluntary actions.

If the causal influence of desires is not constitutive of freedom, why should any other event-causal power be either? Consider our judgements about how we should act. Perhaps, it might be thought, freedom consists in the power of these judgements causally to determine or influence how we act. But there is the intuitive possibility of freely acting against such judgements—I freely decline the nasty medicine that I know I should take. And even if someone denies that we can freely act against our own judgements about how we should act, there can still be free decisions that simply are not accompanied by any such judgements.

For, as we have already seen, often there are options between which I am to choose where I simply have no view at all about what I should do. Should I carry on my walk, stay where I am, or go home? I may well think that I could as well do one thing as another—even that at this moment it does not particularly matter whether I decide and act at all. So if, nevertheless, I do now take some decision and act, it will be as my own whim, not because I am driven to do so by any conviction. There is simply no judgement that I make whose causal power would push me towards one of these options rather than another, or indeed towards doing anything at all.

But it does not follow that I must therefore lack control of what I do or be failing to exercise it. Suppose that, just as a whim, I do simply decide to continue with my walk. If I do so decide, I can still be fully in control. It is my decision, and I determine for myself that I take it. But if my decision is indeed just taken on a whim, there will have been no kind of judgement—a judgement that I should take this decision in particular—that will have determined that I take this particular decision, and with causal power of which my freedom can be identified.

If such exercise of control is a conceptual possibility, compatibilists can no longer continue to define freedom as a causal power of passive motivations to effect their satisfaction—or indeed of any other prior passive occurrence causally to influence how we act. We shall need therefore to frame compatibilism in somewhat different terms—terms that do not appeal to event-causal powers to characterize what freedom is. We shall need to detach compatibilism, which is a doctrine about the compatibility of freedom and causal determinism, from a reductive account of freedom in terms of event-causation. Compatibilism, I shall be arguing, is a doctrine that might be true, at least as a conceptual possibility. But such a reductionism about freedom is certainly false.

In the next chapter we shall see that the conceptual distinction between freedom and event-causal power is confirmed, by the way we experience our own action. It is a conceptual distinction that shows up in phenomenology. But before we turn to that claim, we need first to consider the rival causal theory of freedom, as a power of agent-causes.

14.3 Freedom as an Agent-Causal Power?

We have seen that modern libertarians have been gripped by the dogma that generates the randomness problem. If freedom is not some kind of causal power, they suppose, there is nothing else for freedom to be. Like O'Connor and Clarke, they assume that all power is causal, so that to determine outcomes is to determine them causally. Action that was causally undetermined would not be determined or controlled in any other way. It would simply be action that was random. So these libertarians have sought to identify libertarian freedom as a causal power: not as a power of any occurrence, but attaching to and exercised directly by our own selves.

Freedom must be a causal power, not of some prior action-influencing occurrence in an agent's life, but of a persisting substance—the agent himself. And, since freedom is understood by us as a multi-way power, a power to do or to refrain, this causal power must be similarly exercisable in more than one way. This multi-wayness is a condition, we have seen, of the freedom to do otherwise mattering to moral responsibility. The causal power which constitutes our freedom must be usable both to produce a given effect and to prevent its occurrence. And so we arrive at one very influential and popular theory of libertarian freedom—the theory which appeals to what philosophers term *agent-causation*. Freedom is supposed to be a special multi-way causal power over actions; a causal power possessed and exercised, though, not by any unfree event but by free substances—by free agents themselves. Freedom is supposed to be an agent-causal power. The agent-causal theory of freedom says:

Take some change or occurrence E over which the agent might or might not have control: for E to occur through an exercise of the agent's control is for the agent as substance to cause E.

Why should libertarians want to characterize freedom as an agent-causal power?

The agent-causal theory is really doing two jobs. First, it is identifying freedom with another kind of power, revealing it to be a special case of a phenomenon, causal power, found more widely throughout nature. So we have the satisfaction of identifying even something so (supposedly) unnatural and exceptional as libertarian freedom with a phenomenon found more generally in nature. But secondly, insofar as we are identifying freedom with causation in wider nature, we can use the properties there found in causation, properties already familiar to us, as a means of solving the randomness problem. If when we exercise freedom, we as agents causally determine how we act, then our libertarianly free action cannot be random. Free action cannot be random because it is causally determined—not by some prior freedom-threatening happening but by us ourselves as free agents. And one thing is clear and agreed on by everyone. As it occurs in wider nature, causal determination precludes all randomness in what is causally determined. The exercise of libertarian freedom is being very clearly distinguished, then, from mere chance.

So when some action A occurs through an agent's exercise of his freedom, the agent himself is operating as a cause. Not any mere event or happening, not any desire or motivation, but the agent himself is causally determining whether or not he does A (Figure 14.1)[4].

The occurrence of action A is not random, because it is causally determined. But its occurrence can still be an exercise of the agent's control because it is determined, not by an uncontrolled cause, but by the agent himself, as a freely operative cause.

---

[4] Figure 4.1 implies only a causal, not a temporal priority of agent over effect. It is supposed to leave it open that the agent operates as cause simultaneously with the occurrence of his effect—a point that is of some significance, and that the main text will return to.

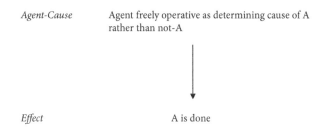

Agent-Cause   Agent freely operative as determining cause of A
rather than not-A

Effect   A is done

Figure 14.1. The agent as cause.

This seems to be the model. But there is a dispute even at this point. Helen Steward has denied that free actions occur as effects determined by their agents, even on an agent-causal conception of freedom. In Steward's view, the agent's action is not something causally determined by the agent, but rather constitutes the agent's very exercise of their agent-causal power—a power that is exercised not to determine the action itself, but the action's further outcomes. Otherwise the exercise of freedom is turned into something mysteriously prior to the agent's action—a sort of mysterious and further action-generating action in its own right, and we are on the way to a vicious regress:

But it is fatal to a proper understanding of actions to suppose that they are caused by agents. Agents cause things, at any rate when they do so qua agents, by *acting*. So it cannot be that they also cause their actions, unless we are to suppose that for each caused action there is another action by means of which it is caused.[5]

But it is unclear that a supporter of the agent-causal theory such as Steward can afford to exclude decisions and actions from being agent-caused. Decisions and actions may surely be taken or performed freely, and fall within agents' control if anything does. What free agents immediately determine, if they determine anything, are their own actions and decisions. We immediately control what we decide and do, and only through that control of how we ourselves act do we exercise control over anything else. But then it does seem to follow that actions and decisions must, on an agent-causal theory of freedom, occur as effects which free agents causally determine. For if we were to take Steward's view, then either we should have to deny that agents determine for themselves what they decide and do—which, as an account of freedom, seems just false—or we should have to maintain that free agents determine their own decisions and actions, but do not determine them causally. But the last option would surely just commit us to my own view of freedom as a non-causal power—a power to determine, but without determining causally. In effect we would have given up the agent-causal theory of freedom.

But suppose we do allow that actions and decisions are causally determined. Does not Steward's problem then arise? What are we to say of the exercise of freedom that determines these actions and decisions? Is it not a kind of action the agent's control

[5] Helen Steward, *A Metaphysics for Freedom*, p. 38.

over which needs to be explained? In fact it is a very familiar worry that theories of freedom as an agent-causal power are incoherent because viciously regressive. Where there is an event E which the agent controls through freely causing it, the agent-causationist is supposedly committed to the existence of a further event—the agent's causing of E—the agent's control over which has to be explained in similar terms, namely in terms of his causing that causing, and so on ad infinitum.[6] But in my view this particular worry is misplaced. Agent-causal theories of freedom are not committed by their very nature to any such regress. It is important to see why.

Consider any occurrence E which the agent might or might not control. Since the occurrence of E does not of itself imply any freedom or control over it, control over E involves some added element, something more than E's mere occurrence, which relates the controlling agent to E. The agent-causal theory is a theory of this added element, which it characterizes as a causal power, so the controlled event E occurs as an effect produced by a controlling agent-cause.

Now it may be true that whenever the agent does exercise his causal power to cause E, there is a further and additional event—namely the event of his so exercising his causal power. The important point is that even if there is such a further event, it is not an event the agent's control over which would plausibly involve anything beyond its mere occurrence. For the exercise of the agent's causal power just is the exercise of his freedom. And freedom, by its very nature, is a power the exercise of which is up to the agent.

Remember what our ordinary understanding of freedom involves. First it involves the idea of a multi-way power—a single power that can be exercised in more than one way, to produce more than one outcome. That multi-wayness is what makes the freedom to do otherwise a condition of moral responsibility, as we ordinarily understand that freedom to be. Only if the power that bases an agent's moral responsibility for what he actually does—the power exercised to determine what he actually does—is also the power to do otherwise, will the power to do otherwise be a condition of moral responsibility at all, as opposed to being some quite distinct power the presence or absence of which is unconnected with what the agent is actually doing. On the agent causal-theory, the causal power must likewise be multi-way. One and the same power must be usable to produce more than one outcome.

But secondly, as we have also seen, the multi-way power involves a freedom of specification. It must be up to the agent how he exercises his power—to produce this outcome or that. So the agent-causal power must not only be usable to produce more than one outcome, but it must be up to the agent how he exercises it. And of course this freedom of specification is vital to any libertarian reading of the agent-causal theory. The agent must control how he exercises his agent-causal power; he must control whether he causes or prevents A's doing. Otherwise, even though causally determined by the agent himself, A's doing would still be determined by a cause

---

[6] Roderick Chisholm in his 'Reflections on human agency', *Idealistic Studies* 1, (1971): pp. 33–46 defended an agent-causal theory of freedom—while supposing that it was committed to just this regress.

outside the agent's control, and libertarian control over whether A is done would be removed.

But this freedom of specification does not regressively involve a further and distinct exercise of power to determine the power controlled. Multi-wayness and freedom of specification are features of one single power—the first feature marking the power's relation to outcomes, the second the agent's relation to the power. And it is the very nature of the power for the agent to have control over its exercise. As freedom, the power does not sometimes fall within the agent's control and sometimes outside. By its very nature as freedom, it is up to the agent how he exercises it—to produce this outcome or that.

In the case of an inherently controlled event such as the exercise of freedom, then, the causal theorist can simply deny that the agent's control over the event involves anything more than the event's mere occurrence. And it is clear why. The agent-causal theory is an attempt to characterize what control of an event involves—but only in so far as that control really is something over and above the mere occurrence of the event controlled. So, obviously enough, the theory applies, not to every event which the agent controls, but only to those events where that is what control of it really is—something over and above the mere occurrence of the event controlled. This restriction to the theory's application is not ad hoc, but self-evident. And it stops the regress.

The agent-causal theory of freedom, then, does not have to apply to the exercise of freedom itself. But it does have to apply to decisions and actions—for these are events that may or may not fall within the agent's control. Their nature is to be goal-directed and purposive, as we have seen, not to be determined by the agent. Where action is controlled or determined by the agent, this is a further feature of it beyond its character as purposive action—and so something which then has to be explained in terms of the agent-causal theory. If the agent-causal theory does not apply to control of actions and decisions, it does not apply at all.

I shall now develop a series of criticisms of this theory of freedom as agent-causal power—as involving causation by a substance. Let me emphasize that in making these criticisms I do not mean to attack the possibility of substance-causation as such. For all I know, causation may be exercised by substances, including substances that are agents, as well as by events. One point is worth making about substance-causation at the outset, however. Substance-causation as such cannot be identified with freedom.

This was always recognized in the past. For historically believers in substance-causation certainly have not restricted it to free agents. Substance-causes have been held to include also unfree inanimate objects such as sticks and stones. Indeed, on some Stoic and scholastic views, all causes, whether free or unfree, are substances.[7] Evidently substance-causation was not being used on its own by these Stoic and scholastic thinkers to explain what freedom is. And in this they were being wise. For

---

[7] For an important discussion of Stoic theories, see Susanne Bobzien, *Determinism and Freedom in Stoic Philosophy* (Oxford: Oxford University Press, 1998).

ordinary causation, whether exercised by occurrences or by substances, does not amount to freedom—an inherently multi-way power the exercise of which is up to its possessor. The existence in a substance of a power to cause one outcome clearly does not imply any power to cause otherwise, let alone a freedom of specification governing how the power is exercised. But for freedom we need both elements—multi-wayness and a freedom of specification in relation to how the power is exercised. Freedom can only be identified with substance-causal power if that power is possessed in this special and inherently freedom-involving form.

14.4 How Freedom Excludes Randomness

But this now gives rise to an obvious problem for the agent-causal theory. This is that the appeal to agent-causation is really chasing up an explanatory dead end. In characterizing freedom as a special, agent-causal power, we are not using what we already know about causation to inform us about freedom. We are simply postulating causation in a novel and highly peculiar form—one to which we are attributing all the special characteristics, such as multi-wayness, freedom of specification, and restriction to agency, which we ordinarily attribute to freedom. In other words, we are simply re-conceiving causation in terms of the prior understanding which we already have of freedom. And so ad hoc a move is hardly going to shed much new light on freedom. In particular, no new light is being shed on how freedom excludes randomness. And that is because, although freedom and causation both exclude randomness, they exclude it in completely different ways.

As we have seen, there is only one way for an ordinary cause to determine the occurrence of its effect. It must be true that, given all the relevant circumstances and the cause, the occurrence of any alternative effect is left impossible. Should more than one effect be left possible, then the cause is probabilistic, and which finally results must remain dependent on simple chance. But when an agent determines what will happen by exercising freedom, things are quite different. For, as we have already noted, freedom involves contingency of determination. Suppose the agent has the options of doing A or not-A. And suppose that given the circumstances and his presence as a free agent, either of A or not-A remains equally possible. Which action the agent performs need not be left random and undetermined. The power of freedom—his being in control—still allows it to be the agent who determines, say, that he does A, so that which he finally does is not a matter of pure chance. But that surely implies that freedom is a quite different kind of power from causation. An ordinary cause determines its effects and excludes randomness only when its very presence leaves alternatives impossible. But a free agent determines his actions and excludes randomness in a quite different way. Why then suppose that way is causal too?[8]

---

[8] This argument was first proposed in my *Free Will: A Very Short Introduction*, p. 115.

The consequence is obvious. Because the two powers, freedom and ordinary causation, work to determine outcomes and exclude randomness in very different ways, the fact that ordinary causal determination is randomness-excluding does nothing to explain how the exercise of freedom might also be randomness-excluding. If there really were a problem about distinguishing freedom from randomness, appealing to causation would not solve it. You may label the power of freedom as 'causal' too, if you like—but attaching that label to it does no explanatory work. For the labelling is merely that. It does not increase our understanding of how the exercise of freedom prevents the final outcome being a matter of pure chance.

Not only does a free agent have the power to determine more than one outcome, but a freedom of specification is involved in relation to that power: it is up to the agent how he exercises it, to determine this outcome or that. This too distinguishes freedom from any causal power in multi-way form. Ordinary causes do not determine for themselves how they operate. Either an ordinary cause's operation is already predetermined, to produce one specific effect, so its operation is not up to the cause to determine; or as with probabilistic causation, the operation of the cause depends on mere chance, in which case nothing determines how the cause operates, and the operation of the probabilistic cause is random.

We can only turn causation into freedom, then, by adding a freedom of specification, so that causation occurs as a special multi-way power the exercise of which is not predetermined or random because up to the agent to determine. But, again, we are not then using causation to explain how randomness is excluded from freedom. Rather we are relying on freedom to exclude randomness from causation. In which case the appeal to causation is redundant.[9]

The appeal to agent-causation was supposed to explain freedom's nature by assimilating it to a familiar power found in wider nature. And it was supposed to explain how the exercise of libertarian freedom really is distinct from randomness. Neither job has been done. For the causal powers found more widely in nature, it is very clear, are nothing like freedom. So why suppose that freedom is a further case of causal power? And no solution has been provided to the randomness problem.

For freedom is particularly unlike causal power at the very point where there was supposed to be a parallel: namely in the way that the two powers preclude randomness in respect of their operation and their outcomes. With ordinary causation the availability of alternatives brings randomness with it. Randomness is precluded only through the exclusion of all outcomes but one. But freedom is quite a different power—a power that precludes randomness while still, by its very nature, making alternatives available. Both powers remove randomness by determining outcomes;

---

[9] Each of freedom of specification and contingency of determination precludes the multi-way power that includes them from involving randomness. Each removes dependence on mere chance. That is not surprising if, as Chapter 8 argued, each is really one and the same feature of freedom as a multi-way power.

but they determine outcomes in quite different ways—by excluding alternatives as causation, or by providing them as freedom.

Already, then, we have grounds fully sufficient for rejecting the substance-causal theory. But as if things were not bad enough, the theory faces further problems. As the practical reason-based model of action now reveals, the substance-causal theory commits us to detaching the exercise of freedom from our aims and goals—and in ways which are counter-intuitive and absurd.

14.5 Freedom and Purposiveness

The practical reason-based model, as we have seen, vindicates an important view of decision-making. The goal-direction or purposiveness in what we do can itself be our own doing. And as such, it can be true that the adoption of an outcome as one's goal or end is, as Kant put it, 'an act of *freedom* on the part of the acting subject, not an effect of *nature*'.

When we take a decision or form an intention, we are doing something as a means to the attainment of the intention's object. We are directing ourselves towards that object as our goal. To intend something is to have it as one's goal—as one's aim or objective. Not only that, but the forming of that intention can be the moment when that object is first adopted by us as our goal. Consider again that walk by the river that we discussed before. Resting while out for a walk, I just decided to continue it rather than stay where I am or go back home. Remember that until the moment when I actually took that decision to continue my walk, continuing my walk need not have been something I even wanted or in any way favoured—let alone had as my goal.

In forming that intention, then, I was intentionally and deliberately acquiring a goal—an aim not had prior to the intention's being held. In fact, that is just what it is deliberately to acquire the goal or aim of performing a voluntary action; it is simply to form an intention to perform it. Now such an event, when it occurs, is a change in us; a change in attitude or motivation, and so a genuine psychological change on a level with, say, coming to hold a belief or want. We are left with a psychological attitude, that of intention, not previously possessed. Moreover, as with the acquisition of any other attitude, it is a kind of change which an agent might or might not control, and the nature of his control over which needs therefore as much as any other to be explained in terms of agent-causal power.

We suppose that we ordinarily do control what goals and aims we acquire—that we ordinarily do control what actions and outcomes we decide on and intend. My decision to continue my walk, I naturally think, was quite probably taken by me freely -as an exercise of my freedom to decide on any one of a variety of options and so to adopt any one of a variety of goals. On the other hand, this freedom cannot be taken for granted. Just as much as with any other action, decisions might be taken and intentions formed unfreely. That an attitude involves a distinctively purposive mode of direction towards its object does not settle what if anything determined the occurrence of that attitude. Sometimes our goals and intentions might be causally predetermined by events beyond our control; or they might even be adopted randomly. The believer in freedom as an agent-causal power needs therefore to apply their theory to explain what it is for us to control what goals we adopt—what actions and outcomes we come to intend.

But this will not be easy. If we identify freedom as an agent-causal power, we shall have to abandon some deeply intuitive truths about what it is to exercise freedom. For, as we ordinarily conceive things, freedom is not something we exercise blindly. Its exercise is directed towards definite goals or ends—and to certain specific goals or ends in particular. Two claims seem particularly intuitive:

- whenever I exercise my freedom to form an intention to do A, that freedom is something which I am exercising towards a goal—that I eventually do A.
- whenever in order to attain some ends I freely cause some means to their attainment, my goal in the exercise of my freedom must include the production of the means. I am exercising my freedom in that way for a purpose—in order to attain the ends through the production of the means.

The problem for the agent-causal theory of freedom is that these are claims which it must reject. The account it implies of free goal-adoption—free decision-making and intention-formation—entails their falsehood.

Remember what the theory of freedom as agent-causation teaches. Take some change or occurrence E over which the agent might or might not have control: for E to occur through an exercise of the agent's control is for the agent as substance to cause E. Moreover, the agent must have control, not only over the effect E which he causes, but also over whether he causes E.

As for control over other such changes, so too for the control which we think we have over intention-formations and goal-adoptions. To control intention-formations,

(a) such changes must occur as effects produced by us as substances, and
(b) we must be exercising control over which such changes we cause.

There are two entities involved in free intention-formation—entities that are clearly distinct—the agent and the intention formed. The agent-causal theory relates these entities causally. There is the agent functioning as cause—and so exercising freedom; and then the agent's effect—his intention to do A, an attitude of intention or goal-direction, a state within him which he freely causes (Figure 14.2).

But as freely operative cause, as exercising control over what goals we adopt—in, say, causing ourselves to start intending to do A—we cannot already be aiming at A as our goal. For our adoption of this goal is supposed to occur through and under our control—and as controlled by us it can occur only as an effect which we freely produce as agent-cause. So, as controlled by us, our possession of the goal can occur only as our effect. It therefore cannot be a feature which already applies to us as its freely operative cause.

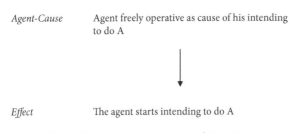

Agent-Cause	Agent freely operative as cause of his intending to do A
	↓
Effect	The agent starts intending to do A

Figure 14.2. Agent-causation and intention.

So what are we aiming at in exercising our free causal power to cause ourselves to intend to do A? Not at the doing of A. *Ex hypothesi*, that aim and intention arises in us only as our effect. It is not a feature of us as cause. Perhaps, then, as free cause we are aiming, not at attaining the intention's object, but simply at forming that particular intention. But why aim at forming that particular intention unless our aim is to attain A thereby? When we exercise control over our intentions, we do not do so out of a simple concern with what we intend. Our aim is never simply to end up holding one intention rather than another. Our aims are surely always to do with the actions and outcomes which are to result from our intentions. That is what exercising our freedom of decision is all about—determining which of the actions to be decided upon we are to perform. So we return to the thought that in so exercising our freedom, our aim must be to ensure not simply that we intend to do A, but that we do A. But, as we saw, on the agent-causal theory, when that goal of doing A is one which we are freely adopting, it cannot already be our goal as freely operative cause of its adoption.

But what of the further ends which we expect or hope to attain through doing A? Perhaps these provide us with our aim. Perhaps as the free cause of our intention to do A, we already intend these further ends, and our aim in causing the intention is simply to attain them. Two points need to be made about this suggestion. First, there need not be any such further ends—not if the action A is something to be intended and done by us for its own sake. In which case there is only one goal we can have when freely causing the intention—the goal of ensuring that we do A. And that is precisely the goal which, as free cause, we cannot have.

Secondly, suppose we do already intend these further ends—and these ends are what are motivating us to cause our intention. Why should it be an intention to do A in particular which they are motivating us to cause? The obvious answer is that our aim in causing that particular intention is to attain these further ends by first ensuring that we do A. But, again, on the agent-causal theory that cannot be our aim. In freely causing an intention specifically to do A, *ex hypothesi* our aim is not to use A as a means to any further ends. For as free cause the doing of A cannot be our aim at all. The aim of doing A is one we only acquire as our effect. And that, I submit, leaves our free causation both of that particular intention and thereby of the action intended unintelligible. Ordinarily, if we freely cause some means, and we do so in order to attain certain ends—ends which we expect to attain through the means—then our aim in so doing must, at the very least, include the attainment of the means. That, after all, is precisely why we are exercising our freedom in that way. Our aim is to secure the means, and thereby attain the further ends.

On the agent-causal theory, our free formation of an intention to do A looks unintelligible. For in freely forming the intention, we are supposed to be operating as a free cause of our adoption of its object as our goal. As something which occurs within and through our control, having that object as our intended aim must be an effect which we produce. But if so, then it cannot be a feature of us as operating to produce it. Properties that are supposed to arise as effects cannot already be features of the cause as operative to produce them. As free cause that goal of doing A cannot be ours already. In exercising our freedom, our aim can be neither to attain A itself, nor to attain further ends through attaining A. And this is absurd. For what else could be our purpose in freely forming an intention to do A, but to ensure that we do A? One thing surely must be true—whenever I exercise control to form an intention to do A, I must be doing so in a goal-directed way, to the end that I eventually do A.

The theory of freedom as agent-causal power separates the exercise of freedom from goal direction. And it is this separation of freedom and goal-directedness which is absurd. Notice that the problematic separation to which the theory of freedom as an agent-causal power is committed need not be temporal. The problem is not that an agent is supposed to be operative as free cause at some time prior to his becoming goal-directed. The problem would still arise even if the agent were freely causing his goal-directedness only as the goal-directedness occurred. Cause and effect could be wholly simultaneous, but a problematic separation of freedom and goal-direction would still arise—a separation which is causal, not temporal. Simultaneous or not, we must distinguish the agent as exercising freedom, and his features as causally operative, from the effect that he produces, intending to do A. His coming to aim at A as a goal—to intend to do A—is precisely the kind of change or event the agent's control over which was supposed to be explained by the agent-causal theory; and explained by its being an effect of him as freely operative cause. That goal-direction therefore remains, on the agent-causal theory, an effect of the freely operative cause, not a feature of the cause as freely operative. We are still left with the view that the agent exercises his freedom blindly, without having the doing of A as his goal.[10]

[10] In a personal communication Randolph Clarke has objected to me that the intention-acquisition is not distinct from the exercise of agent-causal freedom, but a constituent of it. So goal-directedness is to be found in the exercise of freedom after all. But the problem cannot be evaded so easily.

True, the intention-acquisition is part of what that particular exercise of freedom involves. For the intention-acquisition is the event controlled or—on the agent-causal theory—the event caused. And, certainly, any exercise of causal power will involve as one constituent or stage the occurrence of an effect. So we do find goal-direction at the effect end of things, and in that respect as part of the exercise of agent-causal freedom. The real problem, though, has to do, not with the effect, but with its cause. The problem lies in whether the agent exercising freedom can do so in a goal-directed way.

Of course, believers in freedom as an agent-causal power may at this point seek to revise their doctrine. They may seek to agree with common sense that any agent who exercises his freedom to decide to do A cannot be exercising it without already having the doing of A as his goal. Goal-directedness must be a feature of any exercise of agent-causal power.[11] But that just means that throughout his operation as free cause of the act intended A, the agent must already be aiming and intending to do A. The agent operating as free cause is no longer causally prior to his holding that intention. But then, though it is freely formed, that intention can no longer commence as the agent's freely produced effect. It follows that there are some attitudes which we may or may not control, but which, when we do, we control other than through freely causing them. And that is to abandon the agent-causal theory of freedom. For remember the doctrine which that theory teaches:

Take some change or occurrence E over which the agent might or might not have control: for E to occur through an exercise of the agent's control is for the agent as substance to cause E.

This doctrine is now admitted to be false. Freedom is not essentially a causal power.

The point can be made in more detail as follows. As the agent-causationist now explains free goal-direction, it appears that when we freely form intentions and adopt goals, the intention's acquisition or the adoption of the goal is not an effect which as substances we freely produce, but an aspect of our operation as free substance-causes. So at the very beginning of the causal chain leading to the rest of what as agents we freely bring about, we have the situation illustrated in Figure 14.3.

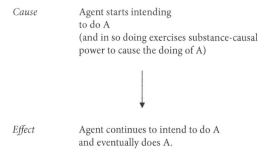

Cause   Agent starts intending
           to do A
           (and in so doing exercises substance-causal
           power to cause the doing of A)

Effect   Agent continues to intend to do A
           and eventually does A.

Figure 14.3. Intention-control and causation.

The cause of the intention-acquisition is not an event, but a substance—the agent, who as exercising freedom or agent-causal power is causally prior to his effect, the decision or intention-acquisition. Now in operating as free cause the agent cannot be supposed already to be functioning with properties that only arise in him as his effect. Goal-directedness is such a property. So in exercising freedom to cause the intention the agent cannot be supposed already to enjoy the goal-direction that only the intention gives. And thus we have the problem—freedom and goal-directedness are being separated when, in the free agent, they should be found together.

[11] As one correspondent seeking to defend the agent-causal theory to me insisted.

But then why think of this process in terms of agent-causation at all? We are now characterizing the initial cause not, or not simply as an agent exercising substance-causal power to cause the doing of A. We are also characterizing it as an altogether more familiar kind of ordinary psychological event or change—a deciding or starting to intend to do A. And this ordinary psychological change is supposed to be controlled by the agent, but without its occurring as the agent's effect.

So there are some events, such as events of deliberate goal-adoption, of deciding and starting to intend, which we might or might not control—but which when we do control them, we control immediately, though without causing them; and other events or states which we can then control in advance through the effects of those events of goal-adoption. But then freedom is exercisable non-causally; it is no longer essentially a causal power. And, at any rate for the purpose of making sense of freedom, any causation which does occur looks like ordinary event-causation. For such causal power as is involved in the exercise of our freedom is, very clearly, the causal power of an ordinary event—namely, our deciding or starting to intend to do A. Which is just what an opponent of agent-causation would say. In which case, to insist that at the cause stage we have the free operation of a substance-cause is entirely gratuitous. All reference to agent-causation can drop out of the picture as an entirely idle wheel.

14.6 Freedom as a Non-Causal Power

We should conclude, then, that freedom is not a causal power. My initial exercise of control over my action, such as, for example, over a decision which I take, does not involve that action occurring as an effect—whether of desires or other passive occurrences or of myself as agent-cause.

But if freedom is not a causal power, what is the relation of a free agent to his free actions—the actions that he controls? For a positive story consider other cases where we exercise non-causal powers to determine outcomes—such as when we exercise moral or legal powers to impose obligations or remove them. The exercise of such powers does not cause the outcomes determined but constitutes their occurrence. Thus, I might exercise my legal power to release you from a debt to me by declaring your release; and that very exercise of my power to release you then constitutes your release. What outcomes are constituted by the exercise of a given power depends on the nature of the power and on the non-causal principles that govern it—in this case legal principles governing the powers of creditors.

If freedom is a further case of non-causal power, then the same kind of story can apply to freedom too. The outcomes immediately determined by the exercise of freedom are actions or decisions. So, on the view now being proposed, freedom is exercised not to cause the taking of decisions but to constitute their being taken. So, for example, my freedom or control over what I decide would be exercised not to cause a decision to do A, but as the taking of a decision to do A. What principles govern the power of freedom—and govern, in particular, what actions and decisions its exercise might constitute? We have seen that these principles include multi-wayness: the power can be exercised to determine more than one action or decision. They also include freedom of specification: in relation to actions or decisions subject to the power, how the power is exercised is up to the agent. So freedom can be exercised to constitute the taking of any one of a variety of decisions; and which particular decisions agents exercise their freedom to take is up to them to determine. Whether an agent exercises his power over what he decides as a decision to do A or as a decision to refrain is up to him.

The exercise of freedom occurs as or constitutes the performance of a particular action or the taking of a particular decision. And because goal-direction is a feature of the decision or action that the exercise of freedom constitutes, so too it is shared with the exercise of power constitutive of it. If the agent's exercise of freedom occurs as a given goal-directed decision, the agent's exercise of his freedom must share that goal-direction too. A freely taken decision's goal-direction is not some effect—an effect that must be absent from the operation of the free agent as its cause. That goal-direction is itself a feature of the exercise of freedom that determines it. And that is because freedom is exercised as the very taking of that decision, not to cause the taking of that decision.

Goal-direction is something common both to freedom and to the decisions and actions that freedom is used to determine. This enables us to explain something which needs to be explained, and for which agent-causal theories provide no explanation. This is the tie of freedom to the exercise of deliberate agency.

Remember that, if it exists at all, freedom is very clearly a power that is agency-specific. Freedom can only be exercised in agency that is deliberate—through intentional action or intentional refraining from action. I have already given an example. To exercise control over whether the lights are on or off there must be something that I am deliberately doing or deliberately refraining from doing and that would influence whether the lights are on or off. If there is nothing of that kind being deliberately done by me or deliberately omitted, then, quite clearly, I cannot be exercising any control over the illumination of the room.

On the agent-causal theory, as we have seen, the properties essential to freedom, far from being explained in causal terms, are just read into causation. These include not only multi-wayness and freedom of specification, but also a tie to agency. It must just be stipulated that, as freedom, causation not only takes a multi-way form the exercise of which is up to us, but that in this form it is immediately exercised to cause only intentional agency—deliberate actions or refrainings. There is nothing in causation itself to explain why this tie to agency should hold; for non-agency can just as much be causally produced as agency.

But when freedom is understood as a non-causal power, an explanation for the restriction of freedom to agency can be provided. For with a shared object-direction, there can be a mode of rationality common to freedom and agency. Indeed, the way that reason governs any exercise of freedom will be just that mode of rationality constitutive of intentional agency.

Suppose that a person had control over something X. What would it be for them to exercise this control rationally? There is only one plausible answer. It would be for them to exercise their control over X in a way likely to have a desirable outcome, or at least an outcome that was not undesirable; and for their exercise of freedom to be aimed at that outcome. In other words, reason in the form in which it governs any exercise of control is reason as concerned with attaining desirable goals or outcomes. But the capacity which is governed by reason in this goal-related form is our capacity for intentional agency—our capacity to exercise rationality practically, or in a goal-directed manner. It follows that when we exercise freedom, what we immediately determine is intentional agency. It is always as deliberate action or deliberate refraining that we exercise our freedom. This account of the tie of freedom to agency obviously depends on the exercise of freedom itself being something goal-directed. And that it can be if freedom is a non-causal power, exercised as the taking of a particular decision, not to cause the taking of a particular decision.

14.7 Causal Theories of Freedom and the Bias to the Voluntary

Why so strong an urge to understand freedom in causal terms? We should see causal theories of freedom, compatibilist and libertarian alike, as generally sharing a common philosophical bias to the voluntary. They reflect, once again, the theoretically distorting effect on philosophical theories of freedom of the profound salience of action in its voluntary form.

It is obvious that in characterizing freedom as a causal power of events, classical compatibilism takes a feature of much free voluntary action—that it occurs through the effects of prior motivation—and uses it to model free action as such. But it is also important to realize that libertarian appeals to agent-causation are doing fundamentally the same thing. These too take a free agent's possible relation to his voluntary actions and use it to model his relation to his own free agency as a whole.

For theories of freedom as an agent-causal power provide a picture of free agency in general which applies, at best, to a free agent's relation to his voluntary actions. On theories of freedom as involving agent-causation, an agent is supposed freely to cause the performance of his own free actions. And free agents often do this—where the actions caused are voluntary. For free voluntary actions can occur as effects of prior free actions—when they are decided on in advance, and occur as effects of earlier free decisions to perform them. In such cases we certainly do, through exercising our freedom, cause the voluntary actions decided upon to be performed. But the only causation involved here is event-causation—the causation of one action by another.

Believers in agent-causation are trying, wholly unwarrantedly, to apply this familiar relation of free causation in relation to the voluntary to free agency as such. Only this time, of course, since it is control over agency in general that we are modelling, the free cause cannot be a prior action within the agent's control. The free cause must instead be the free agent himself, operating as a substance-cause.

As so often, in the theory of freedom as an agent-causal power we are coming across a philosophers' attempt to model agency or free agency as such in terms that can apply only to agency in its voluntary form. And as with all such attempts, the philosophers concerned inevitably depart both from the common-sense psychology of agency and from intellectual coherence.[12]

14.8 The Randomness Problem Dissolved

We have concluded that freedom is not a causal power. That my own decision is freely taken by me does not make that decision an effect of me, or of my attitudes or of any power that I possess. The decision stands to my control or freedom, not as its effect, but as something constituted by its exercise. I do not exercise my freedom to cause the decision. Rather my freedom is exercised as the decision's very taking.

Not that the exercise of freedom actually precludes my decision being an effect. My free decisions can perfectly well occur as effects of prior attitudes and motives, and often do—perhaps provided (as libertarians at least will insist) any prior passions which influence those decisions do not of themselves determine how I decide. But a decision's status as one's own deliberate action, and an exercise of one's own freedom—this is not owed to its being an effect of any cause. In thinking of decisions as our own free actions we are not thinking of them in causal terms at all.

We can see now why the randomness problem is not a real problem. It was supposed to arise as soon as freedom was understood in libertarian terms—as excluding causal determination. But there is no such immediate collapse of libertarian freedom into randomness. The collapse is prevented by the very nature of freedom, whether conceived in libertarian terms or not, as a form of self-determination—a non-causal power involving contingency of determination. There can perfectly well be outcomes which are causally undetermined, but without depending on pure chance. Just because they are causally undetermined, things aren't just happening randomly. And that is because we can still be controlling what is happening—determining actions or outcomes, but non-causally. If the argument so far is sound, then the randomness problem is solved. Or rather, it is dissolved, in that there was no real problem or threat in the first place. There can be all the difference in the world between freedom, even libertarian freedom, and randomness.

---

[12] It is perhaps not surprising that voluntariness-*tied* scholastic accounts of freedom—accounts that were voluntariness-tied because of the salience of the voluntary in free action—also often viewed freedom as an agent-causal power. We have already noted, in Chapter 5, footnote 8, that Suarez tied the exercise of freedom to a form of reflexive voluntariness. Any freely formed intention is reflexively intended. Suarez was also insistent that freedom is an efficient causal power—a power exercised by the agent as a substance-cause: see his *Metaphysical Disputations*, disputation 19, in *Francisco Suarez, S.J. on Efficient Causality*.

15

Freedom as a Power

15.1 Self-Determination

There is a conceptual core to self-determination—a set of features constitutive of any power by which agents determine for themselves what they do. Essential to the power is the determining role of the agent. That role cannot be reduced to one played by mere occurrences or properties. So the power of self-determination must immediately belong to the agent, and not, say, to his motivations. And if the agent is to count as determining actions and outcomes *for himself*, the exercise of the power must not be a simple function of factors not the agent's responsibility, such as chance, or his very nature and capacities as an agent.

Self-determination must therefore involve contingency of determination. The outcome determined must be down to the agent, and not imposed on him by his nature. The agent's mere capacity to determine under given circumstances a specific outcome must not of itself dictate that in those circumstances he automatically produces that very outcome. And nor should the operation of the power to produce a given outcome be a matter of mere chance. The operation of the power must depend not on mere chance, but on the agent. And this seems to involve some sort of freedom in relation to the power. It must be up to the agent whether he exercises the power to produce that outcome.

Self-determination is therefore quite different from causation of any kind, whether determining or probabilistic. But this conceptual core leaves open two central aspects of self-determination as we ordinarily understand it. The first is whether the power is multi-way or one-way: do we have a power the very nature of which is to determine alternatives? And secondly there is the still unresolved debate between compatibilists and incompatibilists: is our exercise of the power compatible with our being causally determined to exercise it as we do?

Both issues have important implications for our moral responsibility. Multi-wayness leaves moral responsibility dependent on a freedom to do otherwise. Incompatibilism makes moral responsibility dependent on the falsehood of causal determinism. Yet the very concept of self-determination does not seem to settle whether multi-wayness or incompatibilism hold true. It seems that we could be determining for ourselves what we do, and so, by consequence, be morally responsible for what we do, whether or not this power took multi-way form, and whether or not an incompatibilist or a compatibilist account of it proved true.

The core to self-determination is that the agent himself plays a distinctive role in determining what he does. So the agent's mere possession of the power must not dictate its exercise; instead the power's exercise must be up to the agent. But could these conditions be met, and the agent's exercise of the power still on occasion be causally determined? As yet, there seems no compelling conceptual argument, from the very nature of self-determination thus described, why this should not be possible. There still seems to be conceptual space for compatibilism about the power. On the other hand, the distinctive role played by the agent as determinant leaves conceptual space for incompatibilism too. Even if an agent's actions are undetermined by prior causes, that need not leave those actions random—a matter of simple chance. Those actions can still be determined, non-causally, by the agent. So there is room too for an incompatibilism that is not sceptical—for libertarianism.

Hence the very possibility, and the intractability, of the dispute about the nature of self-determination between incompatibilists and compatibilists: we have a concept of determining for ourselves what we do that does not immediately resolve that dispute in one direction or the other. Likewise the possibility of theories of self-determination that deny its multi-wayness: there is nothing in the very concept of self-determination to prove those theories false.

But if much about self-determination is conceptually unresolved, that leaves us with an important puzzle. For it seems that ordinary opinion has arrived at a very much more determinate conception of our actual power of self-determination—a conception that goes well beyond the essential core. And the question arises where this more detailed conception might have come from, and how we are to establish whether it applies. Do we really possess a power of which this conception is true?

Our ordinary conception of self-determination is very definitely of a multi-way power. Our immediate understanding of the power is as control of how we act—as making alternatives available to us, as its being up to us how we act. We do not seem to think of or characterize the power in any other terms. That is the very nature of the power of freedom as we ordinarily understand it—to leave it up to us what we do and which actions we perform. Moreover, we treat the up-to-usness of our action as immediately relevant to our moral responsibility for what we do. The power we exercise to determine what we do—the power that is the actual basis of our moral responsibility—is also the power to determine otherwise. Incompatibilism about self-determination, by contrast, seems not quite so universally believed. But there still seems to be a widespread prejudice in incompatibilism's favour, and one which pre-dates exposure to philosophical argument. Very many people are strongly inclined to suppose that if prior causes determine what we do, what we do cannot be determined by us. Again, where do specifically incompatibilist intuitions about self-determination come from?

Multi-wayness and incompatibilism certainly feed into people's conception of moral responsibility. If the power that bases our moral responsibility is conceived as multi-way, or in incompatibilist terms, then moral responsibility will be understood to depend on a freedom to do otherwise, or to depend on the falsehood of causal determinism. But though these ways of conceiving self-determination feed into the conditions we put on moral responsibility, they are not obviously ethically generated themselves. And this is because, as we have noted, these conceptions seem not to be demanded by the very idea of self-determination—by the very idea of a power that leaves action the responsibility of the agent, and not just a function of factors not the agent's responsibility.

Indeed, the very reality of self-determination as ordinarily conceived has not yet been established. The question becomes even more pressing on the supposition that incompatibilism is true. For how could we ever know that our actions and decisions are not causally determined in advance by prior occurrences not of our doing? It is to these connected questions to do with the reality and nature of human freedom as ordinarily conceived that we must now turn.

15.2 Powers and Concepts

The free will problem is first and foremost about a power—about its nature, its significance to us, and its reality. Does the power of freedom really exist; what depends for us on whether it does; and what is the nature of this power and its relation to power in other forms? Such an investigation into power may involve much more than conceptual analysis. The properties of a power may not be determined just by concepts or linguistic meanings. Nevertheless, the model of the free will problem as a conceptual problem still dominates. Yet this conceptual reading of the problem is, I shall suggest, very questionable.

As we have seen, those philosophers who do not just write in general terms of 'capacities to do otherwise'—who do take seriously freedom's identity as a power—generally view the power as causal; and this view is based on a more general assumption that power in general is a causal phenomenon. But even those who espouse a causal theory of freedom still tend to assume that the free will problem is a purely conceptual problem. Even in their case, the implications for freedom of causal determinism are still assumed to be determinable a priori, by arguments appealing to what our concepts imply. But for philosophers who suppose freedom to be a causal power, the assumption that the free will problem is purely conceptual becomes especially peculiar. If freedom is a causal power, why suppose that its relations to all other forms of causal power need be determinable a priori? Thus, for example, why should libertarians who believe in the agent-causal theory—who suppose that freedom is a causal power of substances—think that it need be a conceptual matter whether the operation of this power can itself be causally determinable? Why not, for example, look to see? For we generally rely on experience to determine which forms of causal power are compatible with which; and which defeat or preclude the operation of which.

A particular danger of treating an enquiry into power as a simple enquiry into concepts, is that we may infer too much from thought experiments. Conceptual possibilities may be treated as proofs of what is actually the case. We may fall into the equivalent of an armchair physics. The mere fact that powers could, as a conceptual possibility, take a certain form, does not establish that they actually do so, any more than armchair physics, no matter how internally coherent, immediately provides good explanations for what actually happens.

We already saw Frankfurt and his supporters fall into exactly this trap. Their project was to show that the freedom to do otherwise, even if it exists, is irrelevant to moral responsibility. To do this they devised elaborate and ingenious thought experiments. These were cases of moral responsibility divorced from the freedom to do otherwise. But even if we grant that such cases are conceptually possible, they establish nothing about the actual case. It may be conceptually possible that we possess a power of self-determination that takes one-way form. But that is not enough to make freedom irrelevant to moral responsibility. For the power we actually possess to determine for ourselves what we do might still be multi-way. In which case, as human nature is actually constituted, to remove the freedom to do otherwise would be to remove our power of self-determination altogether—so that the freedom to do otherwise is still very relevant to our moral responsibility.

The conceptual possibility of self-determination in one-way form does not establish that self-determination is actually one-way. Similarly, should compatibilism about self-determination be a conceptual possibility, that does not imply that such compatibilism is actually true. The same general error that lies behind Frankfurt's attempt to detach moral responsibility from a freedom to do otherwise, also afflicts arguments for compatibilism about moral responsibility. For modern English-language compatibilists have been particularly fond of thought experiments to undermine incompatibilism, if not about the freedom to do otherwise itself, at least about moral responsibility. The line of argument is very familiar, and seductive. It is familiar from Peter Strawson's famous paper 'Freedom and resentment', and we find it more recently in Ronald Dworkin's *Justice for Hedgehogs*.[1] The compatibilist plausibly observes that we might quite well not give up our belief in moral responsibility even if we were to discover that ordinary human actions—the familiar, everyday actions for which we generally hold each other responsible—were generally causally determined. So we have a concept of moral responsibility that we would continue to apply even if causal determinism were established to be true. From this it is inferred that our moral responsibility for what we do must actually be compatible with causal determinism.

We can now see the problem with such an argument. True, it may be conceptually possible both that agents should determine for themselves what they do, and that

---

[1] See P.F. Strawson, *Freedom and Resentment and Other Essays* (London: Methuen, 1974), and Ronald Dworkin, *Justice for Hedgehogs* (Cambridge, MA: Harvard University Press, 2011), especially Chapter 10, 'Free will and responsibility'.

how they exercise this power should be causally determined. So there may be a conceptually possible deterministic world in which agents possess a moral responsibility for what they do. And perhaps were we to discover that our actions were quite generally causally pre-determined by past events, rather than give up our belief in our moral responsibility, we might conclude that we did live in such a world. But that establishes nothing about the actual case. For though it is conceptually possible that things should have been otherwise, the power of self-determination which we actually possess and exercise might not be compatible with past causal determination at all. It might be a fundamental property of self-determination as it actually is, that our possession and exercise of the power would be precluded by past determining causes. In which case incompatibilism is true—not conceptually true of self-determination and moral responsibility in general, but of the power of self-determination we actually possess, and so of the moral responsibility which that power actually bases.

It is often alleged that there is a confusion in people's understanding of moral responsibility. People are supposed to veer inconsistently between incompatibilism about moral responsibility and compatibilism. When people are asked to consider the implications of causal determinism in general terms, a majority treat it as removing moral responsibility. But when asked to consider a specific case of morally criticizable action under the supposition of causal determinism, they incline to hold the agent still morally responsible.

But there need be no strict inconsistency. Invited to consider subjunctively the implications of causal determinism alone, we might suppose the natures of the powers to be found in that deterministic world to remain in other respects as they actually are—and so, if incompatibilist in our view of self-determination, infer to an absence of morally responsible action. But invited to consider a case where not only is causal determinism supposed true, but people are portrayed as still performing specific actions in a way they normally do, we may be inclined to retain the supposition that they are still determining their own actions as they actually do, but give up our incompatibilism. This involves no inconsistency in our conception of what moral responsibility is actually like. There is nothing more involved than a familiar feature of conditional reasoning—variation, given different counterfactual antecedents, in what contingent truths we retain as true, and what we suppose false.

Thus Joshua Knobe records that when asked to imagine, in very general terms,

> ...a universe (Universe A) in which everything that happens is *completely caused* by whatever happened before it. This is true from the very beginning of the universe, so what happened in the beginning of the universe caused what happened next, and so on right up until the present.[2]

---

[2] Joshua Knobe, 'Free will and the scientific vision', in *Current Controversies in Experimental Philosophy*, eds Edouard Machery and Elizabeth O'Neill (London: Routledge, 2014), p. 71—my emphasis.

a majority of people tend to deny that people in such a world would be morally responsible for what they do. And there seems an obvious reason for this. The invitation to see everything as *completely caused* by what preceded it is very naturally heard as an invitation just to imagine away everything as an explanatory factor beyond ordinary causal power—and so in particular to imagine away any power people might have to determine for themselves what they do.

On the other hand, as Knobe observes, when people are invited specifically to imagine what is presented as recognizable human action, though in a deterministic world:

> In Universe A, a man named Bill has become attracted to his secretary, and he decides that the only way to be with her is to kill his wife and 3 children. He knows that it is impossible to escape from his house in the event of a fire. Before he leaves on a business trip, he sets up a device in his basement that burns down the house and kills his family.[3]

a similar majority incline to hold the agent morally responsible. Again there seems a plausible explanation—the one already given. Once invited to imagine the performance of what is presented as a very familiar kind of human action, with emphasis on the occurrence of a decision, people retain along with all its other features the power of self-determination that they take such fully intentional, decision-involving agency ordinarily to involve—but in a form compatible with the causal determinism that is also supposed to hold.

15.3 Aphenomenalism about Power

Where certain powers are concerned, if we want to find out whether one power is present, or whether its operation precludes the operation of another, there may be no other way of telling than by, so to speak, 'going and looking'—by attending to experience. In such cases our deepest convictions about power may be very much bound up with how experience presents things to us. At this point conceptual analysis may have nothing to do with the matter.

This is very clearly the case with causal power. Whether a given causal power is present at all, and whether one form of causal power precludes or is precluded by the operation of another—these are questions that often have to be settled by some form of observation and not by conceptual means alone. And though freedom is not the same as causal power, the same may prove to be true of it. The presence or absence of freedom and its relation to causation may have to be determined by reference to experience too, and not just by conceptual argument.

There is a particular reason why, where freedom is concerned, no one nowadays much bothers to proceed by looking. The free will problem has come to be dominated by theories of freedom that are, as I shall term it, *aphenomenal. Aphenomenalism*

---

[3] 'Free will and the scientific vision', p. 74.

about a given power claims that conclusions about the nature and reality of the power are rationally to be arrived at without any reliance, even partial, on experiential representation of that power. Either there is no experiential representation of the power at all; or even if there is, it is for some reason supposed not rational to rely at all on such representation to determine whether the power exists or what it might be like. An aphenomenal approach to understanding freedom has become dominant. This has been encouraged partly by scepticism about the possibility of experiential representation of freedom in particular, especially freedom as conceived in libertarian terms. But this scepticism has also been reinforced by a powerful tendency in the modern English-language tradition to aphenomenalism about power in general.

Aphenomenalism about power may be plausible for some cases. Not all forms of power seem to be represented in experience. For example, it is not clear that many legal or normative powers of agents are so represented. Even if as a promisee I possess the right and power to release you from your promise to me, it is not clear that this power is ever phenomenologically presented either to its possessor or to others. If we believe in the power, that's because its existence and operation in particular cases is dictated by the moral principles governing promising—principles that seem themselves conceptually given, and not presented in experience. But perhaps some powers are experienced, and freedom may be one such, as some forms of causal power may be too.

Since Hume, though, there has been a tendency to aphenomenalism about all forms of power. Even causal power, on the Humean view, is not represented in experience—only the regularities that lead us to infer to the operation of underlying causal laws. In the causal case, of course, experience can at least represent the regularities that license causal hypotheses. But with freedom conceived, not as an event-causal power but instead as some inherently multi-way power of quite a different kind from event-causation, the operation of the power is not guaranteed even to generate such give-away regularities. One day X may freely choose to do A. But under like circumstances he could equally employ the power to act otherwise. That is the very nature of the power—not to underpin a regularity from one kind of cause to a given kind of effect, but to leave more than one kind of outcome available to its possessor. Since it is not the nature of the power to reveal itself indirectly through regularities, without representation of the power itself, multi-way freedom threatens to become wholly invisible to experience. And so libertarians especially have tacitly come to treat it. Hence the assumption which so many modern libertarians make, that the relation of freedom to other kinds of power must be resoluble, not on the basis of our experience of the power, but a priori and conceptually.

Aphenomenalism about multi-way freedom has only been confirmed by the Kantian tradition. According to a dominant interpretation of Kant, we may certainly have a consciousness or awareness of our own freedom. But this awareness is not derived from any experience of freedom. Freedom is not a phenomenon, a thing which is represented to us in experience. And so our awareness of freedom is not knowledge of a phenomenon. It is not a case of theoretical knowledge.[4] Freedom is invisible to us, and arguments for its reality have to proceed without recourse to experience. Any knowledge we have of our freedom can only be practical, arising out of rational commitment belonging to our agency.

Unfortunately it is far from clear how we could ever come to know of a multi-way power of freedom without some experiential representation of it. As far as theoretical knowledge is concerned, we have already noted the difficulty. If freedom were understood in reductive terms, as a causal power of prior events, perhaps its operation might be inferred from the existence of regularities involving those events. But if freedom is a multi-way power that is not event-causal, it cannot be relied on to reveal itself in regular conjunctions of events. How else might it be revealed as an object of theory, then, but by direct experiential representation of the power itself?

The supposed practical route to knowledge is not a plausible substitute. Kantians might suppose that once we think of ourselves as agents who are rational, who act on the basis of deliberation about reasons, that will rationally commit us to thinking of ourselves as enjoying a power of freedom to determine how we act. But why should there be any such commitment? There is certainly no general inference from the fact that something, such as action, is based on and guided by deliberation to its being free—to the outcome of that deliberation's being subject to our determination and control. After all, our beliefs and desires can as much be based on deliberation and as much occur through the exercise of rationality as our actions. But which beliefs or desires our deliberation leads to need not be something we determine or have control over. A desire, for example, is a passion and not an action. Our deliberations lead desires to wax and wane within us, but as things which come over us and which we do not control directly.

True, there is something distinctive about the exercise of our rationality in action. That exercise of rationality is justified in a specific way: as a means to the attainment of its object—and so by the desirability of the object, not its truth; and not by the object's desirability alone, but also by the likelihood of the response helping attain the object. So in action an object of thought is being responded to in a very special way— as a goal to be attained. But there is nothing in this that directly implies any special power on the responder's part over whether he makes the response. For, as we have already observed, what is essential to and distinctive of action and its rationality, purposiveness or goal-direction, has to do with the action's relation to its object—not with the agent's relation to the action.

---

[4] For this interpretation of Kant see, for example, Henry Allison, *Kant's Theory of Freedom* (Cambridge: Cambridge University Press, 1990), especially Chapter 2, 'Empirical and intelligible character'. Of course, it does not matter whether this interpretation of Kant is correct. The important point is that it is a typical and popular mode of interpretation, and it excludes what we believe about our freedom from being based on or inferred from experience.

So it is certainly true that any exercise of freedom presupposes deliberate agency—the exercise of rationality in purposive form. That, as we have seen, is because of how the rationality of any exercise of freedom or control must be determined. The rationality of any exercise of control is determined practically—by reference to the desirability of its goal, and by the likelihood of its actually helping attain that goal. But if any exercise of freedom must involve the exercise of reason in purposive form, it is not obvious that the opposite is true—that by its very nature the exercise of reason in purposive form must always be free and subject to the agent's control.

It is often observed that practical deliberation involves a certain epistemic openness about which action we will perform. For in deliberating practically we do so assuming that our eventual decision depends on what practical conclusion we arrive at. Since we must remain ignorant of what that conclusion will be until we actually arrive at it—until our deliberation is concluded—we must until then remain correspondingly ignorant of how we will eventually act. Might this epistemic openness constitute or establish freedom, at least as some kind of power involving alternatives? It is clear that mere epistemic openness is not enough. Ignorance of the outcome on our part certainly does not imply our possession of any particular power over it. We should not confuse a lack of predetermination, be this lack of predetermination epistemic or be it causal, with the presence of any actual power on our part to determine.[5]

Belief in human freedom cannot be grounded just on the claim that we are rational agents. Conceptually, it seems, we could perfectly well be rational agents without being free. By contrast, of course, the thought that we are morally responsible agents does commit us to the belief that we are capable of some form of self-determination. But as we have seen, freedom as involving alternatives is not conceptually required for moral responsibility. Unless we have some prior reason to suppose that the power of self-determination that we possess is multi-way, we have no reason to tie moral responsibility to the freedom to do otherwise. So we still require some basis for our belief in self-determination in that particular multi-way form. And apart from some experience of the multi-way power as something we actually possess, it is not clear what basis there could be. In any case, nothing in the relation between moral responsibility and self-determination helps establish the reality even of self-determination in some form or other. For how can we be sure that we really are morally responsible for how we act, unless we have independent reason to suppose that we really have some such power to determine action?

---

[5] It is sometimes suggested, by sceptical opponents, that belief in libertarian freedom has its root in epistemic openness, and involves a misreading of epistemic openness as a genuinely causal openness. As Dennett put it, epistemic possibility is 'a building stone in the foundation of free will.' (*Elbow Room*, p. 151). But as we shall see, the basis both of belief in freedom, and of a libertarian understanding of freedom, is not epistemic openness, but the experiential representation of power—power that is represented to us as existing and possessed by us even in cases where epistemic openness is lacking, and when we know full well that we shall not act as we suppose ourselves perfectly free to act.

Freedom is a power that goes beyond any capacity for rationality or for rational agency. Its multi-way nature seems not to follow even from our belief in our possession of a distinctively moral responsibility for what we do. Apart from some direct experience of our own freedom, there seems nothing about our agency and our awareness of it in other respects, and certainly nothing in its nature simply as rational or as morally responsible agency, which guarantees or directly implies the presence of such a multi-way power over how we act, or explains why we should even have developed a conception of its presence. Yet we all do believe that it is up to us how we act; that what we do is within our control. This belief is deep-seated. It is as irresistible as the beliefs about the objects surrounding us that experience represents as there. Perhaps the belief in this power over how we act has a like basis in experience—in the way that experience represents how our agency is determined, a way that has no parallel in relation to modes of rationality that are merely passive.

The most discussed modern argument for incompatibilism about the freedom to do otherwise—van Inwagen's consequence argument—is thoroughly aphenomenal.[6] The truth of incompatibilism about such a power is supposed to be deducible by logic, and from assumptions about freedom's nature that have nothing to do with any experience of freedom, but which are common property to all users of the concept, compatibilist and incompatibilist alike. The argument runs as follows.

Suppose it is already causally determined that someone will perform a given action A. Then a, the proposition that they perform this action, will be entailed by the conjunction of two truths: l, reporting the laws of nature, and p reporting past history to date—a history that includes those prior events which, given the laws, causally determine that A will be done. Now to have the freedom not to do A is to have the power to falsify a. And since the conjunction of l and p entails a's truth, for a to be false, one of l or p would have to be false too. In which case to have the power to falsify a surely implies having the power to falsify one of l and p. But clearly we lack the power to falsify truths about the laws of nature and the past. So the agent must lack the power to falsify a. They must lack freedom.

However, this argument is notoriously open to challenge. For the compatibilist will ask what falsifying l and p is supposed to involve. If it involves changing or influencing the laws of nature or the past, then of course we lack the power to do that. But it seems the compatibilist can coherently deny that the freedom not to do A implies such a power; certainly the implication is not obvious, and there is nothing in the argument to establish it. If, on the other hand, falsifying l and p simply involves acting in such a way that if we did so act, then one of l or p would already have to be false, then indeed the freedom not to do A does imply the power so to act; a could not be false unless one of l or p were false too. But of course the compatibilist thinks that the agent in this case may perfectly well possess such a power. That is just the

---

[6] Peter van Inwagen, 'The incompatibility of free will and determinism', *Philosophical Studies* 27, (1975).

compatibilist position: that though it be causally predetermined that *a* is true, the agent may still have the power to make *a* false—and so to act in a way that if he did so act, the laws of nature or history to date would have to be different. What is there so far to prove the compatibilist wrong?[7]

The consequence argument is quite inconclusive. It has not shown incompatibilism to follow from assumptions about freedom common to all users of the concept.[8] In fact, no conceptual argument has managed clearly to convict compatibilists of any purely intellectual confusion or logical error. There is certainly no general conceptual argument from the existence of a power to do or determine otherwise to the falsehood of causal determinism. For example, I can have the legal or moral power to determine otherwise even if it is causally determined that I shall not exercise it. Why, conceptually, just as a power to determine otherwise, should freedom be any different?

Modern compatibilism does not seem to be a philosophical tradition marked out by any particular lack of conceptual clarity or acuity amongst its defenders. Perhaps, then, the issue is not a purely conceptual one. Perhaps it needs to be resolved quite differently, by reference to the properties which our experience of freedom reveals that power to have.

15.4 Freedom and Phenomenology

Intuitions in favour of multi-wayness or of incompatibilism seem to have no clear basis in a priori argument. They do not appear to be based on any particularly refined philosophical or conceptual considerations. If anything, exposure to contemporary philosophical argument tends to be weakening of them. And that is perhaps because a purely conceptual approach to self-determination—the approach that dominates current philosophical culture—provides these intuitions with no particular support. There is nothing conceptually problematic about understanding self-determination as a one-way power. Such an understanding could still preserve the essential core of self-determination—contingency of determination, and the use of the power being up to the agent. And not only does the consequence argument—the main conceptual argument in favour of incompatibilism about the freedom to do otherwise—not work, but we shall see that it is actually in deep conflict with the form that incompatibilism takes in ordinary intuition.

In fact, I shall now suggest that the main effect of much modern philosophical argument in both directions, compatibilist and incompatibilist alike, has been to

---

[7] For this line of argument, see David Lewis, 'Are we free to break the laws?', in *Philosophical Papers* (Oxford: Oxford University Press, 1986), vol. 2.

[8] Compatibilists have certainly had no difficulty in finding plausible grounds for rejecting the argument. Besides Lewis, see John Martin Fischer, 'Incompatibilism', *Philosophical Studies* 43, (1983), and Michael Slote, 'Selective necessity and the free will problem', *Journal of Philosophy* 79, (1982).

detach us from the true source of our intuitions about what kind of power of self-determination we actually possess. The source of these intuitions seems to lie not in the concept of self-determination, but in phenomenology—in the workings of experience and the imagination.

To ignore altogether the phenomenology of freedom must be a mistake. For freedom, whatever its ultimate nature, is something we clearly do *feel* ourselves to possess. For example, we can and do feel change in the degree of our possession of it. Arguing over the telephone with a selfish and deeply exasperating colleague, I raise my voice, deliberately speak ever more woundingly—and then, as my temper mounts, finish by quite intentionally delivering a gross insult and smashing down the phone. I feel myself doing all this—and I feel my control over what I do lessening progressively as I do it. I can feel myself just *losing it*. I feel it is increasingly my anger which is determining how I am acting, not I. What we describe colloquially as the 'feeling of losing it' seems to be nothing else than an experiential representation, whether veridical or otherwise, of my being driven by anger, and in a way that deprives me of my power to determine for myself what I do.

Notice that, as in the example just given, my experience may include representation of change in what I actually do—but it need not. For what I experience myself doing could remain the same throughout. My feeling that I am 'losing it' may be the simple sense that as I continue to do what I am doing all along, thanks to the growing power over me of my passions and emotions, I have a lessening power to act otherwise. The change in what I feel represents no change in what I do, but just that lessening power that I possess over what I do. And the feeling really is a feeling and not a belief. For I may feel that I am losing control but at the same time be wondering whether I really am.

Why do I illustrate our experience of freedom by reference to a feeling or experience of its decrease or loss? There is an obvious reason. A feeling of loss of control is a feeling that is particularly hard to miss. We may never remark on the experience we have of our control—until we feel that power over what we do begin to ebb away. Through vivid representation of the change in power we are reminded that experience can represent the power. Though one could equally have considered a case where power is represented as increasing rather than decreasing. The emotion that overcame us earlier lessens and we feel ourselves regaining our control.

Notice that experience not only represents to me my control over what I do and its diminishment. It also represents *how* it is diminished. It is not that as I feel my action being increasingly determined by my anger, I happen quite coincidentally to feel that how I act is less and less determined by me—without any suggestion of a connection between the two experienced changes. For I feel my anger taking my control of what I do away. I feel my control over what I do being removed by the force of something that comes over me—that is not my doing. And note that the loss of control is felt as the loss of my very power to determine for myself what I do. To feel the anger removing my power to do otherwise is to feel my action to be determined by my anger rather than by me. The power to determine for myself what I do is represented in experience to me as a multi-way power—as consisting in, and depending on, control over alternatives.

Contrast a case where I feel the force not of some passion that comes over me, such as a fit of anger or of fear, but of my own free will. Consider the decision I freely took five minutes ago, as a strong-willed and resolute decision maker, to return a sum of money in five minutes' time. I am sure as I take this decision that I will carry it out. Particularly if subject to strong contrary pressure from the persuasion of others or from temptation, I may very well feel my handing over the money to be something I am determined to do by the power of my own will exerting itself against this pressure. Highlighted as it is against the pressure it resists, I clearly feel this determining force of my own will—of my own decision, already taken, to hand the money over; a decision that I freely made, that had the goal of causing me to hand the money back, and that I remain intent on carrying out. But though I feel the force of my own will I do not experience my action as thereby removed from my control. I do not feel myself to be imprisoned by my own decision as I might feel imprisoned into a course of action by some overwhelming passion or desire. I do not experience my own past decision as ending my control of what I do and removing my power to do otherwise. I feel that how I act remains fully up to me—that I remain in full control of what I do. My control is retained throughout, embodied in my own persisting will to carry out my original free decision and act exactly as I have decided.

What is the crucial difference between the two cases? In each case we have a content-bearing attitude, anger at my colleague's selfishness, or a decision to return the money. Each appears with equal plausibility a cause determining in advance how I shall act. In each case I feel that a given action is sure to be performed by me, and I feel what cause it is that makes that action sure to happen: in the one case the anger that is gripping me, in the other case my own fierce decision and resolve so to act. In both cases I feel a force—a force that, it seems, is determining me to act.

Nor does the distinction lie in the greater rationality of the decision compared to the fit of anger. For my decision might be foolish and lacking in justification; while the anger might be fully justified, and an emotion that I am gripped by only because it is so evidently justified. What is so emotionally overwhelming, after all, is the blatant and glaring nature of my colleague's selfishness. Why, then, do the two cases feel so different? In both cases I feel something determining me to act in a certain way. But in the decision case, the determination is felt as coming from my own free decision—and so from me. As I withstand temptations or persuasions to the contrary I feel the force of my own will. Whereas in the other case the determination is felt as coming from outside my will—and so not from me at all. I feel something other than my own free decision determining what I do. And when we consider what such an experience of external determination involves, we find it includes a representation of our own lack of control.

If we feel our actions to be determined by something other than our own free will, we feel them not to be determined by us. And that is because in feeling something outside our own will to be determining how we act, we feel our own control of what we do to be removed. This is a distinctive and crucial feature of the phenomenology of self-determination, and it shapes not only our experience but our imagination. Imagine feeling that your action is being determined by something outside your will. Imagine feeling that you are being determined to do something by fear, or by anger, or by exhaustion, or by the operation of a drug. You will *ipso facto* imagine the emotion or the tiredness or the drug to be taking over—to be removing your control of what you do. For that is how, in your imagination, it will also feel. To feel the determination of your action other than by your own will—to feel your action being determined by such states as anger or exhaustion—is to feel the loss of your own control.

A possible basis for widespread intuitions in favour of multi-wayness and incompatibilism becomes clearer. People believe that self-determination takes the form of multi-way freedom because that is how experience represents the power to them. And the belief that freedom is inconsistent with causal determinism has a similar explanation. When we feel that our action is being causally determined other than by our own free decision, so we feel our control to be removed—and with that control, our very capacity to determine action for ourselves.

Notice too why intuition might be more universally committed to multi-wayness than it is to incompatibilism. To feel capable of determining for myself what I do just is to feel that what I do is up to me; and to feel that what I do is no longer up to me is to feel that what I do is no longer for me to determine. Whenever it is represented to us at all, our power to determine for ourselves what we do is represented to us as control over alternatives—as its being up to us how we act. But there is no such constant representation of the relation of the power of self-determination to causal power. It is not as if whenever it is represented to us at all, the power of self-determination is represented to us as taking incompatibilist form. Rather, there is a general character to what it feels like when we do feel something outside the will causally determining what we do: we feel ourselves to be losing control. And we might or might not pick up on this general feature to arrive at an incompatibilist view of self-determination—though it would be very natural for many people to do so.

Notice what will happen if people enter an argumentative culture that treats the case for and against multi-wayness or incompatibilism as purely conceptual—as having nothing to do with phenomenology. Intuition will be cut off from attending to its basis and source, in what self-determination feels like. And that will weaken intuition, or at any rate change its nature.

One of the harder pedagogic challenges facing the inexperienced philosophy lecturer is to introduce new students to the subject by presenting the free will problem as philosophers in modern times have understood it. For the lecturer immediately faces the problem of persuading the audience, not just to abandon any natural libertarianism, but to take reductive post-Hobbesian English-language compatibilism seriously. And that is never an easy task. We now see the nature of the difficulty. It is not that the lecturer has to get the students to become doubtful of their own freedom when all along they still feel themselves to be in control. People in our culture rather expect philosophy to be about bracketing experience to a degree, at least initially. The real task is harder. For of course, classic English-language compatibilism does not ask the students to become doubtful about their own freedom at all. What this compatibilism asks of them is far more intuitively repugnant. It asks that they actually identify freedom with the very causal power—of passions or passive motivations to determine action—that their own experience and imagination tends to represent as directly freedom-threatening.

True, modern compatibilism in reductive form has become more sophisticated than it ever was in its original and unvarnished version. The doctrine has gone beyond claiming that a simple capacity to act as one wants is sufficient for freedom. It now accepts the possibility of psychological compulsion—of certain wants removing freedom. It allows that there might be *some* passive motivations, not all but only those special ones that count as genuinely compulsive, whose causal influence might be freedom-threatening. It therefore strives to pick those compulsive motivations out—though other than as incompatibilism does with its appeal to causal predetermination. So it is not supposed to be decisive just that the compulsive passions are passive motivations which causally determine how we act. What supposedly makes them compulsive is, say, that they are notably resistant to reason, or are attitudes that we would prefer not to be motivated by.[9] But such considerations are simply not relevant to what we really feel is depriving us of our freedom when we feel psychologically compelled. When the anger rises in me, I feel myself losing control; and I feel that as happening not because I would prefer not to be so moved by my anger (it might be an enjoyable and welcome release), nor because my anger is resistant to reason (as already noted, it may be quite obvious to me that I am so angry only because such anger is so plainly justified), but because I feel my action being determined not by my own free will but by a passion. It is precisely this feeling that we report when we describe the anger as 'overwhelming', and of ourselves as being 'driven' to act by it.

Faithfulness to phenomenology is not a concern for modern compatibilists. And there is an obvious reason for this. Compatibilism in the English-language tradition inherits a tradition of scepticism about the experiential representation of power that goes back to Hume, and applies both to causal power and to freedom. My experience is supposed not to represent the causal force of my anger on what I do. For how could

---

[9] For the common view that psychological compulsion involves a failure of responsiveness to reason, see Fischer and Ravizza's *Responsibility and Control*; for the view that to be taken over by a passion involves being motivated by desires we prefer not to be motivated by, see Harry Frankfurt's 'Identification and externality' (p. 63) and other writings in his *The Importance of What We Care About*.

experience represent a causal force? All that experience represents is events or happenings the causal relation of which to other events must be a matter of inference. And how could I experience the control and its loss? For control is a multi-way power. But all that experience represents, or represents veridically, is what is actual; not the non-actual alternate possibility on which the freedom to do otherwise depends.[10]

These quasi-Humean restrictions on what experience could represent run up against our clear sense of what we feel as the anger grows; that we are being driven by the anger to the point of being overwhelmed by it, so that it is no longer up to us to determine what we do. Nor do these restrictions on possible experience have any particularly compelling rationale. If what we experience must be actual, why cannot that extend to the actual presence or absence of a power to do otherwise? For the existence of freedom does not come simply to there being some unactualized state of affairs, a possibility of doing otherwise, distinct and apart from anything that might actually be present to us and veridically experienced. It is not the non-actual state of affairs I experience, but a power to produce it. Freedom is not a bare alternative, a mere unactualized possibility that cannot be experienced. As I have emphasized from the outset, freedom is a power, and one that could equally be used to do what is actually done or some alternative. What is actual and experienced as such is not, of course, the state of affairs that the power makes available, but the power itself—a power whose nature is to determine things either way. If such a power really can exist and be possessed by us (a question which the Humean objector had better not be begging), then why can it not be as present to us and as real as anything it determines actually to occur? As for the claim that experience cannot represent causal force, that claim would make it impossible to give a full and accurate description of all that we feel when we feel ourselves being overcome by anger. As the anger grows, how else to describe the feeling of its driving, action-determining force than as just that—an experience of *force*?[11]

But there is a second and essentially dogmatic pressure within modern compatibilism especially, which so generally takes a naturalistically reductive form. This is the pressure to integrate freedom as a power within a wider, broadly mechanical world view centred on ordinary causation. There could be no power of freedom that was not a power causally to determine the actions controlled, and that was not a power exercised over those actions by prior events that, as preceding action, are

[10] My thanks to James Harris for emphasizing to me this common argument against an experiential representation of freedom.

[11] Within the psychological literature Alan Leslie has provided rather different but important arguments for the experiential representation of causal power—arguments based on experiments in infant perception. See Leslie's 'Spatiotemporal continuity and the perception of causality in infants', *Perception* 13, (1984); and also with Stephanie Keeble, his 'Do six-month-old infants perceive causality?', *Cognition* 25, (1987). Another and very recent defence of the perceptibility of causation is Stephen Butterfill's 'Seeing causings and hearing gestures' in *The Philosophical Quarterly* 59, (2009).

passive. So either our action is causally determined by prior passions, or its occurrence is random and undetermined by any power. And it is assumed in advance that experience could never oppose this world view.

But this contradicts what our experience is really like, which supports a third possibility: that even if causally undetermined by prior occurrences, our action can still be determined by us, as occurring under our control. For any power of the passive over my decisions that fits the reductive compatibilist's prescription is felt as freedom-depriving—as in tension with freedom as quite another kind of power. To feel my decision being causally determined by something passive from outside my will, whether this be fear, or desire, or anger, or the operation of a drug—that is to feel imprisoned and driven, to feel myself as deprived of freedom.

What the best, practical reason-based model of our action revealed as at least a conceptual possibility is in fact what experience represents as actually and often happening; our actions are determined by us through a power, freedom, which experience represents as exercised by us independently of, and even in tension with, the causal power of passions. No wonder, then, that out walking I can think of my decision to go on or not as being up to me and within my control—without viewing it as at the same time determined or even influenced by my prior passions. Experience represents freedom to me as just such a desire-independent power.

There is a considerable irony here. The theory of freedom which has most associated itself with and endorsed empiricism—the tradition of English-language compatibilism which runs through Locke to Ayer—has proved most resolute in its indifference to experience. Remember how from Hobbes onward belief in libertarian freedom was always characterized by that tradition as an illicit inference from ignorance, quite unsupported by experience:

Commonly when we see and know the strength that moves us, we acknowledge necessity, but when we see not, or mark not the force that moves us, we then think there is none, and that it is not causes but liberty that produceth the action.[12]

But it seems our belief in the existence of freedom is based as much on an experience of power as our belief in any force of motivating passion.

It might still be wondered how this could be so, especially if incompatibilism is supposed true. The line of thought is obvious enough. To represent the possession by us of freedom in incompatibilist terms, experience would have to represent to us a condition of that freedom—the absence of determining causes for our action. But how is it possible for experience to represent that? At best experience can fail to reveal causal determination. It cannot directly represent causal determination's absence. In which case, the Hobbesian accusation returns: belief in libertarian freedom is based

---

[12] Thomas Hobbes, in *The Questions Concerning Liberty, Necessity and Chance, clearly stated between Dr Bramhall Bishop of Derry, and Thomas Hobbes of Malmesbury* (London 1656), p. 217.

not on any experiential representation that its conditions are met, but just on a lack of representation that they are unmet.

But remember that in representing our freedom to us, experience does not have to represent a lack of causal determination to us, at least directly. What experience represents is one kind of determination—the presence and operation of one power— and then, in further cases, what would diminish or remove that power. In other words, experience represents the incompatibility of one power with the operation of certain other kinds of power. That means that when experience does represent the power as present, it thereby supports belief in the absence of certain other kinds of power—the very powers that experience has shown would be in conflict with that power and would remove it were they present. So if experience consistently shows that certain forms of causal predetermination—those operating from outside the will—are incompatible with freedom, in representing the presence of freedom it also supports belief that those forms of causal predetermination are absent. It is no different from the experiential representation of any other kind of power. If experience represents the operation of one kind of causal power, it supports belief in the absence of causal powers of other kinds—those kinds that experience has already shown to be inconsistent with the causal power represented as actually operative.

So Hobbes was wrong to deny the possibility of an experiential representation of libertarian freedom. Experience may perfectly well support belief in the reality of such a power. But of course it does not follow that the support need be conclusive. The question of whether we really do possess such a power requires much further examination. What does seem clear is that our intuitions about self-determination are profoundly shaped, for good or ill, by how things feel to us.

English-language philosophy has had great difficulty accommodating our natural beliefs about our own freedom. Part of the explanation is, of course, a profound bias towards mechanism—towards assuming that any power we possessed as free agents to determine how we act would have to be ordinary causation. But there is a deeper explanation. And this lies in our philosophical tradition's ambivalent relation to the very idea of power—an ambivalence based on the assumption, inherited from Hume, that powers can never be directly represented in experience. The case for the existence of any power must, then, lie either in our experience of regularities—as with causation—or it must be conceptual.

But our belief in our own freedom as a multi-way power seems not to be based on any experience of regularities between events, nor does it appear to be conceptual in origin. It seems instead to be based on how that power is phenomenologically represented to us. What our philosophical tradition currently lacks, and has lacked since the days of Hobbes and Hume, is an epistemology of the power of freedom, or indeed of any other kind of power, that is based on a convincing account of its phenomenology—on its representation in experience and the imagination. But until we have such a linked account of the epistemology and phenomenology of power, much about the nature and origins of our belief in freedom will remain mysterious.

The tenacity and character of our belief in freedom as a multi-way power certainly cannot be made intelligible in conceptual terms alone.

It is not just the compatibilist and sceptical philosophers of freedom who have ignored experience and even contradicted it. Modern libertarian philosophers have done so too—as their reliance on the consequence argument shows.

15.5 Incompatibilism—Time-Centred or Will-Centred?

Consider the kind of incompatibilism which the consequence argument supports. Kant stated this incompatibilism very clearly:

...what we want to discern, and never shall, is this: how can pre-determinism co-exist with freedom, when according to predeterminism freely chosen actions, as occurrences, have their determining grounds in antecedent time (which, together with what is contained therein, no longer lies in our control), whereas according to freedom, the action, as well as its contrary, must be in the control of the subject at the moment of its happening.[13]

And that, of course, is precisely what, if the consequence argument were sound, would remove our freedom. What would then remove our freedom would be the causal determination of our action by any past event. For what is crucial to establishing my lack of control over a causally predetermined action, according to the consequence argument, is that my performance of this action is entailed, together with the laws, by statements reporting past action-determining events—statements which, because they concern the past, I now lack the power to falsify. It does not matter what action-determining events are being reported. It is enough that they are action-determining, past and, because past, outside my present control. I shall call this a *time-centred* incompatibilism.

According to time-centred incompatibilism, any past action-determining cause is equally removing of our present power to act otherwise. And that includes our own past decisions. Past decisions can only leave us free to act otherwise to the extent that they fail causally to determine how we act, and leave us with some actual chance of changing our mind and acting otherwise. Of course, this view is not immediately intuitive. It runs up against our own experience. I do not have to feel that there is some chance that I will actually change my mind in order to feel that I retain the power to change my mind. And this is an obvious and very important truth about the way we experience our own freedom. I may be quite sure that no new information will arise to change my mind, and I may feel absolutely resolute. But I can perfectly well feel, at the very same time, that it still remains fully up to

---

[13] Immanuel Kant, *Religion within the Boundaries of Mere Reason*, in *The Cambridge Edition of the Works of Immanuel Kant: Religion and Rational Theology*, eds Allen W. Wood and George di Giovanni (Cambridge: Cambridge University Press, 1996), p. 94.

me how I act; that it remains fully within my control whether or not I continue to adhere to my own decision.

Defenders of the consequence argument show, at some level, a certain sensitivity to this weakness in the time-centred incompatibilism they are arguing for. In the process of softening up that usually precedes any statement of the consequence argument, we are generally asked to consider examples of various intuitive threats to freedom—examples that implicate some sort of prior causal predetermination as fundamental to the threat. But the selling rhetoric is usually careful in what examples it selects. The usual choices are some past state or event that clearly precedes any free doing or decision of the agent, and so which is clearly distinct from any exercise of the agent's free will—such as the state of the world when dinosaurs walked the earth, or the genes the agent was born with and so forth. We are not asked to contemplate the dreadful threat to our own continuing control of what we do posed by the fact that we may already have freely decided for ourselves how we shall act.

If we attend to experience we find support for a different kind of incompatibilism from that believed in by Kant or supported by the consequence argument. The kind of incompatibilism which experience supports is what I call a *will-centred* incompatibilism. What removes my freedom is not the causal power of just any past event, but a causal power that operates from outside my own free will. Freedom is represented by experience as that power of control over what we do that is exercisable in and through the free will, through our own free decisions and intentions—a power which our free will embodies and which its mere exercise can never of itself remove. The view is still incompatibilist. If my actions are predetermined from without the will, by other than my own free decisions, then it is not up to me what I do. A causally deterministic world in which our decisions and actions are already determined before our birth is a world in which we lack any freedom to do otherwise. But the threat to our freedom can no longer come from our own free will, but only from outside it. And it is this intuitively will-centred conception of freedom that defenders of the consequence argument tacitly respect by their careful choice of example; though going just by the logic of their own position they have no rationale for taking such a care.[14]

Of course we can still use our own free will to imprison our future selves. Ulysses can freely decide to have himself tied to the mast, and I can freely decide to take a compulsion-inducing drug. In both cases the end result of these decisions may well be a loss of freedom. But these are cases where the exercise of free will is not the only

---

[14] The distinction between a time-centred and a will-centred incompatibilism was drawn by me before, in slightly different terminology, in *The Psychology of Freedom*, Chapter 3. For an example of modern philosophy's tendency to identify incompatibilism with time-centred incompatibilism, consider David Lewis in 'Are we free to break the laws?'. There Lewis defined compatibilism as the doctrine that it may be true that: '…one freely does what one is predetermined to do;…that in such a case one is able to act otherwise though past history and the laws of nature determine that one will not act otherwise.' *Collected Papers*, vol. 2, p. 291. For Lewis, the dispute between incompatibilism and compatibilism is a dispute about time-centred incompatibilism. Any other doctrine would just be compatibilism.

factor. In these cases, freedom is removed not by the mere taking of the decision, but by intervening changes outside the will which the decision causes. It is these changes that are freedom-depriving. Thus Ulysses loses his freedom to act otherwise only when his decision leads him actually to be tied up. It is ropes that deprive him of his freedom, and not the mere exercise of his own free will. And I lose my freedom to act otherwise only once I have actually taken the drug. It is the drug which takes away my freedom when it, rather than just a free decision of my own, causally determines what I subsequently do. What cannot remove our freedom to do otherwise is the mere decision to act as we actually do. On its own and of itself, a free decision leaves us perfectly free to change our minds and act otherwise. We are not imprisoned and overwhelmed by our own free will. Or so the experience we have of our own free decision-making would suggest.[15]

Can time-centred incompatibilism be saved by introducing a special sense of 'free'—a sense which applies to those actions that are predetermined by prior free decisions? On this approach it is still true that once we have decided what to do, we remain in *some sense* free to act otherwise. But this is supposedly a different sense of 'freedom' from the sense that applied to the original free decision. It is a sense that implies only that the action is motivated by a prior free decision—not that the same multi-way power that was initially possessed over both decision and action is still retained. Unfortunately for this proposal, there just does not appear to be any such variation in our ordinary understanding of our freedom to do otherwise. And that is because there is no relevant change in the experience that underlies that understanding. As before the decision, so too afterwards—I think it all along entirely up to me what I do and how I act. I do not believe that I possess any kind of control over what I do that I would lose just by taking a decision. And that is because experience represents no such loss of control. As before my decisions, so after—I think I remain fully in control of what I do because that's exactly how it feels.

When I first formulated the idea of a will-centred incompatibilism, I was asked why anyone should be an incompatibilist at all if they could not accept the consequence argument.[16] And how could anyone coherently distinguish between past

---

[15] Go back to Martha Klein's fantasy case, mentioned in Chapter 8, of the eternal agent whose every act is predetermined by a previous action of their own. Since their every action is causally predetermined, at no stage is there ever any chance of such an agent acting otherwise. Klein thinks that it obviously follows, given incompatibilism, that such an agent can never be free to act otherwise. But this is obvious only on a time-centred version of incompatibilism. On the will-centred version of the doctrine it could still be that the agent was perfectly free to act otherwise. What if every voluntary action that the agent performed was directly causally determined by a prior decision of the agent's own will to perform that action as a means; which decision was in turn the determined product of yet earlier decisions to attain various ends; and these decisions determined by yet earlier decisions to attain yet further ends—and so on back ad infinitum? If all this action-predetermination was just through the direct operation of the agent's will, what need be freedom-depriving about that?

[16] Randolph Clarke pressed me with just this question in his *Libertarian Accounts of Free Will*, when (p. 128) he notes that since I do not accept the consequence argument for incompatibilism, it is 'unclear' why I am not immediately, and just for that reason, a compatibilist.

action-determining events outside the agent's will which are supposed to remove freedom, and past action-determining free decisions which are supposed not to? The answer to the first question is that so many people incline towards incompatibilism, not because of the consequence argument, the soundness of which has never been established, but because that is how experience represents their freedom to them. And we discriminate between past action-determining events as we do, because experience leads us to, representing the causal powers of some events as freedom-threatening but not others.

There is no good way of reconstructing the incompatibilism which experience supports by purely conceptual means that bypass experience. For then, as the consequence argument's inconclusive fortunes show, we fail to provide any compelling grounds for believing in incompatibilism at all; and we are liable radically to change the kind of incompatibilism to be believed. In fact, we risk alienating freedom from what experience and intuition suggest to be its true basis and source and its sure embodiment—the operation of a free will.[17]

15.6 Scepticism about Freedom: Naturalism and Rationalism

We have already observed an interesting alliance against multi-way freedom—between ethical rationalism on the one hand and metaphysical naturalism on the other.

The ethical rationalist wishes to understand ethical normativity in terms of general reason and rationality. The aim, as we have seen, is to understand blame and responsibility just in terms of reason and rational criticism, without introducing anything as dubious or problematic as a power of self-determination.

The naturalist dislikes the idea of a power of self-determination too. For the naturalist wishes to understand human psychology and its capacities entirely in terms of properties found in wider nature, and in the inanimate and non-mental world as much as the animate and minded. Self-determination seems radically unlike anything in wider nature—and, in particular, it seems unlike ordinary causal power. So for the naturalist too there is the project either of taming self-determination, such as by reducing it to some ordinary form of causal power, or of removing it from the theory of human psychology and capacities altogether.

There may be much in common between many of the moves immediately favoured by the naturalist and rationalist alike. We find in the contemporary subject revisionary models of human self-determination that owe much to a rationalist

[17] As noted earlier against Dennett, the root of our belief in free will, and the nature and content of that belief, is to be found not in epistemic openness but in the way that experience represents power to us—a way that does not tie what we are free to do to its epistemic possibility. Our decisions may remove actions as epistemic possibilities for us. But they do not remove them as actions we are perfectly free to perform.

project, favouring the replacement of any unvarnished appeal to freedom as an unreduced metaphysical power by appeal to some general conception of reason; but equally the same models may also owe much to naturalist projects that aim to replace appeals to phenomena that threaten to be too distinctively human, by appeal to phenomena found in wider nature. Thus ethical rationalists such as Scanlon have commonly endorsed a model of action that has nothing immediately to do with a theory of human rationality and the capacity for reason, but which understands intentional action in broadly Hobbesian terms, as voluntariness, the expression of prior motivations so to act—a phenomenon that might equally occur in non-rational animals.

Yet of course there is a threatening tension between the naturalist and rationalist projects. For by what right do philosophers reject freedom as a metaphysical power, while still holding onto the categories in terms of which we ordinarily understand the operation of human reason and rationality? They condemn as superstition, or at least as highly problematic, the idea that, as we ordinarily suppose we do, we have the power to determine for ourselves which of a range of actions we perform. But they treat as supposedly less problematic our ordinary ways of thinking of ourselves as responding rationally to objects of thought. But these ways of thinking involve powers other than causation too. For we think of ourselves as determined or moved to believe things by overwhelming justifications for so doing, or as moved to want or intend things by their clear desirability.

There is one figure who would have regarded the ethical rationalist as no more respectable a figure than the believer in metaphysical freedom. That figure is David Hume, who no more allowed for a capacity on our part to be moved by the normative properties of objects of thought, than he allowed for our possession of a distinctive metaphysical power over alternatives. In Hume we arrive at a vastly interesting and, at a certain level, profoundly consistent enterprise—that of constructing a theory of normativity and of the role of ethical standards in human life that avoids appeal either to self-determination or to the capacity for reason as ordinarily conceived. It is that enterprise, and the nature of ethical normativity in general, that we shall be considering in Volume 2.

Bibliography

Adams, Robert Merrihew, 'Involuntary sins', *Philosophical Review* 94, (1985)

Allison, Henry, *Kant's Theory of Freedom* (Cambridge: Cambridge University Press, 1990)

Alvarez, Maria, 'Actions, thought experiments and the "Principle of Alternate Possibilities"', *Australasian Journal of Philosophy* 87, (2009)

Anscombe, G.E.M., *Intention* (Oxford: Blackwell, 1957)

Aquinas, Thomas, *Summa Theologiae* (Turin: Marietti, 1950)

Aquinas, Thomas, *In decem libros Ethicorum Aristotelis ad Nicomachum expositio* (Turin: Marietti, 1964)

Aristotle, *Nicomachean Ethics*, in *The Complete Works of Aristotle*, ed. Jonathan Barnes (Princeton: Princeton University Press, 1984) vol. 2, pp. 1729–867

Augustine, *On Free Choice of the Will*, ed. Thomas Williams (Indianapolis: Hackett, 1993)

Bobzien, Susanne, *Determinism and Freedom in Stoic Philosophy* (Oxford: Oxford University Press, 1998)

Bratman, Michael, *Intention, Plans and Practical Reason* (Cambridge, MA: Harvard University Press, 1987)

Butler, Joseph, *Fifteen Sermons Preached at the Rolls Chapel* (London, 1729)

Butterfill, Stephen, 'Seeing causings and hearing gestures', *The Philosophical Quarterly* 59, (2009)

Calvin, John, *Institutes of the Christian Religion*, ed. John T. McNeill (Philadelphia: Westminster Press, 1960)

Chisholm, Roderick, 'Reflections on human agency', *Idealistic Studies* 1, (1971)

Clarke, Randolph, 'Libertarian views: critical survey' in *The Oxford Handbook to Free Will* ed. Robert Kane (Oxford: Oxford University Press, 2002)

Clarke, Randolph, *Libertarian Accounts of Free Will* (Oxford: Oxford University Press, 2003)

Dancy, Jonathan, 'Intention and permissibility: Scanlon's principles', *Aristotelian Society Supplementary Volume* 74, (2000)

Davidson, Donald, *Essays on Actions and Events* (Oxford: Clarendon Press, 1980)

Dennett, Daniel, *Elbow Room* (Oxford: Oxford University Press, 1985)

Dworkin, Ronald, *Justice for Hedgehogs* (Cambridge, MA: Harvard University Press, 2011)

Epictetus, *Discourses* (Cambridge, MA: Loeb Classical Library, 1925)

Fischer, John Martin, 'Incompatibilism', *Philosophical Studies* 43, (1983)

Fischer, John Martin, and Ravizza, Mark, *Responsibility and Control* (Cambridge: Cambridge University Press, 1998)

Frankfurt, Harry, *The Importance of What We Care About* (Cambridge: Cambridge University Press, 1988)

Gibbard, Allan, *Wise Choices, Apt Feelings* (Oxford: Oxford University Press, 1990)

Harman, Gilbert, 'Practical reasoning', *Review of Metaphysics* 29, (1976)

Harre, Rom, and Madden, E.H., *Causal Powers: A Theory of Natural Necessity* (Oxford: Blackwell, 1975)

Hobart, R., 'Free will as involving determinism and inconceivable without it', *Mind* 43, (1934)

Hobbes, Thomas, *Leviathan*, ed. Noel Malcolm (Oxford: Clarendon Press, 2012)

Hobbes, Thomas and Bramhall, John, *The Questions Concerning Liberty, Necessity and Chance, clearly stated between Dr Bramhall Bishop of Derry, and Thomas Hobbes of Malmesbury* (London, 1656)

Holton, Richard, *Willing, Wanting, Waiting* (Oxford: Oxford University Press, 2009)

Hume, David, *An Enquiry Concerning the Principles of Morals*, ed. P.H. Nidditch (Oxford: Clarendon Press, 1975)

Hume, David, *A Treatise of Human Nature*, ed. P.H. Nidditch (Oxford: Clarendon Press, 1978)

Kane, Robert, *The Significance of Free Will* (Oxford: Oxford University Press, 1998)

Kant, Immanuel, *The Cambridge Edition of the Works of Immanuel Kant: Practical Philosophy*, ed. Mary Gregor (Cambridge: Cambridge University Press, 1996)

Kant, Immanuel, *The Cambridge Edition of the Works of Immanuel Kant: Religion and Rational Theology*, eds Allen W. Wood and George di Giovanni (Cambridge: Cambridge University Press, 1996)

Kavka, Gregory, 'The toxin puzzle', *Analysis* 43, (1983)

Klein, Martha, *Determinism, Blameworthiness and Deprivation* (Oxford: Oxford University Press, 1990)

Knobe, Joshua, 'Free will and the scientific vision', in *Current Controversies in Experimental Philosophy*, eds Edouard Machery and Elizabeth O'Neill (London: Routledge, 2014)

Leslie, Alan, 'Spatiotemporal continuity and the perception of causality in infants', *Perception* 13, (1984)

Leslie, Alan and Keeble, Stephanie, 'Do six-month-old infants perceive causality?' *Cognition* 25, (1987)

Lewis, David, 'Devil's bargains and the real world', in *The Security Gamble: Deterrence in the Nuclear Age*, ed. Douglas MacLean (Ottowa: Rowman and Allenheld, 1984)

Lewis, David, 'Are we free to break the laws?', in *Philosophical Papers* (Oxford: Oxford University Press, 1986), vol. 2

List, Christian, 'Free will, determinism, and the possibility of doing otherwise', *Nous* 48, (2014)

Locke, John, *An Essay Concerning Human Understanding*, ed. P.H. Nidditch (Oxford: Clarendon Press, 1975)

Lombard, Peter, *Sententiae in IV libris distinctae* (Grottaferrata: St Bonaventure, 1971)

McCann, Hugh, *The Works of Agency: On Human Action, Will, and Freedom* (Ithaca: Cornell University Press, 1998)

McDowell, John, *Having the World in View: Essays on Kant, Hegel, and Sellars* (Cambridge, MA: Harvard University Press, 2009)

Mayr, Erasmus, *Understanding Human Agency* (Oxford: Oxford University Press, 2011)

Mele, Alfred, *Springs of Action* (Oxford: Oxford University Press, 1992)

Mele, Alfred, *Motivation and Agency* (Oxford: Oxford University Press, 2003)

Mumford, Stephen, and Anjum, Rani Lill, *Getting Causes from Powers* (Oxford: University Press, 2011)

O'Connor, Timothy, *Persons and Causes: The Metaphysics of Free Will* (Oxford: Oxford University Press, 2000)

O'Shaughnessy, Brian, *The Will: A Dual Aspect Theory* (Cambridge: Cambridge University Press, 1980)

Pink, Thomas, *The Psychology of Freedom* (Cambridge: Cambridge University Press, 1996)

Pink, Thomas, 'Reason and agency', *Aristotelian Society Proceedings* 97, (1997)

Pink, Thomas, *Free Will: A Very Short Introduction* (Oxford: Oxford University Press, 2004)

Pink, Thomas, 'Suarez, Hobbes and the scholastic tradition in action theory', in *The Will and Human Action: from Antiquity to the Present Day*, eds Thomas Pink and Martin Stone (London: Routledge, 2004)

Pink, Thomas, 'Thomas Hobbes and the ethics of freedom', *Inquiry* 54, (2011)

Pink, Thomas, 'Law and the normativity of obligation', *The Jurisprudence Annual Lecture 2014, Jurisprudence* 5, no. 1 (2014)

Pufendorf, Samuel, *De iure naturae et gentium* (Amsterdam, 1688)

Ryle, Gilbert, *The Concept of Mind* (London: Hutchinson, 1949)

Scanlon, T.M., *What We Owe to Each Other* (Cambridge, MA: Harvard University Press, 1998)

Sehon, Scott, *Teleological Realism: Mind, Agency, and Explanation* (Cambridge, MA: MIT Press, 2005)

Slote, Michael, 'Selective necessity and the free will problem', *Journal of Philosophy* 79, (1982)

Steward, Helen, *A Metaphysics for Freedom* (Oxford: Oxford University Press, 2012)

Strawson, Galen, *Freedom and Belief* (Oxford: Oxford University Press, 1986)

Strawson, Galen, 'Consciousness, free will, and the unimportance of determinism', *Inquiry* 32, (1989)

Strawson, P. F., *Freedom and Resentment and Other Essays* (London: Methuen, 1974)

Stump, Eleonore, 'Libertarian freedom and the principle of alternate possibilities', in *Faith, Freedom and Rationality*, eds Daniel Howard-Snyder and Jeff Jordan (Lanham: Rowman and Littlefield, 1996)

Stump, Eleonore, 'Moral responsibility without alternative possibilities' in *Moral Responsibility and Alternative Possibilities*, eds David Widerker and Michael McKenna (Aldershot: Ashgate, 2003)

Suarez, Francisco, *Commentaria una cum quaestionibus in libros Aristotelis De Anima* (Madrid: Sociedad de Estudios y Publicaciones, 1991)

Suarez, Francisco, *Metaphysical Disputations*, disputation 19: *On causes that act necessarily and causes that act freely or contingently; also, on fate, fortune, and chance* in *Francisco Suarez S.J. on Efficient Causality*, ed. Alfred Freddoso (New Haven: Yale University Press, 1994)

Thompson, Michael, *Life and Action: Elementary Structures of Practice and Practical Thought* (Cambridge, MA: Harvard University Press, 2008)

van Inwagen, Peter, 'The incompatibility of free will and determinism', *Philosophical Studies* 27, (1975)

Velleman, David, *Practical Reflection* (Princeton: Princeton University Press, 1989)

Vermazen, B. and Hintikka, M. (eds), *Essays on Davidson* (Oxford: Oxford University Press, 1985)

Wallace, R. Jay, *Normativity and the Will* (Oxford: Oxford University Press, 2006)

Widerker, David, and McKenna, Michael (eds), *Moral Responsibility and Alternative Possibilities* (Aldershot: Ashgate, 2003)

Wiggins, David, 'Towards a reasonable libertarianism', in *Essays on Freedom of Action*, ed. Ted Honderich (London: Routledge, 1973)

Williams, Bernard, *Shame and Necessity* (Berkeley: University of California Press, 1993)

Williams, Bernard, *Making Sense of Humanity, and Other Philosophical Papers 1982–93* (Cambridge: Cambridge University Press, 1995)

Wolf, Susan, *Freedom and Reason* (Oxford: Oxford University Press, 1990)

Wolter, Allan (ed.), *Duns Scotus on the Will and Morality* (Washington: CUA Press, 1986)

Index

"The ability to get to the verge w/o getting into war is the necessary art. If you run away from it, [afraid] to go to the brink, you are lost."
— John Foster Dulles —

B/c not raised as a defense does not bar the court from determining whether the K was valid and if it is not valid, from relying on it for legal reasoning.

Impeachment is strictly a leg've fxn. In the exercise of their constitutional fxn is Congress going to allow the Executive branch or defer to the Executive branch's exercise such as invading another country w/o actual provocation

Printed and bound by CPI Group (UK) Ltd, Croydon, CR0 4YY